PEOPLE, MARKETS, GOODS:
ECONOMIES AND SOCIETIES IN HISTORY

Volume 3

Publishing Business in Eighteenth-Century England

T0341677

PEOPLE, MARKETS, GOODS:
ECONOMIES AND SOCIETIES IN HISTORY

ISSN: 2051–7467

Series editors
Barry Doyle – University of Huddersfield
Nigel R. Goose – University of Hertfordshire
Steve Hindle – The Huntington Library
Jane Humphries – University of Oxford
Kevin O'Rourke – University of Oxford

The interactions of economy and society, people and goods, transactions and actions are at the root of most human behaviours. Economic and social historians are participants in the same conversation about how markets have developed historically and how they have been constituted by economic actors and agencies in various social, institutional and geographical contexts. New debates now underpin much research in economic and social, cultural, demographic, urban and political history. Their themes have enduring resonance – financial stability and instability, the costs of health and welfare, the implications of poverty and riches, flows of trade and the centrality of communications. This new paperback series aims to attract historians interested in economics and economists with an interest in history by publishing high quality, cutting edge academic research in the broad field of economic and social history from the late medieval/early modern period to the present day. It encourages the interaction of qualitative and quantitative methods through both excellent monographs and collections offering path-breaking overviews of key research concerns. Taking as its benchmark international relevance and excellence it is open to scholars and subjects of any geographical areas from the case study to the multi-nation comparison.

PREVIOUS TITLES

1. *Landlords and Tenants in Britain, 1440–1660: Tawney's Agrarian Problem Revisited*, edited by Jane Whittle, 2013

2. *Child Workers and Industrial Health in Britain, 1780–1850*, Peter Kirby, 2013

Publishing Business in Eighteenth-Century England

James Raven

THE BOYDELL PRESS

First published 2014
The Boydell Press, Woodbridge

ISBN 978 1 84383 910 1

The Boydell Press is an imprint of Boydell & Brewer Ltd
PO Box 9, Woodbridge, Suffolk IP12 3DF, UK
and of Boydell & Brewer Inc.
668 Mt Hope Avenue, Rochester, NY 14620-2731, USA
website: www.boydellandbrewer.com

A catalogue record for this book is available
from the British Library

Typeset by BBR, Sheffield

For Neil McKendrick

Contents

Acknowledgements

I am especially grateful to D'Maris Coffman, the late Donald Coleman, Elizabeth Eisenstein, Christine Ferdinand, Perry Gauci, James N. Green, Nigel Hall, the late István Hont, Julian Hoppit, Arnold Hunt, Kazuhiko Kondo, Sarah Lloyd, John McCusker, Jason McElligott, Neil McKendrick, Ian Maclean, Craig Muldrew, Peter Stallybrass, Alan Sterenberg, Michael Suarez, Rosemary Sweet, Dominique Varry, Calhoun Winton and Keith Wrightson, for shrewd and generous criticism and for letting me see completed work in advance of print. I am also indebted to Nicolas Barker, Iain Beavan, Charles Benson, Mark Goldie, R. J. Goulden, John Hetet, the late Vincent Kinane, the late Sheila Lambert, David McKitterick, Robin Myers, the late Mary (Paul) Pollard, Michael Twyman and Laurence Worms for comments and references about specific aspects of printing history. Editorial advice from Megan Milan at Boydell & Brewer and the meticulous and stimulating copy-editing of Amanda Thompson at BBR have been invaluable. Other debts are acknowledged in relevant notes.

My search for surviving small-item and jobbing printing and printing records has led me on circuitous routes through Britain, Ireland and North America. It has benefited from the patience and wisdom of numerous keepers of scattered civic, corporation and business records and many dozens of miscellaneous collections which contained (or sometimes didn't) taxation records, printed valuations, business orders, specimens of printing or other printers' ephemera. I owe much to the advice and expertise of the archivists, curators and librarians of the following institutions: Aberdeen University Library; the American Antiquarian Society, Worcester, MA; the Bank of England Archives; Barclays Bank, Lombard Street; Bedfordshire County Record Office, Bedford; the Beinecke Library, Yale; Berkshire County Record Office, Reading; the Bodleian Library; the British Library; Cambridge University Library; Cambridgeshire Record Office, Cambridge; the then Cheshire Record Office, Chester; the then Chester City Record Office; Cork Archives Institute; Cork City Library; Corporation of London Records Office; the Dorset County Museum and Naturalist and Archaeological Society, Dorchester; the then Dorset County Record Office; Edinburgh University Library; Essex County Record Office, Chelmsford; Gloucester Public Library; Goldsmiths Library, London; Guildhall Library, London; Hampshire County Record Office, Winchester; Hereford City Library; Herefordshire Record Office, Hereford (now Herefordshire Archive Service); Hereford and Worcester Record Office, Worcester; the Institute of Historical Research, London; Ipswich Public Library; John Rylands University Library of Manchester; Leeds City Archives; the Lewis Walpole Library, Farmington, CN; the library of the Worshipful Company of Papermakers and Stationers, Stationers' Hall; the London Metropolitan Archives; the National Archives, Kew; National Library of Scotland; Norfolk Record Office, Norwich; Nottingham Central Library; Raynham Hall, Norfolk; Reading University Library and Archives; Scottish Record Office, Edinburgh; Shropshire Record Office, Shrewsbury; Society of Antiquaries, London; Staffordshire Record Office, Stafford; [East] Suffolk Record Office, Ipswich branch; [West] Suffolk Record Office, Bury St Edmunds branch; Sun Life Assurance, Bartholomew Lane; and Trinity College, Dublin. I am also particularly grateful to the British Academy, the Royal Historical Society and the Bibliographical Society for grants for travel and photography. Such grants are indispensable for a study of this sort.

The consultation of materials has continued during years when other projects developed and were completed. I am especially grateful for the support, suggestions and the warmth of hospitality offered by my many colleagues at the University of Essex; Mansfield College, Oxford; Clare College, Pembroke College and Magdalene College, Cambridge; the History and English faculties of Cambridge and Oxford; the Albert Sloman Library, Essex; Cambridge University Library; the Bodleian Library; and other university and departmental libraries. It is also a great pleasure to record my gratitude to the Master and Fellows of Magdalene College, Cambridge, for the tenure of a Fellowship that allows this and other books to be completed. Few can claim such supportive communities of scholars and friends. Neil McKendrick, to whom this book is dedicated in friendship and appreciation, has over many years been especially tolerant of my archival adventures and the distractions caused by other books and assignments. Printers, business people and authors know all about schedules: only the constant support and generosity of my wife Karen has enabled me to keep to mine.

Notes on Dates, Booksellers, Founts and Intaglio

Unless specified, all dates are given according to the old style for the day and month, but in new style for the year. In new style the year turns on 1 January. The old English calendar presents particular pitfalls for dates given on newspapers and the business press (among other imprints) where before 1753 the English New Year began on 25 March (whereas in Europe the year began on 1 January as it was to in England from 1753). Double-numbering of years became common in the early eighteenth century so that, for example, a newspaper issued on 15 February 1714 (new style) might bear the date 15 February 1714/15.

The following also retains the eighteenth-century usage of 'bookseller' to refer to wholesale booksellers (often also copyright-owning publishers) as well as to retail booksellers. Distinctions between the trading in books and the printing or publishing of them are, however, fundamental to the following history. These different activities, distinctive in themselves, might also be undertaken by the same men and women at the same premises.

In letterpress printing (and in the phraseology of traditional typography), a fount of type is a set of all the characters of one size and design (roman, italic, bold, etc.), usually cast in at least the necessary quantities to fill the compositor's pair of cases. This includes numerals and punctuation. An individual piece of type is called a sort. The face of any piece of type is the surface inked by the printer to impress its shape on to paper. In modern usage, the advent of digital typography has led to the use of 'typeface' or 'font' to denote letters, etc., that share a common overall design, even if differing in size or weight. Thus, 'roman' and 'italic' indicate upright or sloped forms of a single typeface. Where possible, this study adopts original definitions.

Intaglio printing includes several different methods of working, principally etching and engraving. In etching, a metal plate (usually copper in the eighteenth century) is covered with a waxy ground, resistant to acid. Marks are made through the ground using a pointed etching needle or, additionally an échoppe, a tool with a slanted oval section that can be used to produce swelling and tapering lines. These marks are turned into hollows by bathing the plate with acid. Once the remaining ground has been cleaned off, ink is forced into the hollows of the plate and its surface wiped clean. It is the ink marks in the hollows that make the print. Most intaglio printing, particularly for pictorial work, was first etched and then completed with the burin as in engraving, thus combining the relative cheapness of etching with the 'finish' of engraving. It is often impossible to recover the exact history of the working on the plate, and for this reason such prints are often referred to as 'engravings'. I have used the generic term 'intaglio printing' to avoid inaccurate distinctions between the two methods.

Abbreviations

AAS	American Antiquarian Society, Worcester, MA
BBTI	British Book Trade Index (www.bbti.bham.ac.uk)
BEA	Bank of England Archives (formerly Bank of England Record Office)
BL	British Library
BRO	Bedfordshire County Record Office, Bedford
CCRO	Chester City Record Office (now part of Cheshire Archives & Local Studies)
CRO	Cheshire Record Office, Chester (now part of Cheshire Archives & Local Studies)
DbRO	Derbyshire Record Office, Matlock
DRO	Dorset County Record Office (now The Dorset History Centre, Dorchester)
DvRO	Devon Record Office, Exeter
EcHR	*Economic History Review*
EHR	*English Historical Review*
ESRO	[East] Suffolk Record Office, Ipswich branch
ESTC	*English Short-Title Catalogue* (formerly *Eighteenth-Century Short-Title Catalogue*)
ESxRO	East Sussex Record Office, Lewes
EUL	Edinburgh University Library
GMRO	Greater Manchester County Record Office (and Manchester Archives), Manchester
HCL	Hereford City Library
HfRO	Herefordshire Record Office, Hereford (now the Herefordshire Archive Service)
HMC	Historical Manuscripts Commission

HRO   Hampshire County Record Office, Winchester
HWRO   Hereford and Worcester Record Office, Worcester (now the
               Worcestershire Archive and Archaeology Service)
LCA   Leeds City Archives
LMA   London Metropolitan Archives
LRO   Lancashire Record Office (now Lancashire Archives, Preston)
NA   National Archives, Kew (formerly The Public Record Office)
NCL   Nottingham Central Library
NLS   National Library of Scotland, Edinburgh
NRO   Norfolk Record Office, Norwich
ODNB   *Oxford Dictionary of National Biography*
OBPO   Old Bailey Proceedings Online (www.oldbaileyonline.org)
SH   Stationers' Hall, Ludgate Hill, London
ShRO   Shropshire Record Office, Shrewsbury
SP Dom   State Papers Domestic
StRO   Staffordshire Record Office, Stafford
T&C   *Town and Country Magazine*
TCBS   *Transactions of the Cambridge Bibliographical Society*
WSRO   [West] Suffolk Record Office, Bury St Edmunds branch

I

The Mediation of the Press

Printers and stationers proved potent if fitful agents in religious and
political change in sixteenth- and seventeenth-century Europe but,
during the eighteenth century, print exerted new influence in subtle
and far-reaching ways. The impact of the printing press in finance
and commerce was manifest in England and in the British Isles whose
economies advanced so extensively from the late seventeenth century.
Printers promoted and serviced unprecedented financial and commercial
expansion. The scale of press activity was also exceptional. In England,
book, pamphlet and newspaper production soared, but in the years
between the lapse of the licensing laws in 1695 and the first successful
mechanized printing of a newspaper in 1814, the volume, quality and
location of small-item or 'jobbing' printing was transformed. Nothing
as potent had been seen since the arrival of the printing press in London
in the late fifteenth century. What was even more remarkable was that
printing-house business accelerated despite a virtual technological
standstill in the design of the common printing press. The printed output
of the 120 years after 1695 was the crowning achievement of the manual
press before its replacement by mechanical power. Intaglio engraving
and etching processes greatly advanced. Engravers were busier than ever,
with striking technical improvements to design and illustration. For the
merchant, retailer, manufacturer and investor, the changing products of
the printing house were nothing short of revolutionary.

Increasingly during the eighteenth century, print recorded trading
achievement and debated its consequences. Writers, illustrators and
compilers all became more certain of their audience and of the practi-
cality and effectiveness of their instruction. Printed books introduced and
popularized commercial techniques. Printers and stationers enabled and
refined trading practice by means of paper ledgers and account books
and a vast array of printed materials that ranged from simple documents,
certificates and 'blank' forms, to sophisticated manuals and commentaries. Bound and ruled blank books revolutionized record keeping and the

precision and authority of the balance sheet. Print, chronicling, evaluating and instructing, helped effect a business revolution.

This book updates and revises my first examination of the productive relationship between printing and the publication of financial and commercial news and information.[1] Since then, arguments about the connection between print and the economy have been both strengthened and refined. As a Nobel Prize-winning economist has asserted, the reporting and dissemination of financial news became an integral part of the financial revolution itself.[2] Others have offered a series of more cautionary observations about the role of the press and published financial guides in the early years of new investment and speculative activity in England up to about 1720.[3] As the following chapters will argue, while such caution might sometimes have been too great, underplaying the fundamental role of printing and the press, it is certainly the case that in the late seventeenth century the oral was as important as the written in the dissemination of commercial, market and financial knowledge. As Anne Murphy writes, in a compelling study, 'the majority of people in the late seventeenth century would have heard, rather than read the news and ... given the volatile nature of the financial market, the active investor must have *chosen* to hear, rather than read, the news at the heart of the market where proximity could facilitate swift action, if required'.[4] However, there is much more to be said about the 'written' as both scribal and printed, and about the relationship between script and print, while the provision of certain printed and written materials, however imperfect, occasional and, importantly, with poor survival rates, offered the basis for a much broader and active oral network of information exchange. Furthermore, the emphasis upon the constraints to developments in the late Stuart period only highlights the depth and complexity of the transformation during the rest of the eighteenth century. The following chapters survey the further (if, of course, never complete) supersession of the oral by the

1   J. R. Raven, 'Print and Trade in Eighteenth-Century Britain' (unpubl. prize dissertation, Thirlwall Prize and Seeley Medal, University of Cambridge, 1986, on deposit at Cambridge University Library).
2   Robert J. Shiller, *Irrational Exuberance* (Princeton, NJ and Oxford: Princeton University Press, 2000).
3   Notably, contributions in Natasha Glaisyer and Sara Pennell (eds), *Didactic Literature in England, 1500–1800: Expertise Constructed* (Aldershot: Ashgate, 2003); and Anne L. Murphy, *The Origins of English Financial Markets: Investment and Speculation before the South Sea Bubble* (Cambridge: Cambridge University Press, 2009).
4   Murphy, *Origins of English Financial Markets*, p. 94.

printed, of the changing impact of the printed within what was written and read and, above all, the role of the printed in providing material items that served and affected the conduct of trade and finance.

This book also takes a more radical interpretation of publishing. While the making public of books, journals and newspapers seems quite clear, much other printing actually 'published' information that assisted in selling wares and advertising services. Printing for commercial and financial practice that invited the addition of script (such as the filling in of certificates or the signing of forms) further complicated questions of authority in the material relationship between the printed and the written. In businesses both small and large, efficiency and accuracy was aided and gauged by ready reckoners, trade calculating tables, timetables and charts for travel by road and water. Published print raised subscriptions to public works and helped organize commercial institutions. It promoted new transport, marketing and rating schemes, and it enabled protest against them. Many printers' and booksellers' premises became an integral part of local business development, offering a diverse range of publishing services, including public notification, the circulation of news (orally as well as by print), the carriage and receipt of letters and goods, the provision of convenience addresses and warehousing, and even banking. Publication and print, as the surviving inventories and business ledgers of the printer-stationers show, was to be of crucial importance in the development of financial and commercial organization.

Terminology is problematic. In English, 'jobbing printing' is often used as co-terminus with 'jobbing' and 'job work' (although 'jobbing' work can also convey the sense of the peripatetic and the temporary). Translation into other languages is even more challenging and most European languages seem to have their own problems of definition.[5] This study adopts 'jobbing printing', a choice of terms helpfully validated by an advertisement placed in the London *Daily Advertiser* in late 1782:

Letter-Press Printers. To be disposed of, a Letter-Press, with six or seven different Founts of Letter; also some Flowers, Chaces, Board and Case

---

5   See for example the note by Dominique Varry in James Raven, 'Choses banales, imprimés ordinaires, "travaux de ville": l'économie et le monde de l'imprimerie que nous avons perdus', *Histoire et civilisation du livre: Revue internationale*, 9 (2013 [2014]), 243–58 (p. 243): 'Les termes anglais, sur lesquels il n'y a pas consensus, sont «jobbing» ou «job work». Leurs équivalents français sont: «travaux de ville», «ouvrages de ville», «travaux de labeur», «bibelots», et «bilboquets». Nous utiliserons principalement «travaux de ville»'.

Racks, Frames. Imposing Stones, Galleys, Composing Sticks, &. would suit a Pamphlet and Jobbing-Printing Office; the Whole to be purchased together. Enquiries of Mr Fleming, at the King's Head, Ave-Maria Lane. Brokers in this Business will not be treated with.[6]

Usages of the term 'jobbing printing' and certainly 'jobbing-printing office' are rare in the eighteenth century, despite the obvious everyday nature of the products and the practice. The appearance of the word 'jobbing' is also often ambiguous. The *Daily Advertiser* notice, however, seems to offer evidence of a trade and public meaning. The opening words are addressing likely purchasers: 'To letter-press printers'. The advertisement also nicely describes the sort of equipment attendant on 'jobbing printing'. The place of sale is adjacent to Stationers' Hall and to the great printing and publishing thoroughfares of Paternoster Row and St Paul's Churchyard. There were at least three Flemings printing in London at this date,[7] but none operated in or near Ave Maria Lane. Fleming of the King's Head is most likely to be acting for a nearby printer. No printer closed his or her office or moved out of Ave Maria Lane at or around this date either;[8] the two established printers of the lane in years either side of 1782 were Widow (Mary) Say at nos. 10 and 11 and William Wilson at no. 8. Perhaps the equipment for sale was superfluous to Say's or Wilson's stock, although it is sold as a working lot and might therefore represent the jettisoning of a separate printing operation. Mary Say and her late husband Charles Green Say (d.1775), himself the son of a celebrated printer, were recurrently prosecuted (mostly in high-profile cases). At the time of the *Daily Advertiser* notice, Mary was only recently out of prison having been gaoled for six months for libel in July 1781.[9] Whatever the circumstances, the description is a helpful one in what are muddy definitional waters. The designation 'jobbing-printing office' confirms that the term was recognized and in general use at the time.

The letterpress and the rolling press were essential props to business

---

6 *Daily Advertiser*, Thurs., 12 Dec. 1782 (issue 17126).
7 Listed in BBTI.
8 This is confirmed by the land taxation database used in James Raven, *Bookscape: Geographies of Printing and Publishing in London before 1800* (the Panizzi Lectures 2010) (London: The British Library, 2014).
9 Ian Maxted, *The London Book Trades, 1775–1800* (London: Dawson, 1977), p. 199; Charles Green Say had been summoned before the Commons as printer of the *Gazetteer* for printing the House's proceedings in 1760, and he was informed against as the printer of *The Letters of Junius* in 1770.

expansion in eighteenth-century Britain. The greater activity of attorneys, scriveners, bankers and brokers enormously increased the traffic in paper transactions. Print was midwife to numerous commercial and financial experiments.[10] Despite this, the engraving and print work supporting the swelling market in securities, in Exchequer issues and in other forms of investment and insurance, is poorly appreciated even by students of the book trades. In surveys of the expansion of print in the eighteenth century, jobbing is often dismissed as an embarrassing and vague sideline, largely unrelated to the more glamorous printing, publishing and selling of books.[11] In many studies of the impact of moveable type the survival of business printing and engraving has been of secondary concern in bibliographical archiving and research. Because of this and because jobbing printing covered such a wide range of activity, the circumstances under which many types of presswork were produced are often obscure.

Printing gave material form to the spectacular increase from the early eighteenth century in the volume of bills of exchange, remittance and retail vouchers, mortgage and share certificates, insurance policies and receipts of deposit and credit. The physical presentation of these items, however, was not passive and inert. The design and adaption of these forms and small, practical texts, affected the practices they were intended to serve. Sometimes, original designs proved inadequate or suggestive of improvement and new usages; in many cases, the use of these items had unintended consequences. In the same way that some modern forms provide insufficient space for information to be filled in, and others leave redundant spaces and parts, the use of printed paper intended to service commerce and finance in the eighteenth century did not always follow design. The authority given to the form that required signatures or blank parts filled in by pen and ink similarly evolved and increased with accepted and changing usages.

10   The development of public funds and banking is considered in P. G. M. Dickson, *The Financial Revolution in England: A Study in the Development of Public Credit, 1688–1756* (London: Macmillan, 1967), and L. S. Pressnell, *Country Banking in the Industrial Revolution* (New York: Oxford University Press, 1956). The structure of local credit is discussed by Peter Mathias, 'Capital, Credit and Enterprise in the Industrial Revolution', in *The Transformation of England: Essays in the Economic and Social History of England in the Eighteenth Century* (London: Methuen, 1979), pp. 88–115.

11   This was lamented nearly eighty years ago by John Johnson, 'The Development of Printing, other than Book-Printing', *The Library*, 4th ser., 17 (1937), 22–35. Also, P. M. Handover, *Printing in London from 1476 to Modern Times* (London, George Allen & Unwin Ltd, 1960), pp. 172–95.

The following chapters examine the mediation of print in the transformation of English commercial and financial practice between the late
seventeenth and the early nineteenth centuries. Successive sections consider
much-neglected but also fragile and comparatively rare materials including
ledgers and jobbing printing, news-sheets and ready reckoners, advertising
cuts and trade bills. The great majority of these paper materials, have long
since been lost, reused or consigned to fires and rubbish tips. Much that
does survive is hidden in archives preserved for the estate or business records
of a particular family or individual. Many of these items are rare survivals;
others, such as documents printed for the legal parish settlement of migrant
labourers and of paupers, for taxation and visitation assessment, and for
civic and commercial records of order and receipt, survive in their tens of
thousands. Such records are usually consulted – and catalogued – more
for their contribution to particular topics in social, economic and political
history rather than as historical subjects and material objects in their own
right. Archival evidence of the business of printing is even more elusive.
When a formerly unknown printer's ledger or important item of jobbing
printing reappears it is hailed by a small group of print historians, but the
new resources are often problematic given the contextual uncertainties
of often small, fragmentary or geographically unspecific documents. Past
coverage of printing history in general is also locationally uneven. Some
English country printers have been the subject of modern study, but
discussion of provincial activity has often been at the expense of the larger
and more important operations in London. Even the coverage of London
printing, however, has been selective. Much more attention has been given
to the publication in London of books, periodicals and newspapers than the
production, issue, use and circulation of other products of the 'common
press' of the letterpress printer and 'rolling press' of the intaglio printer.[12]

The neglected history of jobbing printing, however, illuminates a
further lost history: that of how print, however ephemeral and obscure
now, contributed significantly to broader economic and social change.
Self-evidently, the economy of western Europe was transformed between
the mid fifteenth and the mid eighteenth century, but it was certainly not
a story of gradual, linear improvement, but one marked by checks to
the various components of factor growth and by several clear reversals,

---

12   Iron presses, introduced from around 1800, were never referred to as common presses;
similarly, although all the presses used by letterpress printers were generically 'platen'
presses, this term is usually limited to presses made of iron.

especially in the early seventeenth century. The printing and book trades contributed to the broader transformation and were major beneficiaries of the increased wealth of the state. It is very difficult, however, to be precise about many of the constituent changes. Regular commercial statistics were not collected until the late seventeenth century; survival rates for much that was collected are very low, and crucial considerations such as population structure, wage levels and precise price indices are, despite many methodological advances in recent years, beyond exact historical calculation. There was obviously some overlap between the different categories of print productions and the merging of job work into something more discursive. Jobbing was never completely unattached from formal book and pamphlet and newspaper publication. New commercial opportunities offered printers the chance to extend their range of job work. It was a development quite as important, and in many cases much more important, than the chance to print more books. In alliance with the stationery business, the printing press was a forceful instrument beyond its more obvious contribution to intellectual formation and advance. As well as a vehicle for scholarship, learning and entertainment, the press offered practical instruction and agency.

Irrespective of the ability to read or buy books, more people than ever before experienced the effects of the use of moveable type. Printed books and pamphlets advanced new techniques in accounting and business management. Print was used in advertising, billposting and the production of financial and legal documents. It supported local retailing, auctioneering, banking, transportation and private credit arrangements. At a national level, London printing underpinned stock flotation, investments, insurance, and government excise and revenue operations. Printed paper eased, authorized and replicated commercial and financial transactions. Printed 'blanks' lightened the burden of the scrivener's, lawyer's and merchant's clerk, auctioneer, bailiff and postmaster. The printing press provided the authority necessary for the credibility of dozens of different types of commercial operation where institutional development was imperfect and where so many endeavours depended upon face-to-face trustworthiness. Many aspects of this were soon taken for granted, in the easier circulation of capital by printed notes, the more efficient supervision and enforcement of weights and measures, and the wider distribution and acceptance of timetables and maps.

It is important to appreciate the range of ways in which printing and publication assisted commercial and financial activity. Print served the merchant, financier, manufacturer and investor, most obviously (but perhaps not most importantly) by general treatments of the economy from extended philosophies to small essays in moral and what would later be called political economy. The presses also offered printed practical guidance that included books and pamphlets advancing new techniques in accounting and business management. Non-book or jobbing printing, however, not only supported printers in those periods when they were not printing book, pamphlet and periodical publications, but jobbing itself redefined what was meant by publication.

Print authorized and validated particular business practices by the provision of guides, advice manuals and commentaries. These items were available from bookseller-publishers as well as some printers and stationers. Notably, from the second half of the seventeenth century, booksellers, printers and stationers supplied an unparalleled volume of ledgers and account books. Printers undertook a new and vast range of business jobbing, including printed bills, tickets, receipt forms, commercial and financial blanks, promissory notes, warrants, indentures and authorizations. Such jobbing printing proper and allied stationery sales rarely involved a bookseller, unlike much other publishing activity. In retailing and local commerce, the publication of advertising newspapers from the 1690s created new marts and extended commerce.

Although printed forms offered fresh authority, significantly, it was print in relation to script that offered full 'certification'. It was the penned signature, mark or written-in blank on the form that actually authorized many printed documents. The history of the authority given by pens to printed forms adds a new dimension to continuing debates about the relationship between script and print. The question of authority by penned additions further refines notions of the 'fixity' of print where the apparent uniformity offered by replicated printing actually varies when read by different people with different skills and competences, in different ways, for different motives and in different places, at different times or under different conditions. Authorization and certification might helpfully describe both the processes by which material printed and annotated objects were used to validate processes of exchange, identification and registration, and the wider societal, published endorsement and discussion of business practice. Print certified commerce by supplying documentary and material means for ensuring and redesigning transactions.

In his *Histoire des chose banales*, Daniel Roche ventured one comment on the printer's role in the wider economy, although he did not expand upon upon it: 'on n'en a pas encore totalement mesuré la portée et l'impact dans la vie économique française, qui bénéficie moins qu'en Angleterre du support d'un enseignement spécial, animé par les besoins du milieu des négociants avides de manuels techniques'.[13] Roche kindly attributed this point to my early work,[14] and perhaps a comparison between English and French business manuals of the eighteenth century does suggest greater productivity in London than in Paris. An important question raised by the following study is the extent to which the development of English commercial jobbing print far eclipsed in volume and variety that produced by the nation's main commercial rivals, the Netherlands and France. Roche's discussion nevertheless misses the broader point. Jobbing work, not bookwork, sustained so many printers and sustained so many contributions to economic growth. Printers made business in 'l'expérience de l'urbanité'.

The chapters which follow are surveys of relatively uncharted materials, but they seek also to link islands of specialism, ranging from more established histories of economic commentaries and journalism to consideration of printing techniques and diverse printed ephemera including accountancy, book-keeping, advertisements and newspapers. Connections and contrasts are further investigated in relation to the contribution of printing to knowledge, news and information (or 'intelligence'). At issue are questions of the authority given by print and the relationship between text (of whatever kind) and trust. In this respect, in the years since my first consideration of the effect of printing on the economy and commercial practice, numerous advances have been made in our understanding of the relationship between the printing press and the conduct and reception of trade in early modern and eighteenth-century European society.[15]

13 'We have not yet entirely measured the scope and impact [of the printer's work] in French economic life, which was supported less than was the case in England by special instruction inspired by the business community's enthusiasm for technical manuals', Daniel Roche, *Histoire des choses banales: Naissance de la consommation des les sociétés traditionnelles (XVIIe–XIXe siècles)* (Paris: Fayard, 1997), p. 63; my response, in tribute to Roche, is Raven, 'Choses banales, imprimés ordinaires'.

14 Roche, *Histoire des choses banales*, p. 282, n. 45, citing James Raven, 'Imprimé et transactions économiques: représentation et interaction en angleterre aux XVIIe et XVIIIe siècles', *Revue d'histoire moderne et contemporaine*, 43:2 (1996), 234–65.

15 Raven, 'Print and Trade in Eighteenth-Century Britain'; see also Raven, 'Imprimé et transactions économiques', and James Raven, 'Jobbing: Was it the financial mainstay of the printing house?', in *Craft and Capital in Book Trade History. Part I: A Skilled Workforce: Training and Collaboration in the Book Trades. Part II: Balancing the Books:*

In England, the business press features in several important reappraisals
of the activities of English overseas merchants and also of the so-called
'financial revolution' of the late seventeenth century. Perry Gauci has
shown how the commercial acumen and patriotism of merchants raised
the profile of overseas trade and also public interest in mercantile activity.[16]
The increased value placed on trade was proven in the political arena, and
to a much greater degree than in the ambivalent portrayal of commerce,
finance and wealth creation in literature. There is some room for argument
here about the balance between political and literary judgement, and
certainly suggests the need for further exploration of the broader publication of commercial achievement in the crucial years of colonial and
financial development. Literary and dramatic representations highlighted
the inequalities between merchants and paraded arguments about the
national benefits, or not, of economic development. The examination
of relations between gentry and merchants continued throughout the
following century and remained a common trope in appraisals of public
policy, the aims of the trading community and ideals of the common
good.[17]

Print and paper intervened crucially in the calculation of risk and how
this was radically changed by investors in the late seventeenth century as
they developed new methods to exploit and extend stock markets and
speculative schemes. In significant research already noted, Anne Murphy
has re-examined the transformation in public and private finance after
1685, giving particular emphasis to the private equity markets that anticipated the growth in public funds[18] (something that was undervalued in
P. G. M. Dickson's seminal consideration of the financial revolution and
public finance).[19] More than one hundred joint-stock companies were
established in the ten years before 1695, offering an astonishing range of
investment opportunities and encouraging the development of a sophisticated market in equities and derivatives. In order to finance war and
defence, successive governments developed new revenue-raising operations

Financing the Book Trade from the 16th Century, ed. Robin Myers, Michael Harris and
Giles Mandelbrote, 2 vols (forthcoming, 2015).

16   Perry Gauci, *The Politics of Trade: The Overseas Merchant in State and Society,
1660–1720* (Oxford: Oxford University Press, 2001).

17   See James Raven, *Judging New Wealth: Popular Publishing and Responses to
Commerce in England, 1750–1800* (Oxford: Oxford University Press, 1992).

18   Murphy, *Origins of English Financial Markets*.

19   Dickson, *Financial Revolution*.

that included life annuity sales, state lotteries and the incorporation of the Bank of England. The creation of the national debt spawned an energetic and innovative derivative market in that debt. The enabling and representation of this activity was not always successful or positive. Weaknesses in capitalization, fraud and ineptitude, and greater government demands, resulted in financial and commercial calamity and fueled consequent debates in newspapers, pamphlets, books and prints about the practice and ethics of new commercial and financial enterprise. Issues of trust and deceit permeated contemporary economic commentaries and jeremiads. The avalanche of print assisting or condemning business development inevitably affected behaviour: the historical conundrum is how.

Despite the advance on a number of fronts of what might be called the cultural history of business and the economy, relatively little attention has been given to the actual mechanics and dynamics of the relationship between the two advances: that of printing, two hundred years old in England by 1670 but highly mutable during the late Stuart age, and that of the progressive but fitful expansion in commerce, overseas trade and finance. In recent investigations of the social world of print, from the early interest in the 'history of the book' and the 'culture of print' to more recent pursuit of the social history of knowledge and information, there continues to be one weakness, one blind spot. That weakness is economics. Some of my earlier work, including *The Business of Books*, addressed aspects of the commercial history of the printed book in Britain before 1860, but the commercial history of the broader printing revolution is a quite different consideration, with different questions to be asked and different perspectives to be understood. Margaret Hunt's influential discussion of the changing urban environment of the late seventeenth and early eighteenth centuries has importantly analysed 'commercial ephemera', including advertising, contracts, bonds, calendars, lottery tickets and many varieties of lists, in terms of advancing familiarity with commerce and influencing the behaviour and sensibilities of the literate 'middling sort'.[20] Particular objects, and notably trade cards, have been revisited by historians interested in the debate about consumption and the market for luxury goods,[21] but there is much to be done in understanding

---

20   Margaret R. Hunt, *The Middling Sort: Commerce, Gender, and the Family in England 1680–1780* (Berkeley: University of California Press, 1996).
21   See, for example, Maxine Berg and Helen Clifford, 'Selling Consumption in the Eighteenth Century: Advertising and the Trade Card in Britain and France', *Cultural and Social History*, 4:2 (2007), 145–70.

the economic role and effects of the full range of items produced in their tens of thousands by the printers of England in the eighteenth century. As summarized by Sarah Lloyd, 'printed by-products of commercial activities taught new ways of doing business, standardized processes, facilitated wider distribution networks, enabled a firmer control of resources and promoted goods and services'.[22]

By the end of the seventeenth century, the English and western European world of learning and of pseudo and encyclopaedic knowledge included more and more participants,[23] and (as this book will discuss in later chapters) notably expanded to embrace new types of commercial knowledge. Overload might have worried critics of literature and learning, but replication and minutiae were the common currency of jobbing. Four stimulating case studies for the sixty years before 1720 have been presented by Natasha Glaisyer to demonstrate the range of print media, from newspapers and ready reckoners to sermons, and 'the strategies newspaper writers employed to help readers observe stock market fluctuations, from the reading techniques employed by readers of mercantile manuals to the ways in which the trading world could be captured in a picture'.[24] Important studies have addressed specific aspects of the rise of the early financial press, often in miraculous detail,[25] while wide-ranging histories of credit and money have reconsidered the extent to which social situations shaped perceptions of risk, uncertainty and reliability: conditions both effected and evaluated by communication and publication.[26]

22   Sarah Lloyd, 'Ticketing the British Eighteenth Century: "A thing ... never heard of before"', *Journal of Social History*, 46:4 (2013), 843–71.
23   See Anne Goldgar, *Impolite Learning: Conduct and Community in the Republic of Letters 1680–1750* (London and New Haven, CT: Yale University Press, 1995).
24   Natasha Glaisyer, *The Culture of Commerce in England, 1660–1720* (London: The Royal Historical Society and Boydell, 2006), p. 23.
25   Notably John J. McCusker and Cora Gravesteijn, *The Beginnings of Commercial and Financial Journalism: The Commodity Price Currents, Exchange Rate Currents, and Money Currents of Early Modern Europe* (Amsterdam: NEHA, 1991); Larry Neal and Stephen Quinn, 'Networks of Information, Markets, and Institutions in the Rise of London as a Financial Centre, 1660–1720', *Financial History Review*, 8:1 (April 2001), 7–26; and Larry Neal, 'The Rise of a Financial Press: London and Amsterdam, 1681–1810', *Business History*, 30:2 (April 1988), 163–78.
26   Margot C. Finn, *The Character of Credit: Personal Debt in English Culture, 1740–1914* (Cambridge: Cambridge University Press, 2004); and Deborah Valenze, *The Social Life of Money in the English Past* (Cambridge: Cambridge University Press, 2006).

Historians like Hunt, Gauci, Murphy and Glaisyer point suggestively to the reshaping of behaviour and practices by practical print. More recent, and especially British and North American, historical investigation of knowledge has emphasized its social and political construction. The examination of how men and women set out to describe and disseminate practical knowledge has more in common with the consciously undertaken social activities identified by E. P. Thompson and even by Antonio Gramsci than with the Foucauldian elaboration of the unconscious. Historians increasingly interested in the nature and genesis of 'information' are often also associated with investigating precursors to a 'Big Brother state', the beginnings of the surveillance of the individual and of different identifications of citizens and subjects. The development of 'civicness' and of a 'fiscal-military state' is considered in relation to the genesis of both the census and the annual personal tax return, and other anticipations of the modern enumeration, inspection and supervision of individuals.[27] In the early modern world, Ann Blair has identified changes in information and note-taking allowed by advancing technology that also introduced concern about 'information overload'.[28] It is an interpretation that for some offers a riposte to arguments about the residual powers of Church and Crown in the eighteenth century, where the individual was forced to respond to the birth and development of changing administrative structures and efficiencies (and inefficiencies) in which print again proved a versatile midwife. Whatever the import of the replacement of the primarily oral and scribal by the primarily written and printed, we can be certain that information creation, collection, distribution, storage and retrieval was transformed from the late seventeenth century. This was an information shift – in volume, velocity and effect – of the generation and collection of information, of its circulation and of its deployment.

Questions of materiality and authority link these studies of information generation. The meaning that people attribute to things has been of increasing interest to historians and anthropologists. One influential

27 Edward Higgs, *The Information State in England: The Central Collection of Information on Citizens, 1500–2000* (London: Palgrave Macmillan, 2004).
28 Ann M. Blair, *Too Much to Know: Managing Scholarly Information before the Modern Age* (London and New Haven, CT: Yale University Press, 2010); see also contributions in *The Rise of Note-Taking in Early Modern Europe*, special issue of *Intellectual History Review*, 20:3 (Aug. 2010) with introduction by Richard Yeo, and see esp. Jacob Soll, 'From Note-Taking to Data Banks: Personal and Institutional Information Management in Early Modern Europe' (pp. 355–75).

collection of essays edited by Arjun Appadurai examines ways in which a multiplicity of material forms offers different types of worth and value. Manufactured commodities, however simple, turn out to be mechanisms that regulate taste and trade and establish authenticity and expertise.[29] The age of papers, certificates and tickets did not simply celebrate print and paper. People relied on material forms to reassure and organize. In turn, men and women, producers and users, gave greater focus to the physical and typographical character of the product when scrutinizing its authority. Tickets to admissions, for example, encouraged and created order and hierarchy, and also raised issues of authenticity and counterfeit.[30] The comparison with the Internet age is a helpful one. The sense of the 'new' from electronic and digital media is one of greater participation and of new ordering and information retrieval possibilities, but it also engenders fears of information overload, of greater inefficiency as well as efficiency, and, above all, questions about quality and authority. Warnings about the authority of entries on Wikipedia, or the reliability of evidence posted on websites, are the same as warnings about quickly produced, differently approved and sanctioned, or even unauthorized, jobbing print.

Many related concerns remain beyond the scope of this survey. The following is not an investigation of the development of the science of economics. Nor is it an inquiry into eighteenth-century literacy. Both subjects enjoy extensive and distinguished patronage. Similarly, the long-term effect of print upon commercial and financial transactions is not pursued in detail. Here, a study of the effect that presswork, such as printed advertising, has upon pricing and the relative demand for goods is best served at the microlevel of the local case study incorporating an analysis of local printing, local trade and reactions to national regulations and information. Priority in the following chapters is given to understanding the breadth of the contribution of print to the operation, practice and perception of trade. The book takes the materials and the owners

29   Arjun Appadurai (ed.), *The Social Life of Things: Commodities in Cultural Perspective* (Cambridge: Cambridge University Press, 1986).
30   Valentin Groebner, *Who are You? Identification, Deception, and Surveillance in Early Modern Europe* (New York: Zone Books, 2007); Lloyd, 'Ticketing the British Eighteenth Century', pp. 860–1; cf. the consideration of tickets in Gillian Russell, *Women, Sociability and Theatre in Georgian London* (Cambridge: Cambridge University Press, 2007), and questions of identity and material identification in Steve Hindle, 'Dependency, Shame and Belonging: Badging the Deserving Poor, c.1550–1750', *Cultural and Social History*, 1 (2004), 6–35.

of the press as the starting point to the wider questions of message and audience and the way in which printing interested different clients in the practice and consequences of trade.

Like many other projects currently recovering the history of eighteenth-century printing and publishing, this work draws on an abundance of local archive material and an underexploited wealth of evidence which demands further inspection. It also benefits from the continuing labours of bibliographers and historians of print, some of whose work is available only in specialist journals, conference proceedings and privately printed papers. In discussing both the jobbing printing and publications serving businessmen and women and the broadening of general interest in trade, my additional aim is to provide a context for further work about specific businesses of the period and about issues relating to the production and circulation of texts on commercial matters. For those persuaded by the 'new economics' and the 'limits to growth' interpretations of the Industrial Revolution, the appearance in the following chapters of advances, increases and development might seem dangerously old-fashioned and neo-Whiggish. But from the perspective of the researcher in the local record offices and from study of a cross-section of what was actually published at the time, many of the more traditional points of emphasis do not seem so very wrong. Certainly, it is rather unfashionable to begin by suggesting that a very large number of economic and social statistics for the eighteenth century can be reduced to a crude upward curve which accelerates slowly (even levelling off) towards mid-century and then rushes skywards in the final two decades. With obvious short-term fluctuations, population totals, export trends, home consumption levels, the number of separate banking entries, bankruptcy figures and industrial production statistics all follow the curve. So do the statistics for the expansion of the book trades: the production of books and periodicals, the volume of jobbing printing, the number of bookseller-publishers, the number of bookbinders, the book trade apprenticeship figures, the number of retail bookshops, the number of circulating libraries and the number of book piracies. As following chapters will demonstrate, however, growth is not all: setbacks, resistance and disillusion are evident at critical junctures and the course of printing and publishing as much as economic development is pitted with important checks and constraints.

To so map the relationship between print and commerce is not, however, inconsistent with the aims and approaches of much recent revisionism in eighteenth-century history. New studies of early modern and eighteenth-century Britain advocate greater archival contextualization to enhance our understanding of social change. It is argued that various influential interpretations of early modern society were corseted by preconceived ideas of structural dynamics and economic determinism. The same voices have urged the student of eighteenth-century politics, religion and society to return to the contemporary debate and understand the issues of the day in terms familiar to contemporary participants. There are, of course, dangers in this approach. We can all too easily be absorbed by the colour of antique debates and fail to recognize deeper motivations. Yet there is much to be gained from study of surviving publications in the context of the means of their production, circulation and reception. As the following attempts to show, this is certainly true of the contribution of print to the practice and perception of business.

Finally, study of print and the book trades during this period requires an appreciation of geographical boundaries and trade routes. Any history of the book in England and in the British Isles has to take account of imported books as well as later exports of paper, print and related supplies to the colonies. Too often, in fact, publishing histories of England have not only been excessively anglocentric, but have understated the early modern trade in books from the Continent – a weakness partly addressed in *The Business of Books*. Jobbing requirements and responses were, by contrast, much more localized, and the broader study of the business *of print* actually offers a distinction between the (too often ignored) international context of the book trade and publication, and national, regional and community confines of jobbing printing (itself ignored for different reasons). Studies such as this one also point to much greater printing activity in the country towns of eighteenth-century England than has been previously appreciated.

The early chapters of this book examine the practical and instructional role of print in administrative and commercial transactions. These sections consider the new business 'knowledge' and behaviour effected by printing and stationery, jobbing work, commercial information, advertising, and published guides and directories. The remaining chapters examine the contribution of print to the gathering and dissemination of 'intelligence', the generation of popular, public debate and the development of an understanding of trade among different readerships. The final chapter approaches the relationship between print and trade from the perspective of the common reader, familiar with (if not always appreciative of) jobbing print, and seeking practical and general information about trading and monetary matters.

2

England and the Uneven Economic Miracle

Printers' products and services contributed to an economic transformation of startling range and complexity. The 'English miracle'[1] was part of broader British developments, coaxed by changing political frameworks across the three kingdoms and by expansion overseas. At the close of the seventeenth century, England exported goods to the value of £6.5 million per year and imported goods worth about £6 million. By 1816, English, Scottish and Irish exports were worth £39 million in official (constant price) values; imports were worth £33.6 million. An English and Welsh national income of about £48 million in 1688 compares to a combined English, Welsh and Scottish national income of £232 million on the eve of Irish union in 1801.[2] By 1815, textiles, comprising almost four-fifths of total exports, were as dominant a proportion of exports as they had been in 1695, but cotton, not wool, was now king. As a result of colonial consolidation, particularly in the West Indies, the re-export of tobacco, sugar and other overseas produce comprised about a third of all exports from the 1690s until the early 1770s. By then re-exports roughly equalled the value of all domestic exports to Europe.[3]

---

1   The relationship between England and Britain is crucial: Liah Greenfeld, shifting focus sometimes uneasily between the two, has argued that Britain's 'rise was in the nature of a Miracle', best understood by reason that 'nationalism first appeared in England' something which 'liberated natural economic energies from the constraining tutelage of ethical considerations and social concerns, and therefore ... did not inhibit economic growth': *The Spirit of Capitalism: Nationalism and Economic Growth* (Cambridge, MA: Harvard University Press, 2001), pp. 22–4; cf. Julian Hoppit, 'The Nation, the State, and the First Industrial Revolution', *Journal of British Studies*, 50:2 (April 2011), 307–31.
2   François Crouzet, 'Toward an Export Economy: British Exports during the Industrial Revolution', *Explorations in Economic History*, 17 (1980), 48–93 (p. 78); Ralph Davis, *The Industrial Revolution and British Overseas Trade* (Leicester: Leicester University Press, 1979), table 37. Figures are notoriously problematic and should be compared with computed real values and alternative sources offered by Crouzet and Davis.
3   See in particular Martin Daunton, *Progress and Poverty: An Economic and Social*

With the Navigation Acts ensuring that colonial primary produce was sent directly to the home country and not to other European markets, a quarter or more of all imports to England and Scotland were re-exported in the years prior to 1775. The value of the entrepôt trade was halved during the American revolutionary wars, but British naval supremacy ensured an impressive re-export recovery during the European wars after 1793. Between 1814 and 1816 just over a quarter of all goods sent out from English ports were re-exports. Industrial production was based on textiles (predominantly wool and later, cotton), the manufacturing industries of shipbuilding, construction, metal smelting and refining, and a variety of derivative finishing trades. In 1700, Sir Ambrose Crowley's Sunderland iron factory was the largest in Europe, nine years before Abraham Darby established his famous works in Coalbrookdale. In the same decade an average of 16,000 tons of iron were imported and 1,600 tons of iron and steel were exported each year. A century later, between 1810 and 1819, 18,000 tons of iron were imported and 47,000 tons of iron and steel were exported annually.[4]

The organization of industries, most of which remained cottage, domestic crafts, was transformed by the activities of ambitious merchants and entrepreneurs and by a succession of technological improvements. In total, exports of English domestic produce enjoyed a mean annual growth rate of 1.5% between 1697 and 1800, although such an average is also derived from a succession of different phases of expansion and stagnation. A 2.8% growth rate per annum to 1714 was halved between 1714 and 1745, restored to about 3% to 1760 and then cut to a negative rate of −1.5% to 1781. Thereafter, domestic exports surged forward, reaching a mean annual growth rate of 5.1% to the end of the century. Combined English and Scottish domestic exports increased on average by 3.1% per annum between 1802 and 1814.[5]

England benefited also from the transformation in the economies of its nearest neighbours and constituent countries of the British Crown. In both Ireland and Scotland, linen had replaced the cattle trade as the most successful export industry by the end of the seventeenth century. Both nations embraced the cotton industry during the eighteenth century,

History of Britain, 1700–1850 (Oxford: Oxford University Press, 1995); and, for the early decades, Julian Hoppit, A Land of Liberty? England 1689–1727 (Oxford: Clarendon Press, 2000), chs. 10 and 11.

4 B. R. Mitchell, British Historical Statistics (Cambridge: Cambridge University Press, 1988), pp. 292–4, 298, 300.

5 Crouzet, 'Toward an Export Economy', pp. 50–3.

even though it was ultimately successful only in Scotland. Scottish textile spinning redoubled in the three decades following the establishment of the first Scottish cotton mill at Penicuik in 1779. At this date, Ireland continued to import more raw cotton than Scotland, but ten years later the position was reversed. After a further and sudden advance in cotton importation in the last few years of the eighteenth century, Scotland imported three times more raw cotton than Ireland by 1805–10. The official annual value of home produced exports from Scotland had already jumped from just over £0.25 million in 1755 to just under £2 million by 1800.[6]

There can now be no doubt, however, that the fundamental structural shifts which underpinned economic growth derived from demographic expansion and increased agricultural productivity. The British Isles in 1695 comprised three kingdoms with a total population of just over 8 million. In 1814 a United Kingdom of Britain and Ireland contained a population of some 19 million. Although the enormous demographic change in Ireland should not be overlooked (as it often is), English population growth was rapid.[7] By 1814, 11 million people lived in England and Wales, 5.5 million in Ireland and nearly 2 million in Scotland. A further striking demographic feature of this period was the soaring growth of London. In 1695, London, with over 0.5 million people, was twenty times larger than its nearest English rival and contained 10% of the total population of England and Wales. The principal market in the country, the greatest port and the administrative and political centre, the population of Greater London grew to 1.5 million people by 1814. Almost a tenth of all those inhabiting the United Kingdom were then living in the English capital.[8]

Throughout this period, urban centres other than the capitals boasted extraordinary growth rates. In 1695, Bristol, with a population of about 20,000, was rivalling Norwich as the second largest English town after

6   Henry Hamilton, *An Economic History of Scotland in the Eighteenth Century* (Oxford: Oxford University Press, 1963), table, pp. 41, 44–5.

7   As Julian Hoppit observes, England comprises just over 40% of the total surface area of Britain and Ireland; in 1700 England had over 60% of the population of these islands, and thus a population density of about twice that of Ireland and Wales and three times that of Scotland; about 46% of the total population growth over the century took place in Ireland: 'The Nation, the State, and the First Industrial Revolution', p. 313.

8   E. A. Wrigley, 'British population during the "long" eighteenth century, 1680–1840', in *The Cambridge Economic History of Modern Britain*, ed. Roderick Floud and Paul Johnson, 3 vols (Cambridge: Cambridge University Press, 2004), vol. 1, *Industrialisation, 1700–1860*, pp. 57–95; E. A. Wrigley, 'The Growth of Population in Eighteenth-Century England: A Conundrum Resolved', *Past & Present*, 98 (Feb. 1983), 121–50.

London. By about 1750, Bristol was indisputably the fourth largest town of the British Isles (after London, Dublin and Cork), with a population of 50,000 and its port set fair for the Atlantic trade. Although Bristol continued to expand during the century, albeit at a much lower rate, one of the most significant pointers in demographic change was the rapid advance of Glasgow from a population of 23,500 to approximately 83,000 by 1800. Demographic surveys of Britain, however, only serve to highlight the greater advance of English population, urban growth and economic influence by the end of the eighteenth century.

The rate of English urban expansion in the late eighteenth and early nineteenth centuries was unprecedented. Many new towns in the Midlands and the north of England mushroomed from small villages or market settlements in the mid eighteenth century to be manufacturing and trading centres of over 10,000 people by 1814. By 1801 the third largest city in the United Kingdom was Manchester with a population of some 84,000. The next largest English towns at that date were Liverpool with 77,653 inhabitants and Birmingham with 73,670. Both had tripled their populations since 1750. By contrast, the fourth largest town in England in 1801, Bristol, had increased its population by only 10,000 since 1750, and it was soon to be eclipsed by other cities of the new industrial areas. Whereas those living in towns had comprised some 8% of the population of England in 1600, by 1800 the urban population had risen to 28%. By comparison, the urban population of France, 9% in 1600, had increased to only 11% by 1800.[9]

Urban developments were not simply confined to population increase, migration and changes to household size. The advance of the country town, of the regional city and of London was also, most markedly in the mid and late eighteenth century, one of political, economic and cultural transformation.[10] In an urban revolution, social attitudes and religious belief were as affected quite as much as politics by new spaces of activity, modes of communication and the proximity of different peoples, practices and services. The development of new civic and legal structures and responsibilities was one aspect of changing urban formation; another was

9   E. A. Wrigley, *People, Cities and Wealth: the Transformation of Traditional Society* (Oxford: Oxford University Press, 1987), p. 11; the growth of towns is compared in tables 7.1 and 7.2; further details are given in P. J. Corfield, *The Impact of English Towns, 1700–1800* (Oxford: Oxford University Press, 1982).
10 Of many ground-breaking studies in recent years, see Miles Ogborn, *Spaces of Modernity: London's Geographies, 1680–1780* (London: Guilford Press, 1998).

a transformation in social interaction and the creation of new modes of behaviour associated with the culture of politeness and sensibility. Such cultural development was critically counterpointed by new social tensions. A mutable underworld, sometimes under the radar of history, surfaces in criminal records and in the accounts of responses to increased legislation that attempted to control migration, employment and the lives of poor.[11] Unease and often panic accompanied this change, especially in time of dearth, war and external threat. Perception was often as important as practice, and the escalation of a sense of crisis at the end of the century was, as will be argued in later chapters, reflected in a reaction against the very printing that enabled and reported many of the new practices.[12]

London has featured prominently in studies of division and disorder, but other cities and towns, notably Bristol, experienced the unrest and instability born of vividly uneven commercial success.[13] Involvements and expectations also varied and changed over the century according to gender, although economic and social status remained a critical filter.[14] Some of the most revealing historical analysis of recent years has concerned change as it affected the lives of women, significant in itself but also an integral part of a developing civic and urban culture in which women played new roles and created new demands.[15] The contribution of women

11 See Tim Hitchcock and Robert B. Shoemaker, *London Lives, 1690–1800: Crime, Poverty and Social Policy in the Metropolis* (ongoing searchable database, www. londonlives.org, accessed 11 June 2014); Robert B. Shoemaker, *Prosecution and Punishment: Petty Crime and the Law in London and Rural Middlesex, ca. 1660–1725* (Cambridge: Cambridge University Press, 1991); and Rosemary Sweet, 'Corrupt and corporate bodies: attitudes to corruption in eighteenth-century and early nineteenth-century towns', in *Corruption in Urban Politics and Society, Britain 1780–1950*, ed. James R. Moore and John Smith (Aldershot: Ashgate, 2007), pp. 41–56.

12 Cf. Marjorie Morgan, *Manners, Morals and Class in England, 1774–1858* (London: Macmillan, 1994).

13 Tim Hitchcock, *Down and Out in Eighteenth-Century London*, 2nd edn (London: Hambledon and London, 2004); Jonathan Barry and Kenneth Morgan (eds), *Reformation and Renewal in Eighteenth-Century Bristol* (Bristol: Bristol Record Society, 1994).

14 See, for example, Pamela Sharpe, *Adapting to Capitalism: Working Women in the English Economy, 1700–1850* (New York: St Martin's Press, 1996); and Isabelle Baudino, Jacques Carré and Cécile Révauger (eds), *The Invisible Woman: Aspects of Women's Work in Eighteenth-Century Britain* (Aldershot: Ashgate, 2005).

15 See in particular Gillian Russell, *Women, Sociability and Theatre in Georgian London* (Cambridge: Cambridge University Press, 2007); Hannah Barker and Elaine Chalus (eds), *Women's History: Britain, 1700–1850* (London: Routledge, 2005); Rosemary Sweet and Penelope Lane (eds), *Women and Urban Life in Eighteenth-Century England* (Aldershot:

to the business life of town, country and city, and to a diversity of trades and occupations, has also been reassessed.[16] Such alterations to urban experience produced multiple economic effects, from the creation of new and local skills, employment and industries to new modes of buying and selling and the adoption of new market strategies. Demand for building, basic necessities and a range of consumables increased sharply, as did new centres of production to serve new needs and market interests. New production sites certainly included workshops and manufacturing works in London (all too often overlooked in the historical accounts).[17]

Urban growth and the confident rebuilding of ancient cities and towns was the consequence of economic growth not only unparalleled in history, but founded upon increased agricultural productivity and the expansion of traditional industries by traditional means. The eighteenth-century English economy turned on the delicate balance between food supply and population growth. Experiments in new crops and crop rotation systems going back many decades ensured marked improvements in agricultural productivity in the first half of the eighteenth century. Agricultural exports are most impressive for this period, but even more important was the ability of both arable and pastoral farming to so increase its output and efficiency that it was able – in most parts of England – to support rather than constrain late-eighteenth-century population growth. Fluctuations in agricultural progress were evident and unsettling, and relations between landlords, farmers and labourers reflected what has been described as 'the warmth of steady if slow expansion' but also 'the chill of uncertainty'.[18] Significantly, grain exports rose to a fifth of all English and Welsh

---

Ashgate, 2003); Hannah Barker and Elaine Chalus (eds), *Gender in Eighteenth-Century England: Roles, Representations and Responsibilities* (London: Longman, 1997); and Robert B. Shoemaker, *Gender in English Society, 1650–1850: The Emergence of Separate Spheres?* (London and New York: Longman, 1998).

16   See, for example, Hannah Barker, *The Business of Women: Female Enterprise and Urban Development in Northern England, 1760–1830* (Oxford: Oxford University Press, 2006); Paula McDowell, *The Women of Grub Street: Press, Politics and Gender in the London Literary Marketplace, 1678–1730* (Oxford: Clarendon Press, 1998); and Hannah Barker and Jane Hamlett, 'Living above the shop: home, business, and family in the English "Industrial Revolution"', *Journal of Family History*, 35:4 (2010), 311–28.

17   An exacting and telling case study is Alan Pryor, *Beer, Brewhouses and Businessmen: The Transformation of the London Brewing Trade 1700–1850* (Manchester: Manchester University Press, 2014) examining the production as much as the consumption of a developing commodity in London.

18   Hoppit, *Land of Liberty*, p. 356.

exports at the mid eighteenth century and then fell back. Thenceforth, improved agricultural productivity served burgeoning home populations. More intensive farming in the second half of the eighteenth century was sustained by higher levels of investment. At the same time, war, in many respects a drain on the economy, stimulated agricultural prices and boosted farming surpluses.[19]

'Revolution' was always an unfortunate *mot juste* when transferred to describe the course of English economic history between the late eighteenth and the mid nineteenth century. At no particular moment was an existing economic citadel stormed, even at the level of an individual region or trading district. There was certainly no abrupt discontinuity between a mercantilist and a free trade system or between a pre-industrial and post-industrial society. Revolution in industry can be applied only to certain key technological transformations, almost all specific to a single trade or location, and most taking several decades to multiply and contribute significantly to economic change. 'Revolution' so narrowly applied is of little explanatory value.

A much more meaningful measure of 'industrial revolution' is of changing levels of investment in terms of real per capita income. As Julian Hoppit writes, self-sustained long-term per capita growth, a defining characteristic of modern economies, 'is rooted in the ability and willingness to forgo current consumption in order to invest in more productive processes'.[20] The incentive to invest includes a broad range of inputs to the composition of the economy, from agrarian, commercial, financial and transport changes, to fundamental shifts in energy sources. Other incentives are more culturally, religiously and politically based (and certainly include the communication and information agencies central to the following study). What cannot be questioned is the fitfulness of economic activity in the late seventeenth century and also the advances in productivity from the late seventeenth to the late eighteenth century. Even the most convinced proponent of 'slow growth' is impressed by the structural changes experienced by the eighteenth-century economy,[21] although there can be no denying that expansion in the first quarter of

19 For greater detail, see Mark Overton, *Agricultural Revolution in England: The Transformation of the Agrarian Economy, 1500–1850* (Cambridge: Cambridge University Press, 1996).
20 Hoppit, *Land of Liberty*, p. 313.
21 N. F. R. Crafts, *British Economic Growth during the Industrial Revolution* (Oxford: Oxford University Press, 1985).

the eighteenth century remained modest, burdened by difficulties faced in trying to improve output and productivity.[22] Overseas trade, conducted mostly by private merchants, was both an initial and a continuing stimulus. The expansion of foreign trade in the final third of the seventeenth century boosted levels of wealth and savings and enlarged existing markets. It served as a vital spark to the economic engine, even though the momentum of change in the next century was to be propelled far more by the interplay between population, agriculture and the restructuring of traditional industries. The harnessing of water power and the exploitation of fossil fuels relieved industrial dependence on simple manual labour. The energy revolution, substituting water and coal for muscle power in a range of productive processes, transformed the efficiency and organization of many separate trades and industries. Even so, adoption of new processes and machinery was comparatively slow where the predominantly domestic system of manufacture was resistant to improvements in either productivity per worker or quality of output, or where few possessed what we might think of as the modern desire to advance technologies.

Technically, the first of the new factories was the silk throwing mill which used the power of the River Derwent near Derby to prepare yarn for weaving. In spinning, John Kay's 1733 flying shuttle, Richard Arkwright's 1769 water-powered frame and Samuel Crompton's 1779 mule, successively transformed the industry. The great beneficiary of this technology was to be cotton. The first water-powered cotton mills date from the early 1770s, with the first steam engine introduced to cotton spinning in 1785. With plentiful supplies of water required in the production and finishing processes, water remained an important locational factor. In the final third of the century, the cotton industry in particular achieved extraordinary rates of growth, even if the industry's 1% contribution to English and Scottish national income in 1780 gives the lie to its being an early 'leading sector' of economic expansion. The transition to new manufacturing processes after about 1760 included the development of machine tools following on from advanced chemical and iron production techniques. Innovation spanned several generations, from Abraham Darby's use of coke to produce pig iron from about 1705 to Henry Cort's 1784 puddling furnaces and rolling mills that revolutionized the refining of iron.

Critical also to the support of economic growth was the development of intermediary financial mechanisms and the expansion of domestic

22   Hoppit, *Land of Liberty*, pp. 324–5.

demand for manufactured goods and imports. Walt Rostow suggested that the reinvestment of 10% of Gross National Product was necessary for self-sustained growth.[23] The raising of the rate of investment was an obvious feature of commercial and industrial growth, even if rates required for 'take-off' did not reach Rostovian levels until the 1840s (and then only briefly). The establishment of the Bank of England in 1694 was followed by numerous experiments in investment, joint-stock, insurance and credit-raising schemes.[24] Public finance advanced but so, crucially, did the private equity market. A hundred new joint-stock companies were established between 1685 and 1695, but the market (with advances in both public finance and the private equity market) was still circumscribed. An archivally based estimate, that the total number of joint-stock companies represented no more than 2% of the total wealth of England in 1695, has itself been further refined by the disclosure that two-thirds of the combined joint-stock wealth resided in two stocks, those of the Bank of England and of the East India Company.[25] Nevertheless, the development of what we might anachronistically term the financial services industry dates from the late seventeenth century, from fire and marine insurance in the 1670s and life insurance offers that followed the speculative boom of the 1690s.[26] The increase in the insurance market contributed to the advance of finance capitalism in its own right and boosted confidence by safeguarding wealth while promoting a 'growing sense in English society that the hazards of life and commerce could be converted into calculable, manageable risks'.[27] As will be discussed below, preprinted contracts flourished, notably in relation to the development of trading options and the derivative market that was intended to manage risk and encourage greater investment. Increased complexity of allocation, transfer and information arrangements was a natural consequence of the expansion of secondary and options markets.

23 W. W. Rostow, 'The Take-Off into Self-Sustained Growth', *Economic Journal*, 66:261 (Mar. 1956), 25–48.
24 See W. R. Bisschop, *The Rise of the London Money Market, 1640–1826* (London: Cass, 1968), and pre-eminently, P. G. M. Dickson, *The Financial Revolution in England: A Study in the Development of Public Credit, 1688–1756* (London: Macmillan, 1967).
25 Brian Parsons, 'The Behaviour of Prices on the London Stock Market in the Early Eighteenth Century' (unpubl. Ph.D. dissertation, University of Chicago, 1974), pp. 23, 30; Anne L. Murphy, *The Origins of English Financial Markets: Investment and Speculation before the South Sea Bubble* (Cambridge: Cambridge University Press, 2009), p. 37.
26 Geoffrey Wilson Clark, *Betting on Lives: The Culture of Life Insurance in England, 1695–1775* (Manchester: Manchester University Press, 1999).
27 Murphy, *Origins of English Financial Markets*, p. 14.

In comparison, the credit needs of new industry and industrial servicing (such as transportation) were small, especially when compared to the capital tied up in government stock. Given the scale of the eighteenth-century economy and the modesty of technological advances when compared to those of the next century, capital accumulation was held back less by shortages of savings than by difficulties in transferring economic surpluses to those sectors and individuals requiring start-up or tie-over credit. Almost all credit requirements were short-term and bound not to servicing fixed assets, but to supplying the purchase of materials and to discounting bills of exchange to cash.

In this face-to-face society, in which individual economic transactions depended largely on the trust and hence moral reputation of individuals, the authority of paper, of the printed and written word, gained central significance.[28] Even when replaced by more institutional support from the extension of country banks, for example, by the end of the eighteenth century, the trust in pledges turned on the repute of both creditor and debtor. Credit was paramount in an early modern economy where demand for money escalated during the second half of the sixteenth century, but its supply increased by only a small amount. Surviving inventories record the pervasiveness of debt, all the greater in urban areas, and especially in London. It also proved almost impossible to keep track of the webs of personal obligations where legal uncertainties only exacerbated the crisis of trust and confidence.[29] One result was the thirty-two Acts passed by the Westminster parliament in the eighteenth century to clear or assist debtors, as well as the striking development of borough courts, courts of record, courts baron, hundred courts and county courts, all to hear disputes about debt and credit transactions. Courts apparently preoccupied by justice, civil disputes and administration were in fact mostly concerned with money debt in a rapidly changing economy.[30]

By the end of the eighteenth century, the fledgling country banking system was underwriting the largest credit needs of industry. A steepening increase in the number of bankruptcies was evidence more of advancing

28   See in particular Peter Mathias, *The Transformation of England: Essays in the Economic and Social History of England in the Eighteenth Century* (London: Methuen, 1979), ch. 5.
29   Craig Muldrew, *The Economy of Obligation: The Culture of Credit and Social Relations in Early Modern England* (New York: St Martin's Press, 1998).
30   See Edward Higgs, *Identifying the English: A History of Personal Identification from 1500 to the Present* (London and New York: Continuum, 2011), p. 44.

enterprise, higher risk activity and continuing problems in credit organization, than of permanent commercial or financial impediments.
Institutional development ensured the more efficient use of savings, even
though one should not underestimate the importance of face-to-face
and individually formulated transactions to the very end of this period,
particularly in country districts.

By means of a variety of banking and financial conduits, agricultural
and manufacturing wealth was invested in improving land and transport
during the second half of the eighteenth century. Landlords' profits in
particular were ploughed back into improving the rural infrastructure.
Various major river improvement schemes were undertaken before
mid-century, but it was the Bridgewater canal in 1761 which set the model
for later developments. By 1800, canals linked the Mersey, Severn, Thames
and Trent, and a network of navigations served most major towns in the
country. In England, turnpike trusts also engaged in the management
of many sections of the main radial roads from London during the first
three decades of the eighteenth century. In the 1750s, trusts were formed
to maintain the cross-routes between the Great Roads radiating from
London. In South Wales, the roads of complete counties were put under
single turnpike trusts in the 1760s.

Associated with such investments in transport and the social infrastructure was the impetus given to home demand and its further contribution to economic growth. This has been shown to be particularly
effective in the final third of the eighteenth century.[31] Certainly, the decline
in the level of domestic exports between 1761 and 1780 reaffirms the vital
compensatory support of the home market during these years of rising
national wealth. Similarly, the wars of the second half of the century
increased the burden of government on the economy after several decades
of decline in real levels of taxation. Despite this, and despite no evidence
of a rise in the real wages of the labouring population between 1750 and
1805,[32] domestic demand increased significantly. Income redistribution

31 A. H. John, 'Aspects of English Economic Growth in the First Half of the Eighteenth
Century', Economica, n.s., 28:110 (May 1961), 176–90; D. E. C. Eversley, 'The Home
Market and Economic Growth in England, 1750–1780', in Land, Labour and Population
in the Industrial Revolution, ed. E. L. Jones and G. E. Mingay (London: Edward Arnold,
1967), pp. 206–59.
32 W. A. Cole, 'Factors in Demand, 1700–80', in The Economic History of Britain
since 1700, ed. Roderick Floud and Donald McCloskey, 2 vols (Cambridge: Cambridge
University Press, 1981), vol. 1, pp. 36–65 (p. 57).

was one key to this expansion in the home market, but it is also clear that additional earnings and benefits over and above labourers' money wages provided the basis for a general increase in per capita consumption of home products.

The importance of home demand is extensively contested in historical studies and some have insisted that its contribution to economic transformation has been exaggerated.[33] Certainly, it is no first or even early cause of factor growth, and it is also obvious that there were great regional differences in consumption patterns. Nevertheless, the statistics for increased mass consumption in the final decades of the eighteenth century are impressive. Excised commodities, such as soap, candles, beer and spirits, were bought at a rate which increased more than twice as fast as that of population growth.[34] Boulton, Watt and Wedgwood, and hundreds of lesser entrepreneurs, derived their profits from the apparently increasing discretionary incomes of the middle classes – and their imitators.[35]

The least satisfactory outcome of argument about economic growth in England in the eighteenth century, however, has been the neglect of the comparative economic development of the different parts of the British Isles. At least until recent times, economic histories of the three kingdoms have proceeded on largely separate lines, rarely arriving at the same junctions, and even passing each other in different directions. Thus revisionist accounts of the pre-industrial period in Ireland and Scotland, written in the 1970s, now have much in common with recent limits-to-growth and traditional sector interpretations of the eighteenth-century English economy. The only major difference between these histories is in the scale of their subject and the dependence outside England upon fewer staple industries. Few parallels have been explored, however, and as research on the English economy proceeds upon new tracks stressing slow growth and continuity, historians of the Scottish and the Irish economies

33   Notably, J. Mokyr, 'Demand vs. Supply in the Industrial Revolution', *Journal of Economic History*, 37 (1977), 981–1008.

34   Neil McKendrick, 'The Consumer Revolution of Eighteenth-Century England', in *The Birth of a Consumer Society: The Commercialization of Eighteenth-Century England*, ed. Neil McKendrick, John Brewer and J. H. Plumb (London: Europa, 1982), pp. 9–33 (p. 29).

35   For a recent contribution see Jon Stobart, *Sugar and Spice. Grocers and Groceries in Provincial England, c.1650–1830* (Oxford: Oxford University Press, 2013); see also John Brewer and Roy Porter (eds), *Consumption and the World of Goods* (London: Routledge, 1993).

of the eighteenth century have returned to investigating types of industrial 'take-off' – or reasons for their delay or failure.[36]

In this context, Ireland appears more colonial than domestic, but its developing market supported many English industries. After London, Dublin was easily the second city of the British Isles before 1800. In the longer view Dublin was more of a shock city even than London. The 20,000–30,000 population of Edinburgh in 1650 far exceeded the then population of the Irish capital. In the late seventeenth century, as the Scottish economy faltered, Dublin raced ahead, reaching a population of 60,000 by 1700, or more than double that of Edinburgh. Sometime in the first decades of the next century, Cork, the second city of Ireland, became the third most populous town in the three kingdoms after London and Dublin. While Cork claimed a population of 70,000 by 1750, Dublin's population totalled 140,000 by 1760, 182,000 by 1800 and well over 200,000 by 1814. By 1800 Dublin was more than three times the size of Edinburgh and among the ten largest cities of Europe.

Related questions of the political relationship between the three kingdoms of the British Isles are also critical to the unevenness of commercial development. The century of English naval and mercantile consolidation, English overseas exploration, and confident English architecture and literature, was also one of perilous Jacobite and Irish rebellion, Irish trade disputes and smouldering resentments about commercial organization and national identities. Union with Scotland was enacted in 1707 and, under the settlement, Scotland remained distinct from England in its administration and law. In many other areas – notably currency and financial organization – theoretical unity with England was countered for many decades by the continuance of traditional practices.

The distinctiveness of Ireland was one contained by the Williamite penal laws and the Protestant ascendancy. Union with England was long advocated by those anxious to confirm Ascendancy or to circumvent the Navigation Acts and other legislative restrictions on Irish commerce.

36   Bruce Lenman, *An Economic and Social History of Modern Scotland, 1660–1976* (London: Harper Collins, 1977); L. M. Cullen and T. C. Smout, 'Economic Growth in Scotland and Ireland', in *Comparative Aspects of Scottish and Irish Economic and Social History, 1600–1900*, ed L. M. Cullen and T. C. Smout (Edinburgh: John Donald, 1977), pp. 3–18; c.f. K. J. Cullen, *Famine in Scotland: The 'Ill Years' of the 1690s* (Edinburgh: Edinburgh University Press, 2010); T. M. Devine, C. H. Lee and G. C. Peden (eds), *The Transformation of Scotland: The Economy Since 1700* (Edinburgh: Edinburgh University Press, 2005).

Four years before the Scottish union, the Irish House of Commons had also petitioned the Crown for union, and the Irish Lords followed with a similar petition in 1709. Parliamentary union was eventually concluded in 1801, but under domestic conditions very different from those of a century earlier. Indeed, union with England transformed the Scottish economy at the beginning of the eighteenth century in a way that Irish union at the beginning of the nineteenth century was never able to do. Resentment about English controls over Irish trade should not disguise what was in effect a productive age for the Irish economy. Even so, Irish development was largely a result of the surge in the British market. England took more than half of Ireland's exports, while Ireland continued to import more than she exported. Despite the great boom in the Irish economy, by the end of the century progress was faltering.

All three nations owed most of their growth in the eighteenth century to a strongly improved performance in overseas trade. Ireland, however, was prevented until union in 1801 from direct trading with the colonies, an advantage enjoyed by Scotland from 1707. English demand was more important to both Scotland and Ireland. In any reassessment of the economic relationship between the three kingdoms, therefore, the economic power of England remains the obvious and overwhelming feature.[37] English predominance is seen in every sector of the economy, consistently and overwhelmingly, in the tonnage of shipping, imports, exports, agriculture, and workshop and industrial production. Agriculture in Ireland, the basic economic activity of the island throughout this period, was much inferior to agrarian productivity in England. Scotland indeed was to have more balanced growth than Ireland by the early nineteenth century. This growth in the English economy undoubtedly acted as the greatest stimulus to the course of the Scottish and Irish economies, more so than even internal developments.

In England the proportion of those working outside agriculture grew dramatically, even though the majority remained living in country locations, supplying goods and services for local markets. On all of this, war was a tremendous burden. Government loans, raised mostly for military purposes, amounted to some £500 million between 1793

---

37   General calculations based on figures in Mitchell, *British Historical Statistics*, pp. 448–50, 468–70; Cullen and Smout, 'Economic Growth in Scotland and Ireland', pp. 4–5; and population totals for England and Wales in E. A. Wrigley and R. S. Schofield, *The Population History of England, 1541–1871: A Reconstruction* (Cambridge, MA: Harvard University Press, 1981), pp. 533–4.

and 1815. This compares to about £20 million invested in the building of canals between 1750 and 1815.[38] War, both external and internal, was also, however, a crucial agent in trade expansion and recession. The English economy, stronger and more versatile, was most plagued by the costs of war and defence. The relative strengths of the different British economies are also suggested by trends in emigration patterns. The eighteenth century is notably sandwiched between large-scale entry of Scottish migrants to Ulster in the seventeenth century, and the evacuation of Irishmen to Scotland and England in the nineteenth century.

It is within such a transformative economic history that we need to appreciate the activities of the printing sector and its sponsorship both of trade and of administrative, social and political change. Not only did economic behaviour alter in eighteenth-century England, but so also did its range of contributors and the ways in which all these different changes were perceived. All these aspects appear in the following chapters: investors were informed and encouraged by new modes of printed communication; brokers were given new tools to evaluate risk and exchange; agriculture markets were serviced by printer-stationers; overseas trade was boosted by jobbing as much as by printed manuals – early commercial projects flourished and industrial schemes were organized by document and form. The press assisted organizational features of banking, credit supply and investment funding, and the press assisted in the raising of private capital for projects in transport and the domestic infrastructure. Although print unified features of exchange, at the same time differences between town and country, between Britain and Europe, and between the three British kingdoms, were also echoed by developments in printing. In particular, in what follows, the importance of traditional industries, of agrarian markets, is seen in the print that serviced domestic trade. It is as much about local autonomy as about national advertisements for fashion goods from the metropolis. It is also, however, often about centrally, London-produced reckoners, guides and other manuals, many of which needed certain modification in use, wherever that was. Just as print invited (and sometimes required) augmentation or alteration by pen, so much might also be used in rather different ways from that intended by its author or manufacturer.

Change and its perception also concerned language. While some documents and forms were printed in foreign languages – notably alien

38 Peter Mathias, *The First Industrial Nation: An Economic History of Britain, 1700–1914* (London: Methuen & Co. Ltd, 1969), p. 14.

registration, surveillance, passports and shipping dockets (among others) – English remained the staple of the jobbing printer. But English itself was not static. Forms in standardized language (and abbreviations and terms of art) buttressed English identity as well, eventually, to the idea of a unity to the British Isles (and their colonies) often riding roughshod over national or regional differences and grievances. The availability of long-distance, widely circulating print servicing trade brought a uniformity and non-controversial reality to economic practicalities. Standardized English became the language not only of political but also of commercial ascendancy. The imposition of English as the medium of trade was a key constituent of success. It was also controversial and resisted, much as the role of English is now at the centre of global debate. In the British Isles at the close of the eighteenth century, as in the world today, the triumph of English as the language of business was virtually complete.

3

The Printed and the Printers

'Publishing' is a very broad activity. It is the making public, to a lesser or greater extent, of material items that are scribal, printed or a mixture of both, and textual or pictorial or a mixture of both. Publishing is the dissemination of materials that are books, pamphlets, newspapers, periodicals, single sheets, or a great range of small printed items such as forms and advertisements, or an indeterminate amalgam or blend of these formats. As the commercial market for books and print developed in early modern and eighteenth-century England, so did the different profiles of demand, distribution and financial mediation. The resulting precautionary and punitive regulation by Church and state was much abetted by the property interests of leading booksellers, printers and stationers. The book trade advanced as a trade in argument, in knowledge, in belief, in instruction and in entertainment. The trade brought for its promoters and craftsmen fortunes as well as financial and personal disaster, and jobbing printing (that is the printing of small items other than books) supported the business of the printer more than any other type of custom.

From the late seventeenth century in particular, the volume, quality and location of printing, publication and jobbing printing in England was transformed. The scale of press activity was unprecedented. Nothing as potent had been seen since the arrival of the printing press across Europe in the mid to late fifteenth century. What was even more remarkable was that printing-house business accelerated despite a virtual technological standstill in the design of the common printing press.[1]

Unsurprisingly, early modern book publishing in Britain was dominated by publishing in England, and book publishing in England dominated in turn by publishing in London. Yet even London book production and

1 For further implications, see James Raven, *The Business of Books: Booksellers and the English Book Trade 1450–1850* (London and New Haven, CT: Yale University Press, 2007).

marketing appeared, in relative terms, to be limited before the eighteenth century, and although the endeavours of printers in provincial cities and market towns throughout the three kingdoms were crucial, they have been lost to historical view. Many of the productions were ephemeral and no longer survive, although numerous records attest to the commission, manufacture and consumption of their products, and most particularly in the country towns as well as in the financial centre of London.

All European cities participated in a Europe-wide book traffic in which England proved a rather distant recipient.[2] Early modern London was most obviously surpassed by Paris,[3] but also by other Continental trading centres from Brussels and Hamburg to Venice, Lyons and Milan, and by ancient university towns including Bologna, Pavia, Padua, Florence, Prague, Cologne, Nuremberg, Leiden and Cordova. During the seventeenth century London did, however, move up on some of its Continental rivals, especially in broadside and small-piece print production (although not to the extent that it did in the miracle century after 1680 or so). English and Continental printers alike issued high-status works alongside more commonplace and cheaper productions including single-sheet indulgences, carols and ballads. The printing of the non-book items and many of the smaller books required only a single press – the norm in the great majority of printing houses before 1800.

At the opening of the eighteenth century, some two thousand imprints of books and pamphlets were, according to entries in the *ESTC*, published annually in Britain and Ireland.[4] These imprints include, of course, many works issued in more than one edition and any exercise in the counting of *ESTC* entries is hazardous and cannot account for variation in edition quantities. Sheet counts would be the only real measure of changing output but this is impossible. The best estimate of annual book and pamphlet output at the opening of the eighteenth century is of about

2   In David McKitterick's words, 'contributing little and depending much': 'Histories of the Book', *The Book Collector* (Spring 2000), 9–26 (p. 14). Richard Sharpe estimates that the *surviving* 30,000 books of medieval England represent some 4,000 separate works: index to the Corpus of British Medieval Library Catalogues compiled by Richard Sharpe (www.history.ox.ac.uk/sharpe/index.htm).

3   See Richard R. Rouse and Mary A. Rouse, *Manuscripts and their Makers: Commercial Book Production in Medieval Paris 1200–1500* (Turnhout: Harvey Miller Publishers, 2000).

4   See the estimates – and health warnings for unwary users – given by Michael F. Suarez, 'Towards a Bibliometric Analysis of the Surviving Record, 1701–1800', in *The Cambridge History of the Book in Britain: Volume V*, ed. Michael F. Suarez and Michael L. Turner (Cambridge: Cambridge University Press, 2009), pp. 39–65 (pp. 39–44).

two thousand different items and perhaps 1,500 or so different titles. Of these, a very large proportion were not registered officially, as they should have been, at Stationers' Hall, and perhaps the most obvious result of the searches available in the *ESTC* has been to glimpse a world of rapid, ephemeral and risky publishing, much removed from earlier surveys of late Stuart literature. The Grub Street and the pamphleteering of the age of Defoe, Addison and Steele, often studied as separate spheres, now seem much closer to a printing and bookselling trade at once more integrated in its connections and more diffuse in its output. The *ESTC* item counts also exclude newspaper printing and those books and pamphlets declared (however accurately) to be published in surviving newspaper advertisements (and what has been estimated to be about a tenth of the then total number of title publications).[5] Above all, the scope of the *ESTC* – ambitious and impressive in its own right – concerns books, periodicals and pamphlets and excludes a vast terrain of printed output that comprised items of a sheet and parts of sheets of paper.

In 1700 booksellers anticipated, with some wariness, new opportunities after a turbulent period of censorship and legal constraints, while debates inspired by royal succession, both English and Spanish, offered a new stimulus to journalism, propaganda and even scholarship. Nevertheless, the first two decades of the eighteenth century are no obvious watershed in the volume or quality of book publishing. By contrast, general non-book printing enjoyed an unprecedented expansion. Following the lapse of restrictive English Printing Acts or 'licensing laws' in 1695, printing presses were set up in parts of England for the first time (and returned to some centres where they had existed before 1662 and the first of the new licensing laws). Printers extended their range of jobbing printing in response to fresh commercial opportunities in London, in the towns and in the local marketplace.

Government recognized the new activity as a revenue-raising opportunity, dressed in claims of military fiscal need and of political and legal control. By the early eighteenth century, producers and receivers of documents, and soon of the newspaper press, found stamp duty an

5   Suarez, 'Towards a Bibliometric Analysis', p. 40; by comparison, based on surviving reviews of published titles (more reliable than newspaper advertisements and puffs), my work suggests that about 7% of all novels known to be published 1770–1800 have not survived in any known copy: James Raven, 'The Novel Comes of Age', in *The English Novel 1770–1829*, ed. Peter Garside, James Raven and Rainer Schöwerling, 2 vols (Oxford: Oxford University Press, 2000), vol. 1, pp. 15–121 (pp. 18–21).

unavoidable and invasive presence, with legislation under a series of Stamp Acts requiring tax to be paid on the transfer of documents. Those paying the tax received an official stamp on their documents, thereby making them legal. First devised in the Netherlands in 1624, Stamp Acts were to tax bills of exchange, contracts, playing cards, patent medicines and newspapers (among other products). Following payment of duties, the taxed items were usually physically stamped at approved government offices. A stamp duty was first introduced in England in 1694 as 'An act for granting to Their Majesties several duties on Vellum, Parchment and Paper for 10 years, towards carrying on the war against France'.[6] The duty amounted to between one penny and several shillings on a range of legal documents including insurance policies, documents used as evidence in court, grants of honour, grants of probate and letters of administration. In its first few years the Act annually garnered about £50,000 for the Treasury and what had been proclaimed to be a temporary measure was found to be indispensable – and capable of extension to other written and printed texts.

Unlike many later commercial take-offs, the greater productivity of the printer was not related to major technological change within the industry. Attempts to improve the wooden press, to make printing more efficient and reduce manual effort, eventually resulted in successful all-metal presses, but the first of these, the Stanhope press, did not appear until 1798. It was to be a further thirteen years before Friedrich Koenig's steam-driven presses were working and, even then, the wooden press was not replaced quickly. Whatever mechanization was introduced in the printing process, the basic techniques of composition, hand-setting type, arranging formes, and folding and cutting printed sheets all remained unchanged. William Caxton would have been at home in the printing house of *The Times* in 1800. With minimal technological improvement, increased output from the eighteenth-century presses was the consequence of national commercial and financial expansion, and of the demand created by the changing incomes and literary interests of the propertied classes. The spread of print was enabled by new road and transport developments and by a relaxation of restrictive legislation and *de facto* trade controls.

The statistical increase in the number of working printers in Britain over the century is impressive, even though such tallies are based on patchy evidence and necessarily include craftsmen who were also engaged

6   5 & 6 Wlm & Mary, c. 21.

in other book and non-book trades. In 1700 about seventy master printers were working in London.[7] In the English provinces at that time there were about a dozen master printers, all of whom had migrated from the capital within the previous five years. By comparison, twenty master printers were working in Scotland, and in Dublin, about ten. By 1740, there were some forty master printers in English towns outside London, twenty-seven in Edinburgh, ten in Glasgow and half a dozen elsewhere in Scotland. By 1760 there were well over 250 active presses in London, Edinburgh, Glasgow and Dublin. Twenty-five years later, a conservative estimate by John Pendred suggested that 124 London letterpress printers were then operating at some 300 presses.[8] In 1808 Caleb Stower listed 216 master letterpress printers at work. He also recorded five letter-founder companies in London and seven London firms of printers' smiths.[9] By 1818, 233 London master printers were established, together with 1,882 journeyman and apprentice compositors and an estimated 1,250 journeyman and apprentice pressmen.[10]

As early as 1695, the year of the lapse of the English licensing laws, the printer William Bonney petitioned the elders of Bristol to set up a press there. Thomas Jones arrived in Shrewsbury in 1696, Samuel Darker in Exeter before 1698, and Francis Burges was established in Norwich by 1701. Some thirteen towns claimed their own printer at sometime between 1701 and 1710. Twenty-five towns hosted a printer between 1711 and 1720.[11]

---

7   The following account is indebted to the pioneering work of Jim Mitchell and Michael Treadwell. In a 1668 survey there were twenty-six masters, twenty-four apprentices and 148 journeymen working sixty-five presses (NA, SP 29/243/126,181). Other lists were made in 1675 (NA, SP 29/369/97), 1686 (SH, Box A, folder 4a), 1705 (BL, Harley Papers, Loan 29/130) and 1722 (Negus list [as 1724] reprinted in John Nichols, *Literary Anecdotes of the Eighteenth Century*, 9 vols, 2nd rev. edn (London, 1812–20), vol. 1, pp. 288–312). Details are reproduced in H. R. Plomer, *A Short History of English Printing* (London: Kegan Paul, Trench, Trubner & Co. Ltd, 1915); C. J. Mitchell, 'Provincial Printing in Eighteenth-Century Britain', *Publishing History*, 21 (1987), 5–24; Michael Treadwell, 'A New List of English Master Printers, c.1686', *The Library*, 6th ser., 4 (1982), 57–61; and Michael Treadwell, 'London Printers and Printing Houses in 1705', *Publishing History*, 7 (1980), 5–44.
8   J[ohn] Pendred, *The London and Country Printers, Booksellers and Stationers Vade Mecum* (London, 1785).
9   Caleb Stower, *The Compositor's and Pressman's Guide to the Art of Printing* (London, 1808), pp. 127–34.
10   Letter to Francis Place, BL, Add. MSS 27,799:99, with correction by Ian Maxted, *The London Book Trades, 1775–1800* (London: Dawson, 1977), p. x.
11   Mitchell, 'Provincial Printing', p. 11.

Liverpool gained its first printer, Samuel Terry, in 1712, and Birmingham, in 1717. Prominent arrivals in country towns before 1720 included Edward Ince and William Cooke in Chester, William Craighton in Ipswich, James Abree in Canterbury and Samuel Hodgkinson in Derby. Printing was practised in Ludlow in 1720, in Coventry and Northampton in 1721 and in Leeds in 1726. In 1727 even Carmarthen had its own press and during the 1730s further towns were able to boast of a local printer: Colchester in 1733, Scarborough in 1734, Malton in 1738 and Bury St Edmunds in 1739. In 1740 Samuel and Felix Farley were advertising the arrival of the 'Art and Mystery of Printing' at Pontypool, Monmouthshire.[12]

At mid-century the rate of provincial expansion slowed. By 1760, some forty-five towns boasted a working press, although a much greater number of country merchants and retailers also sold and distributed print. Even by the late 1740s, about 400 traders in books, stationery and printed items operated in 180 English towns. Among the most active of the regional printer-stationers were William and Cluer Dicey of Northampton (who extended their operations to London),[13] John Binns of Leeds, Thomas Saint of Newcastle and, in the south, the Farleys of Exeter and Bristol, Samuel Hazard of Bath, Benjamin Collins of Salisbury and Robert Goadby of Sherborne. After 1760, the number of towns with printers increased again, at the rate of about two new towns per annum during the 1760s and of about seven new towns per annum in the 1790s.[14] By the 1780s, many bookseller-stationers had opened branch shops. John Clay of Daventry, Northamptonshire, established a branch shop at Rugby in about 1744 and, fourteen years later, a further shop at Lutterworth in Leicestershire.[15] The Loder family maintained branches in both Ipswich and Woodbridge.[16] William Edwards of Halifax set up several permanent shops in the West Riding in addition to his market-day stalls in various Yorkshire towns. The Dagnall dynasty of Aylesbury opened shops in Chesham and Leighton Buzzard.[17] In Birmingham, where twelve presses

---

12   A reference table is given in Mitchell, 'Provincial Printing', pp. 17–19 (table 1).

13   See David Stoker, 'Another Look at the Dicey-Marshall Publications: 1736–1806', *The Library*, 7th ser., 15 (2014), 111–57.

14   Mitchell, 'Provincial Printing', pp. 17–19 (table 1) and p. 21 (figure 1).

15   John Feather, 'John Clay of Daventry: The Business of an Eighteenth-Century Stationer', *Studies in Bibliography*, 37 (1984), 198–209 (p. 200).

16   ESRO, IC/AA1/194/75, IC/AA2/112/49, IC/AA1/231/22. Loder wills, 1773 and 1812; and ESRO, HD20/1–6, Loder papers.

17   NA, Prob. 11/1227/19. Other examples are given in John Feather, *The Provincial Book*

were established by 1800,[18] William Hutton and Robert Bage made their fortunes from selling stationery to dozens of local outlets.[19] In many of the rapidly growing towns of the final third of the century there was a further major increase in the number of firms in the book trades sector. In Newcastle, for example, where there had been two firms in 1700 and about fifteen throughout the period between 1730 and 1770, there were twenty-six in 1776, thirty in 1782 and thirty-five in 1790.

Throughout the eighteenth century, London remained the hub of the English trade in books. The majority of operatives in the book trades were trained or at some time worked in the metropolis. For most of the century, London booksellers retained control over distribution and copyright, excluding regional booksellers from copyright and wholesale marts and dominating publication and production. Few books were published outside the capital before the end of the century. Almost all commercial tracts, for example, were published in London and distributed regionally by the country booksellers or by direct order. Since at least the early seventeenth century, London publishers had been served by booksellers in major provincial towns, with chapmen providing the mainstay for country distribution.[20] The sixty or so shops retailing books in London in 1700 were supplemented by dozens of regional agents. Most agents were general storekeepers and many boasted diverse business interests. By mid-century powerful bookseller-publishers, including Andrew Millar, Thomas Cadell, and Robert and James Dodsley, had joined or succeeded the trade leadership of Jacob Tonson the elder, Bernard Lintot and John Knapton and his sons (among others). All used a complex distributional network of agents and retailing journeymen. The wealth and influence of the new publishing families was founded on investment in the copyright

Trade in Eighteenth-Century England (Cambridge: Cambridge University Press, 1981), ch. 2.

18   Paul Morgan, *Warwickshire Printers' Notices, 1799–1866* (Oxford: Dugdale Society, 1970), p. xxi.

19   Llewellyn Jewitt (ed.), *The Life of William Hutton* (London: Frederick Warne, 1872); Joseph Hill, *The Book Makers of Old Birmingham* (Birmingham: Shakespeare Press for Cornish Bros Ltd, 1907).

20   Margaret Spufford, *Small Books and Pleasant Histories: Popular Fiction and its Readership in Seventeenth-Century England* (Cambridge: Cambridge University Press, 1981), pp. 111–28; Margaret Spufford, *The Great Reclothing of Rural England: Petty Chapmen and their Wares in the Seventeenth Century* (London: Continuum, 1984); and D. F. McKenzie, 'The London Book Trade in the Later Seventeenth Century' (unpubl. typescript of the Sandars Lectures, Cambridge, 1975–76), pp. 24–9.

to literary property and trade within the virtually closed London trade sales. Their congers and trade associations were in turn challenged in the second half of the century by new entrants to the business of publishing and bookselling and by new types of operation. John Bell, the Donaldsons, George Robinson, William Lane, John Cooke, James Lackington and Alexander Hogg all reinvigorated the trade with novel ranges of work and commercial techniques.[21]

The concealment of workaday printing in general accounts of publishing began in this period. The pivotal change, apparent from the late seventeenth century, was the increased separation of printers from bookseller-publishers, from the skilled artisan to the bookseller-financier who might have no prior training in the printing house but who took up the publication or the sale of books as another commodity. Like John [Mac]Murray the immigrant Scotsman in London, many leading eighteenth-century booksellers were not guild trained. Murray, a former sea captain, assessed the London market for enterprising ventures and nearly entered the china trade before establishing the family book firm in 1768. The fresh generation of bookseller-entrepreneurs employed printers on a contract basis. With a certain justification, many printers increasingly claimed to be 'meer mechanics'. Great and successful printers such as the Strahans, William and his son Andrew, with an almost industrialized plant in the narrow courts off Fleet Street by the second half of the eighteenth century, were the exception. In contrast to their sixteenth- and early-seventeenth-century predecessors, many of whom acted as publishers and arbiters of printed material in their own right, most eighteenth-century printers served as virtual employees of the booksellers.[22]

This separation between many printers and bookseller-publishers, helped further raise the profile of books (already and understandably, the most prominent of the products of the printing press) and also periodicals and even newspapers, marginalizing in popular discussion the day-to-day printing of small and simple printed items. Another, although far from straightforward, aspect to this reappraisal of print was the reassessment of the status and value of standard chapbooks. These small productions, conveying time-honoured stories with traditional typographical design and woodcut illustration, were increasingly associated with

21   See Raven, *Business of Books*, esp. ch. 7.
22   Stephen Botein, 'Meer Mechanics and an Open Press: The Business and Political Strategies of Colonial American Printers', *Perspectives in American History*, 9 (1975), 127–225.

ruder readerships than the more cultivated audiences for learned and technical works as well as for novels and finely printed verse and plays. The associated development of a literary infrastructure of periodical reviews, critical reviewers and consequent debate and evaluation created a new hierarchy of print. The printed Bible and Prayerbook had always been obviously different in size and worth from other work coming from the printing house, but printed type did fashion a recognizable common bond across a broad range of publications. Now (although we shall return to certain fundamental associations), printed tickets and other small, everyday items, hugely expanded in volume and variety, appeared increasingly disconnected from published books.

Common printing

From the late fifteenth century, demand for books appeared brisk. It was a demand that increasingly came from merchants and the lesser gentry.[23] Monastic, cathedral and great church precincts, long the home of scribes, stationers and book makers, sheltered some of the earliest manufacturers and sellers of printed books. From these confines began the advance of an industry that was to popularize the communication of learning, literature and instruction. By itself, however, the demand for printed books did not support the operations of the new and increasingly widespread printing houses. Caxton, the pre-eminent early English example of a printer-bookseller, stands for hundreds of successor firms before 1800. Stationed in the precincts of Westminster Abbey, Caxton issued more than a hundred printed books, but jobbing printing, although now obscured by its paltry survival, provided essential support for Caxton's bespoke and then speculative editions.[24] After Caxton's death, his long-serving Dutch foreman, Wynkyn de Worde, took over the Westminster premises, and was to prove the most enterprising and innovative of the early businessmen of

23   Alexandra Gillespie, 'Caxton and After', in *A Companion to Middle English Prose*, ed. A. S. G. Edwards (Cambridge: D. S. Brewer, 2004), pp. 307–25; Alexandra Gillespie, 'Balliol MS 354: Histories of the Book at the End of the Middle Ages', *Poetica*, 60 (2003), 47–63.
24   See David R. Carlson, 'A Theory of the Early English Printing Firm', in *Caxton's Trace: Studies in the History of English Printing*, ed. William Kuskin (Notre Dame: University of Notre Dame Press, 2006), pp. 35–68.

print.[25] De Worde was a jobbing printer as much as he was a producer of exceptional books. His subsequent move to establish a printing house at the sign of the Sun in Fleet Street in 1500 suggests a certain migration of trade and a growing market for books, but also for servicing print among the rich merchants of the city of London and its western fringes (even if this was more downmarket trade than Caxton's).

In his analysis of publishing in Reformation Europe, Andrew Pettegree offers compelling evidence that the printing houses of early modern Europe were sustained by piecework and jobbing print.[26] Even so, modern bibliographical assistance to an understanding of small-item printing is variable. The printing house is rather selectively viewed by use of current short-title catalogues, as opposed to published output of books. Of the major European retrospective bibliographical projects, the German *VD 16* [sixteenth-century] short-title catalogue excludes single-sheet productions. This is all the more extraordinary because broadsheets are included in the *Incunabula Short-Title Catalogue* of fifteenth-century European printing (and 80% of them were published in Germany). Broadsheets are also included in the seventeenth-century *VD 17*. This presents a fundamental difficulty for anyone studying sixteenth-century German printing, disguising the total output of even surviving items. For the Low Countries, the *Short-Title Catalogue Flanders* (*STCV*), with its seventeenth-century coverage, does include single-sheet items, but it only surveys some five libraries and cannot serve as a full bibliography of seventeenth-century Southern Netherlands. In new work for 1601–50, the *Universal Short-Title Catalogue* project has discovered a collection of another 1,400 single-sheet items in the Museum Plantin Moretus, hinting at other survivals that might yet be discovered and not currently incorporated into *STCV*. As for the northern Netherlands, the *Short-Title Catalogue Netherlands* (*STCN*) includes very few broadsheet items, for reasons that remain unclear, but certainly misrepresents even the surviving examples of single-sheet pieces. The *ESTC* is not exempt from this blindness, as new projects on local printing in England, such as that by Norbert Schürer, are demonstrating.[27] As Keith Maslen anticipated, the *ESTC*, 'having cast its net wide to take

25   See the verdict of A. S. G. Edwards and Carol M. Meale, 'The Marketing of Printed Books in Late Medieval England', *The Library*, 6th ser., 15 (1993), 95–124 (esp. p. 124).

26   Andrew Pettegree, *The Book in the Renaissance* (London and New Haven, CT: Yale University Press, 2010).

27   See the many non-*ESTC* items in Norbert Schürer (with Chris Mounsey and Debbie Welham), *Jane Austen's Bookshop: An Exhibition* (Alton, Hampshire: Chawton House

in much jobbing and having made some rich hauls, must perforce have left many small fish in the sea'.[28]

The absence of single-sheet items from many short-title and union catalogues is indeed a cause of regret, but further misunderstanding can arise from the categorization of jobbing items. From a library point of view there is a good case for considering some materials, such as blanks and forms that include or invite manuscript annotation, to belong more to an archival deposit status of 'ephemera'.[29] This, however, can confuse, obscuring the historical context in which small-item production took place, the reasons for it and its place within the business operations of printing houses.

The importance of jobbing to the printing house is supported by related market considerations. The international book trade supplied bookshops and printing houses without the need for domestic or local book production. The established shops of bookseller-stationers proved essential to emergent print publication. Even the greatest early modern Continental printing houses, such as those founded by Aldus Manutius, the Birckmanns and the Plantins, depended upon a wholesale bookselling structure, whereby they sold to other booksellers and merchants multiple copies of their printed volumes at discounted prices. Without these networks (which included the great fairs), the publishing printers and booksellers could not have sold sufficient books from their own premises

Library, 2012); his further examination of local printing in Winchester in the long eighteenth century is in progress.

28 Keith Maslen, *An Early London Printing House at Work: Studies in the Bowyer Ledgers* (New York: Bibliographical Society of America, 1993), p. 191.

29 Timothy G. Young, 'Evidence: Toward a Library Definition of Ephemera', *RBM: A Journal of Rare Books, Manuscripts, and Cultural Heritage*, 4 (2003), 11–26 (p. 12); for more on 'ephemera' from a collection-management perspective, see also Falk Eisermann, 'Mixing Pop and Politics: Origins, Transmission, and Readers of Illustrated Broadsides in Fifteenth-Century Germany', in *Incunabula and their Readers: Printing, Selling and Using Books in the Fifteenth Century*, ed. Kristian Jensen (London: British Library, 2003), pp. 159–77 and R. N. Swanson, 'Printing for Purgatory: Indulgences and Related Documents in England, 1476 to 1536', *Journal of the Early Book Society*, 14 (2011), 115–44; see also John Lewis, *Printed Ephemera: The Changing Uses of Type and Letterforms in English and American Printing* (Ipswich: W. S. Cowell, 1962); Maurice Rickards, *The Encyclopaedia of Ephemera: A Guide to the Fragmentary Documents of Everyday Life for the Collector, Curator and Historian*, ed. Michael Twyman, Sarah du Boscq de Beaumont and Amoret Tanner (London: British Library, 2000), p. v; and Laurie Dolphin (ed.), *Evidence: The Art of Candy Jernigan* (San Francisco: Chronicle Books, 1999).

to reclaim production costs. A transnational trade focused on Latin texts, and the great majority of Latin and scholarly books in London continued to arrive from the Continent. Before 1700, great English book collections (and especially royal ones) attest to the exporting prowess of Paris, Venice, Cologne and other European printing centres.[30]

Home production of books was in effect very limited and not sufficient in terms of size or efficiency to support the presses. Just as England was not a net exporter of books until the early eighteenth century and was dependent on importation for its books and for its paper supply for printing, so the presses operated under capacity and thus the reliance on jobbing had to be all the greater. As a consequence of the limitations of the market, but also of guild and government regulation and policing, the productive capacity of the English press probably changed little before 1642 (and indeed, if the use of the presses had been maximized, redundant overcapacity in book production would have resulted). Printing schedules reflected the strains, including concurrent printing techniques where several printers shared in the production of one book, but also the undercapacity and irregular employment of many – if not most – printing houses.

It is important to stress just how risky the production of books was – and continued to be for centuries. The most successful manufacturing stationers had commanded long lines of credit sufficient to sustain manuscript production by expenditure on parchment, vellum and, later, paper. Customers' advance pledges of security only partly assisted the outlays required by publishers.[31] And the early modern 'Latin trade', as the importation of foreign-printed books to England was generally known, required secure credit arrangements. Drawing on reputation and the support of a larger community, the merchants and booksellers, Frederick

30   Lotte Hellinga, 'Importation of Books Printed on the Continent into England and Scotland before c.1520', in *Printing the Written Word: The Social History of Books circa 1450–1520*, ed. Sandra Hindman (Ithaca and London: Cornell University Press, 1991), pp. 205–24 (sample of Continental production of British-owned books, pp. 210, 211); see also Paul Needham, 'The Customs Rolls as Documents for the Printed-Book Trade in England', in *The Cambridge History of the Book in Britain: Volume III 1400–1557*, ed. Lotte Hellinga and Joseph B. Trapp (Cambridge: Cambridge University Press, 1999), pp. 148–63.

31   C. Paul Christianson, 'Evidence for the Study of London's Late Medieval Manuscript-Book Trade', in *Book Production and Publishing in Britain, 1375–1475*, ed. J. Griffiths and D. Pearsall (Cambridge: Cambridge University Press, 1989), pp. 87–108 (p. 91).

Egmont, de Worde, Franz Birckmann, John Reynes and Arnold Harrison, handled great quantities of imported printed books, setting the price and sending them on to other retailers.[32] Traditionally, the financing of a book was largely predetermined by direct patronage or assured custom, but the printing of books also encouraged the modest creation of stock, that is of certain speculative custom other than for 'bespoke' books. Early sale records suggest that some books left unsold had been printed in anticipation of a particular custom, with early speculative publishing little regularized or standardized.[33] Printing gave greater impetus to financing decisions based on perceptions of market taste for developing forms of 'publication', whether bespoke or the making of a prepared, unordered book available through public retail. As the risks involved in book production were passed on to the resting printer (who might also, of course, be the bookseller), he or she needed the relief of regular, quick turnover, relatively simple jobbing.

Variety and flexibility remained the watchwords of the book trade; and whatever the editorial and literary interests of the more learned booksellers, it was their envisaging of secure income, profits and market potential that encouraged them to develop the range of their productions. As Geoffrey Elton also long ago concluded, in a study of the earliest printing of the statutes, innovation resided as much in the cheapness, celerity, distribution and reliability of the product as in the printing itself.[34] These features of the history of the book trade remained essential to successful bookselling careers over four centuries: first, the prerequisite of available financial assets rather than prior skills in printing or an existing knowledge of literary concerns; second, a productive versatility

32   C. Paul Christianson, 'The Rise of London's Book-Trade', in Hellinga and Trapp (eds), *Cambridge History of the Book in Britain: Volume III*, pp. 128–47 (p. 141).

33   For the debate, see Alexandra Gillespie, *Print Culture and the Medieval Author: Chaucer, Lydgate, and their Books, 1473–1557* (Oxford: Oxford University Press, 2006); Vincent Gillespie, 'Vernacular Books of Religion', in Griffiths and Pearsall (eds), *Book Production and Publishing*, pp. 317–41; Linne R. Mooney, 'Scribes and Booklets of Trinity College, Cambridge, MSS R.3.19 and R.3.21', in *Middle English Poetry: Texts and Traditions: Essays in Honour of Derek Pearsall*, ed. Alastair Minnis (Woodbridge: Boydell and Brewer, 2001), pp. 241–66; and David R. Carlson, *English Humanist Books: Writers and Patrons, Manuscript and Print, 1475–1525* (Toronto, Buffalo and London: University of Toronto Press, 1993), pp. 131–41.

34   G. R. Elton, 'The Sessional Printing of Statutes, 1484–1547', in *Wealth and Power in Tudor England: Essays Presented to S.T. Bindoff*, ed. E. W. Ives *et al.* (London: Athlone Press, 1978), pp. 68–86 (p. 75).

that juggled large and expensive undertakings with jobbing printing or the publication of relatively simple books with assured custom; and third, the market evaluation and promotion of printed books as much for being marvellous objects and luxury commodities as for their intellectual content.[35]

Printing-house practice

The fundamental importance of jobbing printing is that it helped overcome obstacles and limits to growth that were crucial aspects of the history of the early and the Enlightenment book trade – but aspects of that trade all too often overlooked in otherwise triumphalist accounts, even including those of Henri-Jean Martin. Central to any analysis of these early modern bookselling careers are the constraints imposed by broader resource limitations upon business expansion – and certainly upon technological advance. In his *The Printer's Grammar* of 1808, Caleb Stower includes a scheme to draw up a 'Job-Book' to record all jobbing undertaken in the printing house, offering not only the first mention of jobbing in published printers' manuals, but also the suggestion that it now demanded separate accounting procedures.[36] Before then, we can safely assume on the basis of surviving printing-house ledgers that jobbing – if entered in the main ledger at all – was an integral part of press schedules and accounting.

Across all trades, most fixed capital was invested in ways that produced only indirect gain. The property of the shop and dwelling-house, where almost all booksellers were tenants (and many were subtenants) offered no opportunity for long-term investment (even though the paucity of legal or customary restraints allowed most tenants to repair, rebuild or extend their buildings with ease). Circulating capital – that is raw materials and goods (with books themselves as primary objects of exchange) – comprised whatever long-term business investment there was. By modern standards the overall result supported a very low productivity rate, with

35 For prestige books from the Frankfurt mart, see Ian Maclean, 'The Market for Scholarly Books and Conceptions of Genre in Northern Europe, 1570–1630', in *Die Renaissance im Blick der Nationen Europas*, ed. Georg Kauffmann (Wiesbaden: Harrassowitz, 1991), pp. 17–31 (pp. 28–9, 31).
36 Caleb Stower, *The Printer's Grammar* (London, 1808), p. 436; Maslen, *An Early London Printing House at Work*, p. 140.

high labour intensity and a vast reservoir of underemployed labour. This created very little inducement for cost-reducing innovations in all trades and industries. The book trades were clearly no exception to this and, in the requirement to have so much capital tied up in a specific item of production – an edition – before any part of this could be sold to realize returns, the publishing sector was especially handicapped.

Hugh Amory, John Bidwell, James Green and others have astutely remarked that the printer made sheets, not books, and they pointed (at least in North America) to the role of jobbing in supporting the business of the printing house.[37] Most European accounts so far, however, very largely survey only the early modern period and focus on indulgences and religious and ballad-type production rather than on civic and business jobbing.[38] One striking exception, Keith Maslen's investigations into the Bowyers, found in a case study of the firm's presswork of 1731 that a quarter of the total output in terms of the amount of paper used was in jobbing. Some eighty-six books and pamphlets were printed by Bowyer in 1731, compared to sixty-one jobs of various sizes. The further calculations in sheets used offer the more accurate production picture, in which the four or five presses in the printing house printed books from some 1,850 reams of an estimated total of 2,530 reams worked that year.[39]

Standing type (that is, type left in made-up pages) required extensive storage space and, in any event, the high value of type precluded the keeping of much set type for very long. The only exceptions seem to have been standing type for certain items of up to a total of four sheets (which can, of course, include a range of productions) or occasional title pages and other special and often-repeated settings (usually stored as

37   See, for example, John Bidwell, 'Printers' Supplies and Capitalization', and James N. Green, 'English Books and Printing in the Age of Franklin', in *A History of the Book in America: Volume 1: The Colonial Book in the Atlantic World*, ed. Hugh Amory and David Hall (Cambridge, MA: Cambridge University Press, 2000), pp. 163–82 (pp. 163–76) and pp. 248–97 (pp. 248–52, 257–9) respectively.
38   Importantly, Peter Stallybrass, '"Little Jobs": Broadsides and the Printing Revolution', in *Agent of Change: Print Culture Studies after Elizabeth L. Eisenstein*, ed. Sabrina Alcorn Baron, Eric N. Lindquist and Eleanor F. Shevlin (Amherst, MA: University of Massachusetts Press, 2007), pp. 315–41. Peter Stallybrass has continued to explore the world of jobbing and I am most grateful for his advice and encouragement; several of the examples of Continental jobbing work below, first included, sometimes incidentally, in other printing and publishing histories, were located at his suggestion.
39   Maslen, *An Early London Printing House at Work*, p. 143.

set pages without formes).[40] In England between 1587 and 1637, regulations issued by the Stationers' Company also supposedly forbade formes to be kept standing and limited editions to 1,250–1,500 copies from one setting of type, or 2,500–3,000 copies for certain small publications. Exceptions were admitted in 1635 (with formes allowed to stand for a year, uniquely, for 'the Psalter, the Grammar and accidence, Almanacs and Prognostications, and the primer and ABC'), yet even here we have to be careful – the same decree confirmed that the regulations since 1587 had often been ignored.[41]

There is one further point. Henri-Jean Martin observed that 'we know from the bitter rivalries between printers for the privilege of printing [broadsides] that the business was highly prized, both for its status and profitability'.[42] Status and economics are linked. Early modern, but also Enlightenment bookselling careers cannot be divided simply between the pursuit of commercial advantage and service to a larger network of patronage and protection. Bookselling, as far as we can tell, enhanced the social and economic standing of its leading practitioners, but for the great majority of stationers and booksellers, domestic and business circumstances remained modest.

The economics of the eighteenth-century printing house turned in part upon the reuse of type, inevitably influencing the design of books and other printed productions, but also helping to determine the division of labour as well as the design and layout of the confined space of the printing house. For all leading printers, booksellers and stationers (although we could argue about differences between some of these), the difficulties in raising and managing credit heightened the importance of cash flow and steady turnover. This was why jobbing printing was so crucial. In speculative publication, strength of sales obviously remained the primary determinant of further trade development, while speculation on the market was of its nature fraught with peril. Until an edition was completely printed, it could not, of course, be put on sale; and, with each new book, the publisher could never be certain of how many copies would be sold.

40   Philip Gaskell, A New Introduction to Bibliography (Oxford: Clarendon Press, 1972), pp. 116–17.

41   SP Dom CI 301: 103, 105, orders of 4 Dec. 1587 and of 16 Nov. 1635 (reproduced in W. W. Greg, A Companion to Arber (Oxford: Clarendon Press, 1967), pp. 43, 94–5).

42   Henri-Jean Martin, Print, Power, and People in Seventeenth-Century France, trans. David Gerard (Metuchen, NJ: Scarecrow Press, 1993), pp. 161–75, especially p. 165, cited by Stallybrass, 'Little Jobs', p. 329.

All publishers faced high, up-front and one-off investment coupled with potentially very slow returns. The liquidity predicament heightened the importance of sure-fire, calculable undertakings, notably the classes of patented titles, successfully reprinted time and time again, but also of a much broader, more varied and more voluminous jobbing work.

A fine example, illustrating press rates and precise printing-house practice, comes from the London Bowyer ledgers. Four consignments of 'malt books', ledgers ruled in red for the collection of the tax on malt, were produced using 92 reams of paper in 1731. In the week ending 21 August 1731, a single Bowyer press was dedicated only to printing 23¼ reams of malt books. The two pressmen each earned £1 16s 10d, about twice the amount for an average crew in an average week, handling the usual variety of work. Assuming a six-day week and twelve hours per day, the average rate of production amounts to an impressive 323 impressions per hour. The rate of production, earnings and output were closely related, with jobbing differing from bookwork in as much as pressmen were charged at piece-rates. Production rates at least can be calculated from the Bowyer ledgers, and the malt book example with its extraordinary speed of labour and output is confirmed by a further weekly sampling. This was also offered by the Maslen study, but the comparative inclusion of bookwork (in this case, a sheet of the almanac *Poor Robin* and a sheet from Archbishop John Tillotson's *Sermons*) needs, perhaps, to be made more explicit. In the week ending 28 September 1734, six men working at three presses and one man sharing a press produced 84,033 impressions from a total of forty-six formes. Again assuming a seventy-two-hour week, the fully manned presses each averaged 333 impressions per hour (and this without allowance for composition and other preparations – or 'make-ready' – the washing and cleaning of type, or the night-work that might have been required, for example, in printing parliamentary *Votes* or legal appeal cases). The print runs were exceptionally large: twenty thousand copies of sheet A of *Poor Robin* and two thousand copies of the sheet for Tillotson's *Sermons*. What is striking from the two examples is first, how jobbing and bookwork are close in production rate terms, but second, how both examples far outstrip the standard calculation made by Joseph Moxon in his 1678–93 *Mechanick Exercises* of 250 impressions per hour as the average work rate for two men at a single press. This became translated as a customary unit of production with many editions assessed for print runs in multiples of 250 (500, 750, 1000, 1,500). McKenzie's study of printing practices at Cambridge University Press found 250 impressions per hour to be a 'maximum production not often attained in practice'.[43] The 250-impressions-per-hour rate also seems to hold best for the edition runs of 500 and 750 copies common in bookwork of the manual press period. In much longer runs, the skilled pressmen at the Bowyer Press in London achieved a much higher rate than 250 impressions, for books as well as for jobbing.

The Bowyer ledgers further suggest that paper was supplied by the Bowyer printing house for most of the small jobs completed, for with a small stock of paper on hand for such purposes the printer could begin work at once. However, paper intended for the printing of books was usually sent in by the bookseller or other client. The bookseller, in this eighteenth-century sense, became the undertaker, the 'publisher', wholesaler and retailer. Some other work also usually involved paper being supplied by the client, as was apparently the case in the orders placed by the Corporation of London. In such situations the great capital burden of paper was therefore lifted from the printer. He might now be one of the 'mechanicks', but one who was not threatened by the risks involved in publication and of risking all on an unknown market. Much jobbing was probably in effect a client-based economy, following specific orders and with limited risks. The only danger was long and overdue credit, the bane and undoing of countless traders and craftsmen of the age.

Beyond this, it is not possible to relate job labour rates to those for bookwork. In the mid nineteenth century, William Savage recorded that 'jobs' (defined as 'any thing which printed does not exceed a sheet') were 'paid extra to the compositor, because there is no return of furniture [wooden sticks and quoins, etc., used in the imposition of formes] or letter [type]: he has generally to put up fresh cases, and has some additional trouble in getting the right letter, and in making up the furniture'.[44] Each job stood alone as a separate piece of work, with its own difficulties, design and composing issues. The malt books do not at first sight appear to have been complex to produce, but the tedious process of continual pulling to print and reprint the ruled pages must nevertheless have been arduous, and the quality of the impression had to be maintained. As Maslen also observed of this malt book example, the rate paid for jobbing was as much determined by 'inspection' as by 'custom', terms borrowed

43   D. F. McKenzie, *The Cambridge University Press, 1696–1712: A Bibliographical Study*, 2 vols (Cambridge: Cambridge University Press, 1966), vol. 1, p. 138.
44   William Savage, *A Dictionary of the Art of Printing* (London: Longman, Brown, Green and Longmans, 1841), p. 428, entry for 'Job'.

from printer Samuel Richardson.[45] Price-setting decisions very largely remain beyond our gaze. We cannot now recover how particular printing-house prices for jobbing work were fully calculated by the printer, given that even surviving ledgers and their entries do not detail the size of type and the amount to be set. We can, however, from records to be discussed below, gain some sense of the rates charged per sheet, general labour costs, the prices of certain-sized items and the prices charged for finishing procedures.

Type and intaglio

Of the technological changes within the book trades during the eighteenth century the most significant were those concerned with engraving, intaglio printing and the design and manufacture of type.[46] Until at least the 1720s much of the type used in Britain was of variable standard. The majority of type and most quality founts were imported from the Low Countries and from Germany. In 1674 Thomas Grover set up his London type foundry in Aldersgate Street, which produced the dramatic script type used by Ichabod Dawks in his *News-Letter* from 1696 until at least 1716. The type was also employed by Hugh Meere, the printer of the Sun Fire Office's *British Mercury*. In the *Observator* of 1708 Meere advertised 'Scriptographia; or Written Print Hand (which can't be imitated by any other printer) fit for bills of lading, Bills of Sale, Bonds of all Sorts ... or any other blank Law forms'.[47] By the time of the first work of William Caslon (1693–1766) in the early 1720s, the older firms of English founders had been absorbed by the business of Thomas James which continued after 1736 under the direction of James's son, also called Thomas. It is their type and that of their predecessors which still appears in the matrices of the few surviving detailed inventories of the English jobbing-printing firm.

English type founding continued to lead in quality and productivity within Britain. The first type foundry in Scotland, that of John Baine and

---

45 Richardson as quoted by I. G. Philip, *William Blackstone and the Reform of the Oxford University Press in the Eighteenth Century* (Oxford: Oxford Bibliographical Society, 1955 [1957]), p. 41; Maslen, *An Early London Printing House at Work*, p. 144.
46 Daniel Berkeley Updike, *Printing Types: Their History, Forms and Use: A Study in Survivals*, 2 vols (Cambridge, MA: Harvard University Press, 1962), vol. 2, pp. 101–24.
47 *Observator*, 7 Feb. 1708.

Alexander Wilson, was not established until 1742 in St Andrews. By 1750, however, Caslon founts had also been introduced to Edinburgh printing houses. Wilson relocated his foundry to Glasgow in 1744, Baine moving to Dublin in 1747 and dissolving their partnership in 1749. Despite competition from several new foundries, including that of Baine, Wilson and his successors had established a virtual monopoly in both Irish and Scottish founding by the end of the century.[48] English type continued to predominate, however. Although the Edinburgh printer, John Reid, used the products of Baine and Wilson, Caslon type dominated Reid's 1768 *Specimen of Printing Types*.[49] One notable example of English type founding occurred outside of London: in Birmingham, John Baskerville (1706–75) set new standards in the manufacture of both type and paper.[50] The Baskerville founts, cast for their maker's own book printing, were not widely adopted during his lifetime, but they were of particular importance in influencing the development of letterpress type. Wilson's first specimen book, not issued until 1772, included large types heavily modelled on Baskerville. In the final quarter of the century, the work of Joseph and Edmund Fry rivalled the specimen books of the Caslons as they competed with six or more other English firms in producing fine and exotic founts.[51]

Most eighteenth-century London printers were able to take swift advantage of technical innovations in typography. From the 1730s substantial printers, and especially those engaged in bookwork, experimented with new type. Most prized was that made by Caslon. Puffs for the printers also show that cast ornaments were of great attraction. Founders sent out specimen sheets to the printers, and printers circulated specimens of printing with newly purchased type to show local traders what was possible. For the simple conveyance of information, many of the new founts and ornaments were clearly an embellishment rather than

48   Cf. NLS Ledger of Adam Neill, prefatory inventory of type, 1767. Also Talbot Baines Reed, *A History of the Development of Old English Letter Foundries*, ed. and rev. A. F. Johnson (London: Faber and Faber, 1952).

49   Details in A. F. Johnson, 'Type-Designs and Type-Founding in Scotland', *Edinburgh Bibliographical Society Transactions*, 2 (1938–45), 255–61 (p. 258); D. J. Bryden, 'A Short Catalogue of the Types used by John Reid, Printer in Edinburgh, 1761–74', *Bibliotheck*, 6:1 (1971), 17–21.

50   F. E. Pardoe, *John Baskerville of Birmingham: Letter-Founder and Printer* (London: Frederick Muller, 1975).

51   Johnson Ball, *William Caslon, 1693–1766: The Ancestry, Life and Connections of England's Foremost Letter-Engraver and Type-Founder* (Kineton: Roundwood Press, 1973).

a necessity. Their value in attracting customers and satisfying clients was swiftly appreciated, however. As well as begging attention, finely printed decoration became a status symbol, much in the manner of modern letter-heads and printed logos. The trademark and the die-stamp were widely adopted by expanding businesses.

These were still 'book types', however, and almost all new typefaces remained within that convention. Despite experiments with head and tail pieces and the 'flowers' used for border decoration, familiar proportions were continued in the cutting of letters. Imported Dutch founts did provide large and decorative letters from early in the century. The 1713 specimen sheet of James Watson the younger, printer of Edinburgh (d.1722), and part of his *History of the Art of Printing*, contained no less than five sets of Dutch capitals and 'blooming letters' (decorated capitals) in different sizes. In the largest set the capitals were 1⁵⁄₁₆ in. high, and the blooming letters, 1½ in. high. Even the second size of letters contained capitals of ¹⁵⁄₁₆ in. and blooming letters of 1¼ in. Such founts, however, were the prestige possessions of a printing elite, and then, used almost exclusively in expensive bookwork. Development of display type was comparatively slow. In France, Pierre-Simon Fournier (d.1768) followed his prodigious typecutting of the late 1730s with the radical set of founts shown in the 'Avis' preface to his 1742 *Modègraveles*. These included an eighteen-point (¼ in.) *gros romain* and a thirty-six-point (½ in.) *trisméiste*. After further series of italics, Fournier experimented in the 1760s with a range of floriated letters particularly suited to advertisements and other jobbing work.[52] Some twenty years later, William Caslon III and Edmund Fry sent out their first specimen sheets of decorative letters. Much simpler than the Fournier designs, both Fry and Caslon included inline faces with a single white line engraved within the bold strokes of the letters.

For most of the century, the absence of type of a height greater than about three-quarters of an inch was a serious limitation to display printing. Decorative founts from the Low Countries were expensive to import and not obviously suitable for many new forms of jobbing. In 1765 Thomas Cottrell, founder at Nevil's Court, Fetter Lane between 1758 and his death in 1785, issued a twelve-line pica (nearly 2 in. high), but other type founders were slow to follow. Surviving examples of jobbing work from the 1770s and 1780s rarely contain large display type. Fry's castings

52   Allen Hutt, *Fournier: The Compleat Typographer* (London: Frederick Muller, 1972), pp. 21–41.

were among the earliest of the large sorts of type available for poster work. In jobbing printing, Fry's ornaments and large founts, such as his five-line pica (⅚ in. high), were therefore especially prized. *A Specimen of Printing-Types, made by Joseph Fry and Sons* issued in 1785 went through annual editions, each with numerous type and flower additions. Each specimen book opened with an example of Fry's new ten-line pica (1⅔ in. high), clear poster-size letters for jobbing work on the standard manual press.

The early Fry specimens were also notable for the great variety of flowers. Of these the larger four-line pica flowers (⅔ in. in height) were but one of several sizes (and it is notable that 'flowers' headed the list of additions to 'Founts of Letter' in the 1782 *Daily Advertiser* jobbing-printing office advertisement noted above).[53] Successive specimens built up an extensive selection of type and space-lines for printing numerical tables or notices requiring statistical sections. Except for various designs of sailing ships, however, the Fry specimens of 1785–89 offered few single cast ornaments. Many were probably available in addition or as made to order, but the full Fry repertoire was not released until the 1794 *Specimen of Metal Cast Ornaments*. This included 103 ornamental pieces ranging from crowns, houses, ships, horses, masons' marks and various illustrative pieces typically used for printing newspaper advertisements, business vouchers and receipts, and public notices. The page of ornaments included further variants of houses used for sales and lettings, and ships for sailing or unlading notices, a runaway slave used in colonial newspaper columns, a horse sale design, and a superb small casting for an auction. A slightly smaller version of the 'protection' medallion, printed by Fry on the Phoenix Company proposals, was also offered as a specimen and priced at 1s 6d. In addition, Fry's new 'ornamented two-line letters' ranged from five-line pica to great primer and even included a 'black open' for a very striking display effect. The ten-line pica was supplemented by a new italic version particularly suited for the printing of large notices. The metal cast ornaments also included an unprecedented selection of flowers of diverse heights comprising three types of the large four-line pica, seven types of double pica, thirty-three types of great primer, thirty-four types of English, twenty-eight types of pica, thirty-three types of small pica, forty-nine types of long primer, twenty-eight types of brevier, sixteen types of nonpareil and fourteen types of the miniature pearl. Flowers were

53   Above, chapter 1, pp. 3–4.

further presented in typical border arrangements, including on 'blank cards', and various crowns, lions, funerary urns and Prince of Wales feathers were among the new cast ornaments.[54] In Fry's patterns, even the most unimaginative printer must have seen how he could use a new stock of flowers to improve the quality and range of his jobbing.

Despite such responses from the type founders, printers in remote country towns were rarely well placed to acquire modern founts. The most obvious feature of jobbing printing of the period was the enormous variation in the type owned by different printers. The country printer, dependent upon old and often worn book type, was particularly handicapped. Printers setting up in the country and specializing in jobbing printing were often too poor to buy modern type or modish ornaments. Woodcut blocks of letters and engraved designs were already being adapted for new business but, for accompanying letterpress printing, veteran type continued to be used. In many cases, it is possible only to guess at the sort of type used in country jobbing. For John Cheney of Banbury, for example, no specimens of his jobbing type survive. The small country printer was often forced to modify the wording of posters and other commercial orders because of shortages of certain letters. This was particularly true of large display lettering. Necessity as much as aesthetics often demanded variations in the size of type. Surviving jobbing printing from the country town of Lewes reveals a chaotic mixture of uppercasing and italic in posters and public notices.[55] John Soulby in Ulverston started in 1792 with a wooden press and a motley assortment of type, most apparently from Fry's foundry, but also including three sizes of ancient black letter, a French roman and italic, and a script. By the close of the century he also had use of an open letter with engraved inline that was his only option for display lettering. Soulby possessed an extremely modest range of flowers and borders which he nevertheless used with great flair. He had at least one wood block – of a racehorse – but his other pictorial printing was achieved by cast ornaments of the type produced by Caslon and Fry. Soulby boasted a flying eagle, a cow, a group of musical instruments and a garland.[56] Most of his posters were necessarily small. Over

54   [Joseph Fry], *Specimen of Metal Cast Ornaments, Curiously Adjusted to Paper, By Edmund Fry and Isaac Steele* (London, 1794).
55   Illustrated in Stanley Goodman, 'A Collection of Lewes Handbills, 1768–1777', *Sussex Archaeological Collections*, 97 (1959), 58–68.
56   All found in Caslon's *Specimen of Cast Ornaments* of 1798, and reproduced in Michael Twyman and William Rollinson, *John Soulby, Printer, Ulverston: A Study of the*

80% of the items by Soulby at the Museum of English Rural Life in Reading are foolscap folio (13 x 8 in.), demy quarto (11 x 9 in.) or smaller. By the end of the century, decorative printing remained a modest and London-based craft, even though it was practised increasingly widely.

Other country printers showed great ingenuity in designing notices and advertising copy from poor and eccentric mixtures of type. Difficult or embarrassing editorial decisions were often presented to clients by printers working with incomplete sets or limited sizes and styles of founts. The conservatism and crudity of local jobbing printing contrasted with examples of locally sold printing from London, although the common availability of London material probably continued to provide an encouragement to many overambitious requests from country customers. The printer had rather to explain his ability in creating a range of effects from a given stock of type. Italics were a common resort for emphasis or moderation. Many country printers proved extremely resourceful in combining different type sizes and styles, and in using white space and treasured decorative cuts to maximum advantage. The overall effect, however, was often unsatisfactory. Both in size and in design, type cast for book printing was rarely appropriate for jobbing orders, which was particularly true of the new sorts of jobbing requested at the end of the century. In display, the types looked thin and unconfident. As Maurice Rickards describes surviving examples of display work using book types, 'though they attempt to shout, they only whisper'.[57]

The design of new display types was in fact heavily dependent upon technical advances to the printing press. The iron presses introduced at the end of the eighteenth century finally enabled larger and heavier areas of type to be printed. Radical new display type was was cast for specified use by the jobbing printer. By 1825 most of the leading type founders issued specimen books of display faces. An early innovator in display type was Robert Thorne, who had been active since at least the mid-1780s, and had bought Thomas Cottrell's Barbican foundry in 1794. In turn, Thorne was succeeded at the foundry in 1820 by William Thorowgood. Another leader in this area was Vincent Figgins, type founder at White Swan Yard, Holborn, from 1792.[58] By 1820, type founders' specimen sheets, notably

---

Work Printed by John Soulby, father and son, between 1796 and 1827 with an account of Ulverston at the time (Reading: Museum of English Rural Life, 1966), pp. 7, 15–35.

57   Maurice Rickards, The Public Notice: An Illustrated History (Newton Abbot: David & Charles, 1973), p. 10.

58   Vincent Figgins, Specimen of Printing Types, reproduced in Michael Twyman,

those of Figgins and Thorowgood, were posted or sent with type founders' salesmen to the most distant of country printers.[59]

For jobbing work requiring intricate design, the obvious alternative to the common press of the letterpress printer was the rolling press of the intaglio printer. Here, surviving examples range from crude woodcuts to ornate metal engraving. The work of particular engravers in security printing for banknotes and counterfoils, with meshes of intricate and swirling engraved flourishes, will be considered below, but use of fine engraving also extended to many types of transaction papers. In 1713 the *British Mercury* carried a good early example of engraving used for blanks, when the news-sheet reproduced one of the receipt forms to be used by clients for quarteridge payments. Like the Bank of England commissioning engraving for banknotes, the *Mercury* announced of its new blanks that 'the Company have thought fit to print 'em *on fine Paper separately* in the Form and Character following, to avoid being counterfeited'.[60] Although it hardly seems reassuring that potential forgers were given advance and exact copies of the new forms, at least these images do survive to show what the receipt slips looked like. Much other security stationery, now also lost, probably bore the same sort of open lettering and scrollwork.

Woodcut illustration and frontispiece embellishment had been integral to Tudor and Stuart bookselling.[61] Superbly illustrated texts ranged from the iconic horror pictures of Foxe's *Book of Martyrs* and the sober woodcuts of the Bishops' Bible of 1568, to the fantastical likenesses in books of prognostication and the lively, if crude, illustrations to ballads, chapbooks and news books. Illustration had become commonplace in small books for the popular market. Some 80% of all ballads published between 1600 and 1640, for example, incorporated woodcut images. As posted on tavern walls, illustrated pages from ballads, like separate

Printing, 1770–1970: An Illustrated History of its Development and Uses in England (London: Eyre and Spottiswoode, 1970), pp. 68–9.

59 Peter C. G. Isaac, *William Davison of Alnwick: Pharmacist and Printer, 1781–1858* (Oxford: Clarendon Press, 1968), p. vii.

60 *British Mercury*, no. 429, 30 Sept. 1713; no. 442, 16 Dec. 1713; no. 455, 17 Mar. 1714.

61 Edward Hodnett, *Francis Barlow, First Master of English Book Illustration* (London: Scolar Press, 1978) and Margery Corbett and Ronald Lightbown, *The Comely Frontispiece: The Emblematic Title-Page in England 1550–1660* (London: Routledge and Kegan Paul, 1979); see also David McKitterick, *Print, Manuscripts and the Search for Order, 1450–1830* (Cambridge: Cambridge University Press, 2003).

promotional title pages, served as advertisements to purchase more print.[62] From the mid sixteenth century, advances in metal engraving ensured much finer illustrations, particularly for books of anatomy and cartography. In contrast to woodcuts and wood engraving where ink was applied to the uppermost surfaces, metal engraving and etching involved intaglio printing from the ink left in the incisions after the plate was wiped clean. Copper intaglio work, in particular, required separate printing techniques and most originating booksellers bound engravings between letterpress sheets or even pasted them onto blank or part-printed pages.[63]

The striking technical improvements of the eighteenth century enabled many fresh applications. The intaglio and engraving processes popularized in France in the early years of the century[64] transformed both book and promotional illustration. For publications in the mid-price range, Robert Dodsley led the London trade in commissioning illustrations to enliven popular texts. Before Dodsley's death in 1764, fine-line engravings had replaced cruder cuts as the expected accompaniment to fashionable literature.[65] Illustration by engraved plates and vignettes contributed increasingly to the success of new part-issues, periodicals and 'collected' editions. Engravings by Paul (sometimes referred to as Pierre) Fourdrinier, for example, enlivened the cheap and immense editions of Shakespeare plays issued in duodecimo in 1734 by Jacob Tonson and others. An unprecedented number of engravers executed plates to insert in magazines or to add practical illustrations to works of utility and topography, as well as portraits of authors and biographical subjects.

In the second half of the eighteenth century, copperplate engravers and the producers of intaglio work offered new levels of technical accomplishment, adding to the distinctions between types of publication. In elegance and quantity, many engravings lived up to their publishers' relentless promotion of the beauty of the 'embellishment' and 'adornment'; in other cases, the speed of production (to satisfy,

62 Adam Fox, *Oral and Literate Culture in England 1500–1700* (Oxford: Oxford University Press, 2000), pp. 5–6, 335–405.

63 Antony Griffiths, *Prints and Printmaking: An Introduction to the History and Techniques*, 2nd edn (London: British Museum, 1996), pp. 29–39.

64 See Griffiths, *Prints and Printmaking*, p. 54.

65 Hanns Hammelmann and T. S. R. Boase, *Book Illustrators in Eighteenth-Century England* (New Haven, CT: Yale University Press, 1975); further references are given in Vito J. Brenni, *Book Illustration and Decoration: A Guide to Research* (Westport, CT: Greenwood Press, 1980).

perhaps, the demand to supply an image of a Sheridan or a Garrick in a recent role) resulted in something short of the bookseller's boast. In the last three decades of the century, entrepreneurial bookselling publishers like John Bell and John Cooke (among many others) relied heavily upon Richard Corbould (1757–1831), Thomas Stothard (1755–1834), Edward Francis Burney (1760–1848), Edward Edwards and many more, to create the frontispieces of magazines and periodical reviews, and illustrative engraved plates for part-issue series, magazines, collected works and cheap pocket editions. Stothard's exquisite and hugely popular designs further depended on craftsmen such as William Sharp (1749–1824) and the young James Heath (1779–1878), whose fine and rapid engraving skills enabled new standards of magazine and periodical illustration.[66] With numerous blunders and botches, but also with increasing confidence and sophistication, booksellers combined relief printing with engraved ornaments, tailpieces, vignettes and full-page plates.

In contrast to many of those known as contributors to magazines and fashionable *belles lettres*, the engravers employed by City businesses remain shadowy figures. Heal's study, which is still the basis for modern knowledge of the engravers, lists 115 London engraving firms active between 1688 and 1790.[67] William Pennock, whose trade card of 1709 shows him based in Newgate Street and offering both wood and copper engraving, was one of the earliest to serve City banks and insurers. Others, such as one Kirkall of St Martin's le Grand or Thomas Oughtibridge of Holborn, seem to have specialized in engraving shopkeepers' bills and 'bills of Parcells and Lading'. William and Cluer Dicey of Northampton and Bow Church Yard advertised the engraving of labels and tickets, while Benjamin Cole and Fourdrinier, both active during the second third of the century, worked for small London tradesmen as well as City merchants and financial companies. The majority of engravers of plates used for printing were also engravers of silver and metal comestibles. Ellis Gamble, to whom Hogarth was apprenticed c.1714–20, specialized in engraving plate, watch cases, bookplates and jewellery at his Leicester Fields shop. He undertook far more engraving than was carried out at the goldsmith's

66 David Alexander, '"Alone Worth Treble the Price": Illustrations in 18th-Century English Magazines', in *A Millennium of the Book: Production, Design and Illustration in Manuscript & Print 900–1900*, ed. Robin Myers and Michael Harris (Winchester and New Castle, DE: Oak Knoll, 1994), pp. 107–33 (pp. 123–6).
67 Ambrose Heal, 'The Trade-Cards of Engravers', *Print Collector's Quarterly*, 14:3 (July 1927), 219–50; he also lists seven firms outside London.

or silversmith's premises, where only the simplest engraving was normally practised.[68] Adam Sadler (d.1768), printer and engraver of Liverpool, was also an engraver of silver tobacco boxes and household items.[69] Even for the great engraver Thomas Bewick in Newcastle upon Tyne, book illustration, in the words of his historian, 'formed an insignificant part of the workshop's turnover', while he designed extensively for commerce, turning out commercial trade cards, invoices, banknotes, insurance receipts, bar bills and visiting cards (as well as thimbles, dog collars, buckles and all manner of other engraved items).[70]

Retailing, which also demanded much paper and print, further enlisted the services of the engraver. Cheney in Banbury, like Thomas Lockett in Dorchester or the White family in Canterbury, printed auctioneers' bills and sales catalogues and used illustrative cuts within both. The engraving and printing of trade cards was an important accompaniment to the expansion of small businesses.[71] Many cards were wholly engraved and were printed on the rolling press which was now commonly set up next to the main letterpress in the printing house. Dozens of firms specifically advertised as printers and engravers of tradesmen's stationery. The Diceys announced that 'Shop-keepers Bills are curiously Engrav'd On Copper-Plates ... Likewise All manner of Business Printed with the greatest Expedition at the Lowest Rates'.[72] Their advertisements showed both a letterpress and a rolling press in action. By the side of the Dicey rolling press stands a customer with his design in his hand. In the illustration of the Dicey letterpress, a customer examines the finished work as the printer inks the type. Many other provincial printers in the second half of the century boasted of their ownership of both types of presses.

68   Ronald Paulson, *Hogarth: His Life, Art and Times*, 2 vols (London and New Haven, CT: Yale University Press, 1971), vol. 1, pp. 48–54.
69   A. H. Arkle, 'Early Liverpool Printers', *Transactions of the Historic Society of Lancashire and Cheshire*, n.s., 32 (1917), 73–84 (p. 77).
70   See Nigel Tattersfield, *Thomas Bewick, The Complete Illustrative Work*, 3 vols (London and New Castle, DE: British Library, Bibliographical Society and Oak Knoll, 2011), vol. 1, p. 68, and see plate of printed ephemera p. 70; and Ian Bain, 'Thomas Bewick and his Contemporaries', in *Maps and Prints*, ed. Robin Myers and Michael Harris (Oxford: Oxford Polytechnic Press, 1984), pp. 67–80.
71   See Maxine Berg and Helen Clifford, 'Selling Consumption in the Eighteenth Century: Advertising and the Trade Card in Britain and France', *Cultural and Social History*, 4:2 (2007), 145–70.
72   Dicey trade card, reproduced in Ambrose Heal, *London Tradesmen's Cards of the XVIII Century* (London: Batsford Ltd, 1925), plate 29.

Of those whose cards and advertisements survive, Richard Mountaine of Portsmouth and Phillip Sandford of Shrewsbury both engraved customers' orders and conducted a full printing service from their shop.[73]

The number of shop-card engravers increased fourfold between 1740 and 1770, with firms such as George Bickham, father and son, of St Martin in the Fields, James Cole and his (presumed) sons, George and William, of Hatton Garden (also engravers and printers to the Bank of England), and Paul Fourdrinier, challenging tradesmen to submit proposals that could not be engraved.[74] Such businesses, like the modern and numerous high-street photocopying and digital copy shops, competed fiercely on speed and quality of service. Most of the 'cards' were printed on thin paper and extended to half-sheet size. Many were deliberately designed for multiple use, including serving as an invoice, a further demand for payment, a receipt, an announcement piece, or as the bearer for lists of wares and services. In 1735, one Reynells launched a series of printed cards for tradesmen to remind masters and customers of the advantage of sending out Christmas gratuities. Funeral and visiting cards became very popular with the middle classes. Theatre tickets and other tickets of admission and engagement were printed in their thousands.[75]

At the same time, the cutting and printing of much cruder wooden blocks continued as a specialist trade in the craft of the tilleter. From at least the sixteenth century, carved wooden 'tillet blocks' were used to stamp bales of cloth (wrapped in rough fabrics or papers known as tillets) and other goods for transport abroad and sometimes domestically. Each tillet carried distinctive designs stamped on it from the tillet block that offered details of the bale's contents for customs and also usually carried the name of the manufacturer as an advertisement for potential buyers. Fine examples of tillet blocks survive in the Ledger collection of the Museum of London, including one used to stamp bales of wool produced by the Exeter firm Banfill and Shute. The Horselydown printing works established by Robert Ledger in Southwark in the 1760s traded as 'buckram stiffeners' and tilleters in both Southwark and the City of London. The Ledger examples typically feature ornate symbolic carving

73 ShRO, Lloyd MSS Sandford (Jnr) billhead; Richard Mountaine, tradesman's card, c.1760.
74 A. D. Mackenzie, *The Bank of England Note: A History of its Printing* (Cambridge: Cambridge University Press, 1953), pp. 37–40.
75 Sarah Lloyd, 'Ticketing the British Eighteenth Century: "A thing ... never heard of before"', *Journal of Social History*, 46:4 (2013), 843–71.

around oval 'blanks' to be filled in by thick ink with the name and destination of the cargo.

By the end of the eighteenth century, therefore (and just as new experiments began from 1796 in lithographic printing using a stone or metal plate), letterpress and intaglio printing offered a kaleidoscopic range of document presentation methods to commerce and finance in town and in country. Production runs and quality of work varied hugely, but the profusion of image and word in clear, stylish and speedily (and usually cheaply) produced signage, anchored the aesthetics and the security of business. The sheer diversity of these items, some self-contained (like the wholly engraved trade card) and others made up of composite additions (like engraved mastheads or part-printed or engraved blank forms), defies summation (as it did at the time). But there was, nonetheless, an important commonality to these productions. Print, however applied, offered a culturally recognized authority to transactions and the imparting of information. Drawing upon historic and traditional visual associations, but also refined by recent English innovations in design and application, type and engraving presented and adorned paper (and sometimes other) items in increasingly specific ways. Much of this design registered – subtly, ingeniously or flagrantly – those particular economic, political, religious, local, institutional and business associations. Buyers and clients were informed, entertained and reassured; security was enhanced; confidence was asserted; trust was developed.

4

Serviced by Stationery and Printing

The business strategies of the printers reflected their locality as well as the strength of their client and market relationships. Long-term contracts and sustained demand for a specific publication were relatively rare. Flexibility and diversity of operation was usually the basis of survival. This was especially so given the underdevelopment of regional and local markets where the products of the printing house and the skills of the printer were adapted to an increasingly wide and experimental range of business needs.

Recovering the business profile of the eighteenth-century printer's office is problematic. Much of the actual servicing of commerce by print has left fragmentary evidence and the diversity of the printers' operations only adds to the confusion. Many sources seem unpromising. Original constituent contracts of the 'financial revolution' do survive, but usually they have featured only incidentally, if at all, in surveys of the development of joint-stock companies or government revenue operations. The history of overseas and inland trade has been constructed from diverse sources, but surviving printed chits of exchange are rarely considered in terms of their origination, design and use. Accounts of local retailing are even patchier, reliant upon the survival of shop accounts and trading advertisements.[1] Business historians have faced similar difficulties with the unevenness of eighteenth-century commercial and industrial records. Few examples survive of the many printed items that were ordered by businesses, revenue-raising bodies, or financial companies and it is often impossible to gauge their representativeness. The fragments of such jobbing printing are also treated very differently according to the wide variety of archives in which they reside. In many business and family archives, many such items remain uncatalogued, to be found simply by accident in boxes and files of named papers and letters. At the other extreme, some filled-in printed

---

1   An eclectic but rich assortment of such pieces can be found in the John Johnson Collection, Bodleian Library, described generally in M. L. Turner (comp.), *The John Johnson Collection: Catalogue of an Exhibition* (Oxford: Bodleian Library, 1971).

blanks, including receipt slips, promissory notes and cargo dockets, are individually catalogued components of cherished institutional collections.[2] The removal of these slender items from their original working business archive, however, only heightens their isolation and the difficulty in interpreting their original use and significance.

Evidence of orders sent to printers and corresponding evidence of production compensate for some of the archival and interpretational complications of surviving printed and part-printed jobbing items. Sources range from the well-known products of individual presses, notably newspapers and printed trade lists and catalogues, to a few surviving printers' business records. Much evidence of the functional connections between printing and commercial and financial transactions can also be retrieved from local legal and municipal administrative records. The articles of exchange between printers, stationers and their customers offer significant help in understanding the complementary relationship between new printing and new trade. The records of what clients ordered, received and paid for are particularly underused resources for printing history. This study includes an initial trawl of their riches.

In 1721, William Craighton, bookseller of Ipswich, died unexpectedly. The resulting inventory of his goods allows one insight into the early-eighteenth-century provincial printing, book and newspaper trade.[3] Numerically, a tenth of Craighton's investment in his stock of books was in a selection of copybooks, shop and account books sold for the use of local businesses. Proportionately, his ready-to-use account books (which might be customized according to particular needs) were the much more valuable. Together with unbound paper and stationery, Craighton's stock of account books amounted to over a third of his total valued commercial assets. Craighton's son took over the business when he came of age in 1727, advertising his wares in the *Ipswich Journal* then owned by John Bagnall, but soon bought up and printed by the younger Craighton himself. In the newspaper, Craighton junior gave notice of printing account books and copy books made up, ruled, bound and delivered to order. Craighton's weekly *Ipswich Journal* became a major commercial force in East Suffolk. Each issue carried up to a hundred advertisements

---

2   Of many such examples, the copyright transaction receipts in the Osborn Collection, Beinecke Rare Book and Manuscript Library, Yale, and the various cargo dockets in the archives of the South Carolina Historical Society, Charleston, SC.

3   ESRO, FE1/15/96; all existing accounts of 'William Craighton' confuse his contribution with that of his more productive son, William Craighton II.

for goods, services and employment. Private properties and commercial premises were sold and let. Auctions, share prices, sailings, coaches and parcel deliveries were all announced. Available by order from the shop were the latest, mostly London-printed guides designed for the merchant, the counting-house clerk, the specialist trader or the gentleman anxious to learn more about estate or personal financial management.

The Craightons' services for local traders were repeated in every large town in England. In the first half of the eighteenth century, towns like Canterbury, Exeter, Cambridge, Norwich and Oxford were centres of stationery production and jobbing printing, serving growing provincial trades. In Exeter, civic orders for print included many sheets printed on one side only for public display on a wall or noticeboard.[4] William and Benjamin Collins commenced book and stationery selling in Salisbury and launched, and then relaunched, the *Salisbury Journal* in 1729 and 1736.[5] The newspaper carried thousands of local and some metropolitan traders' advertisements to the south and south-west of England. Benjamin Collins developed close trading relations with a number of London firms, such that his local customers were able to obtain locally printed works as well as publications produced in partnership with a major London bookseller. By 1750, Collins had opened his 'publick register' where 'Masters and Mistresses may be informed of servants of all kinds; Gentlemen may likewise be informed of houses and lodgings to be lett ... [and] of estates to be bought and sold'.[6] In Shrewsbury, Thomas Durston advertised a wide variety of stationery for local businesses.[7] From the late 1750s, William Cruttwell and Robert Goadby were in competition in Sherborne, Dorset, not only with their rival newspapers and political lobbying but also in the supply of stationery and jobbing printing to local traders.[8] In Tunbridge Wells, Jasper Sprange was offering similar services from the early 1770s. In a collection of 650 items printed by Sprange, mostly from the years 1794–97, 200 are playbills or advertisements for entertainments, 190 are

---

4 Ian Maxted, 'Single Sheets from a County Town: The Example of Exeter', in *Spreading the Word: The Distribution Networks of Print, 1550–1850*, ed. Robin Myers and Michael Harris (Winchester: St Paul's Bibliographies, 1990), pp. 109–29 (pp. 114–15).

5 Their careers are extensively analysed in C. Y. Ferdinand, *Benjamin Collins and the Provincial Newspaper Trade in the Eighteenth Century* (Oxford: Clarendon Press, 1997).

6 Cited by C. Y. Ferdinand, 'Benjamin Collins: Salisbury Printer', in *Searching the Eighteenth Century*, ed. M. Crump and M. Harris (London: British Library, 1983), pp. 74–92 (p. 81).

7 ShRO, Lloyd MSS 2118/294, Durston advertisement.

8 Newspaper files, Dorset County Museum, Dorchester.

announcements of auctions, 35 are the title pages to auction catalogues, 80 are notices for local tradesmen, and the remainder, a typically rich assortment of jobbing including trade cards, official notices, blank forms, tickets and labels for bottles.[9] An even greater variety is seen in another collection, that of over a thousand items printed by John Soulby and son, printers at Ulverston in north Lancashire from the 1790s. In a town of just under three thousand people in 1800, John Soulby senior printed general trade cards, notices of cattle fairs and freight charges, advertisements for labourers, the letting of contracts, sales of ships and ships' parts, and notices of coach departures, services and mail coach arrivals. The majority are posters advertising sales of goods and produce and the sale or leasing of land and property, with most being specifically notices for auction sales.[10]

Paper, ledgers and binding

With sharply increased business demands for writing materials and stationery, many customers faced frequent bottlenecks in the provision of paper and its processing by suppliers and printers. Throughout the century, most civic corporations remained anxious about the availability of paper both for their own use and for the supply to their commissioned printers.[11] The majority of clients provided the paper to be sent to the printers (and, at the very least, paid for the paper to be collected by printers). The earliest newspapers were constrained as much by paper shortages and costs as they were by stamp duty or the technical limitations of the press. Even local tradesmen, who came to rely upon particular suppliers of paper and bound books, often found themselves the victims of regional shortages. Such frustrations could only have increased as the variety of papers available expanded. Details given in the Stamp Act show that as early as 1712 paper mills were manufacturing an immense range of weights, dimensions and finishes in the paper produced. Although

9 David Knott, 'Aspects of Research into English Provincial Printing', *Journal of the Printing Historical Society*, 9 (1973–74), 6–21 (p. 7).
10 Michael Twyman and William Rollinson, *John Soulby, Printer, Ulverston: A Study of the Work Printed by John Soulby, father and son, between 1796 and 1827 with an account of Ulverston at the time* (Reading: Museum of English Rural Life, 1966).
11 Of many examples, HRO, Q.T.10: 10, account of John Measey, stationer (with enclosure).

the problem has received hardly any attention in the histories of early accounting practice, the supply of paper for the keeping of accounts was no easy matter. This was especially so if the tradesman was to follow some of the grandiose schemes proposed by many contemporary accountancy advice books.

From modest beginnings at the turn of the seventeenth century, the home production of paper increased from some two thousand tons in 1700 to about fifteen thousand tons per annum in 1800. In 1700 nearly two hundred paper mills, scattered across the country, were supplying regional stationers and feeding an increasing demand for paper for wrapping, writing and printing.[12] In 1738, 278 paper mills were recorded in the Excise returns for England and Wales, three-quarters of which manufactured coarse papers only. In 1785, 381 licences were issued to paper makers in England and Wales. By 1800, the number of licences issued had risen to 417.[13] Throughout the century, the greatest concentration of paper mills remained in south Buckinghamshire, Hertfordshire and Middlesex, with a further large scattering of mills throughout Kent.

Changes in the types of paper made for printing were particularly marked. Many new patents for the manufacture of white papers were granted in late Stuart Britain. White paper production, together with that of blue paper and millboard, used (among other things) for binding, attracted much comment at the turn of the century. In Scotland, where twelve mills had been established before 1700, there was a massive increase in output from an annual production of board and paper of some 100,000 lb in 1750 to over two million lb by 1800.[14] Production, however, was still by manual labour. All early papers were laid papers made by hand from a pulp of linen rags with a wire-screen mould and strengthening frame. A paper mill driven by a Boulton and Watt steam engine was set up at Wilmington near Hull in 1786, but it was a short-lived experiment. The first successful paper-making machines, adapted from an invention attributed to Nicolas Louis Robert at the Essonne mill near Paris in 1798, were established by Henry and Sealy Fourdrinier at Two Waters, Hemel Hempstead in 1803, and by John Gamble at St Neots in the same year.

---

12 D. C. Coleman, *The Paper Industry, 1495–1860: A Study in Industrial Growth* (Oxford: Clarendon Press, 1958).

13 Alfred H. Shorter, *Water Paper Mills in England* (London: Society for the Protection of Ancient Buildings, 1966), p. 10.

14 Alistair G. Thomson, *The Paper Industry in Scotland, 1590–1861* (Edinburgh: Scottish Academic Press, 1974), p. 74.

These machines introduced a continuous process of paper manufacture from a belt of wire mesh over which the pulp flowed to felt rollers and steam-heated drying drums.[15] Although the Fourdrinier machine was capable of making 1,000 lb of paper per day, where the maximum daily output from a paper mill had been previously 100 lb, by 1810 only a handful of paper mills had adopted power-driven machinery. In the same year, the Fourdriniers were also declared bankrupt.

One of the most common complaints of the local stationer throughout the century continued to be over shortages of paper. Paper-selling was a common staple of the local general storekeeper – even though it is difficult to retrace the supply of paper from mill to wholesaler and to retail stationer and bookseller. Many bales of paper were sent along newly opened trading routes, and many of the suppliers of paper were local. In Kirkby Stephen in the 1740s, the storekeeper, Abraham Dent, was provided with stock by the main paper suppliers of Kendal, Thomas and James Ashburner.[16] Large numbers of regional mills were established before mid-century and, within a few years of the founding of each mill, local dealers like the Ashburners flourished in most nearby large towns. In order to ensure a sufficient and constant supply of paper, however, it was often necessary for the regional stationer to open commercial negotiations with a London wholesaler rather than with a local manufacturer. Henry Crossgrove in Norwich and Farley and Joseph Bliss, the publishers of two early Exeter newspapers, for example, relied upon a London wholesale stationer.[17] By the 1790s in remote Ulverston, Soulby was selling fifteen types of writing paper and eight types of drawing paper.[18] In London, where the manufacture of paper had moved largely to the surrounding villages even by 1700, a complex system of paper warehousing and distribution had developed.

After the imposition of stamp duty in 1712, the importance of supply from the metropolis was increased.[19] Subsequently, the only legal source

15 Further details are given in Coleman, *Paper Industry*, pp. 180–90.

16 T. S. Willan, *An Eighteenth-century Shopkeeper: Abraham Dent of Kirkby Stephen* (Manchester: Manchester University Press, 1970).

17 BL, Add. MSS 5853 (Cole Collection, vol. 52), p. 108, Crossgrove to the Revd John Strype, 27 June 1715; Ian Maxted, 'Four Rotten Corn Bags and Some Old Books: The Impact of the Printed Work in Devon', in *The Sale and Distribution of Books from 1700, ed. Robin Myers and Michael Harris* (Oxford: Oxford Polytechnic Press, 1982), pp. 37–76 (p. 46).

18 Twyman and Rollinson, *John Soulby*, p. 18.

19 After the first act to impose an excise tax on home-produced paper (1711), some twenty-six further acts were passed in the next 150 years.

of supply for newspaper stamped paper was the warehouse of the Commissioners of Stamps in Serle Court, Lincoln's Inn, to where unsold papers also had to be returned in order to claim a rebate. Other duties were also applicable. In Abraham Dent's area of Cumbria, John Moore supplied the paper for legal instruments, which by 1770 bore a stamp duty of 2s 6d in every sheet used in an indenture, lease, bond or deed without a separate rate.[20]

In addition to stamped and unstamped paper, the stationer also entered into a number of agreements with manufacturers of quills, wafers, slates, sand and other stationery items sold to both business and private customers. In the towns, demand was heavy. From the early eighteenth century at least, local administrations were putting in large orders for their own paper, 'skins' and 'texts' (sheets and blank forms of vellum for legal documents), standishes and ink. Civic and business accounts of the period reveal a quixotic array of other stationery requirements, such as the cords and large cardboard labels extensively used in filing incoming bills and receipts.[21] Among the fullest surviving records of the sales of such items by a bookseller are the ledgers of John Clay of Daventry. Most striking in these ledgers are the great distances from which Clay was prepared to source his wares in order to maintain an adequate stock. Clay's main supplier of pens, pen cases, ink, inkpots and sealing-wax was Heatley Noble of Birmingham. Clay bought his quills from Robert Taylor of Nantwich and Edward Laxton of Peterborough (among others). He ordered blank books from suppliers in Bristol and Louth. He purchased paper from mills in Worcestershire, Gloucestershire, Oxfordshire and Northamptonshire. Clay's chief paper supplier was Robert Allen of Boughton mill outside Northampton, but wrapping paper came from John Jones of North Newington mill near Banbury.[22]

Most of the unprinted paper sold by the stationer for business purposes was almost certainly used for account books and ledgers. As financial and

20 Stephen Dowell, A History of Taxation and Taxes in England, 3 vols, 3rd edn (London: Longmans, 1965), vol. 3, p. 290.

21 Of many examples from this period, StRO, Chamberlaine's Accounts, 1729–44; HfRO, BG11/24/2, Chamberlaine's Book of Accompts, 1732–69 (e.g. fol. 408, order of 23 August 1756).

22 Details from John Feather, 'John Clay of Daventry: The Business of an Eighteenth-Century Stationer', Studies in Bibliography, 37 (1984), 198–209 (pp. 202–6). His general argument is qualified by Jan Fergus and Ruth Portner, 'Provincial Bookselling in Eighteenth-century England: The Case of John Clay Reconsidered', Studies in Bibliography, 40 (1987), 147–63.

commercial practice became more complex, printer-stationers offered more sophisticated services. The supply of specialized ledgers and record books was an indispensable feature of new banking and credit facilities. In many London and major offices, simple creditors' and debtors' ledgers could not cope with the complexities of new forms of financial and trading transactions. Not that the threshold of competence was especially high: the accounting of many businessmen was notoriously modest.[23] New types of business organization required specific stationery tailored to individual operations. Inevitably, however, the history of the production and sale of account books is very difficult to recover. Even where bound business ledgers survive they share with their owners a marked reluctance to reveal much about their origins. In an age when paper was such a scarce and valuable commodity it was also the fate of much of it to be reused until worthless.

Nevertheless, the production of durable ledgers was one of the most heavily advertised skills of the wholesaling and local stationer. Neither Collins of Salisbury nor Bliss of Exeter, for example, was made wealthy by the sale of reading books alone. An important and expanding part of their business was supplying local tradesmen with day and waste books and other business ledgers. The surviving stationers' inventories reveal substantial stocks of account books, but most orders were made up to the individual requirements of the customer whether he was merchant, shopkeeper, farmer, householder, alderman or magistrate. A whole ledger could contain two or three hundred pages and charges could be high. In 1757 Alexander Smiton, bookseller of Edinburgh, charged one customer eight shillings for eighty-two sheets of foolscap, four shillings for binding these in two books, two shillings and fourpence for ruling six lines on each page, and eightpence for a six-sheet index.[24] In Kirkby Stephen, Abraham Dent was selling a variety of paper at between threepence and one shilling a quire, and shop books of five quires bound and ruled for six shillings. Smaller ready-made shop books were sold for about four shillings, and memorandum or waste books for 1s 6d. Stationers also catered for specialist needs according to the locality. At Portsmouth from the 1670s, Robert Hartford manufactured ledgers for shipping accounts and for copying bills of lading.[25] Lockett in Dorchester, in one of his rhyming advertisements, offered for sale

---

23 Julian Hoppit, *A Land of Liberty? England 1689–1727* (Oxford: Clarendon Press, 2000), p. 326.
24 EUL, Special Collections, La II: 694, Account of George Wallace.
25 HRO, QR. Misc. I. 34, pp. 34–43.

> Red Books too, which partly shew,
> How it is our Millions go.
> Books full bound, or only half.
> In Morrocco, Sheep or Calf.
> Marble Paper'd green or blue,
> Neatly gilt and letter'd too.[26]

Many stationers, including Lockett and also William Craighton, who offered to bind their books, usually employed a contracted bookbinder. The binder could also be engaged independently by the purchaser of papers or unbound books. If we are to judge by newspaper advertisements, many booksellers were anxious to secure experienced binders. Of many examples, in April 1780 'an eminent bookseller in the country' was searching, through the mediation of John Bell the London publisher, for a 'steady, sober' journeyman bookbinder 'to engage by the year'.[27] In the 1790s, Soulby offered his Ulverston customers 'pocket books – morocco and black leather, with straps, locks or clasps, made to any pattern'.[28]

Craft bookbinding received little recognition, even in the eighteenth century. Today, most scholarly attention is still reserved for the skilled binding and leatherwork which adorns special collections of printed books.[29] In the eighteenth century, bookbinding was described by one guide to trades as having 'no great Ingenuity in it, and requires few Talents ... a moderate Share of Strength is requisite, which is chiefly employed in beating the Books with a heavy Hammer'. According to the guide, a bookbinder seldom earned more than ten shillings per week and was unemployed for half the year.[30] Surviving wills and inventories confirm bookbinders as men of small means, and not in the same league as bookseller-publishers or the larger stationers.[31] Sanguine of the Strand was one of a select group of binders serving businesses in Cornhill and the main financial quarters of London, and one who also featured

26 *Lockett's Address to his Friends*, broadside handbill, [1788].
27 *London Evening Post*, 11 April 1780.
28 Trade advertisement, reproduced in Twyman and Rollinson, *John Soulby*, p. 18.
29 Exceptions include Bernard C. Middleton, *A History of English Craft Bookbinding Technique*, 4th edn (London: Oak Knoll Press, 1996 [1st edn, 1963]).
30 R. Campbell, *The London Tradesman* (London, 1747), p. 135.
31 John Bewell (d.1705), bookbinder of Ipswich, was worth at death £11 6s 8d, ESRO, FE1/5/121.

regularly in the *Public Advertiser* in the final third of the century.[32] Rarely was bookbinding the sole occupation of the binder, however. Sanguine, for example, also advertised himself as a maker of combs and purveyor of strops and razors. Parchment-making and bookbinding were traditionally combined with window-glazing and several successful booksellers, stationers and binders also served as postmasters and glaziers. Lesser bookbinders practised as saddlers, glovers and other types of leather-worker, but were also dyers, cutlers and even coopers.

By the end of the eighteenth century, booksellers were advertising an extensive choice of business bindings. William Smart, owner of 'a genteel shop adjoining the Town Hall' at Worcester, begged leave 'to inform the Merchant and Tradesman, that he being some Time Stationer to the principal Bank in Bristol has it in his Power of supplying them with all the different Sorts of Books made use of in the Compting House, ruled to any Pattern and bound in any kind of Binding, neat and firm, on the lowest terms'.[33] During the century, red morocco binding became the recognized packaging for small account books. London newspapers in particular are full of binders' notices with numerous advertisements for exclusive morocco work. Late in his career, Sanguine was to specialize in morocco binding and in tambour silk for ladies' pocketbooks. The insuring and hiring man made notorious by the literature against the state lottery was known as the 'morocco man' after the ledger he carried with him. The largest account books, however, were still covered in vellum (or indeed made up from vellum), with leather and calf reserved for special orders.[34] There is also evidence of new tensions between binders and booksellers at mid-century as demand and competition grew. In Ipswich, William Craighton II engaged in a very public dispute with one of his former employees, a journeyman bookbinder, in the columns of his own newspaper.[35] Part of the cause, it would seem, concerned not only printed books, but also the general increase in demand for the binding of blank volumes, notably business ledgers.

32 Recurrent monthly advertisements include the *Public Advertiser*, 5, 19 and 26 Jan. 1780; 3, 4 and 27 April 1780; and 11 May and 21 June 1780.

33 HWRO, b899:31/8a, iii, Palfrey Collection, Foley Scrapbook. Smart advertisement, 28 July 1774.

34 Anon., *A General Description of all Trades* (London, 1747).

35 *Ipswich Journal*, 24 Nov., 1 and 8 Dec. 1750; this is also noted in J. B. Oldham, 'An Ipswich Master-Stationer's Tiff with his Journeyman', *TCBS*, 2 (1958), 381–4.

Local jobbing work and regulation

In London, in the regional capitals, the ports and the country towns, print had many practical effects upon the structural development of new financial and commercial systems. Where business enterprise was local and piecemeal the printer was a partner in many ventures. He or she was frequently consulted by local firms not only on how to execute an order but also on the viability of particular schemes. Many printers advised on the technical format of the application forms and proposal notices for London companies; in the country, printers accepted commissions for bills of receipt and promissory notes. Securing a contract for such work could bring a handsome and, more importantly, regular income for the printer.

By mid-century, most regional jobbing work was ordered directly by local business, and many printing orders from local concerns followed in the wake of new transport and postal routes. In Chester, Peter Joynson, having been an apprentice of William Cooke, printer of the *Weekly Journal*, set up in the 1740s as a specialist jobbing printer serving the local businesses of ironmongers, drapers, salt merchants and joiners. John Read, another apprentice of Cooke, began work as a specialist stationer within the town. In Edinburgh, Patrick Neill, printer to the publishers Gavin Hamilton and John Balfour, took on much jobbing work for local shopkeepers and craftsmen.[36] Many papers in family archives deposited in record offices include printed vouchers and forms that attest to an increasing demand for formal and standardized receipts for spending on household and personal goods. Printed vouchers, with purchases written in the blank spaces and signed and sometimes countersigned, included such items as clothing, furniture, dressmaking and sketching equipment, and chaise hire.[37] John Cheney's ledger in the 1790s shows how important jobbing printing was to local commerce in the district of Banbury by the end of the century.[38] Jobbing printing in the 1790s earned him about £100 per year, double that of his takings in 1767, his first year of operations. Cheney's orders remained primarily related to agriculture.

At the ports, the supply of printed bills of lading was increasingly

36   NLS Ledgers of Patrick and Adam Neill, 1764–73.
37   Of many examples, ESxRO AMS 6005/1–12, printed and signed vouchers for Henrietta, duchess of Newcastle and the Pelham family, 1768–71.
38   C. R. Cheney, *John Cheney and his Descendants: Printers in Banbury since 1767* (Banbury: Cheney and Sons, 1936), pp. 1–20.

necessary to the efficient identification and disposal of cargoes. From the outset, the Collins brothers in Salisbury were advertising their services to print not only releases, warrants of attorney and blank bonds, but also ship bills and bills of lading, which were usually ordered by the shipping company or masters of the local ports. Bills were always blanks with spaces left for the name both of the ship and its master, the points of departure and arrival, the witness and signature on receipt of goods, and a very large space – varying according to the type of cargo or vessel – for itemizing the offloadings. Some lading bills also had stubs such that a copy of the relevant information could be easily made and retained. All had sophisticated numbering for copying and reference in storage and indexing. Similar administrative coupons served inland waterways and roads.

The manufacture of books of tickets became a further staple of local jobbing printing and vital to the expansion of many services and much retail enterprise. Tickets and posters were printed for new navigation and turnpike projects (to be considered again below) as well as for a variety of concerns for leisure and entertainment. In London, and then later in spas and other regional towns, many new ventures demanded admission tickets, most notably concert halls, assembly rooms and pleasure gardens. From the 1730s (at least), proprietors such as Jonathan Tyers of Vauxhall Spring Gardens introduced paper and metal admission tickets, many restricting entry to particular attractions.[39] By 1790, major London printers were undertaking massive orders for business requirements – including in one instance the printing of a complete run of five thousand books each of 350 disposable chits. Tickets that gave entry or egress from any number of institutions now proliferated, some still written by hand but most being printed blanks ordered by the committee or board of trustees from a local printer and stationer. Tickets of leave of varying complexity were similarly issued by schools, hospitals and workhouses, supplementing and often replacing earlier badges and certificates, in an attempt to regulate and control patients, employees, visitors, services and objects. In examples cited by Sarah Lloyd, numbers of confirmation candidates were controlled by tickets and church vestries ordered printers to produce pew tickets to regulate parishioners and prevent the occupation of pews by undesirables.[40]

39   David E. Coke and Alan Borg, *Vauxhall Gardens: A History* (New Haven, CT: Yale University Press, 2011), esp. pp. 178–89, App. 2; Warwick Wroth, 'Tickets of Vauxhall Gardens', *Numismatic Chronicle*, 3rd ser., 18 (1898), 73–92.

40   Sarah Lloyd, 'Ticketing the British Eighteenth Century: "A thing ... never heard of before"', *Journal of Social History*, 46:4 (2013), 843–71 (p. 846).

Much of the earliest regional printing originated from the demands of municipal government rather than from commissions from local traders. Certain country jobbing printing apparently predated the lapse of the licensing laws in 1695. The licensing Act of 1662 actually included special mention of books of blank bills, subjecting these to the same provisions affecting other printed works.[41] Large orders for regional printing were, however, still sent to metropolitan printers and to the licensed centres. In 1682, the town clerk of Norwich had ordered printing from Cambridge (then exempt from the 1662 restrictions) for the articles used by parish officers to certify their aldermen.[42] Within twenty years, production was more local. Samuel Darker was printing apprenticeship indentures for the Exeter council before 1700.[43] In Newcastle-under-Lyme, Samuel Parsons, who set up as stationer and bookseller in the town in 1704, was printing official handbills and borough notices on his own press. In 1732 his business was taken over by John Hewitt and the services to the council continued.[44] Stephen Bryan, founder in 1709 of *The Worcester Post-Man*, one of the earliest provincial newspapers, was printer to the Corporation of Worcester from at least 1718 until 1730.[45] In 1711 John White, the Newcastle printer, advertised through his newspaper, the *Newcastle Courant*, the printing of subpoenas, books of blanks, watch warrants, penances and certificates for burying in woollen.[46] Roger and Orion Adams of Manchester were advertising similar printing services in their *Newsletter* in the 1720s. In 1728, John Collyer of Nottingham printed tickets and programmes for the Corporation. In the 1730s, William Chase of Norwich was earning on average £25 for jobbing for the Norwich Corporation, including printing abstracts of Acts of Parliament, combination papers, and assizes of bread and ale. In all of this jobbing printing, Crossgrove proved a keen competitor.[47] John Garnett, established as the first printer of books in Sheffield by 1736, and his successor, Revill Homfray, were printing at least a dozen different types of documents and

41   14 Car. II, c. 33.

42   David Stoker, 'The establishment of printing in Norwich', *TCBS*, 7:1 (1977), 94–111 (p. 95).

43   John Feather, *The Provincial Book Trade in Eighteenth-Century England* (Cambridge: Cambridge University Press, 1981), p. 104.

44   StRO, Chamberlaine's Accounts, 1729–44, 1745–65.

45   HWRO, Quarter Sessions Order Book, II (1714–31): 84a, 219a, 255a.

46   *Newcastle Courant*, 4 Aug. 1711.

47   Stoker, 'Printing in Norwich', p. 106; NRO, Chamberlain's Accounts and Misc. Chamberlain's Vouchers, 21b (3).

forms for the town trustees during the second third of the century. The disbursements of dozens of surviving borough treasurers' records record similar orders for local printing in almost every large town in Britain.[48] There survives at least one separately stitched town accounts' book relating specifically to the orders for stationery and printing despatched (in this case) by the town clerk.[49]

Many of the official orders for printing which served local commerce derived from the judicial and administrative work of the justices of the peace. Responsibilities varied greatly between towns, something which further complicates the inconclusive debate about the relationship between local economic growth and municipal regulation.[50] Country printers took up thousands of different commissions including market weights and price forms for grain and other crop and farm products, various authorizations, blank printed forms relating to husbandry, and assorted bonds and forms of affirmation.[51] Although not directly related to the businesses of an area, many other regulatory forms contributed to an ordering of men, labour, supervisory practices, and general social and political conditions that indirectly – and sometimes acutely – affected local economies. Such work, contributory to much printed in London and undertaken by local printers at their presses, ranged from vagrant passes and settlement examinations,[52] blank printed forms for military enlistment, local returns of arms, warrants and musters,[53] forms for monthly statistics of officers and inmates at orphan hospitals and other institutions,[54] and a multitude of apprenticeship forms, including those for foundling hospitals.[55] Like

48 The survival of records is variable, however, ranging from the splendid Treasurers' Accompt Books of Hereford and Norwich to the bundles of virtually illegible vouchers and receipts at Shrewsbury and at Reading (from which the original but now lost main ledgers were compiled).

49 ShRO, 3365/664, Mr Loxdale's Accounts.

50 For one (strongly argued) view of this, see P. J. Corfield, *The Impact of English Towns, 1700–1800* (Oxford: Oxford University Press, 1982).

51 Every county record office in England and Wales holds examples of these many different forms, some more accessible through catalogues than others (simply because priority, understandably, is given to the estate, family or business catalogue or collection reference). Much lateral thinking, patience and serendipity is required to unearth them. Particularly good examples are ESxRO DUN 55/17; LRO FRP 17/17; and NRO HIL/3/33A.

52 These survive in quantities at a great many county record offices; a good collection is at DbRO Q/RV 1711/12–1809.

53 Of many examples, GMRO E4/95/14, 17, 22, 26.

54 LMA A/FH/D/02/015/001.

55 LMA, A/FH/D/04/006/001.

many other similar printed forms, those for nominations of overseers of the poor also stated the duties of the overseers.[56]

National parliamentary legislation created a need for much small-item printing, although many of the extensive private bills during the century also spawned, often directly, orders for printed forms (toll-gate receipts and share documents generated by local projects and improvement schemes, for example). The vagrancy and settlement printing, whether originating locally or from London, was typical of many orders driven by national statute. In varying detail, Acts and their schedules specified the printed forms to be completed. Numerous procedures, for example, were prescribed in the Vagrancy Act of 1744,[57] but these echoed in large measure the directives of many earlier Acts, all of which needed the commission of a stationer and printer for their local execution. By the 1744 Act, a Justice of the Peace needed a pass (serving in effect as a removal order) to commit rogues, vagabonds and beggars to the local house of correction. The form was to include an examination of the unfortunate before they were despatched, paper and all, to their last confirmed place of settlement or place of birth. The Act further required that a duplicate of the pass and examination, signed by the justice, was to be sent as a record to the next Quarter Sessions. The requirement for these passes was not repealed until 1824,[58] and county records across England and Wales are replete not only with the eighty years' worth of these part-printed documents but also many of the predecessor forms and chits.[59]

Depending upon the locality, clerks of markets, mayors, aldermen or the local magistracy officiated in assizes of bread, fixing rates according to the local price for corn and requiring town bakers to sell bread at the authorized price. Various orders for 'quires of the weight of bread' were sent to the local press as well as orders for posters relating to the administration of this and other types of assize.[60] Printed notices, for example, announced assessments of charges for land or water carriage from London. Other orders

56 DvRO 239 A – 3/PO 1.

57 7 Geo. II, c. 5 (1744); I am most grateful to Naomi Tadmor for discussions about legal parish settlement.

58 5 Geo. IV, c. 83 (1824).

59 See the excellent discussion of these and other documentary requirements in Steve Hindle, *On the Parish? The Micro-Politics of Poor Relief in Rural England, c.1550–1750* (Oxford: Clarendon Press, 2004).

60 CCRO, Treasurer's Accounts, 1759–73, TAB/7 (and corresponding Treasurer's Day Books for 1756–64, TAY/1–4) provide several examples. A remarkable series of seventy printed forms, 1759–80, for 'Prices of grain meal and flour as sold in the corn market in Kingston-upon-Hull … the day of …', etc., are held at the Goldsmiths Library.

specified how and where notices were to be circulated and displayed.[61] Magistrates' printing orders even include canal and turnpike administration.[62] Local courts engaged printers to supply warrants and bills, blanks for recognizances, summons for juries, items to serve the local militia and even calendars of prisoners.[63] Rare surviving examples of the jobbing of the Collins family in Salisbury include a pair of commitment blanks for stealing wood (after 1775) and a warning against damaging trees (1796).[64] Quarter Sessions records for Hampshire show in great detail the stationery and printing orders given to local stationers such as John Measey and John Wilkes in the 1770s.[65] Procedural books of blanks were manufactured for furthering local administration from the poor law to the window tax.[66] William Dicey used his *Northampton Mercury* in the 1750s to give notice each week that he supplied 'all Sorts of Blank Warrants and Summons's, Orders of Removal, Poors Warrants, Window, Highway, and Land-Tax Warrants &c'. In the 1770s Barnabas Thorn, bookseller of Exeter, was selling 'warrants of all sorts viz land tax, window tax and highway &c'.[67] At Worcester, in an example which will stand for almost any large town during the second half of the century, R. Lewis was printing 'Public Accompts' for the local hospital, lists of subscribers to local charities, orders to be observed on the town's byways and in the local workhouse, and numerous notices to serve locally regulated trades ranging from butchers to alehouse-keepers.[68] Poll books for elections were another staple of local printing.

Country jobbing work increased further with the expansion of local banking facilities. Although printed prospectuses and advertisements survive from the 1690s, country banking came of age only after the mid

---

61   ShRO, Quarter Sessions Records, Orders and Minutes of JPs, 1755–67 'Misc' 3365/2446, and Orders, 1767–78 3365/2447.

62   Notable surviving examples include CRO, Quarter Sessions, enrolment, registration and deposited plans.

63   BRO, Quarter Sessions Records, 1775–95, and considered further in Christopher Pickford, 'Bedford Stationers and Booksellers', *Factotum*, 15 (Oct. 1982), 21–7; also ESRO, HRO, LCA, WSRO Quarter Sessions and municipal records.

64   Salisbury Museum, 104/1964; 197/1945; I am grateful to Christine Ferdinand for these references.

65   HRO, Q.T.1, General Accounts, 1715–60; Q.T.10, County Hall Yearly Accounts, 1769–1806, e.g. 8–12.

66   Of various surviving evidence, DRO, D367/E56, printing accounts, 1740; or for Southampton, NA, E.181–4.

67   *Exeter Journal*, 12 June 1772.

68   HWRO, b899:31/8a, iii, Palfrey Collection, Foley Scrapbook.

eighteenth century. There are examples from the late 1750s of collectors of excise accepting notes from country banks as valid currency.[69] The blanks, notes and stamped papers were often distributed with the newspapers from central printer to local agents, although there is a frustrating dearth of actual banking records relating to local commissions.[70] Several newspaper advertisements boast that stationers have previous experience in supplying banks or mercantile companies.[71] With parliamentary sanction, Liverpool issued municipal printed notes in 1793 up to the value of £200,000. In 1803–04 Samuel Oldknow, muslin manufacturer of Stockport, was issuing notes for denominations as low as 1s 3d. His early experiments of the 1790s were based on handwritten notes, but from July 1793 Oldknow issued printed notes as orders upon the counting-house for cash.[72] Nationwide use of notes, however, was problematic even at the end of this period. Bank of England notes were treated with suspicion outside the metropolis and paper currency found general favour only in the decades after the war of American Independence.

The printer's office and bookshop

No account of the printer-stationer's support of local commerce, however, should be restricted to typography, billposting or even stationery and newspapers. The printer's office, the stationer's or the bookshop were in many other ways continuing service centres for the business of the locality. The printer was at the heart of much local commerce, printing proposals, subscriptions, maps and timetables, but also providing collecting agencies, selling tickets and offering much other assistance. Many booksellers opened employment registers and, in the City, printer-stationers combined with exchange brokers to offer 'Register books for clerks fit for counting houses'.[73] By the end of his career, Benjamin Collins, who had frequently

69   L. S. Pressnell, *Country Banking in the Industrial Revolution* (New York: Oxford University Press, 1956), p. 61.

70   NCL copies of the *Leicester and Nottingham Journal* from the 1760s have various MS marginalia relating to the sale of blanks by the newsmen.

71   Smart of Worcester, for example, in the *Worcester Journal*, 28 July 1774.

72   George Unwin, *Samuel Oldknow and the Arkwrights: the Industrial Revolution at Stockport and Marple* (Manchester: The University Press, and London and New York: Longmans, Green & Co., 1924), pp. 182–3, 185, 190.

73   This title taken from notice of de Missy, *Lloyd's Evening Post*, 5 June 1770.

advertised his shop as 'the Accomptant's Office', was styling himself simply 'banker'.[74] A large number of booksellers operated as money-lenders or as the organizers of credit. Robert Gosling established his bank out of his stationery and bookselling business. When he died in 1741 his son, Sir Francis Gosling, set up as banker proper at the head of the first bank in London to derive from a commercial source.[75]

Many other printers and booksellers established themselves as dealers in tickets. As noted, the tickets sold and exchanged ranged across everything from admission tickets for the opera and cock-fighting to coupons for the turnpike or the lottery. Of the many ticket-selling booksellers operating in London after mid-century, the most famous was probably Thomas Hookham, who acted as broker for a variety of musical and dramatic entertainments as well as business and repair services.[76] Many tickets achieved notable exchange value, rather as tickets applied for today might be sold on the black market or distributed to others for value in kind or as a favour to be called in at a later date. The so-called 'Tyburn ticket', dating from the end of the seventeenth century but increasingly part-printed and circulated in the mid eighteenth century, offered exemption from parish and ward duties to those assisting in the arrest of criminals later convicted of shoplifting or other specific offences. Such tickets (and around five hundred Tyburn tickets are said to have circulated in London in 1816)[77] became an unofficial but often very effective and readily exchanged currency.

There is a contrast here with such jobbing items as the settlement certificate that offered no resale or exchange value, although the extent to which tickets maintained their value in circulation beyond the centres where they were produced is questionable. Recognition of value lies in the possibility of that ticket's use and many usages were restricted to specific districts. A particular economy, for example, operated with the 'seaman's ticket' as analysed by Margaret Hunt, where a numbered paper

---

74 Ferdinand, *Benjamin Collins*, p. 55.
75 Frank Melton, 'Robert and Sir Francis Gosling: Eighteenth-Century Bankers and Stationers', in *Economics of the Book Trade 1605–1939*, ed. R. Myers and M. Harris (Cambridge: Chadwyck-Healey, 1985), pp. 60–77.
76 Hookham often advertised very precise dates and terms for the tickets sold – of many examples, *Public Advertiser*, 13 Jan., 8 Feb. and 8 April 1780.
77 Deborah Valenze, *The Social Life of Money in the English Past* (Cambridge: Cambridge University Press, 2006), pp. 196–9; Lloyd, 'Ticketing the British Eighteenth Century', p. 846.

instrument issued by the Navy Office, guaranteeing future payment and transferable under power of attorney, enabled payments to be deferred. By this means, pay tickets operated within a complex late-seventeenth-century exchange network of agents, moneylenders and discounters in maritime communities, where tickets might serve as types of investment bonds and paralleled the buying of shares in lottery tickets.[78]

Other forms of valued jobbing had wider circulation from printers' and booksellers' offices. As revenue agents, the stationers and booksellers were important distributors and sellers of the stamp duty stamps. By 1800, stamps were long past being temporary and were affixed to almost every transaction, including duties on birth and death certificates, exchange agreements, insurances, licences and wills. Of the fifty stamp distributors in England and Wales in 1790, half were booksellers.[79] All the official and very many of the unofficial agents for tickets in the state lotteries were also booksellers. Official operators such as the Corbetts of Fleet Street advertised their ticket-selling in the books they published; others used their own newspapers both to promote their lottery trade and to announce the winning numbers drawn in London.

Distributional services offered by the booksellers and printer-stationers were often as important to the conduct of local commerce as their printing and stationery operations. Delivery offers were sometimes part of an official arrangement with a company or municipal corporation. There was, for example, close co-operation with the insurance offices. By the 1720s, the Sun Fire Office had appointed 'riding officers' to search for customers. When these failed to deliver, the Office approached regional booksellers, including J. Hogben of Rye, Richard Leggassick of Totnes, Nathaniel Collis of Kettering and Mathias Dagnall of Aylesbury, to act as its agents.[80] Such a charge would not have seemed exceptional. Most regional booksellers already operated as agents for a variety of local trades as well as offering general parcel services. Clients left packages and letters at the shop to be delivered by the newsman or bookseller's journeyman. Newsmen would also take orders for the commodities advertised by local merchants and deliver the goods along the normal newspaper routes. Agents for advertisements

---

78 Margaret R. Hunt, 'Women and the Fiscal-Imperial State in the late 17th and early 18th Centuries', in *A New Imperial History: Culture, Identity and Modernity in Britain and the Empire, 1660–1840*, ed. Kathleen Wilson (Cambridge: Cambridge University Press, 2004), pp. 29–47.

79 Feather, *Provincial Book Trade*, p. 86.

80 'Old Agencies Records File', archives of the Sun-Alliance Insurance Group.

were usually members of the book trades, but other retailers and whole-salers could act as advertising agents. Customers in outlying areas were often expected to pay delivery charges, however. As biographical accounts written from remote parts of the north and south-west of England show, the postboy was used to supply coffee, clothes, repaired watches, even small items of furniture to provincial shopkeepers' customers.

As country distributors for the London quack cures, many printer-stationers also carried large stocks of patent medicines in addition to the normal supplies of printed forms, books and stationery equipment. Here again, storekeepers who also controlled a newspaper had an increasingly effective vehicle for advertising their own wares. The great majority of such notices refer to medicines or printed items, but the range of other goods for sale through the agents of newspapers also increased commensurately with the general expansion of advertising. Clearly, newspaper printers and sellers would be the first to notice the promotional successes of others. As the owners of general stores, dozens of firms also stocked groceries including teas, sugar and other luxury goods. The sale of wallpapers was a common sideline, and the vending of paper for packaging was an increas-ingly important charge. By the 1760s, the manufacture and sale of blue paper had grown markedly, in line with advances in the grocery trades. Craighton was stocking large supplies in Ipswich even in 1721. He was also conducting a brewing operation – one of several secondary occupa-tions, including tanning, cabinet-making and upholstering, to appear in the surviving accounts of country printing and stationery firms.[81] Many country booksellers had permanent but versatile shops by mid-century. According to his inventory, Charles Alexander of Woodbridge had well-equipped rooms with elegant frames, counters and display boards.[82]

New types of commercial agency were also stimulated. The profession of the modern auctioneer dates from the introduction of printed notices of sale for general circulation. Bids could be left at printers' offices. New locations and more regular sales were arranged. Newspaper circula-tions brought larger audiences, greater turnover and marketing speciali-zation. Even the office of 'auctioneer' took on new professional form. In Edinburgh, Balfour, publisher and bookseller with Hamilton since 1733, supported the operation of an auction room at the firm's New Exchange

81   ESRO, FE1/15/96: inventory of Craighton; cf. CRO, WS 1740: inventory of Cook of Thornton; and the entry for James Belcher, *Birmingham Directory*, 1770.
82   ESRO, FE/28/14: inventory of Charles Alexander, 15 Oct. 1744.

premises from the early 1750s. He began organizing auctions himself in 1767 and was still active in the 1780s. In 1777, as a device to raise revenue for the American war, Lord North introduced an annual excise tax of twenty shillings on auction sales in London and Westminster, and of five shillings elsewhere. The *Parliamentary History* reported that

> Auctions were multiplied of late years, in all parts of the kingdom, to that excess, as to be very mischievous to every fair trader; and in many cases were attended with circumstances of gross fraud and imposition … As auctioneering was become so extremely profitable a business, and from which such large fortunes were made, he thought the auctioneers themselves were proper objects of taxation.[83]

Although it is now difficult to distinguish between the priced inventory, the valuer's list and the auction catalogue, all were printed in large numbers, circulated and made available from agents in advance. Soon after the introduction of the tax, the Excise Office was also ordering the printing of blanks to act as receipts of tax for each auctioneer.[84] By the early 1780s, such provincial newspapers as *Aris's Birmingham Gazette* used small cuts to illustrate regular auction advertisements. In *Aris's* the cut repeatedly used for James Payton's auctioneering firm showed a hand and gavel. Fry's specimen book of 1794, with its cast auctioneer ornament, anticipated a demand for such a decoration in the general stock of the town and country printer. By the end of the century, print was a mainstay of sales by auction.

It was therefore striking that attempts to regulate printing at the close of the eighteenth century contrasted with the increasingly service-oriented printers' offices in which many presses were operated. The reaction against printing, both metropolitan and regional, derived from and contributed to the conservative ethos and more repressive legislation of the 1790s that followed from the turbulent response in England to the French Revolution. The Unlawful Societies Act of 1799 introduced new surveillance and

---

83 *Parliamentary History*, xix (1777–78), cols. 246–7; and comment, Robin Myers, 'Sale by Auction: the Rise of Auctioneering Exemplified', in *Sale and Distribution of Books from 1700*, ed. Robin Myers and Michael Harris (Oxford: Oxford Polytechnic Press, 1982), pp. 126–63 (p. 127).
84 Particularly good examples are at ShRO, 3365/664 (Mayor's vouchers); each blank recorded 'the Amount of Rates and Duties payable by Law upon certain Estates, goods, and Effects sold by Public Sale'.

regulation of printers in order to prevent the printing of irreligious, treasonable and seditious papers by certain societies.[85] Ironically, printed documents were to chronicle and enforce control over the printers and the presses throughout England. The 1799 Act required filled-in printed forms to be submitted to local officers. All those working printing presses had to deliver their completed returns to the Clerk of the Peace (the officer appointed to assist, among other duties, justices at Quarter Sessions). The Clerk then dispatched a further copy to the Secretary of State. There survive numerous registers of filed returns (or 'notices') and of persons to whom further printed registration certificates had been granted. Each register provided names of persons filing the notice, their place of abode, and the location at which the printing presses and the types were to be used. Notices continued to be issued at regular intervals thereafter until the final quarter of the nineteenth century.[86] Jobbing 'papers' were as much a threat to authority as larger printed items, albeit that jobbing allowed surveillance and enforcement with greater efficiency than in the past, and that most printers in London, and in the country, supported and were supported by the indispensable demands of local authorities for regulatory and communicative print.

85   39 Geo. III, c. 79 (1799).
86   Excellent examples survive in DbRO Q/RS/5/1–44 (1799–1868).

5

Printing and the City of London

Eighteenth-century London acted as a principal clearing centre for financial and commercial agreements, and for the development of public and private investment in bonds and stocks and in insurance against risk and disaster. In the provinces there followed a gradual enlargement of the money market and of credit and insurance services, but London (and for particular services and printing, particular parts of London) continued to be the hub of affairs.

Without the work of the metropolitan printer it is impossible to explain the success of the financial experiments of the 1690s: the stock-jobbing explosion of the late seventeenth and early eighteenth centuries, the fledgling structure of public credit, confidence in currency transactions, new mercantile and retailing initiatives or even late-eighteenth-century country banking. The sheer weight of paper was dazzling. During the century, many hundreds of printer-stationers were employed in providing the bonds, notes of authorization and redemption, company proposals, certificates, vouchers, policy forms, indentures and other business blanks ordered by both London and country customers. The surviving ledgers of William Strahan, probably the richest printer of the century, reveal not only his printing of editions of Pope or of the *Vicar of Wakefield*, but also major contracts for expensive jobbing work.[1]

From the final quarter of the seventeenth century, the potential for print applications was already obvious to major mercantile houses. Powerful merchants like William Braund or Samuel Eyre clearly appreciated the security and authority offered by overseas trading bills of exchange and part-printed blanks for description, lading and receipt.[2] The market for merchants' bills for investment depended upon the safeguards offered

1   BL, Add. MSS 48,800, Strahan Ledgers, esp., fols 26v, 44v, 69v, 72v; 48,803a, fols 39v, 59, 75, 85; and 48,809, fol. 2.
2   Lucy Stuart Sutherland, *A London Merchant, 1695–1774* (London: Oxford University Press and Humphrey Milford, 1933), pp. 29–30, 35, 37.

by letterpress forms against fraud and misrepresentation. Blanks were produced for a variety of bills of exchange, but also for routine bills drawn by merchants on their overseas correspondents and agents, and for monthly accommodation bills in the bullion trade or special cargoes. The products of London's presses not only quickened exchange procedures, but also meant that the capital was already challenging Amsterdam as a new exchange centre and bill market by the 1720s. By the 1730s, large operators like Samuel Brooks, Abraham Coleman and Joseph Watkins both generated and depended upon a great bulk of blanks and printed bills.

Clients and the city printers

Many business accounts that would allow us to quantify orders for jobbing print and gauge the range of the different jobs have disappeared, both from the printing houses and from the clients. The four extant printing ledgers of William Bowyer, father and son, have been painstakingly studied and reproduced (and already featured above, pp. 49–50),[3] but the Bowyer firm is one of only four similar collections surviving from eighteenth-century London. Of these four survivals, two sets of records are relatively short: the ledger kept by Charles Ackers from 1732 to 1748, and some extremely brief extracts from a ledger of Henry Woodfall I, apparently running from 1734 to 1747 and reproduced in print in 1855, but since lost.[4] The fourth and much more substantial collection of surviving printing-house ledgers, that of William Strahan and his successors from 1738 until the early nineteenth century, has been partly edited (for the early years only) by Patricia Hernlund but otherwise remains an underused treasure trove in the British Library.[5]

3 Keith Maslen and John Lancaster (eds), *The Bowyer Ledgers* (London: The Bibliographical Society, 1991); see also Keith Maslen, *An Early London Printing House at Work: Studies in the Bowyer Ledgers* (New York: Bibliographical Society of America, 1993).
4 D. F. McKenzie and J. C. Ross (eds), *A Ledger of Charles Ackers: Printer of The London Magazine* (Oxford, Oxford Bibliographical Society, 1968); P.T.P., 'Pope and Woodfall' and 'Woodfall's ledger, 1734–1747', *Notes & Queries*, 11 (1855), 377–8, 418–20.
5 Patricia Hernlund, 'William Strahan, Printer' (unpubl. Ph.D. dissertation, University of Chicago, 1965); Patricia Hernlund, 'William Strahan's Ledgers', *Studies in Bibliography*, 20 (1967), 89–111 and 22 (1969), 179–95; Strahan business and personal records, BL, Add. MSS 48,800–918, Strahan Papers: Account books and other business papers, 1739–1880 (123 vols).

Even where extensive ledgers survive – as in the case of the houses of Strahan and Bowyer – doubts remains about how fully jobbing work was recorded in the actual day books. In less than seventy years, the Bowyers printed more than five thousand separate works and although, in the words of Maslen, the ledgers contained 'a great deal of jobbing', ledger B becomes highly selective as the younger Bowyer nears the end of his life. John Nichols, as the younger and more active partner, was by this time evidently keeping the main accounts, which were presumably lost in his disastrous printing-house fire of 8 February 1808. Nevertheless, as we shall see, the Bowyer records, especially the early ones, remain invaluable in charting the productive flow of the printing house, and monitoring the progress of particular jobs and individual works through the presses.

Records of clients, of those who ordered jobs from the printers, present a rather different problem for the historian. Far more of them survive than one might think, but they are scattered in every type of repository, from the archives of small businesses, propertied families and private and public institutions, to civic societies and authorities of every variety. Survival is often patchy within the individual records, or disguised by unhelpful descriptions and indistinct record-keeping. The one thing that can be said with certainty, however, is that the volume of orders, even as glimpsed from the imperfect and scarce survivals, was enormous, and that the range of work is bewildering in its scope and variety. Taking, for example, only the ledger entries of orders sent in to Bowyer, one can begin to appreciate the diversity (and often unexpected nature) of jobbing. Bowyer's job work was also requested by what Maslen called 'a miscellaneous company of clients' including clerks, lawyers, judges, shopkeepers, clerics and officials acting for assorted institutions and corporations.

The surviving printing orders made by town corporations and city authorities are marvellously suggestive of the range of job work undertaken, even though most of the runs of receipts and invoices are incomplete (and are something of a miracle of survival). In London, a public transcript of government might be compiled not only from the systematic bills of mortality and the like, but from the official print commanded by aldermen of the City from the early sixteenth century onward. Such orders were executed by those who, from at least the 1580s, who were given special authority as the 'City Printer'. Numerous other city officers and institutions also ordered printing, some from the official City Printer but much else from other printing houses. Between the 1580s and 1660, the City of London's expenditure on printing increased from about

£3 to £60 per annum, broadly comprising civic orders, mayoral precepts, injunctions and forms to be used for administration and government.[6]

Particularly helpful for understanding the accelerating volume of official print is a bundle of surviving invoices sent by the Corporation of London to its appointed City Printers from the late seventeenth century. The invoices cover, with significant gaps, the period between 1673 and 1722.[7] Four printers served successively in the office of City Printer during these years: three were substantial and indeed celebrated members of the Stationers' Company, and the fourth was the young son of one of them, recently freed from his apprenticeship. All were renowned for their craftsmanship, and also printed official jobs for their own Company. Two of the City Printers were assignees or acquired an interest in the Law Patent (the common-law printing privilege).[8]

Among the earliest surviving invoices sent in by a City Printer was from Andrew Clark, printer in Aldersgate Street since at least 1670. In early February 1674, an invoice from Clark was received by Josiah (or Joseph) Lane, Comptroller to the Corporation. The first recorded Comptroller was appointed in 1311 and, together with the City Solicitor (from 1544 but the two posts were often held by the same person), was responsible for providing all the legal service required by the City of London, especially on its extensive property holdings. Andrew Clark had succeeded James Flesher as printer to the City of London in 1672. A bill for half a year's work, comprising nineteen separate productions printed for the Corporation between 16 July 1673 and 6 January 1674, totalled £26 14s 4d. Although Clark was only paid every six months, payment was prompt. Following his submission of the invoice in February 1674, Clark received the amount in full a month later.[9] Each bill also offers a catalogue of the

6   See the table derived from B. R. Masters (ed.), *Chamber Accounts of the Seventeenth Century* (London: London Record Society, 1984) and the excellent discussion of this printing in Mark Jenner, 'London', in *The Oxford History of Popular Print Culture Volume One: Cheap Print in Britain and Ireland to 1660*, ed. Joad Raymond (Oxford: Oxford University Press, 2011), pp. 294–307 (pp. 301–7).
7   LMA, COL/SJ/27/316 (1673[1674]–1814); the very short 1814 invoice is the only post-1722 survival.
8   See J. H. Baker, 'English Law Books and Legal Publishing', in *The Cambridge History of the Book in Britain: Volume IV 1557–1695*, ed. John Barnard and D. F. McKenzie (Cambridge: Cambridge University Press, 2002), pp. 474–503 (pp. 485–7); and John D. Gordan III, 'John Nutt: Trade Publisher and Printer "In the Savoy"', *The Library*, 7th ser., 15 (2014), 243–60; and below, p. 160.
9   LMA, COL/SJ/27/316, Clark's invoice received by Jos. Lane Comptrllr, 5 Feb. 1673

jobbing required by the City. Clark's Corporation printing for the second half of 1673, for example, included 1,000 Freeman's oaths printed from 10 quires of paper, some 'Instructions for apprentices' from 20 quires, 250 'Orders against fishing with unlawful nets' from 10 quires, 500 tickets for the Commissioners of Assessments from 2½ quires, 100 'Deputations for fishing' from 4 quires, 300 orders concerning pipes and party (that is, shared) pipes 'to bring down water from the tops of houses' from 12 quires, 4,000 Court of Aldermen tickets, many other tickets for admission to courts and to the Guildhall, 1,000 'Orders for the better observation of the Lords Day', and 700 'Orders for the taking down of sheds' printed in half a sheet using 14 quires.[10]

The other five surviving half-yearly bills from Clark to the end of 1677 include numerous tickets and constables' passes, 'Acquittances for Maimed Soldiers', orders for tolls, orders against the concealing of coals, tickets to summon tenants to pay their rents, and 'Tables of Rates, Duties and Tolls for the Muskets'. Some jobs appear simple (and omit mention of the necessary cutting of sheets); others involve more complicated folding and cutting operations, such as that begun on 7 August 1676 for printing '1000 Rates for Wharfage and Cranage [use of dockside cranes] for [the] Fleet Channel' in two sheets from eighty quires. To the charge for these rate sheets of £8 6s 8d, was added £1 'for Sticking and Cutting of them'. When payment for the total six months' bill (of £70 15s 10d for thirty-one separate productions) was received by Clark on the last day of January 1676/77, he had waited for what, by contemporary standards, was a very modest time for full renumeration.[11] The Corporation, and jobbing work, continued to offer a safe, low-risk and lucrative commission.

Andrew Clark printed widely. Some 168 separate items are listed in the *ESTC*, including several books (some in Latin), booksellers' 'term catalogues' and commissions taken on in his role as 'Printer to the Stationers' Company'. Several of Clark's larger publications were undertaken in partnership. Among surviving smaller items are the proclamations 'By the Mayor', which are invoiced in the surviving Corporation records, although the great majority of the invoiced jobbing work does not seem to survive in extant copy. In 1675, Clark printed a news-sheet

---

[1674], and paid 11 Feb. for work to early January. Clark signs it as received of Sir Thomas Player, Chamberlain of London, dated as payment received in full 11 Feb. 1673 [1674].

10   LMA, COL/SJ/27/316, invoice dated as received, 5 Feb. 1673 [1674].

11   LMA, COL/SJ/27/316, invoice for jobbing work, 26 July 1676 to 19 Dec. 1776, dated as paid 31 Jan. 1676 [1677].

called *The City Mercury or Advertisements concerning Trade*, heralded
by the following notice:

> Advertisement. Whereas divers people are at great expence in printing,
> publishing and dispersing of bills of advertisement: observing how
> practical and advantagious to trade and business, &c. this method is in
> parts beyond the seas. These are to give notice, that all persons in such
> cases concerned henceforth may have published in print in the Mercury,
> or Bills of advertisement, which shall come out every week on Thursday
> morning, and be delivered and dispersed in every house where the bills
> of mortallity are received, and elsewhere, the publications and adver-
> tisements of all the matters following, or any other matter or thing not
> herein mentioned, that shall relate to the advertisement of trade, or any
> other lawful business not granted in propriety to any other.[12]

Official weekly bills of mortality are usually associated with the crisis
years of plagues and epidemics, but they were also heir to earlier *Love
have Mercy* publications that also left blank spaces for purchasers to fill in
their own counts, as well as to other printed forms reporting christenings
and burials.[13] The bills are here subsumed within more general types
of bill. Clark's association with commerce and finance was confirmed
by his publication, at the very end of his life, of a twenty-two page,
black letter edition of a 1664 work, *The Death and Burial of Mistress
Money*. Clark's edition of the anonymous pamphlet (the only surviving
copy is in the Pepys Library at Magdalene College, Cambridge) warns
against avarice and usury. A closing poem enumerates those who will
suffer from the abasement of money and her burial by a usurer. As it
concludes:

> Thus Money was so beloved,
> that no man ever did scorn her,
> And now being dead and buried,
> the whole world will be her mourner.[14]

---

12   Wing A625 1 sheet, 1675; *ESTC* R31831.
13   See J. C. Robertson, 'Reckoning with London: Interpreting the *Bills of Mortality*
before John Graunt', *Urban History*, 23:3 (Dec. 1996), 325–50; Jenner, 'London', pp. 297–9.
14   Anon., *The Death and Burial of Mistress Money: with her Will she made at her
departure and what happened afterwards to the Usurer that buried Her* (London, 1678),
[p. 22].

Clark died in late 1677 or early 1678, Samuel Roycroft having been appointed City Printer in succession to Clark in December 1677. Roycroft (1657–1717) was then aged twenty, the son of the distinguished printer, bookseller and stationer, Thomas Roycroft, who had died earlier that year. Roycroft the younger took over his father's printing house in Bartholomew Close within months of becoming a freeman of the Stationers' Company at the end of his apprenticeship. The Corporation seems therefore to have appointed Samuel Roycroft as its Printer because of the reputation of his father's printing house. It is also quite possible that Samuel had distinguished himself during his seven apprenticed years (especially if his father was ailing). Roycroft junior, however, is strangely missing from Plomer's standard dictionary of printers and booksellers, especially as compared to the extensive entry for his more celebrated father. A probable reason for this omission is the further muddling of the Roycrofts by John Nichols whose *Literary Anecdotes* was much used by Plomer. Nichols applauded Roycroft's generosity to the poor, including an annual bequest funded by lottery tickets, but he confused father and son.[15]

The *ESTC* offers fresh assurance of the activity of Samuel Roycroft, recording more than three hundred separate items of his printing. These include surviving examples of larger jobbing enumerated in the invoices such as Acts of Common Council, articles of assistance to wards and parishes, reprinted Acts (including 'Against the Murthering of Bastards'), and numerous sheet proclamations 'By the Mayor', with blank spaces left for relevant parish, ward or officer details. The same printing house supplemented this official printing with thousands of copies of manuals designed to support local government, justice and commerce. From his first year in business, Samuel Roycroft published editions of practical administrative guides such as *The Compleat Clerk*, *The Countrey Justice* and *The Duty and Office of High Constables, of Hundreds, Petty Constanbles, Tythingmen, and such Inferiour Ministers of the Peace*. A year later, in 1678, Roycroft began printing *The Entring Clerk's Vade Mecum*, usually in combination with other bookseller-publishers. Notable among other of Roycroft's productions was Jehudah Stennett's Hebrew grammar *Dikduk mikhlol* of 1685, indicative of changing commercial and financial

---

15   On the poor institution, see Anon., *An Account of Public Charities in England and Wales* (London, 1828), p. 554; John Nichols writes that Samuel rather than Thomas was Master of the Stationers' Company in 1675 and names Thomas 'Captain', when it was Samuel who was known as 'Captain Roycroft': *Literary Anecdotes of the Eighteenth Century*, 9 vols, 2nd rev. edn (London, 1812–20), vol. 3, p. 597.

interests. Although Cromwell never officially readmitted Jews to Britain in the mid-1650s, a small colony of Sephardic Jews was recognized in London by 1660, allowed to remain, and contributed to an English-Jewish population of some three thousand by 1690.

The printing and publication of books such as *Dikduk mikhlol* might have contributed to Roycroft's short-term profits (although, in this high-risk business, we cannot be certain that this was the case),[16] but it was most unlikely to have contributed to a stable income for the printing house. The production, much in partnership, of the practical administrative, legal and commercial manuals offered a more predictable return from an assured custom, but even here guesses had to be made about the extent of demand, the use of existing guides that were still in circulation and the requirements for updated texts. Client-based jobbing work, on the other hand, offered the equivalent of bespoke publication income, even if payment was made after as much as a six-month interval.

Roycroft completed his first job for the Corporation of London on 20 December 1677 and undertook what appears to have been his final order as City Printer almost exactly thirteen years later. The work was diverse and individual items extensive. On 14 August 1678, Roycroft printed 4,200 'Summons for Want of Lights' and, on 20 October, 100 'Proclamations to Prevent the Throwing of Squibbs'. In June 1679, he produced (from two orders) 14,000 summons to appoint a day to bring in inventories. Eight of these summons were printed on a sheet, requiring a total of 70 quires of paper. For 1,500 'Books of Habits' in three sheets from nine reams of paper, completed on 28 October 1680, he charged £18 15s, and a further £1 11s 8d for the folding, stitching and cutting of them. After June 1682, Roycroft was paid for a year's work rather than six months, and from mid-1683 for nearly three year's work, presumably at the Corporation's instigation, resulting of course in much larger invoices but with the carrying of much longer overheads. The annual bill for work completed up to May 1683 amounted to £51 10s 10d, and that for seventy-six items of work undertaken in three years from 13 June 1683 to 10 May 1686 to a total of £147 10s exactly (although the sum paid was reduced to £145 18s 9d after checking by the City Comptroller).

The final settling of Roycroft's accounts does raise questions. In common with the great majority of printers of his time, the average

16 See James Raven, *The Business of Books: Booksellers and the English Book Trade 1450–1850* (London and New Haven, CT: Yale University Press, 2007), ch. 4.

profits from Roycroft's book printing are not known, but a comparison to the general profile of Ackers's later business suggests a similar reliance on jobbing as a staple resource, even in years where income from book publication must *apparently* have been higher (by a factor of ten or more) but equally a far less dependable return in a risky and uncertain market. The reliability of the six-monthly income from the Corporation job work, or even one-receipt annual income, could be calculated and anticipated, and payment was swift with few obvious complications. The later wait of some three years for jobbing work payment is a more difficult proposition, and suggests that by 1686, and Roycroft's ninth year of printing by himself, that he was more confident of his financial footing. Even so, his last extant invoice reverted to a demand for eighteen months' payment (June 1689 to December 1690). Perhaps Roycroft charged when he felt he needed to, calling on the debts from the Corporation as a fail safe when he had cash-flow problems or committed to a particular book publication, or printing-house expenditure or investment. If so, the jobbing proved of great utility. There is also evidence, notably from the Bowyer ledgers, that printers were exploited by the increasingly powerful bookseller-publishers, many co-operating in congers or closed associations and cartels, giving only part of a work to a particular printer, varying the price agreed and in other ways destabilizing printer–publisher relations. In 1752, for example, a resentful note from Bowyer junior reads: 'recd as in full what Mr Longman [commissioning client for a new edition of Robert Ainsworth's *Latin Dictionary*] thought proper to pay'.[17] The Corporation of London seems to have been no Longman.

Whatever the exact balance between jobbing and other publications – and the legal case publications must have been a particularly profitable and regular source of income – Samuel Roycroft died a very rich man. His will and codicil of November 1716 enumerates £1,800 in bound book stock, extensive tenanted lands in Staffordshire, the leasehold (as opposed to freehold, one presumes) on London houses in Southwark, Leicester Fields and Gray's Inn Lane, his shop and house in St Bartholomew Close, further stock in the Stationers' Company, and very large numbers of lottery tickets (a form of investment bond, with capital value and offering further return if successfully drawn).[18]

---

17 Maslen, *An Early London Printing House at Work*, p. 204.
18 NA PROB 11/556, Will of Samuel Roycroft, 1 Nov. 1716, and codicil.

Legal business and official revenues

Much jobbing work derived from the interaction of business and the law. In property matters no less than in City financial dealings, the demand for print redoubled over the period. By the end of the century, estate owners were carrying far heavier burdens of indebtedness than their predecessors. New methods of borrowing followed alterations to mortgaging, family settlements and the leasing out of estates. The changes brought extra business and a greater professionalism to the attorney's practice and all brought new orders to the stationer, engraver and printer. By the 1730s, printed forms had superseded the manuscript instrument as the normal medium for the more formalized and less complicated legal transactions. Parchment and full calligraphy were overwhelmed by demand and their growing expense. Without blanks, clerks – even if lowly paid and plentiful – could neither keep up with the requirements for documentation nor guarantee its accurate and efficient replication. By mid-century, vellum was reserved for deeds, the most important of legal and business settlements, and the 'skins' and 'texts' of municipal commissions.[19] Similarly, blanks soon became a staple resource in new documentation required in the servicing of labour. Set indenture and apprenticeship forms became a staple of the printer. By the end of the century, headed forms for partnership agreements were similarly commissioned from a printing house or a separate engraver.[20]

Many printers expanded their business by furnishing the basic stationery for government revenue collection. Greater yields from official revenues contributed in large measure to the fourfold increase in the government's per capita income between the Restoration and the accession of George II in 1727. In addition to increased internal and overseas trade and the ending of the practice of farming out the collection of government revenues to private individuals, the collection of custom and excise duties benefited from an improved administration in which the work of the printer was crucial. Custom House bills of entry, which were printed under licence from the early sixteenth century, were the basis for customs statistics and fiscal calculations. Long-running printing contracts were arranged for the production of the bills. Josias Long of Mark Lane,

---

19   Above, pp. 37, 68–70.
20   Fine examples of these can be found in miscellaneous collections at the Dorset County Museum (special collections), Dorchester; the Phoenix archives of the Sun-Alliance Insurance Group; and the archives of Barclays Bank, Lombard Street.

for whom there is no evidence of any other commercial presswork, was printing Custom House bills from the mid-1680s.[21] The complex receipts for customs duties were also given on printed blanks from at least 1705. Stamp duties imposed from 1694 were to be a further source of revenue. Duties were imposed on transactions from marriage licences and wills to recognizances and conveyances.[22] If, as has been argued, the extension of the tax in 1712 greatly distressed printer-stationers and caused the collapse of certain early newspapers,[23] stamped paper from the central warehouses also provided regular business. Usually sold with the duty affixed by stamp or impression, the paper was a requirement for legal transactions, including the transfer of annuities. At Abraham Dent's Cumbrian shop, a sheet of stamped paper for deeds and indentures usually cost 2s 6d, including the duty.

Between 1700 and 1785, the Treasury employed a dozen or more printers in the servicing of its revenue devices. Public borrowing schemes, ranging from stock issues to state lotteries, required vast printing operations. After their inauguration in 1694, forty-two government debt lotteries were launched up to 1784, with almost annual revenue lotteries between 1769 and 1826. The printing of tickets for each state lottery was an enormous but indispensable undertaking. For the inaugural lottery, 100,000 tickets were printed during the preceding year, 1693. It is also estimated that between 1693 and 1699 alone, 3½ million lottery tickets were sold.[24] In a single year, in 1737, 125,000 tickets were printed, and in 1757, one million.[25] In 1753, the *Course of the Exchange* listed twenty-one major securities and repayment terms for a further four short-term Exchequer loans. Two-thirds of the securities given were for long-term government loans managed by the Bank and Exchequer. The others were for the three monied corporations, the two insurance corporations, the Equivalent Corporation and the Million Bank. The printing commissioned by all

21   List of printers, SH, Box A, folder 4a. Bills of entry are considered below, pp. 164–5.

22   *Act for granting to theire Majesties severall Dutys upon Velum Parchment and Paper*, 5 & 6 Wlm & Mary, c. 21.

23   The arguments are discussed in Alan Downie, 'The Growth of Government Tolerance of the Press to 1790', in *The Development of the English Book Trade, 1700–1899*, ed. Robin Myers and Michael Harris (Oxford: Oxford Polytechnic Press, 1981), pp. 36–65. Downie does not accept the traditional view of the distress caused by the tax.

24   Anne L. Murphy, 'Lotteries in the 1690s: Investment or Gamble?', *Financial History Review*, 12:2 (2005), 227–46.

25   The question is further considered in James Raven, 'The Abolition of the English State Lotteries', *Historical Journal*, 34 (1991), 371–89.

these was undertaken by a dozen or more printing firms. No evidence exists that such contracts were put out to formal tender, but there is no doubt that competition, especially between engravers, was fierce. The securing of government contracts provided the means for many printing houses to expand. John Barber, having purchased the place of Printer to the City of London, sold the rights to George James in 1724 for £1,500.[26] For more than twenty years, William Strahan enjoyed contracts with the Register Office for printing reams of administrative blanks.[27] Samuel Richardson also undertook state commissions, supporting the nine presses of his mature business by printing bills and Commons' reports.[28]

Stocks, shares and banknotes

Eighteenth-century London was remarkable for the multiplication of marketable, transferable shares and debentures to an investing public. The structure of public credit advanced as government built on the financial experiments in revenue raising of the 1690s, and as investors turned from more speculative short-term schemes to investments in government securities. The press was instrumental in servicing both the joint-stock companies and government revenue and loan operations, from whose vast expansion the printing industry was also a major beneficiary.

Financial business was clustered around the Royal Exchange. Of the five hundred or so London coffee-houses operating at sometime during the reign of Queen Anne, Garraway's, Bridge's, Lloyd's and Jonathan's were at the heart of the business life of the capital.[29] Jonathan's was the stock-jobbing coffee-house and Lloyd's, the centre for negotiating marine insurance. From its original position in Tower Street, Lloyd's had been quickly established as the bustling exchange of news and business described by Ned Ward in the *Wealthy Shopkeeper*.[30] By 1691, when Lloyd moved to

26   H. R. Plomer, *A Dictionary of the Booksellers and Printers Who Were at Work in England, Scotland and Ireland from 1668 to 1725* (London: Bibliographical Society, 1922), p. 20.

27   BL Add. MSS 48,803a 14v, 23v–24, 43.

28   William M. Sale, Jr, *Samuel Richardson: Master Printer* (Ithaca, NY: Cornell University Press, 1950), p. 29.

29   John Ashton, *Social Life in the Reign of Queen Anne: Taken from Original Sources*, 2 vols (London: Chatto and Windus, 1882), vol. 2, pp. 262–8.

30   Edward Ward, *The Wealthy Shopkeeper: or, The Charitable Citizen: A Poem* (London, 1700) described in Howard William Troyer, *Ned Ward of Grubstreet: A Study*

Lombard Street, he was already advertising nationally for the sales of ships and printing for general distribution the inventories of cargoes. Between 1698 and 1712, some 203 newspaper advertisements for Lloyd's have been recorded.[31] By the accession of Anne, many financial intermediaries then operating were also using printed forms to compile private lists of 'prices current' to distribute to their customers and inform correspondents about stock prices and exchange rates. In fact, this was merely an extension of the blank forms of prices current that merchants continued to circulate privately to one another, often using printed blanks to do so.

By the accession of George I, the East India Company, the Bank of England and the South Sea Company were all enmeshed in government funding. Between 1660 and 1719, charters were granted to fifty-four major joint-stock companies. In 1695, incorporated and non-incorporated companies totalled some ninety-three in England and forty-seven in Scotland. Most were short-lived. In 1717, only twenty-one English companies remained.[32] Nevertheless, the existence of investable surpluses was patently demonstrated. Investment outlets soared, however transitory some might have been. Likewise, the government's per capita revenue multiplied fourfold between 1660 and 1730 with the creation of a long-term funded debt by Exchequer bills, receivable in payment of taxes.

The companies, the Treasury, and government revenue offices such as the Audit and Lottery Offices, were all serviced by a succession of leading stationers and printers within and outside the City. The warren of bookshops and printers' offices in the vicinity of the Exchange was linked to printing houses centred, among other areas, in Little Britain (at least until its decline from the mid eighteenth century), Cheapside, Blackfriars and Ludgate. Printers were engaged to produce proposals for the setting up and extension of companies as well as notices for elections, meetings and the reduction or raising of interest and premiums. By the 1720s, set forms ordering the repayment of loans were also being printed. More printed paper listed the charges and dividends for insurance and stock companies. The printer's work became even more diversified as the boom in joint-stock

of Sub-Literary London in the Eighteenth Century (Cambridge, MA: Harvard University Press, 1946), pp. 133–4.

31   Frederick Martin, *The History of Lloyd's and of Marine Insurance in Great Britain: With an appendix containing statistics relating to marine insurance* (London: Macmillan, 1876), pp. 81–5.

32   D. C. Coleman, *The Economy of England, 1450–1750* (Oxford: Oxford University Press, 1977), p. 170.

companies and institutions for overseas investments was swollen by new projects to sponsor trusts for mining, navigations, turnpikes and the like.

Of all these initiatives, securities and stock transactions were particularly dependent upon the skills of the printer and engraver. The Bank of England was providing printed transfer books and certain other ledgers of printed blanks for stock dealings as early as March 1696.[33] By 1700, the exchange of stock expressly relied on trustworthy, marketable share certificates. The other companies seem to have followed in placing orders for printed shares and policy documents. All stock transfers under the old East India Company had been conducted in longhand, but from at least 1709 the new United Company imitated the Bank. The South Sea Company also ordered various printed blanks for its transfers.[34] The mechanics of buying into or selling funds are described by Thomas Mortimer in his guide to the Exchange (actually designed to circumvent the brokers and 'professed sharpers'). He even reproduces an example of a printed application form with advice on how to fill it in.[35] In addition to several enabling blanks, a final signed printed receipt allowed business to be conducted at a speed impossible under the old fully scripted arrangements. Securities could be purchased by direct application to the owner or through the mediation of a broker. Transactions could be made either by printed contracts with blanks or by covenants and indentures drawn up by scriveners. By at least mid-century, printed blanks could be used in arrangements with the broker. When the owner of stock – or his surrogate – came to collect dividends, printed warrants of payment were issued to be cashed at the pay desk.[36] From the early 1720s, engravers and printer-stationers of the City, including Hugh Meere and Matthew Jenour, were commissioned to produce forms of attorney to reduce the difficulties over the acceptance of surrogacy. At the quarterly payout on Lady Day in 1724, some 2,000 of the 4,662 proprietors of Bank stock receiving dividends used an attorney.[37] Without print, in fact, the logistical problems of a bulk payment of dividends could hardly have been overcome.

33   BEA, Bank stock transfer books.
34   No South Sea Company stock transfer books have survived, however.
35   Thomas Mortimer, *Every Man his own Broker: or, A Guide to Exchange-Alley* (London, 1761), pp. 99–114.
36   A bundle of printed warrants for unclaimed East India dividends remains in BEA: P. G. M. Dickson, *The Financial Revolution in England: A Study in the Development of Public Credit, 1688–1756* (London: Macmillan, 1967), p. 460.
37   Dickson, *Financial Revolution*, p. 463.

Printing also enabled the widespread acceptance of paper currency, perhaps the most visible and important types of blanks from their early years, requiring both pen and (mostly engraved) print. Continued problems of specie shortage afflicted many commercial interests from the late seventeenth century. There were increased demands for new methods of raising credit and easing non-barter payment. As London agents and a variety of provincial intermediaries further complicated bill-broking, it became increasingly difficult for merchants and long-distance tradesmen to depend upon handwritten notes of credit and transaction. The increasing scale of operations forced greater uniformity in the production of notes to ensure security and ease of identification. Between 1660 and 1692, the goldsmith's promissory notes and tickets were written rather than printed. Circulating within London, these early notes were transferable by endorsement when payable 'to order' or by delivery when drawn 'to bearer'. Although confidence in such notes was undermined in the final quarter of the seventeenth century by doubts about their legal status, an Act of 1704 accorded English promissory notes the same legal rights as bills of exchange, that is Bank of England notes and others might be assignable.[38]

Banknotes, like lottery tickets and rarer items including admission tickets to great events, required security printing to deter forgery. Engraving allowed the lattice of flourishes, along the top or on a counterfoil which was then cut by scissors. Authentication and counterfeiting worked in relation to each other not simply on banknotes but on other badges and certificates of authority.[39] The very form of a ticket invited fraud and forgery, as evidenced by numerous trials for counterfeit lottery tickets and other security-printed tickets.[40]

---

38 *Act for giving like Remedy upon Promissory Notes as is now used upon Bills of Exchange*, 3 & 4 Anne, c. 8. An earlier decision by Coke that no 'thing-in-action' could be considered as transferable, questioned the legality of promissory deposit notes (of both types) even though it seems that accepted mercantile custom excluded bills of exchange from the Coke ruling. In 1680 a further decision found promissory notes legal when drawn 'to bearer', but this was again reversed by the Court of Queen's Bench in 1691: William Graham, *The One Pound Note in the History of Banking in Great Britain*, 2nd edn (Edinburgh: J. Thin, 1911), p. 4.

39 See Valentin Groebner, *Who are You? Identification, Deception, and Surveillance in Early Modern Europe* (New York: Zone Books, 2007); and cf. Steve Hindle, 'Dependency, Shame and Belonging: Badging the Deserving Poor, c.1550–1750', *Cultural and Social History*, 1 (2004), 6–35.

40 Including OBPO, April 1720, trial of Thomas Day (t17200427–64); Feb. 1746, trial of

From its foundation in 1694, the Bank of England, which remained at the centre of both banking and public finance, issued notes written by hand on engraved forms. Originally the Bank would give depositors a receipt, handwritten, signed by one of the Bank's many cashiers. These notes, as with current issues, bore the familiar words 'I promise to pay', although these early notes held the name of the depositor and the amount deposited in the Bank. The earlier notes from the Bank were also printed on everyday paper bought from the local stationers, and printed outside the Bank. At first, the denomination of the note was handwritten but more fully printed notes appeared in 1695 only a year after the Bank's foundation, when the Court of Directors ordered that 'running cash notes be printed'. In June 1695, some 12,000 notes in seven denominations were delivered by the stationer William Staresmore, together with the plates which he had himself engraved. In its first year £1.2 million was raised in bills of exchange. From 1702 John Sturt engraved the Bank's notes, producing new versions in 1707 and 1712. From 1702 James Child printed the notes from Sturt's engraving.[41] After denomination printing in the first four years, notes issued between 1699 and 1725 were engraved with a blank for the value of the bill to be inserted by hand. Denomination printing was resumed after 1725. James Cole, already an established copperplate engraver, took over the engraving of the notes from Sturt in 1721 and also took over their printing from Child in 1731. Cole's business was carried on at the sign of The Crown in Great Kirby Street, Hatton Garden. He continued to work for the Bank until his death in 1748 when he was succeeded in the family business by George Cole (probably his son), and then after George's death in 1795, by George's brother, William.[42]

Preparing and printing the banknote paper carried obvious security implications. Mary Smith, who made the first moulds for the manufacture of the banknote paper, kept her moulds within the Bank. In 1697, a watermark introduced by Rice Watkins showed a looped border and

John Peter Mayaffree (t17460226–36); Oct. 1724, trial of Abraham Deval (t17241014–42), cited by Sarah Lloyd, 'Ticketing the British Eighteenth Century: "A thing … never heard of before"', *Journal of Social History*, 46:4 (2013), 843–71 (p. 875); of tickets in one case, it was 'scarcely discernible which were the True, and which the Counterfeit ones', OBPO, Mar. 1709, trial of Thomas Trott (t17090302–14).

41   BEA, G4/1, Court of Directors' Minutes 1694–1710, with many entries regarding printing, e.g. fol. 13.

42   Details of this history and other aspects of the note-printing can be found in A. D. Mackenzie, *The Bank of England Note: A History of its Printing* (Cambridge: Cambridge University Press, 1953).

scroll on the left, with the words 'Bank of England' clearly visible. An Act of Parliament prohibited anyone else from using the watermark. In 1724, the Bank entered into an agreement with the firm of the Huguenot émigré Henri Portal (d.1747) of Whitchurch and Laverstoke in north-west Hampshire for the supply of banknote paper, a connection which continued until the company was acquired by De La Rue in 1995. The paper used was despatched by wagon in large locked, iron-bound chests from Portal's paper mills at Laverstoke, travelling somewhat vulnerably to the Bank first by road to Newbury and then via barge along the Kennet and down the Thames. A Bank officer resided in a cottage near to the Portal paper mills to oversee operations. Once at the Bank, the paper remained under the custody of the cashiers, who successively sent a month's supply and no more to Child and then, later, to Cole. Each morning one of the cashiers and a clerk drew the engraved copperplates from the Treasury in the Bank, from where they were taken by the clerk to Great Kirby Street. The clerk remained there to supervise the printing, and to receive and count the sheets as they came from the presses. After each day's work, the clerk returned to the Bank with the plates. Meanwhile, the printed sheets were hung up to dry, under sole custody of the printer. When ten reams, representing four or five days' work, had been produced they were delivered to the Bank. A committee of enquiry reported on the undesirability of the paper and plates leaving the Bank premises, but it was not until 1791 that the Coles' business was transferred within the Bank.

When, after 1725, the Bank resumed printing amounts on notes from the engraved copperplates, such printing remained only partial. A surviving £50 note of 1732, for example, carries a printed pound sign and the figure five, but the nought sign is added by hand. Other aspects appear to be the reverse of what one might expect if part of the note is left blank to be filled in. The amount in words as printed is simply 'fifty', the word 'pounds' being written in by hand (rather than the actual numerical amount). Notes of this kind might be made out for uneven amounts by further handwritten emendation, though the great majority were for round sums. By 1745, notes were being printed in denominations ranging from £20 to as high as £1,000. The word 'pound' or 'pounds' was finally printed on notes for £10 and £15, first issued in 1759, for £25 notes first issued in 1765, for £5 notes first issued in 1793 and for £1 and £2 notes first issued in 1797. The word 'pound' or 'pounds' in words, however, was not printed for other denominations until the very end of the eighteenth century. Before 1798, the name of the payee was written in by hand (since

1782 the name always that of the Chief Cashier). After 1798 the payee was printed, but even by 1805 no fewer than eighty-four clerks were employed in numbering, dating and countersigning the notes. From 1809, a machine, invented by the engineer and locksmith Joseph Bramah, printed both numbers and dates on the notes. Nevertheless, handwritten figures and words were not completely eliminated from the Bank's notes until 1853.[43] The involvement of script in one of the most secure forms of financial transaction in the country, and certainly increasingly one of the most commonplace and iconic, lasted for 160 years after the Bank's foundation.

By 1805, the total number of notes of all denominations produced each day had risen to thirty thousand. By this time the Bank's notes were printed by Garnet Terry, who, like his predecessors, had a private contract with the Bank and full control over his staff. This system was changed in 1808 when Terry was sworn into the Bank's service as their copperplate printer at the magnificent salary of £1,000 per annum. A condition of his appointment, however, was that Terry should give up his private business. Terry, therefore, unlike Child and the Coles, did not benefit from the extensive private jobbing business commanded by those entrusted to produce the notes of the Bank of England. It was also in 1808 that the Bank's Printing Department moved from its confined rooms to new quarters at the north-west corner of the Bank, where the presses remained until 1917.[44]

Print removed some of the principal difficulties in the circulation of large quantities of bills. The authority of the promissory note, share certificate and insurance contract depended upon reducing the likelihood of forgery and other threats to market confidence. Print allowed both an efficient production of notes and banking blanks, and the simple, time-saving replication of otherwise complex formulas of instruction and sanction. The reduction of local variations in the form of agreement (not always an asset to security) was matched by the adoption of new precautions against forgery. Early promissory notes were handwritten, but surging demand soon required the manufacture of special papers and then of letterpress printing with blanks. After 1729, the goldsmiths' notes were printed from engraved copperplates as a form of 'blank' to be filled in by longhand. Bonded and watermarked paper was quickly adopted, together with special engravings. Such initiatives were not without problems. The

43   For further detail, see Sir John Clapham, *The Bank of England: A History 1694–1914*, 2 vols (Cambridge: Cambridge University Press, 1944).
44   William Marston Acres, *The Bank of England from Within, 1694–1900*, 2 vols (London: Oxford University Press, 1931).

copperplates were relatively soft and the engravings needed frequent recutting. Almost all notes still required penned authorization and counter-signature. Nevertheless, banking and other financial operations were hugely advanced by the bulk production of uniform notes and certificates.

By the end of the century many regional businessmen including drapers, coal dealers, ironmongers and corn merchants acted as private bankers. Before 1780 most large local banks, including Smith's of Nottingham, Gurney's of Norwich, Lloyd's of Birmingham and Stuckey's of Somerset, still issued notes printed from plates but with various blanks to be filled in by the clerk. By 1790, however, most banknotes were fully engraved. Thomas Bewick (together with his brother John), skilled exponents of the relief block for the hand press, engraved notes for the Northumberland Bank.[45]

Insurance work

The insurance market was also supported from its earliest years by set blanks and formularized documentation. Early insurance projects served shipping and marine cargoes, but experiments in other types of insurance followed swiftly. Print had also been used for insurance policies in the Low Countries and in France in the 1630s. In England, printed papers relating to insurance had circulated since at least the 1650s, but the contract of insurance was issued in a standard printed form only from about 1680.[46] Before 1720, professional underwriters dealing in nothing but insurance were not common, but contracts were available at the end of the seventeenth century from dozens of mercantile and broking operators, many of whom advertised in the *City Mercury*, its rivals and successors. These printed ship insurance policies remained virtually unchanged in design and wording for nearly a hundred years from 1680 until 1779, just after the founding of New Lloyd's. The only significant alteration was the 'memorandum' additions from 1749, in turn based on printed forms used in underwriting in Bristol (and possibly elsewhere) several decades earlier.[47]

45 For examples, see Nigel Tattersfield, *Thomas Bewick, The Complete Illustrative Work*, 3 vols (London and New Castle, DE: British Library, Bibliographical Society and Oak Knoll, 2011), vol. 1.

46 Charles Wright and C. Ernest Fayle, *A History of Lloyd's from the Founding of Lloyd's Coffee House to the Present Day* (London: Blades, East & Blades, 1928), p. 142.

47 Nicolas Magens, *An Essay on Insurances*, 2 vols (London, 1755), vol. 1, pp. 10, 73.

Marine insurance itself included several distinct types of risk cover, from insurance on the ship, the goods and conveyed bullion, to respondentia bonds[48] and protection against barratry[49] and bottomry.[50] Each were given separate printed policies. There were also different options available for some types of insurance policy. For bottomry, for example, Weskett's 1781 guide for merchants specifically recommended the 'Spanish form'.[51] Until the late eighteenth century, when the organized market and the bill-broker were increasingly assertive, the initiative in much procedural business – including various instructions to the printer – rested with the insurance broker. The broker, or 'office-keeper', served as the agent for the merchant or the shipowner, and presented the insurance policy for signature to the underwriter.

In addition to marine insurance, officially dating from the early seventeenth century, companies were set up to cover against fire and death. Benjamin De Laune had circulated insurance proposals in 1668[52] and Newbold's unsuccessful scheme for house insurance was put forward in 1674. Barbon's Fire Office, the first successful fire insurance scheme, was established in 1680, as 'the Insurance Office at the Backside of the Royal Exchange'. The Friendly Society was founded in 1684, the Hand in Hand Fire Office in 1699, the Phenix in 1705, the Society for Assurance for Widows and Orphans before 1708, the Company of London Insurers, which established the partnership known as the Sun Fire Office in 1710, and the Double Hand in Hand or

---

48   In a contemporary definition, 'if the loan is not upon the vessel, but upon the goods and merchandise, which must necessarily be sold or exchanged in the course of the voyage, then only the borrower, *personally*, is bound to answer the contract; who, therefore, in this case, is said to take up money at respondentia': John Weskett, *A Complete Digest of the Theory, Laws, and Practice of Insurance* (London, 1781), p. 463.

49   The fraudulent alteration of goods or of a ship's course by its Master.

50   'In the nature of a mortgage of a *ship*; when the owner takes up money to enable him to carry on his voyage, and pledges the keel or bottom of the ship (*pars pro toto*) as a security for the repayment:– in which case it is understood, that, if the ship be lost, the lender loses also his whole money; but, if it returns in safety, then he shall receive back his principal, and also the premium or interest agreed upon, however it may exceed the legal rate of interest': Weskett, *Digest of Insurance*, pp. 44–5.

51   Weskett, *Digest of Insurance*, p. 46.

52   Anon., *Proposals modestly offered for the full peopling and inhabiting the City of London, and to restore the same to her ancient flourishing trade, which will suite her splendid structure* (London, 1672); and Boyer Relton, *An Account of the Fire Insurance Companies, Associations, Institutions, Projects and Schemes Established and Projected in Great Britain and Ireland during the Seventeenth and Eighteenth Centuries* (London: Swan Sonnenschein & Co., 1893), p. 22.

Union Fire Insurance Office in 1714. The Westminster Fire Office opened three years later. George Osmond's ambitious but unsuccessful National Insurance Office had been proposed in 1711.[53]

In insurance transactions, belief in the authority offered was clearly of paramount importance. Although much underwriting centred upon the Exchange, many brokers trying to place risks had to pursue potential investors across the city. Underwriting brokers were normally not partners and often risked private fortunes. With no common liability or partnership control, no specific legal power covered either what was written or who wrote it. Where there were several underwriters to a joint venture, the authority required was also that much greater. Charlatanism could, of course, not be prevented by print. Indeed, the false authority provided by numerous printed prospectuses and policies was publicly exposed in the South Sea Bubble of 1720. For those building on proven reputations, however, set forms both eased and enhanced business transactions. The printed policy came to enshrine standard forms of wording, replicated procedures and recognizable worth.

Policies, however, contributed to only about half of the total print work underpinning the expansion of insurance services in the eighteenth century. Conditions of insurance, particularly during the first two-thirds of the century, were not contained in the policy itself but printed in separate 'proposals', often as a wrapper or envelope.[54] Incorporated into the policy in the form of 'according to the exact tenor of their printed proposals dated ... [etc.]', revised or new proposals could be issued by the Insurance Office or underwriter even during the selling of an existing stock of policy blanks. Similarly, the same proposal, with the addition of a new heading or paragraph, could be directed towards a specific market. In December 1709, for example, the Company of London Insurers ordered the printing of a set of 'Proposals for the Country' with which to launch their country scheme.[55] Two years later, 1,500 proposals were printed in French.[56]

53   Early companies are discussed in P. G. M. Dickson, *The Sun Insurance Office, 1710–1960: The History of Two and a Half Centuries of British Insurance* (London: Oxford University Press, 1960), pp. 1–31.
54   Cornelius Walford, *The Insurance Cyclopaedia*, 5 vols & 1 part [unfinished] (London: Charles and Edwin Layton, 1871–80), vol. 3, pp. 407–8.
55   Geoffrey Wilson Clark, *Betting On Lives: The Culture of Life Insurance in England, 1695–1775* (Manchester: Manchester University Press, 1999), pp. 88, 90–1; Relton, *Insurance Companies*, p. 272.
56   Relton, *Insurance Companies*, p. 324.

Current proposals were also sent out to clients on special occasions (such as with the first number of the *Historical Register* in 1716) or as part of a lobbying campaign. Proposal print-runs were therefore considerable. In 1711 the Company of London Insurers had forty thousand proposals printed on quarter-sheet paper.

Even when not intrinsic to an operation, many financial and commercial concerns used print for market advantage. One of the most successful of these undertakings was in insurance company newsletters and circulars. Charles Povey's Traders' Exchange House, established in a rented building in Holborn in 1705 and offering life insurance from 1706, gained fame by its association with the *General Remark on Trade* published by Povey and freely circulated to clients. Its printer, Matthew Jenour, whose premises stood near St Sepulchre's Backgate in Gilt Spur Street, was already the printer of the Whig *Flying Post* and *Daily Advertiser*. Jenour was also employed by the Company of London Insurers (alias the Sun Fire Office) when it too decided to promote its business by distribution of a newspaper, the *British Mercury*. Jenour printed the paper, offered at reduced costs to the clients of the Insurance Office, from March to October 1710. Published three times a week, the *British Mercury* was a popular success, attracting subscriptions during its first fifteen months from nearly all those insured with the Office.[57] Ornamented with a striking sun on the masthead, a further design of a Mercury figure was added after twelve weeks.[58] A fire insurance policy without the newspaper cost two shillings per quarter, and with the *Mercury*, the charge was 2s 6d per quarter, plus stamp duty after 1712. From at least the end of its first year, however, it was also possible to subscribe to the newspaper without holding a Sun insurance policy. As one advertisement read:

> all persons ... who have a mind to continue to have the said *British Mercury* after Christmas without being Insur'd are Desir'd to give notice by the penny post ... in order to be register'd in the Company's Books and regularly serv'd, paying the first quarter before Hand; and if they continue they are to pay their Quarteridge within ten days after every quarter day for which a printed receipt shall be delivered to them, sign'd by two members of the Company, filed and witnessed by the men

---

57 Relton, *Insurance Companies*, p. 304; for Jenour's career and environs see also James Raven, *Bookscape: Geographies of Printing and Publishing in London before 1800* (London: The British Library, 2014), pp. 121–5.
58 *British Mercury*, no. 38, 21 June 1710.

who carry the said *British Mercury* which receipt they are to keep till called for, being their own and the Company's security.[59]

From the first issue, double policyholders entitled to two concessionary *Mercury* subscriptions could also have one of the newspapers sent to a friend or client. The *Mercury* not only promoted the insurance company and the goods and services of its contributory advertisers, but it also served as a sweetener or reward for a further chain of commercial contacts. It was also an ambitious journal, including from February 1712–13 to July 1714 a serialized 'History of the World'. The printer, who from October 1710 was Hugh Meere, was subsequently authorized to publish the 'History' separately. Even more ambitiously, it was announced some seven months after its inauguration that a French version of the journal, *Le Mercurie Brittanique*, would also be available.[60] Remarkably, it seems that the venture survived for two years under the editorship first of Alexander Justice and then of Charles Gildon, both writers for the *Mercury*.[61] According to an early advertisement, it was 'taken in by several hundreds of French inhabitants in this City and suburbs, and also by diverse English, for the easier acquiring of the French tongue, and by others sent to the country and beyond Sea'.[62] Certainly, 'French walkers' were employed to canvass for business.[63] The *Mercury* itself was initially a splendid promotional success. In March 1713 it was reported that within Westminster and London only 189 of a total 2,724 policyholders did not additionally subscribe to the newspaper.[64] It was, however, hit hard by the implementation of the 1712 Stamp Act, and three years later was buffeted by the launch of six-page weeklies. The *British Mercury* was duly changed to a one-and-a-half sheet publication, with stamp duty affixed and published once rather than three times a week,[65] but failed to survive beyond 1715.

From May 1716, Meere, 'at the Black Fryer in Black Fryers', printed a successor to the *Mercury*, the quarterly *Historical Register*. This was distributed free to policyholders by the Office's 'walkers'.[66] The *Register*

---

59   *British Mercury*, no. 116, 18 Dec. 1710.
60   *British Mercury*, no. 84, 4 Oct. 1710.
61   The *Mercury* writers are listed in Dickson, *Sun Insurance*, pp. 37–8.
62   *British Mercury*, no. 125, 8 Jan. 1711.
63   Relton, *Insurance Companies*, p. 369.
64   *British Mercury*, no. 455, 17 Mar. 1714.
65   *British Mercury*, no. 369, 2 Aug. 1712.
66   *The Historical Register, containing an Impartial Relation of all Transactions, Foreign and Domestick, published at the Expence of the Sun Fire Office.*

published a wide range of business news, including summaries of relevant debates in Parliament. The first number was printed in an edition of 4,500 copies. Meere himself became an Acting Member of the Company of London Insurers and then Secretary to the Board from April 1718 to August 1720.[67] It was clear that Meere was not just a contract printer. In addition to his direct participation in the affairs of the Company, he ran an extensive business press. It was also probably his own idea to establish a 'Numerical Table Book of Lotteries' at the Sun Coffee-House in Threadneedle Street and to print multiple copies of it to be sent to other coffee-houses – 'a thing which Mr. Bell the Printer under the Managers for the Royal Lottery makes no pretensions to do'.[68]

At mid-century, the increasing complexity of the insurance market forced the reorganization of Lloyd's and its re-establishment in new premises at Pope's Head Alley in 1769.[69] It also brought the agreed adoption of the 'memorandum' to the printed policy. The addition provided extra protection for the underwriter against special cases of deterioration and damage of goods as well as a more specific description of cargoes and conditions. The agreement of all parties to this, it is argued, confirmed the predominance of Lloyd's in insurance negotiation.[70] The centralized information service at the original coffee-house, together with *Lloyd's List* and daily auction sales of property (including ships), reinforced Lloyd's supremacy. Its position was also enhanced by the absence of external policing as the sole regulatory body was the Office of Assurances, which was concerned merely with registration. What is perhaps most remarkable about this is that so much was achieved without the sanction of law. The acceptance of the standard policy, for example, was a measure of the legitimacy achievable by the professional and reliable duplication of an agreed form of words. In the opinion of the historians of Lloyd's, 'the authority of the printed policy depended entirely on its general and voluntary acceptance by all concerned as embodying, in the most convenient form, the recognized customs and usages of Lombard Street or elsewhere in London'.[71] The subsequent development of case law concerning marine insurance during the second half of the century was little more than an accretion of interpretations

---

67 Relton, *Insurance Companies*, pp. 303, 312.
68 *British Mercury* advertisement, cited by Relton, *Insurance Companies*, p. 306.
69 See below, pp. 162–4, on *Lloyd's List*.
70 Wright and Fayle, *Lloyd's*, pp. 143–7.
71 Wright and Fayle, *Lloyd's*, p. 143. The policy was not prescribed by law until 1795.

of the different clauses of the printed form. According to John Weskett, the compiler of the major eighteenth-century insurance manual, such law was entirely derived from the 'general, settled, *printed* [his italics] Form of Policies'.[72]

Certainly, as early as the 1730s, the function of the insurance broker was both more diverse and more particularized than that of the bill-broker. The number of insurance brokers in London also steadily increased. In 1720 there were about a dozen regular underwriting agencies in the City, although many were engaged mainly in other branches of business and some associations were short-lived and unreliable projects. These were led by the 'Company for the Mutual Insurance of Ships' at Sadler's Hall, an 'Office for Insurance of Loss' near to Garraway's Fisheries and a 'Company for Insuring Ships and Merchandise' at the Marine Coffee-House. All were examined by a House of Commons Select Committee 'to inquire into all undertakings for purchasing Joint Stocks or obsolete Charters' following the South Sea Company crash.[73] All previous marine insurance schemes were suppressed by the 'Bubble Act' of June 1720.[74] In their stead, the Act raised the two great marine insurance houses, the London Assurance Corporation (Company), derived from Lord Chetwynd's proposals of 1719, and the Royal Exchange Assurance Corporation. The Royal Exchange derived in part from the realization of Billingsley's controversial 1716 project for a 'Public Assurance Office' and in part from the determination of the Mines Royal Company to undertake marine insurance.[75] Within a year of their foundation both chartered Offices were also undertaking life and fire insurance.[76] The focus of business remained at Lloyd's, but the number of underwriters and brokers continued to expand. Between 1741 and 1774, the merchant William Braund did business with at least seventy-six different insurance brokers.[77] At the height of the brokers' powers, 130 brokers subscribed

---

72 Weskett, *Digest of Insurance*, p. liii.
73 *House of Commons Journals*, 19: 274–5.
74 *An Act for better securing certain powers and privileges intended to be granted by His Majesty by two Charters for Assurance of Ships and Merchandizes at Sea; or for lending money upon bottomry; and for restraining several extravagant and unwarrantable practices therein mentioned*, 6 Geo. I, c. 18.
75 Relton, *Insurance Companies*, pp. 153–6.
76 A. H. John, 'The London Assurance Company and the Marine Insurance Market of the Eighteenth Century', *Economica*, n.s., 25:98 (May 1958), 126–41.
77 Sutherland, *London Merchant*, p. 61.

to the Register of Lloyd's in 1778.[78] Thereafter merchants turned increasingly to direct dealing with the underwriters.

In all these early schemes the coffee-house network played a prominent part. The Friendly Society was organized through Bridge's Coffee-House and the Hand in Hand through Tom's, both near to the Royal Exchange. Rebuilt in 1747 after the Cornhill fire, Garraway's survived as a major mercantile meeting-house; it vended insurance policies and offered its own news service and auction sales. The venerable Rainbow, near the Temple, Fleet Street, was an early headquarters of the Phoenix Fire Insurance Office. Fierce competition between the different insurance firms was conducted in newspaper columns and by hand-outs from 'walkers' and underwriters. Propaganda for the Double Hand in Hand declared that 'the Directors themselves being barr'd from the least profit but in common with every other Person insuring; whereas in the Sun Office, the few Proprietors take to themselves ten shillings per annum per policy'.[79]

Between 1720 and the founding of the second Phoenix Assurance Company in 1782, six insurance companies were responsible for the great majority of fire insurance policies issued throughout the country. Provincial fire insurance offices were also opened at Bristol in 1718 (the Crown Fire Office), at Bath in 1767 (with a second, rival office in 1776), at Manchester in 1771 and at Liverpool in 1777. The New Bristol Fire Office opened in 1769, with offices at Shrewsbury in 1780, Leeds in 1782, Newcastle upon Tyne in 1783 and Norwich in 1785. By 1800 all large provincial English towns boasted a fire insurance office.[80] Elsewhere in Britain, the first insurance office in Scotland, the Friendly Insurance Society of Edinburgh, opened in January 1719–20. The first fire office in Glasgow, surprisingly, does not seem to have been established until 1785.[81] In Ireland, the Hibernian Insurance Company offered insurance for life,

78   *Annals of Lloyds Registers*, p. 12.

79   *Union or Double Hand in Hand Fire Office for Insuring Goods and Merchandizes by Mutual Contribution in the Way of the Hand in Hand Office for Houses*, June 1716. BL 816.m.10 (105–6 & others).

80   Details of the different insurance companies are given in Relton, *Insurance Companies*; Harold E. Raynes, *A History of British Insurance* (London: Pitman, 1950); Dickson, *Sun Insurance*; Barry Supple, *The Royal Exchange Assurance: A History of British Insurance 1720–1970* (Cambridge: Cambridge University Press, 1970); and Clive Trebilcock, *Phoenix Assurance and the Development of British Insurance*, 2 vols (Cambridge: Cambridge University Press, 1985–99).

81   For further details, see Relton, *Insurance Companies*, pp. 187–90, 231.

fire and shipping in Dublin from 1770. The Royal Exchange Insurance of Ireland was instituted in 1784.

In printing for insurance companies, the early dominance of London was hardly rivalled for the rest of the century. Insurance provided long-lasting engraving and printing contracts. Copying certificates, standardizing procedure and collating written records were famously problematic. Print transformed operations in all areas. One London broking firm alone issued 4,000 certificates (mostly for fire) in one week in 1724. In 1707, Phenix had secured 10,000 buildings' policyholders, the Friendly Society some 18,000, and the Hand in Hand, 13,000. In 1739, the Westminster Fire Office alone issued house insurance policies for 7,852 clients.[82] With the expansion of business, more elaborate counterfoils were engraved to eliminate errors and forgery in insurance claims. Some of the finest workmanship in business engraving appears in the 'New Fire Office' counterfoils for the Phoenix Assurance Company policies from 1782.[83]

As security printing and design requirements increased so did the number of specialist jobbing printers and engravers. One of the earliest of these was Richard Newcomb, operating from Fleet Street between 1691 and 1713. In addition to the commissions from the Bank, skilled engravers were employed by the stock companies and later by the Treasury. From the setting up of the Office for the Issue of Exchequer Bills in 1727, procedures were established for the regular engraving and altering of plates for bills and for the manufacture of special paper at Exeter.[84] Some decades later, transactions in Exchequer annuities were also fully transferred to engraved forms.

In much production work, therefore, engraving and the rolling press superseded letterpress jobbing. The form of policy issued by the first Phenix Office from 1712 was not printed but copperplate engraved, as was the elaborate stationery prepared for the Friendly Society.[85] The original commissions involved an engraver and stationery supplier, but it was usual for engraving orders, like those from the Bank before 1791, to go through an executive printing firm. Printers also sent out work to engravers and, in many cases, inserted the finished cut or plate within

82   Relton, *Insurance Companies*, pp. 113, 263.
83   Policy documents, archives of the Sun-Alliance Insurance Group, Bartholomew Lane.
84   NA E. 407/134, collections of exchequer bills; and BL Add. MSS 31,025 (1697, 1709, 1720, incl. South Sea bills and uncut, unused proof pages of ten bills and one (fol. 9) with counterfoil intact).
85   Examples survive at BL 816.m.10 (scrapbook), incl. 85–9, 99, 102.

their own typesetting. Insurance policies and headed warrants were also frequently the product of combined operations. The Sun Fire Office used several different illustrative cuts to head its letterpress policy blanks from the mid-1720s. From 1725, the Sun's policies were printed on paper larger than the original foolscap and headed by a copperplate engraving ordered from the Company's then printer, Mr Cartwright.[86] The sun emblem was always placed in the centre of the engraving. Until 1744, the sun was supported by a porter with bales and a fireman with a fire-hook, and above the sun was a drawing of an old tub engine. From 1744, a new engraving showed, on either side of the sun, a salvage man with bags and a fireman with an axe, with a large manual engine above. The arrangement of the fire officers was reversed in 1763. The main section of the policy, with its various large blanks for the addition of individual details, used a mixture of bold black letter, italic and small capitals for effect. Between at least the policy relating to the 1741 proposals and that relating to the 1775 proposals, the wording of the blank remained unchanged except for an attempt at emboldening the words 'Sun Fire-Office'.[87]

By the end of the century, printing efforts were increasingly elaborate. The new standard of craftsmanship was exemplified by the superb engraving commissioned for the 1785 Phoenix advertisements and the accompanying policy headings. From at least 1789 these were engraved for the Company by Henry Richter, then seventeen years old and the elder brother of Thomas Richter who was to be Phoenix Company Secretary from 1837. Henry Richter, established in Great Newport Street from 1788, was a close friend of William Blake and a society watercolourist. Although many of his later engravings were actually executed by Charles Rolls, in his early years he used the burin himself[88] and the Phoenix commissions are among his finest work. The successive plates used to head the policies were also numbered (perhaps uniquely for this type of work), such that by 1800 the policies were bearing plate no. 15, another Richter design. In 1797, Richter also engraved the cut used in the policy for the Phoenix's new life insurance venture, the Pelican Life Office. The engraving was made of an exquisite drawing by William Hamilton, the leading book illustrator and member of the Royal Academy since 1789. This design was succeeded

86   LMA, Sun Fire Office, Company Minutes; I have been unable to discover details of Cartwright's business.
87   Policy documents, archives of the Sun-Alliance Insurance Group.
88   John Lewis Roget, *A History of the Old Water-Colour Society*, 2 vols (London and New York: Longmans, Green and Co., 1891), vol. 1, pp. 29, 384–5.

in 1800 by a drawing by Edward Francis Burney (1760–1848) and engraved by Anthony Cardon (1772–1813).[89] Burney was – albeit briefly – one of the most fashionable illustrators of these years. Cardon, a Flemish engraver, was a particularly prolific and gifted contemporary book illustrator.[90] In terms of artistic verve and fine execution, such policies probably represent the high point of jobbing engraving. The policies and proposals were actually printed by Frys and Couchman of Worship Street, Upper Moorfields. Joseph Fry (1730–89), Quaker type founder and printer of Bristol, was also a partner in a Bristol porcelain works and soap factory, and a chemical works in Battersea, and was the founder of Fry's chocolate empire.[91] With William Pyne, Fry established a type foundry in Bristol in 1750 and by 1758 was cutting Greek founts for Oxford University. In 1766, Fry moved to Moorfields where (changing workshops in 1783) he worked for over twenty years. Stephen Couchman joined the printing side of Fry's business in 1779, publishing a new type specimen sheet in 1780. The policy blanks in particular, made effective use of Fry's impressive two-lines great primer black font.[92] Having moved to Throgmorton Street in 1790, Couchman was still printing the proposals and the policies of the Phoenix Company at the end of the century. Couchman retired in 1824.[93]

89   Examples are reproduced in Trebilcock, *Phoenix Assurance*, vol. 1, pp. 61, 94.

90   M. T. S. Raimbach (ed.), *Memoirs and Recollections of the late Abraham Raimbach, Esq., Engraver* (London: Frederick Shoberl, Junior, 1843).

91   In 1759 he bought the patent to Churchman's chocolate (established 1728) and opened his factory. Fry is greatly neglected as a subject for eighteenth-century business history. A brief sketch is given in Arthur Raistrick, *Quakers in Science and Industry*, 2nd edn (Newton Abbot: David & Charles, 1968), pp. 214–16.

92   [Joseph Fry], *A Specimen of Printing Types made by Joseph Fry and Sons, Letter-Founders, Worship-Street, Moorfields* (London, 1785).

93   Ian Maxted, *The London Book Trades, 1775–1800* (London: Dawson, 1977), p. 54.

6

Advertising

The commercial practices and customer services associated with a developing 'consumer mentality' are now standard features of economic histories of eighteenth-century England.[1] Much of this almost wholly domestic consumer activity, whether emulative buying or the entrepreneurial stimulation of demand, would have been impossible without the extension of jobbing printing after 1700. From the first decades of the century, the increase in the number of printing houses and improvements in engraving, letterpress typography and paper-making served merchants, manufacturers and retailers. Less obvious activities of the local printer also encouraged market development. The distributional services of the pressman and stationer were used by many different trades. The printing house became a convenient accommodation address and a centre for the co-ordination of projects and lobbying related to the extension of local business.

The clearest contribution made by print to the promotion of local commerce, however, was in advertising. Advertisements have been studied from a variety of perspectives, and the historical relationship between advertising and the creation of a local mart for goods and services has been the subject of renewed investigation.[2] Much greater understanding

---

1   Eric L. Jones, 'Fashion Manipulators: Consumer Tastes and British Industries, 1660–1800', in *Business Enterprise and Economic Change*, ed. L. P. Cain and P. J. Uselding (Kent State, OH: Kent State University Press, 1973); Neil McKendrick, John Brewer and J. H. Plumb, *The Birth of a Consumer Society: The Commercialization of Eighteenth-Century England* (London: Europa, 1982); Louise Lippincott, *Selling Art in Georgian London: The Rise of Arthur Pond* (New Haven, CT: Yale University Press, 1983); and in a broader perspective, Fernand Braudel, *Capitalism and Material Life, 1400–1800* (New York and London: Harper Collins, 1973).

2   See, for example, Maxine Berg and Helen Clifford, 'Selling Consumption in the Eighteenth Century: Advertising and the Trade Card in Britain and France', *Cultural and Social History*, 4 (2007), 145–70; earlier approaches to the study are surveyed in Donald

of eighteenth-century advertising in England is now possible,[3] especially given advances in newspaper history.[4] Several focused studies of the role of advertising in the eighteenth century have also provoked fierce debate about whether saturation advertising and other related techniques are a sign of weakness or strength.[5] Connections between bibliographical and printing history and the advance of advertising have been meagre, however.

Although printed advertising dates from the first century of moveable type, it was not until the late seventeenth century that the printing of bills and advertisements became a common business practice. Merchants commissioned printed pieces for negotiating and monitoring transactions and for informing agents of wares for sale. Even in London, however, there is little evidence to suggest that many general tradesmen and storekeepers adopted regular printed advertisements much before 1700. At that date, the actual term 'advertisement' had been in common currency for a few decades only. Earlier advertising was sufficiently small in scale to make the new initiatives of the London and regional printers appear both bold and innovatory. During the first decades of the eighteenth century, various promotional leaflets and broadsheets were prepared. Notices were printed for the sale or lease of houses, land or other property. Sales of businesses, horses and ships were featured in a variety of closely worded broadsides. Town corporations and magistrates commissioned bill posters for cattle

Slater, 'Advertising as a Commercial Practice: Business Strategy and Social Theory' (unpubl. Ph.D. dissertation, Cambridge University, 1986).

3   Except for the introductory (and unfortunately inexact) work of Adriano Bruttini, 'Advertising and the Industrial Revolution', *Economic Notes*, 4:2–3 (May–Dec. 1973), 90–[116], the fullest general surveys covering this period are H. Sampson, *A History of Advertising from the Earliest Times* (London: Chatto and Windus, 1874); Frank Presbrey, *The History and Development of Advertising* (New York: Doubleday, Doran & Co., 1929); Blanche B. Elliott, *A History of English Advertising* (London: B. T. Batsford, 1962) and discussion of newspaper advertising in publications given in notes 4 and 11 below.

4   See especially Hannah Barker, *Newspapers, Politics and English Society, 1695–1855* (London: Longman, 2000); Hannah Barker, *Newspapers, Politics and Public Opinion in Late Eighteenth-Century England* (Oxford: Oxford University Press, 1998); and Ian Jackson, 'Print in Provincial England: Reading and Northampton, 1720–1800' (unpubl. D.Phil. dissertation, University of Oxford, 2003).

5   Most notably perhaps, for England, Francis Doherty, *A Study in Eighteenth-Century Advertising Methods: The Anodyne Necklace* (Lewiston, NY: Edwin Mellen Press, 1992), in contrast to Jonathan Barry, 'Publicity and the Public Good: Presenting Medicine in Eighteenth-Century Bristol', in *Medical Fringe and Medical Orthodoxy, 1750–1850*, ed. William Bynum and Roy Porter (London: Croom Helm, 1987), pp. 29–39.

sales, for market regulations, for assizes and for advertising municipal weighing machines.[6]

Many experiments were made in advertising design. Model notices were offered, incorporating 'neater' type, greater use of white space, and combinations of print, woodcuts and engravings. In general retailing, print enabled the production of elaborate advertising trade cards. Before about 1740, the majority of cards were printed from woodcuts, although finer copperplate engraving was already adopted, as discussed in chapter 5, for banknotes and high-end security commissions from affluent London companies. By mid-century, copperplate engraving was also generally favoured by all tradesmen and women who wished to give out a distinctive, informative and attractive trade card, bill poster or other promotional matter. As already noted, the engraving of pictures for advertising, promotional giveaways and labelling was a key supplement to the businesses of London and provincial engravers, even from the opening decades of the century. In tradesmen's rush to be different and to attract custom in increasingly competitive markets, engravers and printers found their skills to be in great demand. In turn, new working strategies were required when the speed with which advertising copy could be made ready was essential to the commission. At the same time, jobbing design and typographical layout assumed new sophistication. Surviving printers' notices issued before mid-century include several announcing the purchase of new founts, ornaments and cuts, and offering traders improved services in setting their advertisements in neat and attractive type.[7]

Except for the newspapers, however, there survive relatively few examples of separately printed advertising executed before about 1760. At Salisbury the only bill poster printed by Collins surviving from the hundreds he must have produced, is for a local gunsmith (c.1766–67). In Kent, Jasper Sprange printed elaborate posters for the 'Annual Diversions at Tonbridge', one of the hiring fairs and shows of livestock and agricultural produce that characterized the rural calendar. Even William Strahan, handling some of the greatest literature of the century, accepted an order to print four thousand advertisements for salad oil.[8] Local printers produced advertisements to be pasted on the side of stagecoaches, wagons and buildings. Alehouses erected their own notice-boards to contain the

---

6   HfRO, BG11/24/2, Chamberlaine's Book of Accompts, 1732–69, fols 360ff, cattle sales, weighing machine and assize.

7   NRO, Heaton MSS Misc. bundles; ShRO, Lloyd MSS.

8   BL, Add. MSS 48,800:69v, Strahan Ledger, June 1745.

paper warfare conducted to the benefit of the local printer-stationer. Such campaigning might have required sudden assaults and swift responses. Richard Lobb and Timothy Toft, whose press was established in Chelmsford in 1758, assured customers that their 'Printing Business is executed in the most elegant Manner, and Hand-bills printed at Two Hours Notice'.[9]

Printed circulars and handbills served such a variety of operations associated with commerce and industry that it is impossible to detail them all. Printers received orders for separate advertisements from all manner of wholesalers, owners of workshops and those offering professional services. Many were bulletins about changing conditions of the trade.[10] The main commissioners of printed notices, however, were shop-men and those selling directly to the public through a mail or carrier service. After mid-century, many changes in retailing practice were publicized by print. Posters and handbills advertised wares and offers of free delivery, part payment and a range of specified credit or abatement terms. The organization required was greatly assisted by printed forms and checklists, both for distribution and internal use. In fact, the services offered were not always as generous as they seemed, often involving trade protection as much as commercial one-upmanship. During the second half of the century, for example, many wholesale and retailing trades introduced strict pricing in the guise of 'never again' offers. By 1800, where credit, delivery, abatement or free packaging might once have been expected, it was now often unavailable unless stipulated in the notice. James Lackington was an early advertiser of bargains by strict dealing and also a member of the book trades. In his second-hand book emporium in Oxford Street in the 1780s, he was clear that no discount could be offered or part-exchange accepted.

Print also changed the addresses and forms by which businesses were known, encouraging standard styles and enumeration instead of the eclectic and visual codes of old. By the final third of the century, advertising specified more exactly the addresses of shops and agencies. In 1762 the Corporation of the City decreed that all large hanging shop signs in London were to be fixed flat against walls and ordered all street houses

9 Subscript to the masthead of the *Chelmsford and Colchester Chronicle* during the 1760s.
10 'Instructions', 1779, reprinted in W. H. Crawford and B. Trainor (eds), *Irish Social History: Aspects of Irish Social History 1750–1800: Documents* (Belfast: HMSO, 1969), pp. 28–9.

to be numbered. The world in which commercial and financial transactions were promoted was increasingly one dominated by print, printed numbering and easily replicated identification.

Newspapers

The greatest boost to advertising came with the transformation of the seventeenth-century corantos and diurnals into the modern newspaper.[11] By the mid eighteenth century, notices in national and local advertisers were underpinning selling campaigns in some of the remotest parts of the country. The humble almanac had long carried brief advertisements for fairs, books and professional and commercial services. Some almanacs advertised 'Offices of Intelligence', inviting the submission of more notices. Others advertised practical services ranging from 'horse burning' (branding) to 'amputations of all sorts'.[12] Notices in newspapers, however, were of a quite different order. They were regular, of the instant, and relatively cheap to advertisers. There was also potentially far greater space available, with both readers and advertisers knowing in advance publication dates, costs and expected format. The resulting notices in newspapers and their effect upon the business community varied according to the type of publication. Certain journals were specifically concerned with trade and finance, providing information about prices, imports, shares and financial transactions.[13] Others were designed solely as repositories for public or private advertisements. Still more, either from choice or necessity, included advertisements as part of their general service to the reader.

Most of the earliest business newspapers were partly printed, expecting and requiring the addition of written prices, times or other commercial and financial information in blanks, or of news and even correspondence

---

11   Early newspapers are studied by Joseph Frank, *The Beginnings of the English Newspaper, 1620–1660* (Cambridge, MA: Harvard University Press, 1961); E. S. de Beer, 'The English Newspapers from 1695 to 1702', in *William III and Louis XIV*, ed. R. Hatton and J. S. Bromley (Liverpool: Liverpool University Press, 1968), pp. 117–29; R. B. Walker, 'The Newspaper Press in the Reign of William III', *Historical Journal*, 17:4 (Dec. 1974), 691–709; and, focusing on 1679–82, James Sutherland, *The Restoration Newspaper and its Development* (Cambridge: Cambridge University Press, 1986).

12   As in Forbes' Aberdeen *Almanack* from the 1680s.

13   These are considered as specialist guides in chapters 8 and 9 below.

in the large spaces left for that purpose. John J. McCusker and Cora Gravesteijn noted that the partly printed newspapers 'look like forms of some kind which further helps to explain why they have not always been recognised as published periodicals'.[14] But in fact one might reverse that point and say that the rather basic idea of what 'publication' involved has meant that newspapers have not been regarded as jobbing printing, itself not simply an also-ran activity but a wide-ranging achievement that published all kinds of print and part-printed forms and reading materials for very precise reasons and circulation. Publishers were also diverse and certainly not confined to printers, stationers or booksellers, but for financial advertisers and guides they were more usually merchants and businessmen.

Printed registers of notices were the direct successors to those short-lived attempts dating back to 1611 to establish a 'Publique Register for General Commerce'. In 1649, Henry Walker's *Perfect Occurrences* and his Office of Entries were suppressed by the government. Eight years later, the *Publick Adviser*, printed weekly by 'the devil's half-crown newsmonger', Marchamont Nedham (or Needham, d.1678), communicated 'unto the whole nation the several occasions of all persons that are in any way concerned in matter of Buying and Selling or in any kind of Employment or dealings whatsoever'. The complex scale of advertising rates that was used did not take into account the size of the entry or 'advice', but varied according to the profession of the advertiser and the nature of the announcement. Like many of the first publications devoted solely to private notices, the *Publick Adviser* did not last for more than a few months. In 1663, Roger l'Estrange was appointed as 'Surveyor of the Press' and charged with controlling the 'writing, printing and publishing advertisements'. It was under licence from l'Estrange that in 1667 the *City Mercury or Advertisements Concerning Trade* was published by several booksellers as a series of free hand-outs.

By the far busier trading times of the 1690s, such publications served a responsive market. The *City Mercury Published Gratis every Monday for the Promotion of Trade* of 1692 and its successor, the *London Mercury*, offered increasing space to merchants and adventurous tradesmen to advertise goods and services. Both journals were succeeded in 1707 by

14 John J. McCusker and Cora Gravesteijn, *The Beginnings of Commercial and Financial Journalism: The Commodity Price Currents, Exchange Rate Currents, and Money Currents of Early Modern Europe* (Amsterdam: NEHA, 1991), p. 28.

the *Generous Advertiser; or, Weekly Information of Trade and Business*. Perhaps the most famous of the early-eighteenth-century business advertisers was the *General Remark on Trade* (1705 to at least 1708), compiled by Charles Povey of the Traders' Exchange House (1705), which was an agency for employment as well as life and estate insurance. The irrepressible Povey further set up the Exchange House Fire Office in 1708, sold two years later to the Company of London Insurers (and Sun Fire Office), and the transferred paper became the Jenour-printed *British Mercury*. At the same time, Povey covenanted not to continue the paper or establish a competitor.[15] The *British Mercury* solicited custom by reminding advertisers of 'its spreading so far, there being near 4,000 printed every Time, and those carefully distributed into all Parts, not only of the City, but of the whole Nation, being deliver'd throughout London and Parts adjacent, by Men employ'd for that Purpose by the Office, and transmitted to remoter Parts by Post and Parcel'.[16] After 1711 the paper was no longer issued free of charge and it ceased publication four years later. Povey's great rival, John Houghton, used his *Collection for Improvement of Husbandry and Trade* to gauge the market for trade advertising. Following this, he issued a free, if apparently short-lived, bi-weekly advertising sheet, *The Useful Intelligencer for Promoting Trade and Commerce*. Houghton's adverts included a wide variety of services. At first these were announced in the registry office form, with notices written in the first person. No exact details were available before application to the paper's editor. By the late 1690s, however, all advertisements appeared as direct addresses.

Although the potential for printed advertising was clear to the newspaper proprietors, the first examples of free news-sheets supported entirely by advertising revenue were financial disasters. The limited circulation of the papers was probably the main reason for trade advertisers failing to support the ventures. At least one sheet, the *Generous Advertiser*, also proved too generous. With copies distributed for free, the paper charged advertisers threepence for every fifty letters. *The Advertiser* claimed a circulation of four thousand and, on the basis of the number

15   Geoffrey Wilson Clark, *Betting On Lives: The Culture of Life Insurance in England, 1695–1775* (Manchester: Manchester University Press, 1999), pp. 80–2; Boyer Relton, *An Account of the Fire Insurance Companies, Associations, Institutions, Projects and Schemes Established and Projected in Great Britain and Ireland during the Seventeenth and Eighteenth Centuries* (London: Swan Sonnenschein & Co., 1893), p. 301.
16   *British Mercury*, 502, 12 Feb. 1715, p. 6.

of advertisements in one surviving copy, the paper returned less than £5
gross, providing only a third of a penny for the production and distribution of each copy.[17] With the notable exception of price currents and
other lists serving trade and finance, the advertising-only journals did not
flourish.

The key to future advertising was its incorporation into strictly *news*-
papers. Advertisers were willing to pay higher charges for notices that
were guaranteed to appear in multi-purpose publications enjoying wide
circulation. Advertisements had provided income for publishers of news-
sheets as early as 1640, and by 1710 advertising brought additional revenue
to a dozen or more London newspapers, some short-lived but others
maintained over decades. Here, a simple review of titles can be misleading.
As Michael Harris cautions, many early 'advertisers' merely adopted a
fashionable title and actually contained little advertising.[18] Nevertheless,
newspaper mastheads increasingly carried the word 'Advertiser' and some
began to fill several columns with adverts. It was especially common to the
weekly standard-bearers of printers setting up in the provinces.[19]

It is difficult to be precise about the readership achieved by most of
these newspapers, especially when a single copy might enjoy a large and
unpredictable tavern or coffee-house circulation. From the first decade of
the eighteenth century, London newspapers were produced in editions of
2,000 or so. One surviving estimate of newspaper sales, in Spring 1704,
lists weekly sales of 12,000 copies of the twice-weekly *London Gazette*,
11,600 copies of the thrice-weekly *Post Man*, and 9,000 copies of the
thrice-weekly *Post Boy*. Total weekly sales of newspapers were put at
43,800.[20] Newspaper historians have generally accepted these estimates,
while highlighting the long 'tail' of less successful newspapers with very
modest circulation figures.[21] In 1712, about twenty single-leaf newspapers

---

17   Calculations by R. B. Walker, 'Advertising in London Newspapers, 1650–1750',
Business History, 15:2 (July 1973), 112–30 (p. 118).
18   Michael Harris, *London Newspapers in the Age of Walpole: A Study of the Origins
of the Modern English Press* (London: Associated University Presses, 1987), p. 58.
19   This has been frequently noted, including by Jeremy Black, *The English Press in the
Eighteenth Century* (London: Croom Helm, 1987), p. 58.
20   NA, T. 1, vol. 129 (4), estimate prepared for a proposal to increase stamp duty, dated
and discussed in James R. Sutherland, 'The Circulation of Newspapers and Literary
Periodicals, 1700–30', *The Library*, 4th ser., 15 (1934), 110–24.
21   Henry L. Snyder, 'The Circulation of Newspapers in the Reign of Queen Anne', *The
Library*, 5th ser., 23 (1968), 206–35; and Henry L. Snyder, 'A Further Note', *The Library*,
5th ser., 31 (1976), 387–9.

were published regularly in London each week.[22] Of the more famous
journals, Defoe's thrice-weekly *Review* seems to have enjoyed a modest
regular edition of between 425 and 500 copies from 1704 to 1713, the
Guardian sold about 850 copies daily, and the *Spectator* enjoyed a daily
sale of between 1,600 and 2,200 copies.[23] Each number of the *British
Merchant*, appearing three time a week, was issued in about 1,200 copies.

After Bolingbroke's 1712 Stamp Act, whole-sheet newspapers were
required to carry a penny stamp or a halfpenny stamp on a half sheet or
less. Undoubtedly this temporarily restricted the growth of the press and
ended the publication of several newspapers. The Act was almost immediately circumvented, however, by newspaper proprietors claiming the right
to register newspapers as pamphlets of more than one sheet and paying the
smaller duty of two shillings per sheet on *one copy* of each edition. An
obvious result of the Stamp Act, therefore, was to hasten the demise of the
old one-sheet weekly and replace it with journals of one-and-a-half or more
sheets. Despite the further Stamp Act of 1725 extending tax to newspapers
of more than one sheet, the number of London weeklies, including *Read's
Weekly Journal; or, British Gazetteer* and *Mist's Weekly Journal*, increased
to twelve during the next decade, before levelling out, in a very competitive market, to five titles in 1750. Of these, journals such as the *Craftsman*
boasted circulations of 13,000 per week. Total sales of all newspapers in
England based on the stamp duty returns amount to some 7.3 million in
1750, 9.4 million in 1760, 12.6 million in 1775 and over 16 million in 1790.[24]
In addition, unstamped weekly newspapers, probably exceeding 50,000
by 1730, were also distributed in the London area. Estimates from the late
1730s put the weekly total at between 50,000 and 80,000 copies.[25]

Most unstamped and cut-price halfpenny and farthing newspapers
were, however, of little consequence in the development of commercial
notices. In press advertising, the clear rival to the weeklies was the daily
journal. The first daily paper, the *Daily Courant*, was published in
London in 1702 by Samuel Buckley. While it remained for the next decade
the sole daily newspaper, the *Courant* gave over half, and often as much
as two-thirds, of its back page to advertising notices. At its low point,
however, the *Courant* was selling only about six hundred copies per day,[26]

22   Harris, *London Newspapers*, p. 19.
23   Snyder, 'Circulation of Newspapers', p. 209.
24   NA A.o.3/950 ff.
25   Harris, *London Newspapers*, pp. 28, 200 n. 60.
26   Snyder, 'Circulation of Newspapers', p. 210.

and newspaper advertising was advanced more by the next two dailies to be published, the *Daily Post* of 1718 and the *Daily Journal* of 1719. Six London daily titles were in publication in 1730 and, albeit with fluctuations, the total stayed at six for the next twenty years. By 1770 the number of daily titles had increased to nine, each with a circulation much larger than any of their predecessors. The first English dailies sold under a thousand copies per issue with sales based in London. By the mid-1740s, the *Daily Post* was printed in editions of 2,500. By 1770, both the *Public Advertiser* and the *Daily Advertiser* sold well over three thousand copies per day. Linked to this advance in publication figures was the separation between morning and evening newspapers. In the early 1730s, the morning papers were overtaken in popularity by evening publications claiming more up-to-the-minute news coverage. These evening journals were led by the *London Evening Post* and the *General Evening Post*, each of which was issued in editions of up to six thousand copies between the 1730s and 1780s. In all, four dozen London evening newspapers and advertisers were established during the century.[27]

In London and later in the larger provincial towns, the coffee-house served as a focal point for the dissemination of trading news. London coffee-houses were confirmed as regular receivers of newspapers after the failure of the coffee-house proprietors in the late 1720s to restrict the number of newspapers printed in order to sponsor their own morning and evening half-sheet papers.[28] During the 1730s, many coffee-houses were taking up to four copies of the leading newspapers for the benefit of their customers. As the coffee-house proprietors complained in their battle with the printers, it was 'plainly a difficult and hazardous Thing for a Coffee-Man to leave off a Paper he has once taken in: For his Customers seeing it once in his House, always expect to see it again'.[29] Despite the furore over supplying the coffee-houses, many of their customers would have bought copies of newspapers prior to arriving at a coffee-house.

27 Michael Harris, 'The Structure, Ownership and Control of the Press, 1620–1780', in *Newspaper History from the Seventeenth Century to the Present Day*, ed. George Boyce, James Curran and Pauline Wingate (London: Constable, 1978), pp. 82–97 (p. 87); for a fuller contextual study, see Barker, *Newspapers, Politics and English Society*; and Barker, *Newspapers, Politics and Public Opinion*.
28 Harris, *London Newspapers*, p. 31.
29 Anon., *The Case of the Coffee-Men of London and Westminster. Or, An Account of the Impositions and Abuses, put upon Them and the Whole Town by the Present Set of News-Writers* (London, 1728), p. 15.

Newspaper printers employed numerous 'walkers' and distributing agents to deliver newspapers to subscribers and retail outlets. In London, hawkers were the sole means for distributing the cheapest newspapers. In addition, many bookshops and general stores became regular suppliers of newspapers. By mid-century, several wholesale dealers or 'publishers' even organized the distribution of rival titles to retailers and other distributors. A further outlet within London was the pamphlet shop. Here, a vendor or 'mercury' had usually bought the newspapers at discount to sell directly to the public or to street hawkers. Many of the mercuries were the wives or widows of printers, including Mrs Elizabeth Nutt, whose son and heir, Richard, married into the Meere printing business.[30]

The other great distributor of newspapers and advertisers was the Post Office. After 1688 the Post Office, no longer in 'grant and farm', was directly accountable to the Treasury. During the next century the cost of newspaper distribution was lowered by the activity of groups with Post Office franking privileges. First the clerks to the Secretaries of State, and then the Post Office Clerks of the Road, served as retailers of newspapers to the town as well as to the provinces. By 1782, some sixty thousand newspapers were said to be distributed by the Post Office in London alone.[31] Five years later, John Palmer established a separate office for newspapers in the Post Office to ease the burden of distribution. A staff of eighteen supervised the receipt, sorting and distribution of news-sheets. In 1785, mail coaches had been made exempt from tolls,[32] and in 1792, franking requirements for newspapers were finally abandoned, largely because of the ease with which the nominal stamps could be forged.

The circulation of newspapers outside London extended trading opportunities and provided vital additional financial support for publication. Newspapers and advertisers carried into the country boosted both local commercial networks and the quantity of advertising sent in from London and the provincial towns. Even by the time of the 1712 Stamp Act, five London morning newspapers were published on Tuesdays, Thursdays and Saturdays, which was when the post left for the country. Michael Harris has shown how the *Post Man* and *Post Boy*, as well as the *Flying Post*, the three great long-running newspapers of the first half of the century, were specifically targeted towards the provinces. Sections of

---

30   See John D. Gordan III, 'John Nutt: Trade Publisher and Printer "In the Savoy"', *The Library*, 7th ser., 15 (2014), 243–60.
31   Post Office Records, 97/6, cited by Harris, 'Structure, Ownership and Control', p. 90.
32   25 Geo. III, c. 57.

the papers were regularly left blank for correspondence and postal use. As the *Flying Post* advertised in its 'Postscript', 'tis done on good Paper, with Blanks so order'd that any one may write of their *Private Affairs* into the Country'.[33] Of the surviving examples of annotated newspapers, one of the most informative is the 1708–20 run of the *Evening Post* in the Burney collection. These copies were originally sent between Gabriel Walker of Chatham and his two sons in the City. In a marginal note, one brother is informed of the arrival of cloth and the despatch of various business orders. He is further advised that 'you may see p[r] this paper what an alteration there is in Bank Stock since I left you. If can get it at 108 or thereat tomorrow I will purchase.'[34] Taking pen to print was once again an essential contribution to advancing news and confidence. Trust in the authenticity and accuracy of printed news might also be confirmed or questioned by written emendation. It is also the beginning of what has been identified for the late eighteenth century as the spreading out of trust, of an increasingly depersonalized and outward-looking guarantee that matched the advancing anonymity of changing urban environments.[35]

In the second third of the century, the London evening papers and the weeklies, including *Applebee's Original Weekly Journal*, *Read's* and *Mist's*, were particularly important in expanding country distribution. The thrice-weekly evening papers, appearing at four or five o'clock in the afternoon, could copy the morning newspapers as well as cover the latest news including the arrivals of foreign ships. As Cranfield noted, the thrice-weekly evening papers were, after the *Gazette*, the most widely tapped news source for the growing number of country-printed newspapers.[36] Of the cheaper newspapers, there is no evidence to show that large numbers of penny or unstamped London thrice-weeklies, published between post days, reached the provinces. At least until the end of the century, no circulation network was available for them.[37] What developed was a tiered market, with a free delivery service available to stamped and

33   'Postscript' notice, *Flying Post*, 23 and 27 June, 28 July 1702.

34   *Evening Post*, 155, 10 Aug. 1710, BL, Burney Collection; similar examples survive at the Dorset County Museum in Dorchester, Leeds City Reference Library and Nottingham Central Library.

35   Hannah Barker, 'Medical Advertising and Trust in Late Georgian England', *Urban History*, 36:3 (2009), 379–98 (p. 397).

36   G. A. Cranfield, *The Development of the Provincial Newspaper, 1700–1760* (Oxford: Oxford University Press, 1962), pp. 31–4.

37   Harris, *London Newspapers*, p. 37.

post-day publications, and with other kinds of unstamped and non-post-day newspapers confined to circulation within London.[38]

In the second half of the century, many more newspapers and advertisers were published in the country towns, eventually offering local tradesmen and readers a more direct and immediate advertising and news service. Of the total newspapers published in the century, about one-fifth were provincial papers with the proportion rising steeply after 1780. In 1700 there were no provincial newspapers in England. Between 1701 and 1721, forty provincial newspapers were started, many proving an important prop to the printers who moved out of London in the early years of the century. William Bonny began the *Bristol Post-Boy* and Francis Burges, the *Norwich Post* in 1702. Farley established the *Exeter Postman* in 1704. Bliss launched the *Exeter Postboy* and Stephen Bryan, the *Worcester Post-Man* in 1709. A *News-Sheet* was also briefly issued by Thomas Jones in Shrewsbury in about 1705.[39] Of longer-lived newspapers, the *Weekly Courant* was published in Nottingham from 1712, the *Newcastle Courant* from 1711 and the *York Courant* from 1725. In 1730 there were about twenty provincial newspapers, about ten of which were of a decade's standing. Newspapers were then printed in Exeter, Reading, Canterbury, Bristol, Gloucester, Ipswich, Northampton, Bury St Edmunds, Worcester, Norwich, Stamford, Nottingham, Derby, Chester, Lincoln, Leeds, York and Newcastle.[40] As judged by tallies (and location counts) of surviving jobbing printing,[41] the 1740s might appear to be a period of consolidation rather than expansion, but between 1740 and 1746 alone, the number of provincial weekly newspapers in production increased from thirty-one to forty-two.[42] By 1760, over 130 had at some time been published. By 1780, over fifty English country newspapers were in production. In 1781, the total number of newspapers from England and Wales was seventy-six.

Throughout England, the array of newspapers was a large one in which long-distance runners were more an exception than the norm. The local newspaper almost always had to succeed against powerful obstacles including stamp taxes, distribution and production difficulties,

---

38   See Barker, *Newspapers, Politics and English Society*.

39   ShRO, Lloyd MSS 2118/290, Lloyd to Wroth, 6 July 1934.

40   R. M. Wiles, *Freshest Advices: Early Provincial Newspapers in England* (Columbus, OH: Ohio State University Press, 1965), provides a chronological chart in appendix B.

41   C. J. Mitchell, 'Provincial Printing in Eighteenth-Century Britain', *Publishing History*, 21 (1987), 5–24 (pp. 11, 18 and 21, fig. 1).

42   Harris, *London Newspapers*, p. 36.

metropolitan and regional competition, and local vested interests.[43] In London also, advertisers in all price and production ranges might be squeezed by new policies or co-operation between competitors, or might fall victim to one of the capital's general and recurrent financial slumps. The stability of long-running publications such as the *Public Advertiser*, the *London Evening Post* and *Lloyd's Evening Post*, all dominating London newspaper circulation from 1770 until the end of the century, contrasted sharply with the extremely short life of many of the advertisers. The greatly increased production of newspapers is, however, perhaps the most impressive feature of printing history in the final two decades of the eighteenth century. In 1782, the Post Office despatched just over three million London newspapers to the country. Ten years later the volume had doubled, and by 1796 the annual postal distribution of London newspapers stood at 8.6 million copies. The growth in provincial newspapers sent into London over these twenty years was even more marked. In 1782, nearly 46,000 country newspapers were mailed to the capital. In 1796, London readers took nearly 200,000 country newspapers via the post.[44]

In Wales (unlike the fast developing newspaper businesses in Scotland and Ireland),[45] local newspaper production lagged significantly behind that of England, largely because of the successful circuits developed by the printers of Bristol, Gloucester, Shrewsbury, Chester and Liverpool. Although Thomas Jones issued a prospectus for a Welsh newspaper in 1706, the first genuine news periodical, the *Cambrian*, was not established until January 1804. Printed at Swansea, the *Cambrian* was followed in 1808 by the publication of the *North Wales Gazette* at Bangor, and the *Carmarthen Journal* in 1810.[46]

In long-running newspapers from both the country towns and the capitals, an increasing proportion of the total space was devoted to advertising. After relatively modest insertions in newspapers of the first decade

43 Wiles, *Freshest Advices*; Cranfield, *Provincial Newspaper*.
44 'Report on Reform and Improvement of the Post Office', *Parliamentary Papers*, 1807, 2: 219, table.
45 See the useful chronological table of Scottish newspapers given in Mary Elizabeth Craig, *The Scottish Periodical Press, 1750–1789* (Edinburgh: Oliver and Boyd, 1931); for Ireland see Robert Munter, *The History of the Irish Newspaper, 1685–1760* (Cambridge: Cambridge University Press, 1967).
46 Details, David Jenkins, 'Newspapers for the Historian', *Journal of the Welsh Bibliographical Society*, 11:1 (1973–74), 68–84 (p. 70).

of the century, over a third of all the columns of a newspaper might be given over to advertisements by 1730. By mid-century, advertising was a financial mainstay for most newspapers published. By 1760, numerous examples can be found of newspapers with more than half of their columns given over to commercial notices. During the final third of the century, total available advertising space more than trebled. By the 1790s, few newspapers retained the traditional full essay on the front page; most were almost entirely filled with the boxes and block cuts of advertising notices and designs. This increase in newspaper advertising was not evenly paced, however. Many have noted the effect of the Stamp Act on the circulation of newspapers, but the Act was also an abrupt disincentive for English (and Scottish) advertisers, applying a shilling duty to each advertisement. The effect was immediate. The *Flying Post* was one of many newspapers not only changing from single sheet to one-and-a-half sheets to evade stamp duty, but also suddenly carrying less than a tenth of its usual number of advertisements. Thereafter, pressures eased, with the advertising tax remaining at one shilling for over forty years. It was eventually doubled in 1757, raised to 2s 6d in 1776 and advanced to three shillings in 1789.

Always a constraint, the advertising tax clearly did greatest damage in its earliest years, and the advertising market seems to have recovered from the first application of tax by the early 1720s. Late in 1727, certain London printers combined to raise advertising charges, even though this had not been a requirement of the recent 1725 Stamp Act. There are no obvious signs that the move reversed the growing demand in commercial notices. Indeed, early in 1728 the *Craftsman* announced a major extension to its advertising service:

> We hope that none of our Readers will take it amiss, that we have of late admitted so great a number of advertisements into this paper ... But as we found that they increased upon us every week (which must be allowed to be of some use to the towns as well as profit to us and the Government) we have put ourselves to a considerable expence by enlarging our paper and widening the columns for that purpose, without encroaching on the entertainment of our readers.[47]

Over the century, aggregate financial returns from such newspaper advertising increased sharply. The total payments of advertising duty

---

47   *The Country Journal: or, the Craftsman*, 2 Mar. 1728.

(even allowing for duty increases) rose from the £912 collected in 1713 to £3,158 in 1734, £7,915 in 1754, £33,662 in 1774, £46,284 in 1784, £69,943 in 1794 and £98,241 in 1798 (the last year for which gross figures are available).[48] The Treasury's covetousness did not jeopardize the health of the most popular newspapers, however. In 1746 the *London Daily Post and Daily Advertiser* carried 12,254 adverts which brought a post-tax profit of £753 10s. In 1771 the *Public Advertiser* carried 24,613 adverts which brought in £2,303 17s.[49] Assuming a three-shilling duty on each advertisement, the total number of advertisements placed in British newspapers (excluding Ireland) in 1798 totalled 654,946.

The increasing proportion of advertising duty paid by provincial newspapers is still the most striking feature of the duty returns for England and Wales in the final two decades of the century. The advertising duty paid by country newspapers amounted to about half of that collected in London by the 1760s, to two-thirds by the late 1770s, and after 1796 was never less than equal to that collected from the capital.[50] Even small provincial advertisers were at this time bringing in average post-tax advertising takings of £2 per week, which comprised almost half the full weekly profit.[51]

The usual cost of placing a newspaper notice after the increases forced by the 1712 Stamp Act was 2s 6d. At first, charges were apparently levied regardless of the length of the advertisement, but set notions of 'moderate length' and even numbers of lines were established by the 1720s. It is, however, impossible to give hard and fast rules about charges made and the costs incurred in printing newspaper advertisements. Most printers seem to have made individual decisions about each submission. In 1715, the *British Mercury* gave notice that 'advertisements not exceeding 10 Lines, will be taken at 2s. each, including the King's Duty, and one Penny for every Line above the said 10 Lines, which is cheaper than in any other Paper'.[52] By the 1730s, a standard ten to twelve lines' block cost between 1s 6d and 3s 6d, based on surviving printers' records. The most notable of these are the annotated advertisements in the *General Evening Post* for 1736, and the series of *London Daily Post* marked up by Henry Woodfall

48 Full tables are provided in A. Aspinall, 'Statistical Accounts of the London Newspapers in the Eighteenth Century', *EHR*, 63 (1948), 201–32.
49 Harris, 'Structure, Ownership and Control', p. 93.
50 NA, Audit Office Papers, A.O. 3/950 ff., cit., Aspinall, 'Statistical Accounts', p. 204.
51 Cranfield, *Provincial Newspaper*, p. 246.
52 *British Mercury*, 502, 12 Feb. 1715, p. 6.

in 1741 and 1743–46. In 1746 the *London Daily Post* published 12,254 advertisements, with an average income from each issue of £2 7s 6d. Discounts were offered for regular or share-owning clients, although it is also possible that proprietors were stepping in to support the newspaper during slack advertising periods.[53] In 1736 the *General Evening Post* published 2,435 advertisements of which 790 were charged at the cut-price rate of one shilling. This brought in an average of just under £1 for each issue. As the number of newspapers increased, so did disputes between local newspaper printers and the frequency of competitive reductions or special offers on advertising rates. In Ipswich in the 1730s, Craighton demanded 2s 6d per week for 'moderate length' advertisements of about an eighth of a column. In 1740 he offered a concessionary rate of two shillings per week for advertisements placed continuously for at least three weeks.[54] In northern Ireland at mid-century, Henry and Robert Joy charged advertisers in the *Belfast News-Letter* '2s.2d. the first Time, and 6d. half-Penny each Continuance'.

As a vehicle for increasing local trade the newspaper had a vested interest in promoting commerce. One study has suggested that, by 1740, a three-tier provincial press can be identified according to the number of advertisements accepted by newspaper proprietors. Leading the country papers were those such as the *Ipswich Journal*, the *Newcastle Courant* and the *York Courant*, accepting over two thousand advertisements per year.[55] As another study has argued, local newspaper development was limited by the potential for advertising in a locality, given geographical considerations and the existence or otherwise of a core–periphery regional network.[56] It is certainly the case that the two thousand or so annual advertisements taken in by the few premier provincial newspapers was well under a sixth of the annual number of notices in most large London journals of the same period. Nevertheless, many local newspapers served towns with far fewer businesses than in the districts most immediate to the metropolitan advertisers. Country newspapers also made connections between regional towns, making many local advertisements far more significant than the staple notices of large but distant manufacturers and retailers of luxury goods. During the second third of the century, the editorial

53   This and the preceding examples are discussed in Harris, *London Newspapers*, pp. 58–61.
54   *Ipswich Journal*, 9 May 1740.
55   Cranfield, *Provincial Newspaper*, p. 210.
56   Black, *English Press*, pp. 55–7.

and organizational labours involved in newspaper advertising certainly increased in line with the volume of new business. By the late 1720s it was already obvious that the potential profits from advertising were related to circulation and access. Indeed, as the coffee-house proprietors pointed out in their struggle with the newspaper publishers, the printers

> stipulate for *News*; not for *Advertisements*: Yet the Papers are ordinarily more than half full of them. The *Daily Post*, for Example, is often equipped with Thirty; which yield *Three Pounds Fifteen Shillings* that Day to the Proprietors, for the least: And sometimes that Paper has more. Well may they divide Twelve Hundred Pounds a Year and upwards: They are paid on both Hands; paid by the *Advertisers* for taking in *Advertisements*; and paid by the Coffee-Men for delivering them out.[57]

In summary, the 'Coffee-Men' argued, 'if the Coffee-Houses were to be shut up, I would ask what would become of *Advertisements*? Whether they would not be driven to their old Habitations, the City-Gates, The Corners of Streets, Tavern-Doors and Pissing Posts? And what would they be worth in such Situations?'[58]

The printers were increasingly keen to employ agents to collect advertisements, and most of those hired frequented the coffee-houses as obvious meeting and collecting points. In their abortive attempt to found their own advertiser, the London coffee-house proprietors proposed to pay an agent sixpence for each advertisement taken in.[59] By the 1750s, the *Gazetteer* was employing a 'Proper Person' to collect advertisements submitted to specified booksellers and coffee-houses.[60] In the provinces, twopence was paid to certain newsmen for taking in advertisements. The newspaper printers continued to trawl widely for new advertisers. By the 1770s most journals listed a dozen or more agents or postmasters taking in adverts in the town of publication and in neighbouring districts. By 1770, *Aris's Birmingham Gazette; or, The General Correspondent* announced that advertisements would be accepted by Richard Baldwin of Paternoster Row and named booksellers and agents in Shrewsbury, Wolverhampton, Worcester,

---

57 Anon., *Case of the Coffee-Men*, p. 16.
58 Anon., *Case of the Coffee-Men*, p. 17.
59 Anon., *Case of the Coffee-Men*, p. 23.
60 Robert Louis Haig, *The Gazetteer, 1735–1797: A Study in the Eighteenth-Century English Newspaper* (Carbondale, IL: Southern Illinois University Press, 1960), p. 31.

Bridgnorth, Lichfield, Stafford, Dudley, Walsall, Stratford, Tamworth, Atherstone and Kidderminster. Edinburgh newspapers also included agents south of the border, in Newcastle, Kendal, Longtown and Durham.

Such advertising was bolstered by the enlargement of the distributional network. The construction of turnpikes and new transport routes was itself a major stimulus to the development of the provincial printing and bookselling trade. The metropolitan papers in particular, benefited from improvements in transport and the increasing ease with which they could be received in the provinces. A radial network from London was supplemented from about 1730 by smaller networks centred on the major regional capitals. The further activity of the six Post Office Clerks of the Road, personally responsible for services to different parts of the country and some of them shareholders in newspapers, ensured that by the mid-1760s over twenty thousand London papers were despatched three times a week to the provinces.[61] With increased access to new routes, the influence of the metropolitan press was advanced while the development of cross-posts for routes between country towns provided new networks for the country advertiser.[62] As early as 1714, Henry Crossgrove was boasting that his *Norwich Gazette* 'spreads all over Norfolk and Suffolk, parts of Lincolnshire and Yorkshire'.[63] The early circulation of the provincial advertisers should not of course be exaggerated – in the 1720s the weekly edition of most of these newspapers was probably about a thousand copies. After mid-century however, many local newspapers also increased their edition sizes. The *York Chronicle* sold well over two thousand copies a week by the 1760s.[64]

The use of agents in conjunction with the postal routes was a further stimulus to the volume and diversity of advertising copy. By 1755, Benjamin Collins had arranged for his *Salisbury Journal* to be sold by booksellers in Andover, Bath, Blandford, Bristol, Chippenham, Devizes, Dorchester, Farringdon, Gloucester, London, Lymington, Marlborough, Newport, Oxford, Poole, Portsmouth, Reading, Shaftsbury, Sherborne

---

61   Parliamentary investigation into the Post Office, Mar. 1764.

62   As early as 1696 an important cross-post was established between Exeter and Bristol. For an authoritative contemporary account of the next century's development, see A. E. Hopkins (ed.), *Ralph Allen's Own Narrative, 1720–1761* (London: Postal History Society, 1960).

63   BL, Add. MSS 5,853 (Cole Collection, vol. 52), pp. 106–7. Crossgrove to the Revd John Strype, 2 Dec. 1714.

64   Wiles, *Freshest Advices*, pp. 96–100.

and Southampton. In the same year, Felix Farley's *Bristol Journal* was distributed through agencies in thirty-eight different towns from Penzance to Liverpool. In the 1740s, the *York Courant* listed forty-three provincial distributors. In addition to the bookseller-agents, the newspaper printers employed newsmen and post-riders to widen circulations. Thanks to the 'disappearance' of many of these men – either through abduction or abscondence – we have lively descriptions of their appearance and likely travelling route. In 1772 Thomas Wood, printer and supplier of the *Shrewsbury Chronicle* to mid-Wales, engaged one Daniel Morris to promote his newspaper throughout Montgomeryshire. Morris set off with newspapers and other property belonging to Wood and was never heard of again. For months afterwards Wood was advertising a reward for the apprehension of a twenty-one-year-old youth who was 'of a dark complexion, speaks rather broken English, lisps a little in his speech and steps very light'. Equally sinister notices in the newspapers of Northampton and Sherborne included descriptions of the likely routes of freckled men with limps carrying stolen newspapers.[65]

The essential question for readers, newspapers proprietors and advertisers was one of trust and confidence. Greater competition between newspapers increased attempts to achieve professional standards of good copy, but there could be no guarantee of the veracity of trade or personal advertisements. The questionable nature of many advertisements, especially for products such as patent medicines, claiming particular effects and cures, tested public trust in advertising throughout the century.[66] The clarity of many of the wordier advertisements improved, as did the quality of descriptive illustrations (although these remained rare). Wording also contained more assurances of reliability, clearer addresses and, for the most part, the promotion of a business or service as one with its own standards, respectability and proven competence. It might also be suggested that trust was spreading geographically. Furthermore, socially, trust was becoming more institutionalized than process-based[67] in the sense that the newspaper produced more objectified evidence that relied more on regularity and familiarity of its material, printed existence

---

65 *Northampton Mercury*, 40, 30 Jan. 1721; *Sherborne Mercury*, 16, 7 June 1737.
66 See Barker, 'Medical Advertising and Trust'.
67 For an elaboration of process-based trust associated with past or present individual exchanges, see Lynne G. Zucker, 'Production of Trust: Institutional Sources of Economic Structure, 1840–1920', in *Research in Organizational Behavior* 8, ed. B. M. Staw and L. L. Cummings (Greenwich, CT: JAI Press, 1986), pp. 55–111 (esp. p. 60).

than on face-to-face confirmation. The advertisements of earlier in the century, conveying letters of appreciation from satisfied customers and crude 'certificates' of inspection and description were replaced by more detailed and, in most cases, less spectacular assertions. Credulous men and women continued to fall for claims about unmatchable cures for venereal disease,[68] and boasts and bravado were not eliminated from front-page advertising columns, especially in some country newspapers. Nonetheless, increased circulation, wider and more experienced readerships and greater familiarity with newspapers and advertising techniques all brought greater confidence and approval. The increasing number of advertisements, carried by the increasing number of newspapers in all their variety of place and time of issue, was of itself testimony to the increased trust placed in them by business communities and their customers and clients. The structure of publishing, supported by the claimed authority of many London and regional city newspapers, well-established networks of delivery, and the longevity of some titles, all contributed to the effectiveness of advertising and the confidence placed in it, even if such considerations could not always reassure the misinformed or dissatisfied.

68   P. S. Brown, 'Medicines Advertised in Eighteenth-Century Bath Newspapers', *Medical History*, 20:2 (Apr. 1976), 152–68 (p. 159).

7

The Advertisers

The surge in advertising copy sent to newspaper proprietors, and the consequent expansion in space allocated to notices and in monies received, are the best testimony to the effectiveness of advertising in the promotion of trade and services. Although claims that over half the population of London was regularly in touch with the content of the newspaper columns[1] must be exaggerated, trading patterns were certainly altered by the intervention of newsprint. In London and at port towns, merchants used the newspapers to detail the latest unloaded or expected goods from overseas or from home coastal districts. Manufacturers used newspapers in much the same way, introducing new products and promoting special lines. Regular and relatively cheaply printed advertising, circulating both locally and at great distance, was adopted as a solution to specific problems in underdeveloped and difficult markets. It is clear that many tradesmen were both optimistic and anxious about the effect of newspaper notices, even though it is difficult to gauge either the extent of each investment or the likely returns of individual advertising outlays without knowing the full turnover of the business.

Nevertheless, the widening of newspaper circulation was the key to the expansion plans of hundreds of small manufacturing, finishing, craft and retailing businesses. As early as the second decade of the eighteenth century, promoters were confident of the potential in printed notices carried from London to the provincial market.[2] Obviously, profit margins on individual goods had to be sufficient to support investment in expensive advertising. Ordinary foodstuffs were never the subject of retail advertisements in metropolitan newspapers and, increasingly during the century, featured in provincial papers only when a particular market price or levy was fixed. Likewise, it is perfectly true that early London newspaper advertising was dominated by notices for books, pamphlets and patent medicines – all

---

1 Adriano Bruttini, 'Advertising and the Industrial Revolution', *Economic Notes*, 4:2–3 (May–Dec. 1973), 90–[116] (p. 109).
2 NA SPD 35, 18/117, examination of Hugh Meere, 1719.

sold and even printed or made up by the printer or agent booksellers and shopkeepers. Most advertisements in Defoe's *Review*, for example, were typically restricted to new publications and popular restoratives. These ranged from 'Rhombi Scoleteini: Or, the Lozenges for Killing Worms' to the 'Famous Chymical Secret for the Tooth-Ach'.

By the late 1720s, however, journal advertising was rapidly diversifying. Certain newspapers and printers maintained old ways or excluded particular types of advertisement, but although there remained an obvious division between advertising in metropolitan and in country newspapers, varying mixes of national and local advertisements appeared in almost all journals. Newspaper advertising as received by country readers was divided between the ubiquitous 'London-style' notices for patent medicines, books and luxury goods, and local notices by local tradesmen and operatives. London merchants and retailers advertised in country newspapers, giving addresses for direct order or for contacting local agents. More obviously, London newspapers also included advertisements of local interest to Londoners as well as those attractive to country readers. In *Mist's Weekly Journal*, for example, property notices dominate the advertising sections which wholly comprise the final two of its four pages. In most London dailies, requests for houses in particular vicinities vied with local employment notices or advertisements for services and goods for those living in the capital.

In developing national advertising through local newspapers, English regional printers established London agents to accept advertisements and leave copies of provincial newspapers in advertised London coffee-houses and printing offices. This was largely so that potential clients could see the newspapers that might feature their adverts. The ledgers of Robert Gosling show him acting as one such intermediary in placing advertisements in the London press in the 1730s.[3] During the early 1740s, the *York Courant*, *Salisbury Journal*, *Leeds Mercury*, *Reading Mercury*, *Norwich Mercury*, *Newcastle Courant* and *Birmingham Gazette* all established metropolitan agencies for advertisements to be taken in and copies of their newspapers read.[4] It is noticeable that in contrast to the variety of local goods and services advertised in the provincial newspapers, the early advertisements placed in metropolitan papers by London agents concerned just two familiar wares: books and medicines. Both could be ordered through the local

3 Bodleian Library, MSS Eng. Misc. c. 296, 'Gentleman's Ledger B'.
4 Michael Harris, *London Newspapers in the Age of Walpole: A Study of the Origins of the Modern English Press* (London: Associated University Presses, 1987), p. 220, n. 25.

bookseller or the agent of the wholesaler or publisher. Thus, at least before the 1770s, the *national* network sponsored by print was largely restricted to wares that the bookseller-stationer was already selling. The same does not obtain for advertising within the locality, where the newspapers served, created and reinforced varied commercial marts and advertised produce sold by those with no connections with the printing trade.

During the final quarter of the century, however, the import and manufacture of a great range of luxury goods was boosted by countrywide newspaper promotion. The successful retailing of many new consumer goods in remote market towns could not have been achieved without the printed advertising and distributional services of the newspaper proprietors and their agents. 'Fashion' required a responsive and adaptable promotional medium. Change was self-generating: the very fact that the provinces could be in contact with the capital underpinned the projection of fashion products, and particular wares took a very high printed profile. Different newspapers with their different readerships, distribution networks and house policies, became associated with the promotion of different forms of advertising. Of the quality newspapers, the *London Evening Post* appears to have refused advertisements for quack medicines – which, with notices for books, continued even by the 1770s to form the staple of most back and front-page columns. In the *Post Boy*, *Flying Post* and other popular newspapers, most advertisements were for books, lotteries, medicines and luxury items. Advertisements for teas litter the provincial newspapers of the second half of the eighteenth century. Promotions for goods aimed at female consumers were especially encouraged, and dress and household items were major advertising features of the century. Some other famous examples of the concern shown by manufacturers in newspaper advertising have been well documented. In the 1770s and 1780s, the products of both Boulton and Wedgwood benefited from promotional puffs, most of which were invented by the manufacturers themselves. Boulton and his main rivals in domestic goods, Taylor and Gimblett, issued dozens of different letters, addresses and other promotional ploys in the final third of the century.[5] Less noticed in business histories of the eighteenth century are the notices

---

5 Examples from the *Birmingham Gazette; or, General Correspondent*, 1760–89, cited in Neil McKendrick, 'The Commercialization of Fashion', and 'Josiah Wedgwood and the Commercialization of the Potteries', in *The Birth of a Consumer Society: The Commercialization of Eighteenth-Century England*, ed. Neil McKendrick, John Brewer and J. H. Plumb (London: Europa, 1982), pp. 34–99, 100–45 (pp. 72–3, 123–6).

inserted by London wholesalers and retailers for manufactured goods from the area served by the local or distributed newspaper. Typical of these is the notice 'To the Founders and Manufacturers of Brass' in *Aris's Birmingham Gazette* in January 1770.

Some fashionable resorts clearly attracted greater than usual attention from advertisers of both luxury goods and the increasingly competitive stalwarts of the newspaper columns, books and cure-alls. P. S. Brown's study of medical adverts in the Bath press records not only the deluge of pills and powders descending on the counters of Bath bookshops at mid-century, but also how these gave way to advertisements for dress fabrics and other fashion items every September–December in the opening months of the new 'season'. By March, 'Daffy's elixir' and 'Dr Anderson's Pills' again ruled the back and front-page columns of the *Bath Chronicle* and *Advertiser*. All the while, the appetite for printed advertising was apparently increasing. In 1750 the *Bath Journal* carried advertisements for thirty different medical products, in 1770 the *Bath Chronicle* featured eighty different products, and in 1790 a total of 114 different medicines were listed in the same paper over the course of the year.[6]

As has been well discussed, many of the consumer industries serviced by print were concerned with the growing leisure market.[7] In this the promotional work of the printer-stationer was particularly important. Bath was itself the most obvious example of a town exploiting print to advertise its attractions. Once Bath's 'season' was established and visitors came in their hundreds to try the waters and parade the rooms, print continued to encourage local trade. From the mid-1720s when *Brice's Weekly Journal* published by Andrew Brice at Exeter was trumpeting the virtues of Bath waters, and from the 1730s when Felix Farley actually began printing in the town, there survive sheet advertisements for hoop petticoats, fashionable periwigs, musical accompaniments and a torrent of consumer wares. Pleasure gardens, concerts and plays were all opened and attended by virtue of printed notice. Where rival newspapers competed for the right to inform the public of local events, popular entertainments could in fact exploit newspapers for financial support. Those advertisers particularly

6 P. S. Brown, 'The Venders of Medicines Advertised in Eighteenth-Century Bath Newspapers', *Medical History*, 19:4 (Oct. 1975), 352–69 (p. 353); and P. S. Brown, 'Medicines Advertised in Eighteenth-Century Bath Newspapers', *Medical History*, 20:2 (April 1976), 152–68.
7 In particular, J. H. Plumb, 'The Commercialization of Leisure in Eighteenth-Century England', in McKendrick, Brewer and Plumb (eds), *Birth of a Consumer Society*, pp. 265–85.

valued by a readership and offering exclusive information could hold the newspaper proprietor to ransom. An advertisement in the first issue of the *London Daily Post* in 1734, for example, shows that the managers of the five leading London theatres used the occasion of a new newspaper to combine and force an advertising monopoly.[8]

Although leisure advertising, including notices for local theatres and race meetings, became increasingly prominent in the provincial press, the staple of most country newspaper advertising was property and the servicing of a predominantly agricultural economy. From almost the first years of the local newspaper, advertisers included craftsmen in search of work and employers wanting assistants, housekeepers and servants. Also announced were local fairs, many of which were for hiring labour, together with the sale of shops, horses and business stock (usually after failure or formal bankruptcy). Property was heavily advertised, especially houses and farms to let, but notices for the sale or lease of parcels of land formed the majority of advertisements in many country newspaper columns. For about the first ten years from the *Belfast News-Letter*'s establishment in 1738, the number of advertisements in each issue increased very gradually, from filling half the third column to filling all the columns of the back page. On average, a third of its space comprised advertisements for local land and properties. From the first issues of many provincial newspapers there was also a large number of advertisements offering rewards for the recovery of lost banknotes, all of which, it was noted, 'have been stopt at the bank'. Numerous other reward notices ranged from requests to apprehend runaway journeymen to pleas to find missing dogs or cattle. Industrial notices, which were few in number until the last two decades of the century, varied from region to region. In the Midlands, newspapers such as the *Nottingham Journal* advertised sales of stocking frames, looms and shares in mills, mines and manufacturing workshops.

Attracting custom

Advertising requirements brought numerous changes in printing display and design. Typographical advances were matched by the adoption of new woodcuts and metal engraving techniques. Printers altered column format with increased advertising demand and inserted cuts according both to

8   Harris, *London Newspapers*, p. 54.

their own preferences and to advertisers' designs. Newspaper printers strove to buy in new sets of type, improve the quality of printing, paper and layout, and compete in finely cut capitals, factotums and mastheads. The most striking of these in the country newspapers included the full-breadth town panoramas of the *Leeds Mercury*, the *Norwich Gazette* from 1725, and the *Derby Mercury* and *Newcastle Courant*.

The changing face of the newspaper fuelled much contemporary comment and, from an early date, not all were happy with what they saw. Addison in 1710 accused newspaper publishers of sharp practice:

> The great Art in writing Advertisements, is the finding out a proper Method to catch the Reader's Eye; without which, a good Thing may pass over unobserved or be lost among Commissions of Bankrupt. Asterisks and Hands were formerly of great Use for this Purpose, of late Years the N.B. has been much in Fashion; as also little Cuts and Figures, the Invention of which we must ascribe to the Author of Spring-Trusses. I must not here omit the blind Italian character, which being scarce legible, always, finds and detains the Eye, and gives the curious Reader something like the Satisfaction of prying into a Secret.[9]

Fifty years later, Dr Johnson was ridiculing the saturation of newspapers with adverts: 'the trade of advertising is now so near to perfection, that it is not easy to propose any improvement'. Adverts had become so common that ever greater extravagance was necessary to catch readers' attention.[10]

The earliest newspaper advertisements were set contiguously with news items. Unless large sections were republished in successive issues, repeat advertisements had to be reconstructed. The more manageable alternative – essential once advertisements numbered twenty or more to an issue – was the use of made-up blocks, preserved between issues and treated like mastheads, colophons and factotums. In fact, repeats of exactly the same positioning were extremely rare, and the efficient ordering of precomposed notices required the use of vertical columns into which the blocks could be repositioned. Despite this, many newspapers – especially those outside London – remained without dividing columns until the second quarter of the century. In some the space to be filled by advertisements had been inflated by the printing of the additional sheet to avoid stamp duty. In such

9   *Tatler*, 224, 12–14 Sept. 1710.
10   Samuel Johnson, *The Idler*, 2 vols (London, 1761), vol. 1, p. 227 (no. 40, 20 Jan. 1759).

newspapers, advertisements often continued to use whatever additional type was available to pack space or to distinguish commercial notices from the surrounding text. Arrangements of asterisks were obvious and favourite ploys, as were small casts of pointing hands (such as ☞ or ☞). Much used in the *London Mercury* from 1682, hands and 'N.B.'s were liberally scattered in many early London journals.

Other alternatives were more individual. The *London Evening Post*, printed by Edward Berrington in Silver Street, Bloomsbury, carried advertisements inset with clusters of special types. It would certainly be a mistake to interpret all eccentric variations of type within early newspapers as design features. Often the printer simply had insufficient body type to serve for the entire newspaper. It has been suggested that this may also explain that frequency of italics mocked by Addison.[11] Throughout the century, type remained an expensive but effective weapon in bids to increase newspaper circulations. Divisions were widened as the more successful printers stocked greater ranges of both very large and very small sizes of body type and modified presses to take larger sheets as a regular item. By mid-century, Caslon type, founded from the 1730s, was taking over from imported Dutch materials in the richer, usually city-based, printing firms.[12] At the same time, the premium on space, accentuated in mainland Britain by the 1712 and 1725 Stamp Acts, often forced reductions in the size of print used in advertisements. Where this was combined with the user of coarser paper, legibility was often disastrously diminished. Repetition of a notice over several editions was probably a wise insurance policy on the part of the advertiser.

Metropolitan competition in design was increasingly severe from the 1740s but, in provincial towns, printers also aspired to buy in new founts to attract greater custom and upstage rivals. In Ipswich, Craighton was quick to abandon the type he inherited from Bagnall and, in Norwich, Henry Crossgrove flamboyantly announced the arrival of his new letters in 1725 and again in 1742. Thomas Boddeley was only one among dozens of local printers between 1740 and 1760 proudly proclaiming their recent investment in new Caslon type. In Boddeley's case he was also anxious to announce his advance order of the founts and that he was ready to

---

11   R. M. Wiles, *Freshest Advices: Early Provincial Newspapers in England* (Columbus, OH: Ohio State University Press, 1965), p. 55.
12   Typographical changes in English newspaper illustration are considered in Stanley Morison, *The English Newspaper, 1622–1932* (Cambridge: Cambridge University Press, 1932).

take priority bookings.[13] Other country printers used standard decorations as ingeniously as they could. Attempting to follow London models, the *Chelmsford and Colchester Chronicle* added increasing numbers of flowers to the divisions between articles during the late 1760s. The match between assorted flowers and elderly type was not always a happy one.

In addition to shortcomings in design, slipshod composition often resulted from the inexperience of printers in the early years, working to the tight and demanding schedules of newspaper jobbing. Even Benjamin Collins's newspaper was not free from blunder. His own advertisement for 'Printed in the neatest Manner ... Warrants of Removal and Misdemeanour, Passes with Certificates, and any particular Sorts of Blanks printedi f [sic] required', was not likely to inspire confidence.[14] Nevertheless, professional standards clearly improved during the second quarter of the century. As the competition for advertising increased between the large circulation newspapers, so frequent modifications were made to the presentation of notices, including the width of column lines, the design of section headings, the use of flowers and dividing space lines, and the separate 'boxing' of advertisements. Black letter 'Advertisement' headings had been adopted in many late seventeenth and early-eighteenth-century London newspapers, but by the 1730s advertisements in several newspapers, including the *Grub Street Journal*, were prefaced by their own black letter titles.

The way in which advertisements were put together and arranged on the page was also revised as more and more of the space in a newspaper was given over to commercial notices. The increasing number of advertisements presented problems for swift and accurate composition at the same time as greater competition between newspapers forced tighter schedules. All printers were aware that finer quality of workmanship was as much an inducement to traders to place advertisements in newspapers as was the greater availability of more versatile type, ornaments and engraving. Even the best products of Caslon or Fry were no substitute for guarantees of accurate and reliable copy. In 1744 the *Evening Post* relocated its advertising to the two inner pages, reserving the outer pages for news and official bulletins. Other metropolitan dailies retained interspersed news, including the *Gazetteer and London Daily Advertiser*, which by 1760 filled at least two of its four columns on the front page with advertisements as

13   *Bath Journal*, 26 Nov. 1750.
14   *Salisbury Journal*, 2 Dec. 1740; reference kindly supplied by Christine Ferdinand.

well as up to all of the third page and three-quarters of the back page. By 1770, all four columns of the front page of the *Public Advertiser* were usually filled by advertisements, as well as almost all of pages three and four. By 1771, however, the *Gazetteer* belatedly followed the *Evening Post*, moving its news from page two to page four in order to expedite rapid and exact composition.[15]

The greatest variation in styles of advertising, however, both between traders and between newspapers, was brought about by the use of woodcuts, metal engraving and cast trade ornaments. It is still not clear how many advertisers arranged for the cutting of illustrations prior to taking the text to the newspaper publisher. Clients using only one newspaper probably commissioned the printer to cut the design himself or to find a suitable engraver. Many printers employed local cutters to prepare the more difficult commercial advertisements and many newspaper offices accumulated large collections of display blocks. Ten parcels of woodcuts were included in the stock of Orion Adams, the son of Manchester's leading jobbing printer and publisher of its first newspaper.[16] By at least the 1720s, however, many advertisers were bringing precut blocks to the newspaper office, probably after initial inquiries as to the appropriate size. Certainly, consultation between advertiser, printer and cutter must have occurred over the incorporated use of large display capitals. It is also apparent that many cuts executed for particular advertisers were taken to several different newspapers. Some may have been sent out from London along with supplies of the product they advertised. Cuts for medicines such as the ever-popular Daffy's elixir (an alcohol-based laxative) were certainly uniform across most of the regional newspapers, proudly displaying recognizable trademarks. After mid-century, the woodcut or *in situ* cut in metal was largely replaced by finer metal or copperplate engraving. The greater expense of the metal cut probably encouraged greater reuse of the same engraving in different newspapers. By then, however, the surge in the number of advertisers forced many printers to exclude or charge heavy premiums for cuts on account of the limited space.

Of the early newspapers, the *Post Boy*, *Post Man* and *Flying Post* led the way in cuts either side of the title in the masthead. In 1711 the printer of

15 Harris, *London Newspapers*, p. 56; Robert Louis Haig, *The Gazetteer, 1735–1797: A Study in the Eighteenth-Century English Newspaper* (Carbondale, IL: Southern Illinois University Press, 1960), pp. 124–5.
16 CCRO SF/180, sale inventory of Adams, 1748.

the *Post Boy*, Lucy Beardwell of Black Friars, introduced large cut capitals on the front page, a feature soon rivalled by the large factotums printed by Dryden Leach in the *Post Man*. The *Flying Post*, now printed by William Hurt of Great Carter Lane, responded with a striking masthead ornament of a gentleman writing for the next post. The first advertisements illustrated by a woodcut were for William Mason, writing master, with his sign of the quill pen in the *Flying Post* for 19 and 26 December 1702, and for Inwood's chocolate, featuring a chocolate-making machine in the *Daily Courant* for 17 March 1703. Another regular early advertising cut in the *Flying Post* featured a globe to advertise the maps and geographical instruments for sale at Willdy's toy shop in Ludgate Street.[17] If Addison was wrong in attributing the introduction of cuts to truss dealers, purveyors of medical instruments and medicines were certainly early commissioners of both simple woodcuts and elegant metal engravings. Most frequent of the notices in Defoe's *Review*, and always accompanied by a cut, was the advertisement for Bartlett's spring-steel trusses and 'divers instruments to help the weak and crooked'. The cut appeared many times in the *Review*, but particularly frequently in issues from summer 1706 to spring 1707. The paucity of surviving runs of many early newspapers frustrates analysis of the recurrence and remodelling of advertising illustrations. Study of all issues of *Mist's* published between June 1725 and June 1726, however, reveals an average of four cuts to each issue. The most popular cuts were the several designs for the 'Anodyne Necklace' and that of the sign of the 'Black Boy and Comb' for the 'Hungary-Water Warehouse'. The Anodyne Necklace, for the ease of teething infants, was featured in numerous newspapers, with frequent changes of new or recut illustration. As included in the *Daily Post* in the 1720s, the Necklace design also represented a major advance in cutting skills as well as a departure from the set square block which framed most early cuts.

Various advertisers introduced or remodelled a display cut in order to invigorate a long-running campaign. Unillustrated notices for the Hungary-Water Warehouse had been a feature of several newspapers' columns, including those of the *Craftsman*, before a new cut for the 'Black Boy and Comb' was introduced on 12 December 1730. This cut became one of the most familiar newspaper illustrations of the second third of the century. Such familiarity was accentuated by the near absence of topical allusion in advertising illustration. Only the most regular

17   As in the edition of 4 April 1713.

investors in advertising designs attempted up-to-the-minute references. A rare example is the use of a large moon-face cut, relating to an imminent eclipse of the sun, inserted by the promoters of the Anodyne Necklace in the *Craftsman* four times in September and October 1725.[18]

More important than the variety or quality of the earliest cuts was the support offered to a particular advertising campaign by the use of a recurring symbol, trade sign or trade illustration. Before mid-century, emblematic cuts were popular, but also increasingly challenged by small portraits of the actual products or services on offer. The Black Boy and Comb cut was, for example, placed against that for Leadbetter and Boddington, blacksmiths, in the *Craftsman* for 2 June 1733. The Hungary-Water advertisement epitomizes the emblematic sign; the black-smiths illustrate their business by an example of their wares. In September 1725, *Mist's* accepted a new cut from the candlemaker, Richard Carter, representing his sign of the half-moon. Two months later, a rival tallow chandler, Thomas Rawlinson, chose not a sign but a beautifully detailed illustration of his craft. Sometimes the choice between an emblem and a craft drawing was obligatory. Certain trades and services were too complex or diverse to be illustrated. It could be misleading or restrictive to depict just one object or activity. In many cases – and the Hungary-Water notice is an instance – the emblem was reproduced on the product itself as a guarantee of quality and authenticity. The choice of design might also be determined by the operations of rivals. In July 1726, John Pindar elected to illustrate his advertisement for trusses by his sign of the Black Boy. With so many newspaper illustrations of trusses then circulating, Pindar's was the more distinctive for portraying his trade sign.

During the second half of the century, however, most London newspapers abandoned the use of the illustrative cut. This was largely for reasons of space, with increasing demand for column inches and rising charges for notices above 'moderate length'. Many provincial newspapers also abandoned cuts. By 1785 Joshua Jenour was printing advertisements in the *Daily Advertiser* in identical format using a large black capital to open each notice. The pages were divided into three columns, each of which contained up to thirty advertisements. With the newspaper now four-fifths full of advertising, the effect was masterly.

The affection for cuts by many English country printers and advertisers

18 See also Francis Doherty, *A Study in Eighteenth-Century Advertising Methods: The Anodyne Necklace* (Lewiston, NY: Edwin Mellen Press, 1992).

also waned. Panoramas in many provincial mastheads were replaced by finely cast display type. Cuts in the *Chelmsford and Colchester Chronicle* were abandoned and the advertisements – many extremely long and verbose – were set out with elegant use of blank space. Chase's *Norwich Mercury* is a standard example of a provincial newspaper taking a variety of cuts in its early numbers, but bereft of cuts by the mid-1760s. In some country newspapers, however, where space was not always so tight, advertising decorations were continued. In the late 1770s and early 1780s, various cuts were still used in *Aris's Birmingham Gazette*, including the mice for James Poulty's rodent-destroying paste and the medallion for Pullin's antiscorbutic pills. Some provincial newspapers even increased their use of advertising ornaments during the second half of the century.

In all newspapers, however, unillustrated notices easily outnumbered those with cuts. Throughout the century, the majority of advertisements remained without illustration. Some provincial newspapers did continue liberal forms of display decoration. By 1761, for example, *Aris's Birmingham Gazette* displayed advertisements in the three columns of its pages in a stylish mix of boxes, notices in different sizes of type, black letter and italic, and introductory capitals. The overall effect, however, was to satisfy advertisers with the appearance of the columns: there was indeed no need to commission a cut. The *Gazette*'s increase from four to five columns on each page in July 1776 also ensured that the number of advertisements could be greatly increased without loss of quality in presentation.

For most advertisers, the message remained strictly letter-bound. Their words-only advertisements ranged from short, boldly printed messages to prolix recommendations and assertions. In 1759, Dr Johnson complained that 'advertisements are now so numerous that they are very negligently perused, and it is therefore become necessary to gain attention by magnificence of promises, and by eloquence sometimes sublime and sometimes pathetic'.[19] Familiar slogans and recommendations were often retained for generations. Daffy's elixir (the second most frequently advertised medicine from P. S. Brown's survey of newspapers, 1744–1800) was still for sale in 1910, and Hooper's 'Female Pills' (the fourth most popular advertisement) was still sold in 1907 at their eighteenth-century price and 'with the advertising copy remarkably like that of 1744, many phrases being identical'.[20] From at least the 1720s, written testimonials were used to convince or

19   Johnson, *The Idler*, vol. 1, p. 225 (no. 40, 20 Jan. 1759).
20   Brown, 'Medicines Advertised', pp. 154–5.

reassure buyers. Most of the famous potions and cures were at some time accompanied by long quotations from satisfied customers. Nathaniel Godbold assembled aristocratic recommendations for his ubiquitous 'Vegetable Balsam', while others competed with rival lists of rectors and civic worthies. In the case of several advertisements for remedies for venereal disease, readers were provided with the names and addresses of satisfied customers prepared to allow personal inspection. By the end of the century, some of the testimony was very skilfully presented. Verse was increasingly popular. The Bath newspapers included 'lines addressed to N. Godbold Esq ... Proprietor of the celebrated Vegetable Balsam, on seeing a print representing a view of his elegant Mansion at Godalming, Surrey: Written by a Young Lady of the City of Bath as a small mark of her gratitude for the restoration of her mother's health.'[21] The originator of the Balsam is revealed to be a man of both wealth and taste, a man who has built a considerable house from the continuing custom of satisfied clients.

Comparative advertising was commonplace, with many notices punctuated by scathing references to rival products. A mid-century advert advised that Godfrey's Cordial was universally known as 'Lord have Mercy', actually the same name as the old mortality lists (see above, pp. 87, 90) but here apparently 'alluding to the affected Squall of hireling Nurses, on finding their Charge dead after administering an over Dose thereof'.[22] There are several surviving agreements, like that between Richard Smith, the bookseller, and Henry Rhodes, the printer, excluding the advertisements of rivals while a particular set of notices ran their course.[23] Advertising duels were fought ferociously. In the late 1720s, that between two manufacturers of 'clock-lamps' ran for over a year in several journals including the *Craftsman* and *Daily Post*. In December 1729, Leonard Ashburne of the Sugar Loaf in Paternoster Row had inserted an illustrated notice for his 'new-invented chamber-lamps: or, the never failing burning light ... being the only true and certain light'. Ashburne's 'new-invented clock-lamp' appeared some months later in 1730 adorned with an intricate cut showing four models of candle and oil lamps. Later that year, J. Walker advertised his 'original new-invented clock-lamp' with a cut of his 'Bell and Horse' trade sign. In the issue of 2 January,

---

21 *Bath Chronicle*, 31 Oct. 1799, cited by Brown, 'Venders of Medicine', p. 354.
22 *Bath Advertiser*, 12 Nov. 1757, cited by Brown, 'Medicines Advertised', p. 156.
23 Cyprian Blagden, 'A Bookseller's Memorandum Book, 1695–1720', in *Studies in the History of Accounting*, ed. A. C. Littleton and B. S. Yamey (Homewood, IL: Richard D. Irwin, and London: Sweet and Maxwell, 1956), pp. 255–65 (p. 257).

the notices of Ashburne and of Walker appeared juxtaposed. In the *Daily Post* of 6 January and the *Craftsman* of 16 January, Walker changed the accompanying cut to that of an illustration of the upright clock-candle, but also altered his written puff, claiming 'it neither daubs the Finger nor the Place whereon it stands, as others do; especially the counterfeit Lamp sold in Pater-noster-Row'. In the *Craftsman* of 23 January, Ashburne complains in a rider to his usual notice that 'a malicious and ill-designing Advertisement was set forth by the Lamp Pretender in Cheapside', and cautions the public to compare the products of both manufacturers. The printer of the *Craftsman*, however, continues to place both clock notices side by side in the advertising columns. Ashburne does not advertise in the *Craftsman* again; Walker continues to place his advertisement in the issue of 30 January and regularly thereafter. It is now impossible to know how the printer played off the two manufacturers. Possibly he accepted a larger payment by Walker not only to continue the knocking copy, but to place the rival advertisements next to each other. Whatever the case, the incident highlighted once more the power of public newspaper advertising and its manipulative possibilities.

8

Intelligence

Print ensured that financial and commercial information was published and circulated with increasing regularity. As publishers' methods and practices evolved during the eighteenth century, greater reliability was also claimed – and, in general, accepted. The gathering of financial and commercial information and the efficiency of its publication became increasingly specialist tasks. Above all, the nature and contemporary perception of 'publication' was of fundamental importance to the collection and dissemination of business and financial intelligence. Distinctions between private and public usage became increasingly important, much perhaps as today's understanding and regulation of insider trading depends critically upon the procedures and rules governing information exchange. If distinctions became more important, however, it was not always because they were universally clearer: what to one person or owner or distributor of the information might be private, to another might be, in some form, 'public'. Publication and what it meant remained a critical variable.

Both the agents employed and the sources used became increasingly familiar resources to the eighteenth-century newspaper proprietor, stationer-publisher and jobbing printer. In many ways newsprint was a form of jobbing, and a highly developed and popular form by the mid eighteenth century. Some 'intelligence' was produced in specific publications, addressed to particular mercantile or financial clients; other types of commercial information were published more generally. Categories of commercial and financial newspaper might be divided, generally, into three: first, reports or 'currents' of local economies, including general and specialized commodity price currents, foreign exchange rate currents, money currents and stock exchange currents; second, reports on overseas trade and shipping, including marine lists and general and specialized ('small') bills of entry; and third, combinations of two or more elements from both types of report and published in the same newspaper (an exchange rate current with a marine list, for example).[1] To contemporaries, early 'newspapers' were certainly not only advertisers and were as much concerned with commercial and economic bulletins and news as they were about politics, either at home or abroad.

The most thorough study to date of financial information gathering in London in the fifty years or so before 1720 concludes that market investors had little option where they gathered and that when they did, 'poor communications forced them into the City where they would have struggled to find pertinent information among rumour, opinion and gossip'.[2] This chapter argues that this situation was transformed in the following decades of the eighteenth century and, although concentration upon the 'City' was true in the sense that the area around Cornhill was the centre of financial affairs and of financial print journalism, that by at least mid-century the newspapers, and the networks of knowledge and news created by them, were spread across London and reached far out into the country. The assessment of risk that was so handicapped by a dearth of information at the beginning of the century was hugely improved such that what has been identified as a market inherently flawed by the absence of plentiful, correct or sufficiently speedy information was much closer to offering what investors needed by the end of the century. As has been pointed out,[3] many other cultural and political factors intervened to temper the commercial practices of merchants and the investment decisions of investors. The accuracy of relevant news was not invariably central to an investment or commercial decision, but that is and always has been the case. Moreover, the extensive role of print serves to inform this more broadly human (and some might say humane) aspect of the investing and commercial market, whereby emotion, loyalty and prejudice are confirmed or altered by newsprint. Markets are constructed by many means; print contributed knowledge and chauvinism, precision and error, indirectly as well as directly. As a historian of the South Sea Bubble observes, 'investment markets may behave anywhere, at any time'.[4]

---

1 A useful succinct guide to these categories is given in John J. McCusker, 'British Commercial and Financial Journalism before 1800', in *The Cambridge History of the Book in Britain: Volume V*, ed. Michael F. Suarez and Michael L. Turner (Cambridge: Cambridge University Press, 2009), pp. 448–65 (table 22.1, pp. 450–1).

2 Anne L. Murphy, *The Origins of English Financial Markets: Investment and Speculation before the South Sea Bubble* (Cambridge: Cambridge University Press, 2009), p. 7.

3 Murphy, *Origins of English Financial Markets*, pp. 7–8.

4 Richard Dale, *The First Crash: Lessons from the South Sea Bubble* (Princeton, NJ: Princeton University Press, 2004), p. 2.

Trade news bulletins and information sheets were generally labelled 'intelligence'.[5] The first newspapers in many senses were commodity price and exchange rate currents. Later newspapers, in particular, incorporated sections of commercial and financial 'intelligence', ranging from details of ships landed or about to depart, and stock prices, to the local assize of bread and the prices of livestock and foodstuffs in local markets. There was little doubt about its being discrete from other news and advertising in newspapers, just as separately printed price currents or commercial lobbying 'news' information bore distinctive material styles and forms. For centuries, 'intelligence' had carried notions both of superior under-standing and of a sense of particularist and exclusive communication, one to another. The application of 'intelligence' to information about trading transactions and industrial projects bolstered the growing confidence in the superiority of trade and finance. It confirmed the intimacy of such news. In the increasingly competitive trading world, 'intelligence' conveyed guarded secrets, closed knowledge, even conspiracy. For the editor of price currents or the editor of the newspaper, 'intelligence' bore the further imprint of a freshness from unique and guarded sources. Once published to a particular audience, the information was shared, yet shared to those party to commercial affairs, who were also able to discern and recognize the originality, authenticity and superiority of the information offered.

Examination of much merchant correspondence confirms the rapid advance of networks of information. The extraordinary growth in mercantile activity centred on London in the late seventeenth century promoted immigration of those with financial and commercial skills. Entrants from abroad brought with them extensive contacts and greatly enlarged the circuits of correspondence. With the expansion of knowledge networks and with the private equity market as important as the devel-opment of public finance, information needs hugely increased.[6] Suppliers of such information, however, have been characterized as inadequate, inept and even miscreant. How investors used the newspapers and bulletins has also been questioned, raising doubts about the historical interpretation of the *effect* of increased print production and circulation.[7]

5   For early bulletins see esp. Larry Neal, *The Rise of Financial Capitalism* (Cambridge: Cambridge University Press, 1990), pp. 20–34.
6   Larry Neal and Stephen Quinn, 'Networks of Information, Markets, and Institutions in the Rise of London as a Financial Centre, 1660–1720', *Financial History Review*, 8:1 (April 2001), 7–26.
7   Murphy, *Origins of English Financial Markets*, esp. pp. 37–8, 189–95.

Cautious assessments of the usefulness of print carrying economic news are matched by the insistence that verbal networks of exchange were as important as the printed ones. This might well be true for the formative years of financial and commercial growth in the late seventeenth century but, by at least the mid eighteenth century, a multitude of printers, publishers and printed materials deepened and expanded the commercial and financial literary infrastructure.

Printed information represented the core communication agency, enabling the further enlargement of verbal and aural networks. As discussed, many printing houses offered various local services beyond that of printing. This broader role of the printer and his or her premises in 'publication' was especially well developed in London and in the particular neighbourhoods, such as Cornhill, Cheapside and Fleet Street, associated with printing, finance and public affairs. Printers' and publishers' offices consequently assumed further importance as nodes in the information network, printers and booksellers acting as postmen and conduits for intelligence. Of many examples, the Baptist minister and prolific hymn-writer, Benjamin Beddome (1717–95), used his co-religionist and Little Britain bookseller, Aaron Ward (d.1747) as receiver of all his correspondence during his visit to London in 1740 (and probably on other occasions). Ward sent some of the letters on to Beddome's London lodgings but, like Pepys and many others before him, Beddome visited Ward and the printing houses of Little Britain as a way of meeting people and learning of the latest news and publications. From Ward, Beddome collected his latest correspondence, leaving notes of reply and letters to others implicated in the latest news.[8]

Currents, bills of entry and marine lists

Specialist works printed to serve the merchant and financier were several: commodity price currents, both specialized and general; currents for the rate of exchange on money and stock; and reports on shipping, which were largely marine lists and bills of entry. The price current was a regularly or occasionally published (and more public than private) statement or list of the prevailing prices of merchandise, stocks, specie or bills of exchange.

---

8   James Raven, *Bookscape: Geographies of Printing and Publishing in London before 1800* (London: The British Library, 2014), p. 90.

The bill of entry comprised a declaration by an importer or exporter of the exact nature, precise quantity and value of goods that had been landed or were being shipped out. Bills were usually prepared by a clerk or broker, and were intended to be examined by customs authorities for their accuracy and conformity with the tariff and regulations. Most of these papers were issued, received and used in London, although the major outports such as Bristol and Southampton generated much similar entry publication besides and, by the late eighteenth century, currents and many other papers circulated much more widely than a century before. These small printed and part-printed papers were the essential tools of a growing army of financial and commercial intermediaries, from bankers, stock and bill-brokers, and dealers in foreign exchange, to underwriters, stock-company and government revenue administrators, and their agents and clerks. These were the daily inhabitants of the streets and coffee-houses in the shadow of the Royal Exchange.

In addition to the leading coffee-houses such as Lloyd's and Jonathan's, instrumental in London's business and financial life,[9] dozens more operated within an alleyway or so of the Exchange, including the Marine Coffee House in Birchin Lane, Elford's in George Yard, Tom's in Pope's Head Alley, the Jamaica in Cornhill. The Jamaica, as its name announced, was, like the Jerusalem and the Pennsilvania, favoured by those with interests in particular trading destinations. All the coffee-houses neighboured the many different establishments of printer-stationers.[10] Most of these printing houses, like many of the coffee-houses, were flourishing enterprises, transferring between generations and celebrated names in London affairs. Custom was easy to find. As the French visitor, César de Saussure, had written in the late 1720s of the Exchange and its immediate environs:

> It is said that this is the wealthiest corner of the earth, as it covers relatively a small space of ground, and brings in more than two thousand pound sterling a year. There are many taverns in the neighbourhood of the Royal Exchange; they are filled from midday till two o'clock with merchants. Change Alley, close by, is also crowded with money-dealers; at times you can scarcely move.[11]

9   See above, p. 96.
10   See Raven, *Bookscape*, pp. 98–108.
11   César de Saussure, *A Foreign View of England in the Reigns of George I and II*, trans. Madame van Muyden (London: John Murray, 1902), p. 80.

In Continental Europe, specialized trade and financial publications dated from the mid sixteenth century. In England, regular commodity price currents date from at least 1608, and bills of entry from 1619, both part of the commercial revolution based on overseas trade,[12] and were appearing weekly by the 1620s. By the final third of the century, the circulation of these lists was aided by preferential postal rates. Later, privileged rates of taxation further boosted list transmission. The lists were exempt from the 1712 Stamp Act,[13] as indeed bills of exchange and account had been exempt from the original 1694 Stamp Act.[14] The Clerk of Roads attempted to ensure trade and commerce were assisted by published newsletters. Bills of exchange and one-page merchants' accounts were exempt from postal duties under a 1710 Act, although bills of lading were taxed fourpence.[15] Both currents and bills were available on set days of the week and from rival publishers.[16] Marine lists and exchange rate currents seem to have been later items, the earliest surviving example of each dated 1697.

As McCusker and Gravesteijn have shown, the English press took many lessons from Antwerp, just as Thomas Gresham had modelled the Royal Exchange in London on the Antwerp bourse. Merchants in both Antwerp and London identified formal business publishing with commodity price currents.[17] Until the 1670s, the London commodity price current appeared under licence from the Crown with the royal and city arms imprinted on the paper. Many of the currents were part printed or mostly printed but with the '£ s d' column left blank for penned additions. Competition was slow to develop, with a second rival commodity price current appearing in the late 1660s, another in the mid-1690s and a fourth by about 1710. By then, no other European city had such service. In 1716, for example, London

---

12   Ralph Davis, *A Commercial Revolution: English Overseas Trade in the Seventeenth and Eighteenth Century* (London: Historical Association, 1967).

13   10 Anne, c. 19, imposed from 1 August 1712.

14   5 & 6 Wlm & Mary, c. 21.

15   9 Anne, c. 11 (1710); 9 Anne, c. 16 (1710).

16   See John J. McCusker, 'The Business Press in England before 1775', *The Library*, 6th ser., 8 (1986), 205–31. The following has greatly benefited from his analysis, although neither of our studies of the price currents discovered more than a few extant runs of this 'instantly ephemeral' material (to use McCusker's phrase) or great detail about their printing history. The early listings were also considered in detail in J. M. Price, 'Notes on some London Price Currents, 1667–1715', *EcHR*, 2nd ser., 7:2 (1954), 240–50.

17   John J. McCusker and Cora Gravesteijn, *The Beginnings of Commercial and Financial Journalism: The Commodity Price Currents, Exchange Rate Currents, and Money Currents of Early Modern Europe* (Amsterdam: NEHA, 1991), p. 292.

merchants were able to subscribe to seven different weekly or semi-weekly business newspapers with information about prices, exchange rates, ship arrivals and departures and their cargoes. The Boston merchant, Thomas Fitch, wrote to Thomas Crouch and Company, merchants of London in 1707, 'Without good and frequent advices it is impossible to manage a trade profitably.'[18] Those financing the publication of price currents from the mid seventeenth century worked for different companies.[19] Notable among the backers was John Day (d.1660) who was still publishing in 1649, but there must have been earlier publishers backing the venture. Between 1660 and 1667 Humphrey Broome, successor to John Day, published *The Prices of Merchandise in London*. He was succeeded as editor first by William Bannister and then by Robert Woolley (or Wooley), a major London merchant, who published the current from 1671.

When Woolley died in 1696 there were several price currents available. The bi-weekly *Currant Intelligencer* was first issued in February 1680 with new emphasis given to shipping returns. For the first time, arrivals and departures of more than London ships were listed. James Whiston's *Merchants Remembrancer* began publication in 1680, continued under slightly different titles until 1707 and was then relaunched by Francis Robinson, running until 1714.[20] It appeared on Mondays and was published in editions of between five hundred and a thousand copies. At first, Whiston printed symbols to indicate the highest or lowest levels reached rather than the actual prices. A rival price current was launched in 1692 by John Houghton, apothecary and Fellow of the Royal Society. Houghton was already editor of the *Collection for Improvement*, which also included prices of commodities and was, as its title announced, 'the Saturday-Paper extracted from the Custom-House Bills'.[21] Houghton's *Current* gave the price of corn and meats, of actions in companies, lists of London ships in and out of port, and abstracts of bills of mortality. It was intended for 'the advantage of tenant, landlord, corn-merchant, mealman, baker, brewer, feeder of cattel, farmer, maulster, grazier, seller

---

18   AAS, Thomas Fitch letterbook 1703–11, Thomas Fitch to Thomas Crouch and Co., fol. 182, cited in McCusker and Gravesteijn, *Beginnings of Commercial and Financial Journalism*, p. 291.
19   McCusker and Gravesteijn, *Beginnings of Commercial and Financial Journalism*, p. 293.
20   *The Merchants Remembrancer*, 1680–86; *Whiston's Merchants Weekly Remembrancer of the Present-Money-Prices of their Goods Ashoar in London*, ?1689–1707; *Robinson's Merchants Weekly Remembrancer of the Present-Money-Prices, etc.* 1708–?1714.
21   In 1681 he had published a similar 22-page pamphlet, the *Collection of Letters*.

and buyer of coals, hop-merchant, soap-boyler, tallow-chandler, wool merchant &c'. Of the other price currents, Samuel Proctor's was launched sometime before 1694 and was still running in 1731.

Publishers of all types of lists must have employed printers on regular contractual terms, and agents were hired to gather the required weekly or daily information. The demands made on such men, both for the speed and accuracy of their data collection, increased at the end of the seventeenth century when the previously part-printed lists, with prices and figures filled in by hand, were replaced by fully printed records of transactions and valuations. Most works bore no imprint and almost none of their early printers can now be identified. Even the number of surviving copies of the printed lists is small, making printed currents (together with printed bills of entry) some of the most ephemeral of all the business literature of the period. After the 1670s, the printed London current appears far less associated with royal approval and its history becomes more fragmentary. During the 1720s, only a single price current was published, something which might seem consistent with the overall numerical decline in commercial and financial publications of that post-South Sea Bubble decade, although not with the rising proportion of business items among overall publication totals.[22] Whatever the cause, the publication of the price current became effectively a monopoly issued from the Exchange.[23] From about 1730, London brokers at the Royal Exchange took control over the commodity price current.

The evolution of the price current also points to an important aspect of 'publication'. The authority given to the price current became distinct from the perception and use of the mercantile firm's own list which might have seemed to the business community to be partial in both senses of the word: as incomplete and as biased. The published commodity price list presented a different order from the merchant's letter or own price list production, whether scribal or perhaps part printed for ease, but, in any case, usually restricted to clients' interests. Nevertheless, many types of list probably circulated, with varying degrees of authority and popularity, and where the distinction between private and public seems, and seemed at the time, problematic. Certainly, there was variation in the information given in the lists, in their material form and regularity, and in

22 See below, p. 214.
23 A list of surviving London Commodity Price Currents 1608–1770, with their known location, is given in McCusker and Gravesteijn, *Beginnings of Commercial and Financial Journalism*, table 25.2, pp. 308–11.

the expectations attendant on them, but both producers and consumers might not always have adhered to strict and agreed divisions between the private clientele network and the public anonymous market.

For 'insiders' it was essential to provide the very latest intelligence with the widest possible choice of purchases, whereas for those not within private circulation, or 'outsiders', more general information was usually adequate.[24] In 1772, a very revealing guide to business practices was written and published by one Jürgen Elert Kruse,[25] in which he explained to his readers what commodity prices looked like and how to use them. As McCusker and Gravesteijn have speculated, Kruse's guide suggests that a very large number of scripted lists also circulated, given that Kruse provides lists that are truncated and, for the widening market, inadequate. Evidence is poor and the contextual history of the currents is beset by unknowns. Nevertheless, Kruse's example listed only thirty-four imported goods and no exported goods. The suggestion is, therefore, that when William Prince began publication of his *London Price Current* in 1776, he responded to a major market opportunity.

Identification of readerships and the types of list circulating remains difficult, even by the 1770s. It is possible that Kruse simply reprinted for his guide a particular mercantile firm's price list and that Prince actually took over an ongoing but now lost *London Price Current on the Royal Exchange*, as published by Peter Fearon, a London commodity and insurance broker of St Nicholas Lane, Lombard Street.[26] Fearon had advertised in January 1747 that he was to begin publication of 'a new and correct price current', implying, perhaps, that he saw an opportunity for improvement and revision to existing publications and possibly of a then less than completive market (and probably one marked by complaint about imperfect information). Fearon's list was to be published every Thursday and for a subscription of half a guinea per annum. A surviving copy of Fearon's *Current* of 1754 reveals it to be published by four brokers,

---

24 See Larry Neal, 'The Rise of a Financial Press: London and Amsterdam, 1681–1810', *Business History*, 30:2 (April 1988), 163–78.

25 Jürgen Elert Kruse, *Allgemeiner und besonders Hamburgischer Contorist*, 3rd edn, 3 vols (Erfurt, 1772), vol. 3, pp. 279–80; its origins are not quite clear but we know that the second edition of volume 1 was printed in 1761, and that the first edition of volume 3 appeared in 1768: McCusker and Gravesteijn, *Beginnings of Commercial and Financial Journalism*, pp. 160, 242, n. 33.

26 Fearon appears in the 1749 fourth edition of *A Compleat Guide to All Persons Who Have Any Trade or Concern with the City of London and Parts Adjacent*, 4th edn (London, 1749).

probably a committee of 'price courantiers' of Edward Taylor, William Vaughan, Benjamin Vaughan and Mark Hudson. At least these (and publishers of other currents) are known: we have no such information about their printers and the table of 'Printers' given in the most authoritative listing of eighteenth-century London commodity price currents is devastatingly blank.[27] Only Daniel Bridge, printer of Samuel Proctor's current in 1717, is readily identified, and he is not among printers for whom much record remains. We know that he joined his father, Samuel Bridge, at a Little Moor-Fields printing office when he was the printer of *The English Post*. He was also at Austin Friars near to the Royal Exchange at different periods in his working life and is probably the Bridge who appears in Samuel Negus's 1724 'List of Printing Houses', described there as 'well affected to King George'.[28]

The accounts are problematic because the scant evidence apparently attests to something that is piecemeal and suggestive of amateur operations, which simply could not have been the case. Many lists were, of course, written not printed and hundreds of scribbled lists survive in business papers in Europe and North America (and even wider afield). Some bear the names of the firms commissioning or receiving the lists but many more are anonymous, obviously rapidly produced and for a specific and urgent purpose. The extraordinarily wide range of repositories holding such lists and the profusion of the lists themselves confirm the dense circulation of the currents, although their relation to more public and publicly announced currents is difficult to gauge. The history is made the more complex by the appearance of still more currents announced in newspapers now digitally and more readily searchable than when research first began on these lists. Without the actual lists themselves, however, judgements about their extensiveness and use remain limited.

The *London Price Current on the Royal Exchange*, as has been pointed out, was published from at least 1754[29] and was succeeded in 1776 by the *London Price Current* which was to run for over a century. This current's great rival was the *New London Price Courant*, first printed in 1786. A

---

27   McCusker and Gravesteijn, *Beginnings of Commercial and Financial Journalism*, table 25.1 VI. D, p. 308.
28   See Michael Treadwell, 'London Printers and Printing Houses in 1705', *Publishing History*, 7 (1980), 5–44.
29   It seems highly probable that the same or a similar publication had been running for some years but no evidence – certainly no extant copies – could be found; cf. McCusker, 'Business Press', pp. 221–2.

third such publication, the *Universal Price Current*, rivalled these two between 1784 and 1795.[30] Apart from two short-lived experiments at Liverpool and Hull, no provincial price currents appear to have been published. During the second half of the eighteenth century, the compilation and publication of the currents continued to be a major commercial undertaking, even though the profits and the size of each run is unclear. As advertisements reveal, lists were available on a regular subscription basis or alternatively could be purchased singly from agent bookshops and coffee-houses.

Supplementing the publications recording commodity prices were serials in a consistently presented form that broadcast prices of stocks and shares and acted as guides to securities and investments. The authority generated by publications similarly boosted confidence in the dealings in London's international market. In early modern Europe, the bill of exchange was the leading negotiable instrument of overseas trade. The provision of authoritative, up-to-the-minute and updatable checks on exchange rates and transaction costs secured confidence and avoided additional time-wasting labours. Just like the first commodity price currents, the first exchange rate currents were partly printed forms and intended to be filled in by hand for merchants to inform their own network of agents and correspondents and, in the case of the exchange rate forms, for brokers to advise their investors and correspondents. These early productions (technically lists of 'prices current') have been sharply contrasted with the development of the public, usually fully printed, 'price currents',[31] but much again depends on what private circulation or 'publication' actually meant in practice.

From March 1697, John Castaing, of Huguenot origins, living in Cornhill and a stockbroker on the Royal Exchange, published his *Course of the Exchange* from 'next the General Post Office in Lombard Street where his Interest Books are sold'. Printed to monitor stocks and shares, it appeared initially on Tuesdays and Fridays and later three times a week.[32] His earliest known venture was a 1687 *Vente faite à Londres Sold by the East India Company*, a serial that continued to be published into the eighteenth century. As broker and publisher, Castaing also introduced

---

30   Other currents were very short-lived; those printed before 1775 are listed in McCusker, 'Business Press', table 2, pp. 216–20.

31   McCusker, 'British Commercial and Financial Journalism', p. 451.

32   Clerk's papers, King's Remembrancer, Exchequer Office, NA, E.219/448, cited by McCusker, 'Business Press', p. 230.

the first exchange rate current in 1696, not then known in London although several were by then published in mainland Europe. The London commodity price currents regularly included exchange rate quotations, and Houghton and then Proctor also presented exchange rates. Castaing, however, presented the exchange rate far more regularly and separately. From his first advert for the *Course*, Castaing assured clients that it 'delivers the Course of the Exchange, the Price of Bank-Notes, Bank Stock East India Stock, and other things every Post-Day, for 10s. Per Annum'.

From the first issue, *Course of the Exchange* included rates for the exchange of both stocks, currency and bonds, providing in one section tabulated lists of European cities and the current Royal Exchange selling-price of their bills. Castaing and his successors employed clerks to collect details of the latest share dealings, and also to provide an increasingly wide-ranging variety of miscellaneous information relating to the financial life of London. Taken over by Castaing's son in 1707, the *Course* was published continuously throughout the century with the active involvement of the elder Castaing's daughter Arabella until at least 1779.[33] Arabella Castaing appears, despite contemporary publishing procedures and the conde-scension of history, to have been a decisive figure in mid-eighteenth-century London business life. Like Elizabeth Nutt, the widow of the business and legal publisher John Nutt, Arabella held the business together but in a way that, especially in Arabella's case, is quite hidden as she appears in no imprint of the *Course of the Exchange*. She married the broker Edward Jackson (d.1735), became Mrs Wharton in about 1742 and also became a partner of the broker Richard Shergold, an arrangement that might have been specified by her father's will. She seems to have been involved in the publication of the paper between at least 1707 and 1779, and more certainly managing its affairs for more than forty years from 1735 after the death of her first husband.[34] According to the imprint, however, the main publishers after the death of Castaing junior were Jackson and then, between 1735 and 1763, the Shergolds, first Richard and then George. Whoever led the financing and organization of the publication, what is clear is that, by the end of Arabella's life, the *Course of the Exchange* was acknowledged as the authoritative monitor of the Stock Exchange.

The printer of the *Course* is unknown, as are those of its early rivals,

33   McCusker, 'Business Press', p. 227.
34   See McCusker and Gravesteijn, *Beginnings of Commercial and Financial Journalism*, p. 313.

Freke's Prices of Stocks, etc. published by John Freke and running continuously from 1714 until 1722, and *The London Course of the Exchange*
published by Francis Viouja and Benjamin Cole in about 1736, who
duplicated Castaing's publication to the extent of adopting his exact title.
The piracy lasted some three years. Even by that date, the guides to the
exchange contained information about a variety of investments, from
company bonds and shares to lottery tickets, annuities and government
securities. The publication of these lists was of major importance to the
development of the financial market. The need for accurate and regular
information on the price of commodities was evidenced by a succession of
post-financial crisis inquests. Regular publication of these lists also enabled
the subsidiary development of financial middlemen, and many of the guides
for merchants adopted costing methods dependent on the availability of
comparative market data. As John Houghton himself had argued:

> the uses of these bills are very great, they tell every one the proper Market
> where to carry such Goods they abound with, or where to fetch the
> Goods they want. They tell the Shop-keeper the name of the Merchant,
> where to buy; and help the Merchant to a variety of Customers, which
> otherwise could not be had, but by the help of Brokers at very great
> Charge: Nay 'tis impossible that Brokers can find out all that would buy,
> or that all such could find out Brokers to shew them choice enough of
> what they wanted.[35]

Whatever the arguments over the local economic results of municipal
regulation, the broadcasting of prices on a more than local basis (with
many of the newspapers reprinting London data in turn collected from
the currents) did much to break down regional anomalies in assize and
the movement of goods. In investment also, the availability of stock and
annuity price changes provided market assurance for both the companies
and the private investor. By mid-century, the lists were offering even
greater sophistication in the monitoring of stocks and price and exchange
movements. Castaing's *Course* had particularly gained in authority from
its use as testimony in the South Sea Bubble inquiry.[36] Stock brokers, on

35 *Collection for Improvement*, no. 6 (27 April 1692), the full first page of which is
devoted to an explanation of bills, continuing in no. 7 (30 April 1692); cf. *Collection of
Letters*, 1: 163 (13 Mar. 1682).
36 NA E.134, 17, deposition of R. Shergold, 16 Nov. 1743, depositions to the
Commission, Exchequer, King's Remembrancer, Geo. II, Mich. no. 7.

and off the Royal Exchange, did their business at much the same time as the foreign exchange brokers. The Exchange was open for business for just two hours, from twelve noon until two o'clock, and the brokers met for dinner at about one o'clock on Tuesdays and Fridays, the days of the publication of the *Course of the Exchange*. Printed copies of the newspaper, based on rapid and accurate gathering of the day's information after the dinners, were published in the afternoon, with most subscribers, it seems, committed to a quarterly or annual subscription.

In tandem with the commodity price currents and the publications relating to the course of the exchange, regular bulletins became available for shipping and customs from at least the 1690s (and almost certainly in a more modest form before). New financial journalism supported the development of financial institutions and practices in the 1690s. Most prominent, perhaps, was the bulletin of 'port letters', *Lloyd's News*, published from about 1696 by Edward Lloyd, the founding proprietor of Lloyd's Coffee-house in Lombard Street, Cornhill and opposite to Exchange Alley. This was a general news-sheet about shipping and later continued as *Lloyd's List*. Lloyd's dual role as 'coffee-man' and publisher, and the location of his operation in this crowded, bustling place of information exchange, exemplify the foundation of modern business publishing as it was to develop during the eighteenth century.

There remains contention over the continuity of the publication of Lloyd's endeavours. *Lloyd's News* appears to have failed after about five months, while, in fact, Lloyd's earliest publication was a weekly marine list issued from about 1692, styled in its running title, *Ships Arrived at, and Departed from several Ports of England, as I have Account of them in London* [and] *An Account of what English Shipping and Foreign Ships for England, I hear of in Foreign Parts*, reporting on the status of English ships around the globe. Lloyd entered into a special agreement with the Post Office that allowed the letters from his rapidly expanding network of correspondents at ports to be sent out post-free and given priority handling, and to be collected by a messenger from the General Post Office, which was located adjacent to his coffee-house. Following the publicity about its closure in 1697, *Lloyd's News* was apparently not revived until 1734.[37] It is tempting to believe that Lloyd used the

---

37   However, McCusker suggests greater continuity for the publication, based on the recent 'discovery of numerous very early numbers': 'Business Press', p. 223. The traditional version is retold by D. E. W. Gibb, *Lloyd's of London: A Study in Individualism* (London: Macmillan and Co., 1957), pp. 7–8.

controversy surrounding a mistake in the *News* early in 1697 to close the paper after just a few months, given the poor quality of the early numbers. There is large variation in the amount of shipping information contained in the different numbers and there is frequently more about naval convoys than commercial cargoes.[38] It is difficult to see how it could be regarded as reliable and authoritative by those with mercantile interests and it was in no way comprehensive in its coverage. Nor was it particularly novel, with other shipping bulletins of varying length contained in the *Flying Post* and other journals such as Proctor's commodity price current; the latter progressively included shipping information, itself imitating the earlier example of John Houghton' *Current*. Certainly, Thomas Jemson can be accredited with the foundation of *Lloyd's List* proper in the year of his own death, 1734.[39] This seems to be a reconfiguring of the Lloyd marine list with a new title. Numbers contained lists of ships arrived and departed. Like the price currents, *Lloyd's* was for sale by casual purchase or by subscription at three shillings per quarter. From 1735, when edited by Richard Baker, *Lloyd's* was published twice weekly, and its editor remained the Master of Lloyd's association of marine insurers. Lloyd's then expanded its business news coverage and included for the first time a complete copy of the *Course of the Exchange*.[40]

Appearing on Tuesdays and Fridays, the nights of the despatch of the foreign mails, *Lloyd's List* shared with Castaing's *Course* the need for rapid copying or verification of the commercial and financial data to ensure its competitive strategy. For a set contractual fee, *Lloyd's* continued to buy preferential service from the Post Office that still consisted of no postal charge made for agents' letters sent to *Lloyd's List* and all such correspondence enjoying separate and priority handling. In 1788 this fee was £200 per annum, a perquisite divided evenly between the Comptroller General of the Inland Department and the Secretary of the Post Office.[41]

---

38 Summaries of the contents of the *News* are given in Frederick Martin, *The History of Lloyd's and of Marine Insurance in Great Britain: With an appendix containing statistics relating to marine insurance* (London: Macmillan, 1876), pp. 67–74.

39 Details are given in Charles Wright and and C. Ernest Fayle, *A History of Lloyd's from the Founding of Lloyd's Coffee House to the Present Day* (London: Blades, East & Blades, 1928), pp. 70–1.

40 Lloyds Marine Collection, Guildhall Library. Extracts are reproduced in A. Cameron and R. Farndon (eds), *Scenes from Sea and City. Lloyds List 1734–1984* (Colchester: Printed for Lloyds, 1984).

41 *Tenth Report of the Commissioners on Fees, Gratuities, &c, of Post Offices*, 30 June 1788, House of Commons Reports 1806, 7: 761, 764, 789, 799, 810.

This does seem to have been a bargain, and one which gave *Lloyd's* an unassailable monopoly on the supply of fast and reliable shipping information. A single sheet normally cost fourpence to send through the mails, a double sheet cost eightpence, and an ounce, 1s 4d. Long-distance post was extremely expensive, with an additional 50% charge made for post arriving from Dublin or Edinburgh. From 1774, the Masters of Lloyd's were personally responsible for paying the fee to the Post Office, and also fees to their agents in the ports.[42] By 1792, *Lloyd's* was receiving reports from at least thirty-two agents and twenty-eight different ports.[43] The publication of the list certainly assisted in the centralizing of private underwriting in the coffee-house and led in 1764 to the biannual publication of a *Register of Shipping*, issued both to subscribers and to members of the association for marine insurers. Even so, Castaing's *Course* continued publication despite *Lloyd's* offering the additional marine list, all for the same price as its rival. Possibly this was related to the Postmaster General's insistence upon the public display of *Lloyd's List* in certain coffee-houses, making separate subscription to the *List* less attractive than it otherwise might have been.

Publications of much longer standing than the lists were the bills of entry, recording the shipment of commodities in and out of port and including specialized as well as general bills. An Office of Clerk of the Bills was in existence by 1619, with London bills published by the patent holder. From 1660 until 1722 the holder was Sir Andrew King and his heirs and thereafter the Lewis family. It is argued that this tight control over the production of the list ensured its accuracy.[44] Certainly the patent effectively controlled the use to which the entry information could be put. Bills were published daily, with information culled from the records of the Custom House. Entries detailed importer or exporter and the type and quality of the merchandise. Again, these lists performed a vital function in commercial expansion, allowing merchants to remain informed of competition and the general trend of the market. *London Imported* was published from at least 1683. From the 1730s, provincial publishers were operating under licence and began printing entry bills at Liverpool and Bristol. Hull bills were published from 1753[45] and those for Dublin from at least 1767. In London,

42   Wright and Fayle, *Lloyd's*, pp. 73–4, 168.
43   Letter by the Secretary of the Post Office, Wright and Fayle, *Lloyd's*, p. 75.
44   John J. McCusker, 'European Bills of Entry and Marine Lists: Early Commercial Publications and the Origins of the Business Press', *Harvard Library Bulletin*, 31:3 (1984), 209–55 and 31:4 (1984), 316–39.
45   The date, at least, of the first printed proposals for Hull bills.

Charles Whitworth produced the rival *Register of the Trade of the Port of London* from 1777, and the General Post Office's *Daily Statement of the Packet Boats* was printed from 1798. At Bristol, Samuel Worrall's printed bills were collected as *Bristol Presentments: Exports for the Year* and also, *Imports for the Year* from 1770, continuing weekly until 1808.[46]

The Treasury was also interested in the volume and composition of marine cargo. Publications such as Henry Crouch's *Complete Guide to ... Out Port Collectors* of 1732 were acknowledged to be an important contribution to the more efficient collection of customs duties.[47] Between ten and thirteen separate rates of duty were levied in the century, with eight hundred separate Acts concerning customs duties passed before 1760 and a further 1,300 Acts between 1760 and the long-awaited Consolidating Act of 1787. As the complexity and the number of duties increased, anxious merchants also looked to fuller guides to explain the levies. The Book of Rates issued after the 1660 Act of Tonnage and Poundage of Charles II superseded the Books of 1558 and 1604 and was itself replaced by new Books of Rates in 1725 and 1757. More duties were imposed under Anne than in the preceding three reigns put together. By 1784, no fewer than a hundred separate accounts of customs had been opened. To give one example, a merchant in 1784 importing twenty reams of French Royal Paper had to pay duties under thirteen different heads, subsidies, imposts and specific duties on French goods and paper.[48] To this was added the increased complexity of the drawbacks redeemable upon re-export. Crouch's other guide, *A Complete View of the Customs containing the Rates of Merchandize*, first published in 1724, was reissued five times up to 1755 and spawned several piracies.

Commercial journalism

Quite aside from specifically commercial and financial newspapers, economic news was increasingly conveyed by general town and country newspapers and journals. In the early eighteenth century the distinction

46 A listing is given to the collection, now in the Central Reference Library, Bristol, in *Bristol Presentments, 1770–1917*, ed. Walter E. Minchinton (Wakefield: Microform Academic Publishers, 1986).

47 The subtitle described the work as 'being forms, precedents and instructions for the execution of every branch of that business of the Revenue'.

48 Example cited by Elizabeth Hoon, *The Organization of the English Customs System, 1696–1786* (London: Greenwood Publishing Group, 1968).

between types of newspaper was perhaps more blurred, and contemporary comments reflect this. By mid-century, however, particular formats of news presentation and the association of particular modes of information categories made the range of published news intelligence more categorized, with clearer boundaries to expectations. Most general newspapers carried shipping reports from the domestic ports but also from foreign cities. Although the shipping reports were inexact and slow in the late seventeenth century, this intelligence speeded up and became more detailed and authoritative. By mid-century, the financial and commercial sections in London and provincial newspapers were both expected features and viewed with confidence. Many newspapers carried, in small discrete columns and boxes, lists of prices of stocks, the course of the exchange, the prices of various foodstuffs and other goods, and the nature of imports and exports. Listed also in many of these columns were bankruptcies, deaths, river-crossing times and tidal information (among other bulletins). Typically, the *British Mercury* announced that its 'Weekly Account of what Houses, Lands, Goods, and Wares, are to be bought or sold, and what lost or stolen, and of all other Businesses of Moment in way of Traffick' was 'to advance Trade in both Town and Country'.[49]

Rivalry between newspapers ensured extensive coverage, even at the risk of error. Despatches in the *Flying Post* were impressive, with reports in from Amsterdam, the Hague, Copenhagen, Stockholm, Hamburg, Danzig, Warsaw, Vienna, Venice, Madrid, Paris, Lisbon and many other cities. The newspaper also carried news from the colonies from Massachusetts to the West Indies and later from India. The organization of its correspondents became a particular concern to newspapers in the more competitive markets of the eighteenth century. 'Notices of transactions' poured in, although Michael Harris is rightly suspicious of such claims as those of Nathaniel Mist in 1717 that he established correspondents at 'the Hague, France, the North, Italy, Germany, and even into Hungary, Turkey and Russia'.[50] Such news gathering was *ad hoc* and – before a rival could be established in any particular city – often probably bogus. How news came into the hands of the agents is now obscure, but it is likely that the 'offices' of correspondents were local taverns and coffee-houses just on the other side of the Channel. By the late 1720s, however, competition between

49   Cited by Michael Harris, *London Newspapers in the Age of Walpole: A Study of the Origins of the Modern English Press* (London: Associated University Presses, 1987), p. 177.
50   *The Weekly Journal; or, Saturday's Post*, 34, 3 Aug. 1717.

news-gathering journals had so increased that much greater accuracy was required. When a mistake was made, rival newspapers might be ready to comment.

In 1727, the London coffee-house proprietors (or 'coffee-men') complained that 'Falshood' was now published as 'Credible Information', that the 'Publick is misled and distracted' and that newspaper printers paid men to spy on other men's affairs, including financial matters: 'the same Persons hang and loiter about the Publick Offices, like House-breakers, waiting for an Interview with some little Clerk, or a Conference with a Door-keeper, in order to come at a little News, or an Account of Transactions; for which the fee is a shilling or a Pint of Wine'.[51] This proved a prolonged dispute between the coffee-house owners and the publishers of newspapers, revealing much about mutual antagonisms and the development of the press and its circulation. News monopolies were seen to be unjust and claims of impartiality must always be tested, in the words of the coffee-men's manifesto:

> It was just and natural, for Example, Twenty Years ago, for: the Coffee-Men of London and Westminster to consider, their Houses as the Staples of News, and Themselves as the fittest Persons in the World to furnish the Town with that Commodity. Yet none of them have thought so far till just now, that the Common Abuse in that Article, is become a Common Complaint; and the Impositions they suffer in it are no longer to be born. Necessity has taught them to think right, and think home; and led them to the Knowledge of their true and natural Interest; which is, to furnish the Town with News themselves, from the Stores of Intelligence in their own Hands, of which they have been the blind Possessors to this Day.[52]

In late 1727, the coffee men combined in an attempt circumvent the £10–20 demanded by newspaper publishers for the annual subscription to one of their newspapers. The coffee men planned to publish a twice-daily newspaper, issued each morning and evening and priced at 1½d, with an estimated break-even circulation of three hundred copies.[53] In

---

51   Anon., *The Case of the Coffee-Men of London and Westminster. Or, An Account of the Impositions and Abuses, put upon Them and the whole Town by the Present Set of News-Writers* (London, 1728), pp. 6, 7, 13.
52   Anon., *Case of the Coffee-Men*, p. 4.
53   Dale, *First Crash*, pp. 10–12.

response to this threat, certain newspaper publishers claimed that they would establish their own coffee-houses, a boast that was probably met with all due scepticism. While the quarrel appeared to have resulted in neither a newspaper owned by a coffee-house nor a coffee-house owned by newspaper publishers, it does point to a fraught and lively market.

The spat also highlights a general concern about the broader authority of news (by 'the present Set of News-Writers, ... the Trade and Credit of the Kingdom are often at a Stand') and the function of publishers and printer in advertisements. For historians it seems a useful protest too far, suggesting the success of printers in attracting custom by good design and typographic skill:

> Who they are that circulate an Advertisement and direct it to its proper Ends. Is any Thing due on this Account to the Genius or Dexterity of the Proprietor of a Paper? Or is it owing to the Care or Ingenuity of a Printer, that an Advertisement passes thro' Twenty Thousand Hands in a Day? The Answers here run both in the Negative: And the Matter can only be affirmed of the Coffee-Men, The Coffee-Men are the Persons who do the Business of the Advertisers. The Coffee-Men are They who circulate Advertisements, and direct them to their proper Ends, The Coffee-Men pass them from Hand to Hand, and make them known to the whole Town. And, if the Coffee-Houses were to be shut up, I would ask what would become of Advertisements?[54]

The further consideration in the dispute over newspapers was, *plus ça change*, what was true in news. The issue, as commentators realized, was of critical importance to commercial and financial intelligence. Critics warned of the dangers and consequences of error, and the importance of reliability and reputation. Here, remarkably, in defending themselves against charges of spreading false news, the newspaper proprietors declared that they 'insert all they hear, but the Publick may believe what they please. But the Coffee-men are to insert nothing that may call their Veracity in question ... The *Scepticks* said that there was no such thing as Truth in the World, and how can they pretend to insert nothing but Truth in their Papers?'[55] The same pamphlet, clearly identifying some coffee-house owners as business newspaper publishers (like Edward Lloyd, who

54   Anon., *Case of the Coffee-Men*, pp. 12–13.
55   Anon., *The Case Between the Proprietors of News-Papers, and the Coffee-Men of London Fairly Stated* (London, 1729), p. 10.

had died in 1713), offered a further dash of cynicism that men of business did not, in any case, not remember anything beyond a day.

The dispute continued to reveal more about perceptions of business publication. Of their own proposals to establish a new newspaper, the coffee-house proprietors wrote that 'there is not a Nation or Country round about us, nor any Part of the Trading World, from whence the Merchants, or other Gentlemen residing in Town, have not often very material Advices, touching Political Transactions and remarkable Occurrences; which, for Want of such a Canal, are rarely communicated to the Publick; but, by this Means, will be published with the greatest Facility'.[56]

The benefit of specialist financial and commercial journalism was established, albeit in debate about ways and means (and, significantly, about both material and intellectual ownership), but the intelligence provided by currents, marine bulletins and other short digests might also be more widely circulated. Economic news and advice was now increasingly conveyed by journals such as *The Weekly Miscellany for the Improvement of Husbandry, Trade, Arts and Sciences*, published for about twenty years after its foundation in 1720. Far more significant in terms of circulation, however, were three further developments: first, the greater distribution of newspapers carrying business news to country towns and men and women in the countryside; second, the inclusion in country newspapers of extracts from the commercial and financial intelligence; and third, the increased reporting of local news relevant to business.

By the end of the century, regional newspapers, all acting as advertisers for local trades and services, now also offered, often alongside national commercial and financial intelligence culled from the London newspapers and bulletins, a detailed range of locally sourced public information intended to inform the local business community. A few examples stand for tens of thousands of insertions. The second page of Raikes and Dicey's *Northampton Mercury* in its earliest issues from 1720 was devoted to goods imported and exported from London, listing these in great detail according to shipments and cargoes. From at least 1745, the *Cambridge Journal and Weekly Flying-Post* printed Bank stock prices and 'Prices of Grain at the following places last Market-Day' including Cambridge, Hitchin, Hertford and St Albans, and Ware. Prices from Bear Key in London were also given, including wheat, flour, horse beans, hog

56   Anon., *Case of the Coffee-Men*, p. 39.

peas, bohea (black) tea, green tea, chocolate, brandy and rum. In 1769, Chase's *Norwich Mercury* gave 'Prices of Corn and Flour' at Bear Key, Norwich, Yarmouth and Downham Bridge.[57]

London price intelligence continued to be carried in some detail. The *Ipswich Journal* supplemented freight and port information with listings of London prices of stocks and rates of exchange. The *Chelmsford and Colchester Chronicle* of the late 1760s included prices of stocks and the price of London foodstuffs under the heading 'Mark Lane', named for the location of the London Corn Exchange. These included wheat, rye, pease, horse beans, barley, oats and malt, showing the range in prices for each. Occasional notes were added, such as 'clover feed somewhat cheaper'. In the 1770s, Henry Kirkby and James Simmons gave the price of grain at the Corn Exchange in their *Kentish Gazette*. Sections such as 'Observations on the State of Yesterday's Market in Mark Lane' appeared in many London newspaper columns, including for example, the *English Chronicle; or, Universal Evening Post*.

News also ran in the other direction, from the countryside to London. In 1795, for example, John Walter's London *Evening Mail* carried many despatches from the country quoting latest prices and views about harvests and markets. The issue of 17 August 1795, for example, contained a report from Shrewsbury dated 14 August:

> At our Fair on Wednesday last, fleece-wool sold from 16s. to 23s. per stone, and lamb's wool as high as 22s. per stone. Old cheese from 48s. to 54s. New ditto from 38s. to 44s. per hundred. Cattle, sheep, and pigs sold well; horses rather lower than at the last fair.

A further paragraph from the Shrewsbury report then gave a detailed description of Britford fair. Such information was vital to farmers and dealers following the prices of foodstuffs and livestock. The same issue gave prices of corn in Birmingham, reports of plentiful harvests in Oxford and Reading, and a variety of news about shipping and new landings.

In the 1760s, the eight-page *Lloyd's Evening Post* regularly included post news, stock prices and 'Price of Grain at the following markets viz: London, Oxford, Abingdon, Farnham, Basingstoke, Henley, Reading,

---

57 For further examples and analysis see C. Y. Ferdinand, *Benjamin Collins and the Provincial Newspaper Trade in the Eighteenth Century* (Oxford: Clarendon Press, 1997); and Ian Jackson, 'Print in Provincial England: Reading and Northampton, 1720–1800' (unpubl. D.Phil. dissertation, University of Oxford, 2003).

Warminster, Devizes, Gloucester, Birmingham.' Thrice-weekly price
ranges were given for foodstuffs usually including wheat, barley, oats,
beans and peas. In whichever direction intelligence was sent, the timing
of reports and of going to press became critical. Printers needed to catch
incoming news and yet also have time to print in order to catch outgoing
mails.

Municipal government made frequent use of the local commercial
advertiser. The activity of town corporations and magistracies is evident
not only because of the survival of so many local official records about
business recording and regulation (the potential of which has still not
been fully recognized in historical studies), but also because of the connections between local trading regulation and the work of the printer. In these
matters, journalism elides with advertisement. Through newspaper advertisements, corporations sought information and the direction of much local
trade. In turn, the printer was assured of a local and relatively regular source
of employment. The weighing machine, for example, was an important
but often troublesome support to local economies based on agricultural
produce (and, indeed, on coal, salt, timber or other raw materials). At
Hereford, York and Derby, regular payments were made to advertise 'the
Machine'. In the case of Hereford, such notices were sent to printers as
far afield as Robert Raikes in Gloucester, Harvey Berrow in Worcester and
Thomas Aris in Birmingham. On at least two occasions advertisements
were placed in seven consecutive issues of the *London Evening Post*.[58]
Deserters from the local militia were also advertised, together with notices
of hop and corn tithes, cattle sales and the assize of bread.[59] Of dozens
of surviving examples, the Breconshire Quarter Sessions record-books list
orders for public advertisements to be inserted in the *Gloucester Journal*
early in 1759 to solicit persons willing to undertake repair work whenever a
bridge appeared to be ready to collapse. All port towns from Bristol to Hull
advertised the arrival and departure of ships, their captains and the destination, origin and sometimes even the goods they carried.

The identity of the collectors of information for the most part remains
unknown. It is likely that most were simply the casual employees of the
local publisher and/or printer, and often, most probably, the printer
him or herself, an apprentice or a member of the printer's own family.

58 HfRO, BG11/24/2, Chamberlaine's Book of Accompts, 1732–69, fol. 341 (Dec. 1754),
fol. 433.
59 CCRO TAB/7:33 Treasurer's Accounts, 1759–73; HfRO, BG11/24/2, Chamberlaine's
Book of Accompts, 1732–69, fols 341ff.

Identity was also not important, especially when there was much obvious plagiarism and the sharing of reports. The *London Gazette* remained a key source. One final aspect of the reporting has been neglected: that various of the types of commercial and economic intelligence, regional and metropolitan, was itself collected on forms, and forms that were printed and sometimes designed by the newspaper printers. As with the part-printed papers that allowed the early price currents or the course of the Exchange to be noted by agents and correspondents and sent to the printer's office or other collecting station, so local prices, weights, measures, arrivals and other information might be provided with printed documents made for this purpose. This was all the more the case when the good or service recorded was subject to government or local regulation. Obvious examples are the many forms printed to record the prices of agrarian goods at local markets. From 1685, inspectors, under royal authority, sent in reports every quarter on the market prices of major agricultural commodities in the English maritime districts. The declared purpose was to review and police customs duties and bounties on imported foreign grains.[60] Legislation in 1770 required market inspectors (as the mayor's representatives) of at least two market towns in each county to supply the weekly quantities and prices of corn being sold there to the Receiver of Corn Rents and duplicate copies to the local Clerk of the Peace.[61] 'Corn' usually (with local variation) comprised separate listings on the printed forms for wheat, rye, barley, oats and peas. The Receiver published these weekly returns in the *London Gazette* and sent a certificate to the Clerk of the Peace and the County Treasurer, who in turn paid the local market inspector two shillings for each return he had made. As noted by a pioneering research project devoted to their study, these price returns critically informed debates about the Corn Laws in the early nineteenth century as well as providing ammunition in contested eighteenth-century moral philosophy and political economy.[62] Many of the original part-printed and filled-in forms have survived. The completed recording forms for the three selected market towns of Middlesex, for example, remain bundled up in the London Metropolitan Archive, much as they were after they had been collected and then recorded in

60   *James the Second, 1685: An Additionall Act for the Improvement of Tillage. Chapter XIX*. Rotulae Parliamentariae, *nu. 19.; Statutes of the Realm: Vol. 6: 1685–94* (1819): 21–3.
61   10 Geo. III, c. 39.
62   Corn Returns Online, directed by D'Maris D. Coffman, Centre for Financial History, Newnham College, Cambridge, www.cornreturnsonline.org.

summary tables sent for central collection.[63] The jobbing work that went into the production of these thousands of forms for a single county was undertaken by the same printers who produced the local newspapers that recorded in their columns local agrarian prices and much other business, economic statistics and news besides.

An encouragement to projects

One of the most obvious results of jobbing printing and circular publication, both in the great towns and in the country, was to boost the effectiveness of private lobbying. The circulation of printed notices, separately or in journals, enabled schemes to be proposed and to succeed. The managers of the English financial experiments of the 1690s relied heavily upon the services of London printer-stationers. Projects for canals were similarly serviced by printed bill and leaflet. Few proposals for turnpikes, canals, and other major building projects were without controversy. Just as print had fuelled religious and political controversy in the previous two centuries, so also did the press enable protest and public debate about commercial and financial proposals.

During the first quarter of the eighteenth century, several prolonged public disputes concerned commercial and financial organization. In all of them, commissioned pamphlets and broadsides streamed from the London presses, all designed to convince or refute. In November 1710, the Sun Fire Office embarked on what appears to be purely self-promoting lobbying. The Office sent some 150 copies of their freely distributed advertiser, the *British Mercury*, each with an insurance proposal attached, to the House of Lords, and a further six hundred copies to the House of Commons.[64] Some eighteen months later, however, in April 1712, the Managers of the Sun Fire Office were faced with the imposition of a new stamp duty on their advertiser (which also carried extensive news from the foreign mails, price currents, lottery ticket numbers and other

---

63   LMA MR/W/G/001–009, weekly lists of corn prices sent from the market inspector to the Clerk of the Peace for Uxbridge market, 1762–1853; MR/W/G/010–016 for Brentford market, 1770–1810; MR/W/G/017 for Staines market, 1796–1806; LMA COL/CHD/DM/08/009 certificates of corn returns for London, 1807–08.

64   Boyer Relton, *An Account of the Fire Insurance Companies, Associations, Institutions, Projects and Schemes Established and Projected in Great Britain and Ireland during the Seventeenth and Eighteenth Centuries* (London: Swan Sonnenschein & Co., 1893), p. 303.

information) and set out to lobby parliament. The Managers' actions were typical of numerous protests from companies and specially formed associations throughout the century. On 26 April 1712, the Managers drew up a petition and resolved that this

> be ingrossed and delivered Munday next to the House of Commons, and the case now agreed to be printed to the Number of 600 and a reme of writing paper ordered. Ordered the Printer to deliver them fold up for Mr Gedney at Eller's Coffee House at Westminster Hall Gate, Munday morning by nine o'clock. Ordered that all Members shall attend Munday at 10 o'clock in the said Coffee House, thence to the Lobby during the Sitting of the House.[65]

The petition was printed as *The Case of the Members of the Sun-Fire Office, London, relating to the Duties on News-Papers*. It noted that the subscribers had

> erected and set up, with very great Expence and Trouble (for the Benefit of the Public), an Office of Insurance of Houses, Goods, Merchandize, Furniture and Wares, for Loss by Fire, all over Great Britain; and have likewise oblig'd themselves by an Instrument or Policy upon Stamp'd Paper, under their Hands and Seals, to furnish Weekly every Person Insur'd with three Printed News-Papers, call'd the *British Mercury* ... nor do make any other Profit or Advantage of the said Paper, other than for carrying on the said Insurance from Fire.

Every member of the Commons (and probably some members of the Lords) were given a copy. It is unclear whether these were despatched in advance or distributed personally in a mass canvas of members in the Lobby. It is most probable that all copies were taken to Parliament and those (the majority presumably) not handed out in person but left for members. The printer, Hugh Meere, probably provided guarantees of the speed and quality of production and contributed to the design, certainly in the typographical presentations to give the best impression to those being lobbied. The surviving copies of *The British Mercury* offer certain encouragement about the quality of Meere's work. The small printed listings of commercial and economic information and the long extracts from the mails are readable and well placed in regular, tidy lined

---

65   LMA, Sun Fire Office, Company Minutes; Relton, *Insurance Companies*, p. 309.

columns. The newspaper is adorned with striking woodcut factotums and small illustrative advertising cuts, almost all neat and well designed. The order that the petitions be folded up echoes the surviving invoices for the jobbing printing for the City printers and the expectation that the printing office do more than simply print but also cut, fold and stitch according to orders.[66] In the usual way, Hugh Meere's imprint on the *British Mercury* named him as 'of the Black Fryar in Black Fryars where Advertisements are taken in and also at the Sun-Fire-Office abovesaid'. A coffee-house (here, Eller's adjacent to Westminster Hall) again provided a focal point for organization. As it happened in this case (and as must have happened in the majority of such cases), the lobbying by the insurers came to nothing.

From 1716 until the Bubble Act four years later, further furious lobbying was undertaken over various proposals for insurance corporations. In 1714, annuities capitalized various mercantile enterprises, including a Beech Oil Company and a Stock for Improving the Fishery.[67] More infamous was the York Buildings Company for Raising Thames Water.[68] Of further annuities schemes, the proposal to establish the Mercer's Hall Marine Company in 1717–18 met with particularly vociferous hostility from those defending the existing underwriting structure. Many critics feared that the establishment of such a major company would effectively bar private dealing. Both the Lords Commissioners appointed in 1718 and the Select Committee of the Commons in 1720 were inundated with petitions and printed broadsides, proposals and counter-proposals.[69]

Between 1716 and 1720, at least 185 different projects were floated, some thirty of which included insurance schemes. The South Sea Company was sponsored by print, recorded by print and destroyed by print. The commercial disputes of the early decades of the century were enflamed by bitter Grub Street pamphleteering as well as by the more restrained output of associations of merchants and landowners. Printers' offices, like the City coffee-houses, were centres for raising subscriptions, many with practical, some with apparently charitable, objectives. The subscription scheme became the primary means of raising moderate sums of serviceable capital for local works. Such schemes encouraged

66   See above, pp. 89, 92.
67   Relton, *Insurance Companies*, p. 119.
68   Cornelius Walford, *The Insurance Cyclopaedia*, 5 vols & 1 part [unfinished] (London: Charles and Edwin Layton, 1871–80), vol. 1, pp. 1, 117.
69   Anon., *A Letter to the Chairman of the Committee by a Merchant, Reasons Humbly Offered Against the Societies of Mines Royal* ([London, 1720]).

the sponsorship of local economic development by small-time investors, an army of whom underpinned the enrichment of the economic infrastructure of eighteenth-century England. The subscription usually acted as a loan to managers of projects and charities and offered, therefore, both an investment with considerable potential financial returns from the interest charged, and potential prestige in the neighbourhood. Buildings might be raised, new products marketed, new poorhouses or almshouses erected by subscriptions, all organized from the stationer's office or through his or her newspaper or distribution services. In John Brewer's words, the subscription 'provided a degree of security in a period of change, enabling the small tradesman or producer to move outside the protected realm of patrician patronage without being totally at the mercy of the open market's vagaries and whims'.[70]

The circulation of pamphlets and single-sheet proposals particularly assisted in the formation of investment trusts for navigations and turnpikes. During the first decade of the century, the proposals for the Weaver navigation and the schemes put forward by Thomas Slyford and the pioneers of the rock-salt trade in Cheshire succeeded only because of the numbers publicly subscribing to their cause. The efficiency with which this lobbying and planning was executed and the often complicated local settlements reached is directly attributable to the prompt printing and circulation of proposals and counter-proposals by both London and local printers.[71] All the early struggles over navigations and turnpikes were marked by pamphlet warfare.[72] The first turnpike authority of 1663 was a much extended form of an otherwise traditional parish repair scheme. The experiment was not repeated until 1695 and Acts to establish turnpike trusts were few until the 1750s, a decade of 186 new trusts. Thereafter development was piecemeal, both on the thirteen main highways radiating from London and on the networks around provincial centres.[73] From

70   John Brewer, 'Commercialization and Politics', in McKendrick, Brewer and Plumb, *Birth of a Consumer Society*, pp. 197–264 (p. 225).

71   CCRO, Minutes of Commissioners and Trustees of the Weaver Navigation; Edward Hughes, *Studies in Administration and Finance, 1558–1825* (Manchester: Manchester University Press, 1934), pp. 249–65; the Weaver Bill received Royal Assent, 17 Mar. 1721.

72   Various printed petitions concerning the Weaver disputes, 1699–1720, are held at BL, Add. MSS 36,914, 29, 86, 87, 117–23; many of the notices were printed in Chester.

73   Development has been superbly researched by William Albert, *The Turnpike Road System in England, 1663–1840* (Cambridge: Cambridge University Press, 1972; new edn 2007); see also B. J. Buchanan, 'The Evolution of the English Turnpike Trusts: Lessons from a Case Study', *EcHR*, n.s., 39:2 (May 1986), 223–43.

mid-century, however, the method of financing turnpiking also changed from searching for investors after the passing of a permissory private Act to the soliciting of subscriptions before the establishment of the trust.

By the end of the 1760s, the subscription method, aided by printed proposal and other documentation, was by far the most popular method of proceeding in road and navigation as well as mining schemes.[74] Other navigation battles such as that over the Don in Yorkshire between 1697 and 1726 were played out from printing houses in London, Sheffield and Leeds.[75] Much the same publicity was required to underwrite new road construction. In 1757 the *Newcastle Journal* published thirteen different turnpike notices. In 1760 the *York Courant* broadcast seventy-five. *Aris's Birmingham Gazette* carried hundreds of announcements concerning road and canal routes during the century.[76] With the exception of the Bridgewater canal projects, all subsequent navigations were advanced as joint-stock companies. With such innovative industrial and commercial schemes it is also easy to overlook the backing given to improve local agriculture and to support the local market in foodstuffs and livestock by land drainage, woodland clearance schemes and a variety of rural building proposals, including the erection of new weighing machines.

The schemes were all launched by initial investments in local and national advertising. Organizers engaged local printers to provide blanks for applications and shares, and regular notices of projectors' meetings. Shares were usually fully or very largely subscribed by the time an enabling Act was approved. Breakdowns of those investing show that subscribers were drawn from wide geographical areas. While most came from the neighbouring counties, important support also came from London and regional mercantile wealth.[77] Among those investing was the pre-eminent London printer, William Strahan.[78]

74   Albert, *Turnpike Road System*, 100.

75   The history of the Don disputes is given in T. S. Willan, *The Early History of the Don Navigation* (Manchester: Manchester University Press, 1965); and cf. his *Navigation of the River Weaver in the Eighteenth Century* (Manchester: Chetham Society Publications, 1951).

76   Illuminating examples are given in John Money, *Experience and Identity: Birmingham and the West Midlands, 1760–1800* (Manchester: Manchester University Press, 1977), 24–33.

77   J. R. Ward, *The Finance of Canal Building in Eighteenth-Century England* (Oxford: Oxford University Press, 1974), p. 17.

78   BL, Add. MSS 48,810: 14, Strahan Ledger, £800 shares in the Trent and Mersey Navigation, 1773.

When both land and water highways were established, local printers continued to be engaged to produce toll stationery, as well as posters concerning fares and alterations to services. Tickets again played a part in the later organization of these projects. The same printer employed for the proposals and lobbying often continued in the paid service of trusts to issue printed paper tickets for the turnpikes.[79] Quires of paper bound for the turnpike were sold by Dent in Kirkby Stephen at 1s 3d each. Cheney printed the tickets for the Oxford canal. John Lawton and Mrs Elizabeth Adams printed 'coal tickets' for the tolls on the canals, river and docks under the control of the Corporation of Chester.[80] Municipal meetings about turnpikes were also regularly advertised in public broadsides.[81] Certain local managers continued to employ London printers. Strahan, for example, was commissioned by Henry Davidson of the Clyde Navigation to print bills, supporting statements and '1,110 cards' (presumably tickets) in 1767 for which Strahan charged £96 4s.[82]

Newspapers continued to service largely localized markets for the exchange and purchase of canal shares. With the early banking system primarily aimed at commercial credit extension and not at all involved with underwriting long-term investment projects, the support of navigations continued to be based on personal connection and, with the exception of a few specialized jobbers and brokers, dependent on general advertising. At the height of the 'canal mania' of the early 1790s, Richard Phillips, bookseller and stationer of Leicester, advertised his premises as 'Navigation Offices', offering his services as canal share broker.[83]

Circulated newsletters also helped to support lobbying by early interest groups, both commercial and industrial. The Society for the Encouragement of Arts, Manufactures and Commerce, founded in 1754 to promote 'improvement', issued printed *Registers* of its plans and

---

79   Of many early examples, City of Westminster Archive Centre, 988/188: photograph of a Marylebone Turnpike Ticket, Aug. 14, 1721, cited by Sarah Lloyd, 'Ticketing the British Eighteenth Century: "A thing ... never heard of before"', *Journal of Social History*, 46:4 (2013), 843–71 (p. 846).

80   CCRO, Treasurer's Accounts 1759–73, TAB/7: 80v (including a payment of £1 14s for twenty quire of coal tickets 'and binding the same in 4 books', Dec. 1766).

81   CCRO, Treasurer's Accounts, 1768, TAB/7: 92.

82   BL, Add. MSS 48,803a: Strahan Ledger, fol. 86v.

83   *Jackson's Oxford Journal*, 18 Aug., 24 Nov., 1 Dec., 1792, cited by Ward, *Canal Building*, p. 107.

pronouncements.[84] By the final third of the century, various mercantile and trading groups were organizing for specific purposes. Of many and diverse examples, in the 1770s two well-developed trade associations, the Staffordshire potters and the ironmasters of the Midlands, were operating to counter local hostility and further their own interests in trade agreements and in private enabling Acts.[85] In an example of a similar type of society, the *Public Advertiser* of 1780 was soliciting membership for a 'Society of Tradesmen &c for the Protection of their Property against the inroads of felons, forgers, cheats &c'. Later announcements gave the dates of their monthly meetings.[86] Also from the early 1780s, a flood of colourful pamphlets, notably those by 'Oliver Quid Tobacconist', denounced the proposed tax on receipts.[87] It was, however, the belief by manufacturing groups that they were excluded from mercantile interests at Westminster that prompted the formation of the most powerful new lobbying groups of this period, the local manufacturers' and trade associations led by Manchester (founded 1774 and reorganized in 1781) and by Birmingham (founded in 1783). Pitt's Irish trade proposals of 1785 provided the catalyst for the organization of one 'General Chamber of Manufacturers' in London in March of that year. The venture was short-lived once the immediate issue was resolved (to the satisfaction of one group in the Chamber at least), but the episode also confirmed the power of having a published plan in co-ordinating action. The *Plan of the General Chamber of Manufacturers of Great Britain* was published in London in 1785, to be followed by regular and widely circulated issues of *The Merchant's and Manufacturer's Magazine of Trade and Commerce*, reproducing accounts of the London Tavern debates and stimulating the publication of further technical discussions. The wider aspects of this debate are considered in the next chapters.

---

84   The early history of the society is charted by D. G. C. Allan, *William Shipley: Founder of the Royal Society of Arts*, new edn (London: Scolar Press, 1979).
85   J. M. Norris, 'Samuel Garbett and the Early Development of Industrial Lobbying in Great Britain', *EcHR*, 2nd ser., 10:3 (April 1958), 450–60.
86   *Public Advertiser*, 20 Jan. 1780.
87   Oliver Quid [pseud.], *A Letter of Advice Addressed to All Merchants, Manufacturers and Traders, of Every Denomination in Great Britain* (London, 1783); Quid's *A Second Letter of Advice* (London, 1783) claimed that its predecessor reached ten editions.

9

Instruction and Guidance

The subject of this chapter comes deliberately late in the organization of a book designed to reimagine the full compass of 'business publishing' and the mundane but critical handling of print that enabled and informed economic concerns. Most historical assessments of the contribution of print to society focus on the reading of books and understand the relationship between books and trade as a history of economic thought. Published works, however, were also responsible for far-reaching changes in the teaching and practice of commercial skills. From the late seventeenth century there was a very obvious increase in the number of small, usually one-man establishments devoted to commercial training, while the expansion in business houses and financial intermediaries had to be serviced by practical guides and commercial aides-memoires. Practical manuals contributed in great measure to the upturn in publications and to the increasing specialization of those engaged in writing for and about trade and industry. By mid-century, advertisements for general commercial schools and publications competed with those for specific courses of instruction in particular branches of trade or for short treatises on accountancy, broking or insurance.

Books and pamphlets intended for use in commerce included both those designed to educate and those designed to inform. There were many different types of publication within each category. Information required in trade and manufacturing was obviously not just of the daily news variety discussed in the preceding chapter. Many instructional works taught numeracy and accounting. Others provided specialist training for the young merchant or retailer. Informational works offered continuing guidance to the trader by way of memoranda, reckoners for calculations, updates of trading news and a variety of other services to the tradesman or his client.

As noted, throughout the eighteenth century the great majority of books sold in Britain continued to be published and printed in London. Provincial booksellers acted as agents for the London wholesale-booksellers, and

very occasionally as joint printers or publishers. The great majority of
books offering instruction on trade were certainly published in London
until mid-century, although thereafter specialist guides were produced
in specific localities. First Edinburgh and later Glasgow became noted
centres for publishing books on accounting. In the final third of the
century, newly thriving port, commercial and manufacturing towns
quickly achieved as strong a specialist book trade serving local needs
and interests as the established centres trading in London-printed books.
With strengthening demand in the provincial towns, the efficiency of the
distributional network was particularly important for works specifically
designed to assist the businessman.

This further point about publication sites highlights another critical
difference between books and much other print, especially jobbing work.
Many national studies of the 'history of the book' have been weakened
by consideration only (or disproportionately) of books and printed items
manufactured in the country under review. Yet 'publication' and books
know no national boundaries – as states anxious to control the importation of foreign material were well aware. Even import bans, however,
could be evaded, while large quantities of books, pamphlets and, later,
newspapers easily crossed borders and the English Channel. For the first
two hundred years of printing in England, many readers, and especially
scholars, were dependent on imported books to supplement often meagre
home productions. By the early eighteenth century, however, English
publications fulfilled most needs and the country was soon to be an
exporter of books. Books and pamphlets aiding merchants and investors
were an example of specialist publication that was almost wholly written
in English for first its English and British and later its colonial audience.
Unlike scholars and the more learned clerics and gentlemen, the trading
community read little classical literature in the original language, and even
French and other modern languages, commonly used by some traders in
their meetings and correspondence, featured little in the books read. In
1622, for example, Gerard de Malynes (1586–1626), overseas merchant
and English commissioner in the Spanish Netherlands, published in
English in London his *Consuetudo, vel Lex Mercatoria: or, The Law
Merchant: Divided into three parts, according to the Essential Parts of
Traffick Necessary for All Statesmen, Judges, Magistrates, Temporal and
Civil Lawyers, Mint-Men, Merchants, Mariners and Others Negotiating
in all Places of the World*. His dedication to King James refers to the book
as 'The Law Merchant' and explains the title as following 'customary law'

usage. The 'Epistle to the Reader' that follows is also almost entirely in English with a light sprinkling of foreign terms. The work, in title at least, was also to be the inspiration behind Wyndham Beawes's publication of his *Lex Mercatoria Rediviva: or the Merchant's Directory* in 1751. As its title went on to proclaim, this was 'a Compleat Guide to all men in Business, whether as Traders, remitters, Owners, Freighters, Captains, Insurers, Brokers, factors, Supercargoes, Agents etc.', giving a description of the occupation of each.[1] Beawes's book, however, was itself largely also a translation from the *Dictionnaire universel de commerce* by Jacques Savary des Brûlons (1657–1716), completed and published posthumously in 1723. A different but more productive influence was upon John Burn (1744–1802), whose publication in 1755 of *The Justice of the Peace and Parish Officer* heralded a description of the legal duties of (and forms and forms of words required by) justices of the peace. It was to be a standard text and assistant to the printers of forms for generations. Burn's four-volume sixteenth edition was published in 1788.

Guides to book-keeping

The publication history of books teaching book-keeping has received some attention from historians of accountancy as well as limited discussion in studies of the rise of industrial and market capitalism.[2] After the first book on accounting printed in English, Hugh Oldcastle's *Profitable Treatyce* of 1543, some forty further works were published before 1700.[3] Most of these enlarged on different double-entry systems and claimed that they enabled the simple calculation of profit and loss, of employed capital and of the current financial condition of the business. After the Restoration, books on commercial accountancy were increasingly domesticated and almost no subsequent work was a direct translation. Most were written

---

1   The work was reprinted in 1754, 1761, 1773, 1783 and 1792.
2   A. C. Littleton and B. S. Yamey (eds), *Studies in the History of Accounting* (Homewood, IL: Richard D. Irwin, and London: Sweet and Maxwell, 1956); B. S. Yamey, H. C. Edey and Hugh W. Thomson (eds), *Accounting in England and Scotland: 1543–1800* (London: Sweet & Maxwell, 1963); B. S. Yamey, *Essays on the History of Accounting* (New York: Arno Press, 1978); B. S. Yamey, 'Scientific Bookkeeping and the Rise of Capitalism', *EcHR*, 2nd ser., 1:2/3 (1949), 99–113; M. F. Bywater and B. S. Yamey (eds), *Historic Accounting Literature: A Companion Guide* (London: Scolar Press, and Tokyo, Yushodo Press, 1982).
3   Yamey, Edey and Thomson (eds), *Accounting*, bibliography, pp. 202–26.

by teachers of book-keeping, many of whom also advertised their services as accountants. A few of the manuals were compiled by practising merchants or tradesmen. At least two of these seventeenth-century works continued to be popular in the next century. John Vernon's 1678 *Compleat Compting-house; or the Young Lad ... Instructed ... in all the Mysteries of a Merchant* was reprinted in large editions in the 1720s and 1730s, and in an eighth edition in 1741. William Mather's *Young Man's Companion*, with its array of accounting tabulations, reached a twenty-fourth edition in 1755. After 1710, however, there were few reprints of the best-selling manuals of the seventeenth century.

By 1720, Scottish contributors were also prominent. The first work on book-keeping published north of the border was Robert Colinson's *Idea Rationaria, or the Perfect Accomptant* of 1683. This was followed in 1718 with books by Lundin, MacGhie and Malcolm. Perhaps the most popular book on accounting practice throughout this period, however, was John Mair's *Book-keeping Methodiz'd*. First published in 1736, at least seventeen reprints were issued from Edinburgh and Dublin before 1765. In 1768, Mair revised the work and as *Book-keeping Moderniz'd* it went through a further nine editions in the next forty years. On the evidence of colonial sales catalogues, library inventories and import lists, Mair was by far the most sought-after work on accounting in the new world.[4] George Washington both owned a copy and recommended its use to others. In Britain, Mair also seems to have been the most popular of the larger book-keeping reference works for both business and private use. It was the only work on book-keeping in Adam Smith's personal library.[5]

Double-entry book-keeping appears to been increasingly practised in the eighteenth century, most notably in surviving ledgers of the East India Company and by some provincial merchants even in the 1690s.[6]

---

4 Based on an examination of sales lists as catalogued in R. B. Winans, *A Descriptive Checklist of Book Catalogues Separately Printed in America 1693–1800* (Worcester, MA: American Antiquarian Society, 1981), and also of MSS and printed listings held at the AAS.
5 Tadao Yanaihara, *A Full and Detailed Catalogue of Books which Belonged to Adam Smith* (Tokyo: Iwanami Shoten, 1951), and Hiroshi Mizuta, *Adam Smith's Library. A Supplement to Bonar's Catalogue with a Checklist of the Whole Library* (Cambridge: Cambridge University Press, 1967).
6 Notably by Samuel Jeake who in 1690 recorded that his ledger entries were made 'after the method set down in Chamberlain's Accomptant's Guide': Michael Hunter and Annabel Gregory, *An Astrological Diary of Samuel Jeake of Rye, 1652–1699* (Oxford: Oxford University Press, 1988), p. 149; see also R. Grassby, 'The Rate of Profit in Seventeenth-Century England', *EHR*, 84 (1969), 721–51.

The practice began to change the contradiction identified by B. S. Yamey and confirmed by Richard Grassby for seventeenth-century England, that although systematic, double-entry book-keeping was explained and extolled by most early modern manuals, actual practice adhered resolutely to single-entry accounting, a method much simpler (and requiring less paper).[7] The balancing of profit and loss remained a sporadic exercise, however, at least according to the evidence of surviving ledgers. Phyllis Whitman Hunter's research, especially concerning the trading accounts of the merchant Timothy Orne (1717–67),[8] shows that despite early training in accounting, many of those succeeding to businesses were unable to overcome shambolic practices, perhaps forced by the pace of trading. The business ledgers of the greatest printers in London in the eighteenth century, the Strahans, discussed above in relation to their jobbing printing, also confirm the practice of recording monies owed to creditors and owed to the firm by debtors, but not calculating ongoing profit and loss. A modern auditor would despair.

As eighteenth-century books on accounting became increasingly specialized and as rival systems were developed, competition between writers intensified. By far the most successful of the early guides was Edward Hatton's *Merchant's Magazine*, even if surviving copies contain clear evidence, from the scribblings of users, that some of the examples Hatton gave needed correction and outran the competence or patience of his readers.[9] First published in 1695, it reached an official ninth edition by 1734, but was also much pirated.[10] A few of the publishing teachers of book-keeping were very prolific. Charles Snell wrote eight different books on accounting between 1701 and 1720, at the same time attempting to exploit the growing market for specialized guides. Snell's general *Rules for Book-keeping* of 1701 was followed, among other works, by his *Accompts for Landed-men* of 1711, his *Merchant's Counting-House* of 1718 and his *Book-keeping in a Method Proper to*

---

7   Yamey, 'Scientific Bookkeeping'.
8   I am most grateful to Phyllis Whitman Hunter, a colleague during my Fellowship at the American Antiquarian Society for the preparation of this book, for sharing then unpublished research with me; see also P. W. Hunter, 'Containing the Marvellous: Instructions to Buyers and Sellers', in *Didactic Literature in England, 1500–1800: Expertise Constructed*, ed. Natasha Glaisyer and Sara Pennell (Aldershot: Ashgate, 2003), pp. 169–85.
9   See examples given in Natasha Glaisyer, *The Culture of Commerce in England, 1660–1720* (London: The Royal Historical Society and Boydell, 2006), p. 138.
10   *London Gazette*, 9 May 1695.

be Observ'd by Super-Cargo's and Factors of 1719. Other works, such as James Dodson's 1750 *The Accountant, or, the Method of Book-keeping,* contained successive examples of book-keeping for different commercial or private concerns. Most works on accounting included model pages or unfinished examples for practice. These were, in effect, part-printed items, like the blanks that need to be filled in to be given authority and perform in the marketplace, stock market or counting-house. Filling in was not obligatory, however, merely an opportunity to practise and get the best out of a book aiming to teach. Rather like many DVDs and downloads abandoned by those attempting modern language courses, many of the book-keeping tutorial books surviving in archives and in original private collections are in almost pristine, unused condition. The further parallel was with the many writing instruction books whose use is debated by historians: were the models used and copied in correspondence or simply books to be read?[11]

During the eighteenth century such sections in tutorial books were made more elaborate and tailored to specific undertakings. Dodson illustrated accounts for the farm, the country estate, the 'considerable' merchant, the business partner, the banker, and a shoemaker who manages his own shop. Technical manuals for the clerk and apprentice merchant included lessons to be learned by rote. Most boasted of their simplicity. Many were in fact extremely complex.

All the major booksellers of the century seem to have been involved in the production of at least one book on accounting, either an academic piece or a practical manual. An increasing number of such works were marketed for a general or amateur audience. Roger North's *Gentleman Accomptant* was issued in 1714 and Richard Hayes's even more popular *Gentleman's Complete Book-keeper*, in 1741. Other all-purpose handbooks and manuals of instruction also appeared. William Webster's *Essay on Book-keeping*, first published in 1719, reached a sixteenth edition in 1779. By 1762 the *Monthly Review*, among other journals, was tiring of the flood of accounting books. Thomas Harper's *Accomptant's Companion* was wearily dismissed as stale and unattractive.[12] As the value of such works to the booksellers

---

11   See Susan Whyman, *The Pen and the People: English Letter Writers* (Oxford: Oxford University Press, 2009), and my consideration of this point in James Raven, 'Letters, correspondents and correspondence', *Electronic Enlightenment On-line* (Oxford: Voltaire Foundation, 2010), www.e-enlightenment.com/letterbook/colloq2010/raven,james.html, accessed 28 June 2014.

12   *Monthly Review*, 26 (March 1762), 235–6.

increased, so did the number of commissions arranged with authors. After mid-century some textbooks were still privately printed by teachers hoping to attract custom, but many books on commerce were actually solicited by the booksellers. In one surviving commissioning agreement from 1765, John Nourse, the London bookseller, agreed to pay John Mills two guineas per sheet for a projected work on overseas trade of between sixty and eighty sheets, with thirty guineas in advance.[13]

Shares in copy of such books were also much transferred between booksellers, again indicating keen competition to buy into a successful accounting book. Although this type of work has not usually been ranked as one of the most lucrative investments for the bookseller of the period, both the Ward and Longman records of copy transactions show high prices for many of the book-keeping manuals and financial guidebooks. Apparently even the good housewife, as Mrs Malaprop was to put it, was anxious to acquire 'a supercilious knowledge in accounts'.[14]

The accountants themselves were hardly reticent in stressing the importance of their work to the new society. Alexander Malcolm's *New Treatise on Arithmetick and Book-Keeping*, published in Edinburgh in 1718, emphasized the social and moral evil of keeping everything to memory and not making written accounts. Certainly there were good reasons for the businessman taking book-keeping seriously. Supplying and receiving materials, retailing and accounting for marketing expenses could be an extremely complex operation. This was especially so in the provinces where barter or at least *ad hoc* exchanges were far from obsolete. Bills of credit drawn on third or fourth parties also produced complicated arrangements in which a written record was vital. Disputes were common. So were bankruptcies and unexpected mortality. In many cases, an inventory or a business record of outstanding debts, balances and stock was demanded. As Defoe intoned, 'next to being prepar'd for death with respect to Heaven and his soul, a tradesman should be always in a state of preparation for death with respect to his books'.[15]

The influence of book-keeping journalism was extensive, even though it is also clear that few businessmen followed the accounting guidebooks

---

13   BL. Add. MSS 38,729, 2: 174–8, assignments, 1703–1822; the average payment to authors at this time was about 10s. per volume.

14   R. B. Sheridan, *The Rivals*, act I, scene ii.

15   'Of the tradesman's keeping his books and casting up his shop': Daniel Defoe, *The Complete English Tradesman, in Familiar Letters; Directing him in all the several Parts and Progressions of Trade*, 2 vols (London, 1726–27), vol. 1, pp. 323–47, (pp. 345–6), letter xx.

with great precision. From what evidence we have of business records, double-entry book-keeping does seem to have been widely adopted in England and Scotland by the end of the sixteenth century,[16] but for the shopkeeper or even small merchant many of the plans presented in print by the eighteenth century were also absurdly ambitious. Alexander MacGhie, for example, recommended the use of no fewer than five account books subsidiary to the waste book, journal and ledger and then went on to leave the fine details of the organization of these to references to Colinson and Hatton.[17]

Few regional merchants in 1718 could have had ready access to a full library of book-keeping manuals. Equally, many books and closely printed broadsides with passages to be learned by heart were not especially short. Across all sections, Hatton provided some seventy-four rules for his students to remember. Snell's 1701 *Book-keeping* had seventy rules and his 1718 *Merchant's Counting-House* only one fewer. Nevertheless, many merchants and tradesmen did attempt some modelling of their accounts on the manuals, and training in book-keeping certainly did benefit from printed instruction. Even if the more subtle and minute details of the works were not copied, the basic guidelines certainly were. It is clear that book-keeping had become an expected and necessary part of all mercantile education by at least the mid eighteenth century and that the relative merits of published manuals on accountancy were eagerly and minutely discussed in print. The ultimate test, however, is that of usage and here the evidence is equivocal. The huge number of editions is the best testimony to the demand for such books, even if need was sometimes more perceived than sustained. The claimed poor quality of much book-keeping in surviving business records of the period is used by those who are sceptical about the widespread use of the manuals, while some authors' pompous and even specious addresses to would-be readers are also used as evidence for the prosecution. In particular, it might be that title-page descriptions of intended readers were used to differentiate between merchants, gentlemen, and other professions and occupations in what was in fact a world of overlapping spheres and inexact professional designation.[18] It is also likely that some manuals were read in order to

16   The earliest known English ledger to be composed in double-entry dates from 1522: Peter Ramsey, 'Some Tudor Merchant Accounts', in Littleton and Yamey (eds.), *Studies in the History of Accounting*, pp. 185–201.
17   Alexander MacGhie, *The Principles of Book-keeping Explain'd* (Edinburgh, 1718).
18   Glaisyer, *Culture of Commerce*, pp. 116–29.

inhabit the persona of the merchant or tradesman, and that even specialist guides appealed to gentlemen readers (discussed in a later chapter).[19]

Against the more cautious assessments of how the manuals were used, there is plentiful evidence, both real and circumstantial, for their popularity and contribution to trading life. It is clear, for example, that many guides and commercial 'assistants' and dictionaries were related to writing manuals and were associated with formal pedagogic practice and even apprenticeship. Evidence also survives that merchants acquired these texts in order to secure not only the good opinion of fellow traders and clients but to reassure themselves of their own value and skills.[20] What is also abundantly clear is that many texts lent themselves to versatile and multiple uses, whether in the schoolroom, the counting-house, the institutional library or at home. The fragmentary evidence of usage confirms a variety of sites, readers and motivations (where motives can be adduced).

For all the emphasis on the currency of the guides, of the importance of having the latest and the best, of the 'improved' text, particularly in comparison with some named rival, many antique texts remained popular. In 1698, John Gilpin, steward to John Lowther in Whitehaven, recommended Malynes's 1622 *Lex Mercatoria* as offering 'us an account of coyns, weights, etc.'. It was also a riposte to Lowther's suggested reading of Robert Morden's *Geography Rectified: or, A Description of the World* published eighteen years earlier (and Lowther might have had access to the then most recent edition of Morden of 1693).[21] Nevertheless, modernity did carry cachet, especially by the mid eighteenth century. Where early-seventeenth-century publications might still have served as standard reference works in the 1690s, half a century later, competition between multiple and rival guides and manuals, many available in new and revised editions, and a much increased market and trading community, ensured that a larger premium was placed on new publications. Greater relevance and accuracy were also attributed to recent writing and revision.

19   See also Lawrence E. Klein, 'Politeness for Plebes: Consumption and Social Identity in Early Eighteenth-Century England', in *The Consumption of Culture, 1600–1800: Image, Object, Text*, ed. Ann Bermingham and John Brewer (London: Routledge, 1995), pp. 362–82.

20   See D. A. Rabuzzi, 'Eighteenth-Century Commercial Mentalities as Reflected and Protected in Business Handbooks', *Eighteenth-Century Studies*, 29 (1995–96), 169–89.

21   D. R. Hainsworth (ed.), *The Correspondence of Sir John Lowther of Whitehaven, 1693–1698, a Provincial Community in Wartime* (New York: Oxford University Press for the British Academy, 1983), pp. 494, 499; also cited in Glaisyer, *Culture of Commerce*, p. 141.

Other business manuals

Instructive guides for merchants took many forms. By 1800, many different disciplines were described in print and great ingenuity shown in devising new ways of teaching them. Booksellers offered specialist textbooks on skills for particular branches of commerce, as well as prestige offerings in the form of grandly sounding grammars and dictionaries of trade. After about 1740, a very large number of humbler, but no less important, assistants appeared for retailing and local business. Books on industrial processes also increased towards the end of the century, although these were very largely restricted to traditional workshop crafts for which there was some market in do-it-yourself instruction.

In the first half of the century, the advance in the number of textbooks on commerce was the subject of much comment. Many of these works were in the vanguard of the books sold by newly established provincial printers from the 1720s. General introductions to the 'principles of trade' were accompanied by a large number of massive reference works. Malachy Postlethwayt's two-volume *Universal Dictionary of Trade and Commerce* of 1751–55 weighs in at nearly two stones.[22] Showroom heavyweights like Postlethwayt and, later, Thomas Mortimer were huge successes. According to its subtitle, Mortimer's 1772 *Elements of Commerce, Politics and Finances* was 'designed as a supplement to the education of British youth, after they quit the public universities or private academies'. William Guthrie's *New Geographical, Historical and Commercial Grammar* reached a fourteenth edition in 1794.

The market for such works was a discerning one, however, and not all of the prestige publications proved to be popular. Richard Rolt's *Dictionary of Trade and Commerce* of 1756 was a commercial catastrophe, despite a preface by Dr Johnson (who later protested that he had not read the book which followed). Within six months, the publishers were trying to sell off

22   The work reached a fourth edition in 1774; it owes much to both Savary and Cantillon, aspects of which are discussed in H. Higgs (ed. and trans.), *Essai sur la Nature du Commerce en géeacuteral by Richard Cantillon* (London: Frank Cass and Co., 1931), introduction. Cf. Jean-Claude Perrot, 'Les dictionnaires de commerce au XVIIIe siècle', *Revue d'histoire moderne et contemporaine*, 28 (1981), 36–67; Maria Colombo Timelli, 'Dictionnaires pour voyageurs, dictionnaires pour marchands, ou la polyglossie au quotidien au XVIe et XVIIe siècle', *Linguisticae Investigationes*, 16:2 (1992), 395–420; and also, more comparatively, Michèle Janin-Thivos, 'Pratiques commerciales, pratiques linguistiques. Les langues du commerce entre gênes et lisbonne (fin XVIIe–début XVIIIe siècle)', *La Revue Historique*, 7 (2010), 59–75.

Rolt's work in cheap part-issues. After a further five years it was reissued with a rearrangement of the pages.[23] The disaster was probably caused by overprinting, further evidence of the demand that publishers saw for such works.

Many publishers of popular material found a profitable sideline in merchants' guides. London Bridge and, after mid-century, Paternoster Row were centres for the publication of cheap, best-selling works for the popular market, but they also produced many books for the merchant and the retailer.[24] Such firms included, most famously, Thomas Norris, Robert Walker and James Hodges of the Bridge, each of whom advertised dozens of cheap guides and pocketbooks. Among many other books for commerce, Hodges published William Markham's *General Introduction to Trade and Business or the Young Merchant and Tradesman's Magazine*. It was announced in the newspapers of the period as available from over 150 provincial sellers. Craighton of Ipswich, Raikes of Gloucester, Dicey of Derby, Thomas Slack of Newcastle and Collins of Salisbury each devoted over a full column of their journals to advertising Markham on the occasion of each of its several editions. Publications offering tradesmen advice on how to avoid financial difficulties had been well publicized in the seventeenth century. In 1695 the stock of Roger Williams, bookseller of Hereford, included Bartholomew Ashford's *The Heavenly Trade; or, the Best Merchandizing. The only way to live well in impoverishing times*, first published in 1688. The bookshop also offered *The Art of Thriving: Or the Way to Keep Money* of 1674.[25]

Personal advisers also included guidance to those entering or trying to choose between trades. An early success was R. Campbell's 200-page *The London Tradesman. Being a Compendious View of all the Trades, Professions, Arts ... Calculated for the Information of Parents and Instruction of Youth in their Choice of Business*, published in 1747. Other manuals offered instruction in particular crafts or in the basic skills of arithmetic, grammar and geography. Joseph Moxon's famous *Mechanick Exercises*, a work issued in parts between 1678 and 1693, was perhaps the first wide-ranging instructional trade manual. G. Bird's *The Practising Scrivener* of 1733 and Joseph Champion's *Practical Arithmetick* of the same year were among the more popular of over fifty such guides published

23   I am indebted to Terry Belanger for this reference.
24   H. R. Plomer, 'The Booksellers of London Bridge', *The Library*, 4 (1903), 28–46.
25   F. C. Morgan, 'A Hereford Bookseller's Catalogue', *Transactions of the Woolhope Naturalists' Field Club*, 1942–44, pt 1, 22–36.

before 1750. Thereafter an average of ten new trade manuals were issued each year, ranging from *The Flax-Husbandman and Flax-dresser instructed*, printed in Glasgow in 1756 and reprinted at least four times by 1760, to guides to navigation and geometry written specifically for the training of merchants. Works teaching navigation could be purchased from the map and print sellers, many of whom also sold mathematical instruments and appropriate stationery.[26]

Basic arithmetic was still the staple fare, however. In 1695, the Hereford stock of Williams included both the *Young Clerk's Guide* in four parts, and the *Young Clerk's Companion; or a Manual for his Dayly Practice*. Edward Hoppus's *Practical Measuring made Easy for the Meanest Capacity* was first published in 1759 and was still being reissued in the 1790s. Hundreds of small academies survived by the use of printed manuals. Advertisements offering a 'commercial education' for young men were often published far from the featured school, with teachers in Lancashire, Derbyshire and Yorkshire advertising in East Anglia and the Home Counties.[27]

The teacher was often no more than a supervisor, and the sudden upsurge in 'accountants' or 'masters of navigation' as dependent on the increased availability of books of instruction as on any surfeit of teachers.[28] In 1716, Thomas Watt's *An Essay on the Proper Method for forming a Man of Business* heralded a wave of classroom works for the apprentice merchant. Martin Clare's 1720 *Youth's Introduction to Trade and Business for the Use of Schools*, Edward Lloyd's *Young Merchant's Assistant* and Peter Hudson's *New Introduction to Trade and Business ... Designed for the Use of Schools* of 1761 were among dozens of books supporting the advance of private academies. Many teaching works provided pupils with working definitions of trading terms. William Kippax's *New Book of Arithmetick*, for example, included definitions of 'discount' for the trainee merchant to copy into his exercise book.

Many schoolbooks taught specific writing skills. Writing was stressed as an essential accomplishment for the merchant and one, the teachers

26   Sarah Tyacke, *London Map-Sellers 1660–1720* (Tring: Herts Map Collector Publications, 1978).

27   Revd Mr Hyde of Wakefield, for example, advertised in the *Ipswich Journal*, 17 Mar. 1749/50, citing East Anglian addresses for testimonials from fathers of present pupils of accounting and navigation.

28   The foundation of many of the private academies is recorded in Nicholas Hans, *New Trends in Education in the Eighteenth Century* (London: Routledge & Kegan Paul, 1951).

insisted, still sorely neglected. The puff for George Bickham's writing manual, *The Universal Penman* of 1735, decided that

> In the politest age we seldom find
> The Man of Business with the Artist join'd
> But in your Genius both these Talents meet
> To make the happy Character complete.[29]

The versatile Snell published his *Art of Writing in Theory and Practice* in 1712 from his Foster Lane writing school 'where youth may board'. Shorthand primers included Thomas Gurney's 1748 *Brachygraphy or Swift Writing Made Easy to the Meanest Capacity*, advertised frequently in Gurney's *Proceedings of the Sessions of the Peace*. Other books announced their intention to enable tradesmen to become civilized and accepted members of society. Campbell's *London Tradesman* of 1747 advised on a number of etiquette matters as well as questions of practical business. By the end of the century, works like those by William Wright provided, in one book, guidance to all areas – commercial, social and moral.[30]

Comparing these genres of skill manuals and advice books, Natasha Glaisyer has offered a perceptive study of the extensive commercial vocabulary developed within them from the late seventeenth century. Edward Hatton's 'A Dictionary, or Alphabetical Explanation of the most difficult Terms commonly used in Merchandise and Trade' appeared in his *Merchant's Magazine* in 1699[31] and provided 330 entries, increasing to 450 entries by its sixth edition in 1712. As a forerunner to the compendious dictionary format of Postlethwayt's commercial dictionary of 1751, Hatton offered a lexical compass in an increasingly complicated world of trade and finance.

---

29 Examples of writing-instructors are reproduced in Ambrose Heal and Stanley Morison, *The English Writing-Masters and their Copy Books* (Cambridge: Cambridge University Press, 1931).

30 William Wright, *The Complete Tradesman: or, A Guide in the Several Parts and Progressions of Trade* (London, 1789); and c.f. anon., *The Compleat Tradesman* (London, 1790). According to the *Monthly Review*, 'The young tradesman will certainly be much benefited by a due observance of most of the directions contained in this useful performance', vol. 81 (1789), 374–5.

31 Edward Hatton, 'A Dictionary, or Alphabetical Explanation of the most difficult Terms commonly used in Merchandise and Trade', *Merchant's Magazine* (1699), 223–39.

Desktop and office guides

Many of the teaching manuals already described were, of course, often kept for reference. Even some of the bulky histories or grammars, such as Beawes's *Lex Mercatoria Rediviva*, were designed to incorporate specialist reference material. Two Edinburgh works, William Gordon's *Universal Accountant and Complete Merchant* of 1763 and Robert Hamilton's *Introduction to Merchandize* of 1777, were sold as compendiums with both an instruction and a reference section, the latter including calculating tables, and tables of weights and measures. Hamilton was the eighth son of Gavin Hamilton, the Edinburgh bookseller, and a keen observer of the market for commercial books. Publications providing information necessary to undertake transactions included indices of trading regulations and customs duties, and collected copies of statutes and treaties relevant to particular trades. After mid-century, several guides to commercial and financial laws were produced for the merchant's office, led in 1760 by the *Laws of Bills of Exchange* and two years later by a two-volume work by Timothy Cunningham, *The Merchant's Lawyer; or, the Law of Trade in General. Containing an abridgment of all the statutes relative to the East India Company, the Bank of England, the South-Sea Company, and all the public annuities, … bankrupts, … money and coinage, … bills of exchange, … promissory notes, … banknotes and insurances, … and customs.* Such collections had to be regularly updated – a need stressed by the booksellers as the commercial return and ease of revision became obvious. Many, such as David Davies's 1780 *Tradesman's Lawyer*, were published in part-issues.

The detailed, often overcomplicated, instructional works on accounting and other mercantile and retail skills were supported by simple charts and pocket reckoners offering continuing assistance to tradesmen, negotiators and investors. In 1633, Ralph Handson had produced a single sheet of rules for the counting-house to remind the clerk of the general principles of book-keeping. Much reprinted, its format was also much copied, with single or double-sided broadsides printed by numerous English and Scottish booksellers. One of the most famous imitations was *The Accurate Accomptant* compiled by Browne in 1670. A form of this work was even included in Postlethwayt's *Dictionary* under the heading 'Mercantile Accountantship'. By then, however, there were cheaper and handier reference works available – as publishers of rival dictionaries were quick to point out. Over the century, the market for the separate guide or table expanded enormously.

Of such charts or pocket works, the best selling was the ready reckoner. The most popular of these were almost certainly William Leybourn's *Panarithmologia: or, the Trader's Sure Guide* of 1693, and Edward Hatton's *Comes Commercii: Or, The Trader's Companion*, first published in 1699. As its title page advertised, Leybourn's *Panarithmologia* was

A Mirror, Breviate, Treasure, Mate, For Merchants, Bankers, Tradesmen, Mechanicks, And a Sure Guide for Purchasers, Sellers, or Mortgagers of Land, Leases, Annuities, Rents, Pensions &c In present Posession or Reversion And A Constant Companion Fitted for All Mens Occasions. In Three Parts. All Performed by tables Ready Cast Up.

The 1709 second edition of this cover-all-bases reckoner boasted a revised title page, with a net cast for a more artisanal reach (although not exclusively so):

Containing Exact, and useful Tables ready cast up, adapted to the Use of Merchants, Bankers, Grocers, Weavers, and Haberdashers: And all that deal by Wholesale or Retale. Also, for Carpenters, Bricklayers, Joyners Glaziers, Plasterers, Plummers and Painters, And all other Mechanicks, As also, For all Purchasers of Houses or Lands: Shewing the Interest of Money, and Discount on prompt Payment.

The official 'twentieth' edition of Leybourn was issued in 1791. The 'twelfth' edition of Hatton was published in 1766. 'As to the subject of the book in general,' the author began, 'I have this satisfaction that morally speaking there is none more useful, because none more advantageous.'[32] Numerous such guides reside in business archives throughout England, some kept with family papers in county record offices. In an often battered state, the reckoners, bearing testimony of great use, also bear numerous scribblings and marginalia – as well as the occasional correction. As Natasha Glaisyer reports, a 1714 edition of Hatton's *Index to Interest*, now in the University of London Library, contains an additional 31 pages of manuscript tables 'Pertinent to the Subject of this Book'. The manuscript insert extended the usefulness of the *Index* by some thirty years.[33]

---

32 Hatton's *Arithmetick Made Easy* was also published in 1726 and went through at least five editions in a year.
33 Glaisyer, *Culture of Commerce*, p. 139.

Certainly production sharply increased from the 1720s with over fifty different titles available by 1750. Most of the reckoners were wholly collections of tables with no other text. With dozens of tables included, mistakes were common. Reckoners were therefore frequently revised and rival works rushed into print, advertising new accuracy. John Hewitt's *Trader's Pocket Accomptant* was written, according to its author, not despite but because of the popularity of the three best-selling works by Hatton, Playford (incorporating Morland) and Leybourn.[34] As Hewitt is at pains to point out, these books contained numerous computational errors and he insists that financial catastrophe and bankruptcy might result from buying them. For anyone who has worked with surviving business records of this period, the claim that even the reckoners were unreliable will not come as a surprise. Accounts and self-made inventories of small businesses are notoriously liable to error. The complex system of weights and measures adopted by different trades and in different parts of the country certainly did not help the cause, whatever textbooks still claim about Britain enjoying a uniform and un-Continental-like system of measurements.

Locally compiled reckoners, providing specialist tables for particular trades, were new to the century. Large numbers of subscription proposals for reckoners and guides were issued. It would seem that local writers and teachers as well as the London and regional printers and booksellers perceived a market among local tradesmen for assistants to accounting and commercial measurement. *The Builder's Bench-mate* of 1747, a re-issue of Batty Langley's very popular *Builder's Director*, was printed exclusively for his son, Archimedes.[35] *The Mariner's Jewel* of 1724 written by James Love, 'Mathematician', was republished many times during the next twenty years. Works offered specialist tables of mensuration for timber merchants, blacksmiths, farriers and corn factors.[36] *The Weaver's Index; or a table shewing how much yarn it will take to warp any web*, published in

34 Edward Hatton, *Comes Commercii: Or, The Trader's Companion* (London, 1699); John Playford, *Vade Mecum; Or, The Necessary Companion*, which included Sir Samuel Morland's *Perpetual Almanack* (London, edns since at least 1679); William Leybourn, *Panarithmologia: Or, The Trader's Sure Guide* (London, 1693).

35 This was just one among many other similar titles published by Batty Langley (1696–51). His work *The Builder's Jewel* (London, 1741) was also reprinted at least fifteen times by 1800: N. L. Savage, 'On the Make-up of Certain Eighteenth-century Architectural Books', *Factotum*, 20 (May 1985), 20–7.

36 Of dozens of examples: Batty Langley's *London Prices of Bricklayers Materials and Works* (London, 1750); William Salmon's much-reprinted 'Vade-mecums' for builders and for blacksmiths; and Anon., *The Coal Dealer's Assistant. Being Tables Calculated for the*

Glasgow in 1753, was reprinted and sold all over the lowlands. Its great rival was David Ramsey's *The Weaver and Housewife's Pocket Book ... wherein is shown what should be the weight of each hank of yarn ... and likewise the number of right telled yarn*, first printed in Edinburgh in 1750.[37]

Many timetables were accompanied by itemized reckoners listing distances between different locations, in order, it was claimed, to prevent the unfortunate number of disputes which arose between driver and passenger. Guides were also published for rent and tax collectors, tidesmen and customs officers. By the final decades of the century, tables were produced in the Midlands and industrial regions for calculating tonnages of raw materials and manufactured goods for carriage or for the levying of duties and tolls.[38] Similar tables served agricultural districts with measurements given for the assessment of corn, dairy produce and even livestock. In Kent, reckoners included tables for calculating values and tonnages of hops. The most sophisticated of these books provided the cost of gross weight of hops reduced to neat weight with the price of the hundredweight at any price per pound and with the duty paid.

Directories

Greater commercial and financial activity generated new demands for the easy identification of a firm or commercial district. The enlargement of inland trade was in large measure dependent on printed maps, guides and easily copied and transported details of location and access. The market for Speed's county maps in the first half of the century is clear from the priority given in booksellers' advertisements. At the same time, however, Speed was gradually replaced by much more detailed district and town guides. Many included postal routes and labelled major properties. Some accompanied trading manuals and a few identified local merchants, retailers and other commercial firms. Edward Hatton, whose production of other literature more directly related to business has already been noted, compiled the

---

ready and easy finding out the true value of any number of chalderns from 1 to 200, at any of the usual prices, first published in 1759 at Newcastle upon Tyne.

37 The various complementary works included [John Collinges], *The Weaver's Pocket-Book; Or, Weaving Spiritualiz'd* (Glasgow, 1766).

38 Of many examples, the most popular of the 1790s was James Goodfellow's *The Ready Calculator ... exhibiting at one view, the solid contents of all kinds of packages* (London, 1794).

leading new survey of London to be published in the first decades of the century. Yet both his 1708 *New View of London* and Strype's update of Stow, expensive at six shillings but very basic, were designed more for the library shelf than for travel. Even Strype, however, did include lists of coaches and carriers, and some street-by-street identification of traders.[39]

Local corporations, at least, were also using the older and larger maps and surveys in their overseeing of local trades and industries. A Mr Summers, bookseller of Hereford, was supplying maps of the surrounding districts to the Mayor and burgesses in the 1730s and probably had been doing so for twenty years.[40] A more obvious advance in providing modern and more extensive local information was the production of county surveys, led nationally in 1721 by the Revd Thomas Cox's *Magna Britannia et Hibernia*. Published in six large volumes before 1732, each county was individually considered and surveys could be sold separately, accompanied by a county map and copperplate. 'Singly sew'd up in blue paper', the county surveys ranged from Yorkshire, the most expensive at six shillings for 47½ sheets, to Cornwall, 7 sheets, and Huntingdon, 3½ sheets, each at ninepence. With the possible exception of their maps, however, Cox and subsequent county guides again probably appealed as much to antiquarians as to tradesmen, even though the surveys did list dates of fairs and markets and describe all new roads and transport facilities.

Far more appropriate for business were the pocket guides for the 'dealer' or 'journeyman'. These were produced in large numbers after 1700. From the London Bridge publishers came Thomas Norris's *Remarks on London* in 1722, a basic but pocket-sized directory. Other early and popular examples included J. Bridge's 24-page *Book of Fairs or a New Guide to West Country Travellers*, printed at Oxford in 1718, and P. W.'s *Description of all the Counties in England or ... the Dealer's Pocket Companion*, enlarged in a second edition of 1728. A brief description of each county was followed by a list of market days, moveable and permanent fairs, carriage and postal routes, and pick-up points for carriers. Like so many works aimed at the business customer, it also included a ready reckoner. All these works, however, paled in comparison to John Ogilby's *Pocket-Book of the Roads*. First issued as *Ogilby's Britannia* in 1676, it went through several titles and over two dozen editions by 1800.

---

39 Rival productions are discussed in Michael Harris, 'London Guidebooks before 1800', in *Maps and Prints. Aspects of the English Booktrade*, ed. Robin Myers and Michael Harris (Oxford: Oxford Polytechnic Press, 1984), pp. 31–66.
40 HfRO, BG11/24/2, Chamberlaine's Book of Accompts, 1732–69.

By the seventh official edition of 1752 it had reached ninety-four pages in length. Throughout the eighteenth century publication rights to the work were keenly contested, with most of the leading booksellers, including Rivington, Baldwin, Lowndes, Newbery, Wilkie and Hazard of Bath, at some time holding shares in its copy.[41]

Other publications were not so stable over the century. Early attempts at national coverage were easily surpassed by the more detailed and versatile local directories. William Owen's countrywide *Book of Fairs* – which was exactly that, a list of fairs with dates and locations – was much reprinted after its appearance in 1773, but it had few competitors and was the last major work of its kind. The portable and locally published guide was again the key to expansion, both in terms of the successful combination of local expertise and growing demand, and in its support of an often vulnerable local printing firm. In London, Samuel Lee had published a seminal form of small directory in 1677 as *A Collection of the Names of Merchants living in and about the City of London … directing to the Place of their Abode*. Cumbersome and inaccurate, it was also hardly comprehensive or systematic. In 1726, John Bowles published his pocket map of London, but a greater turning point came in the late 1730s with the interest shown in guidebooks by the elder Baldwin. Always a bookseller with an eagle eye on the market, Baldwin issued *A Complete Guide to all Persons who have any Trade or Concern with the City of London* in 1740. It reached a sixteenth edition in 1783. Some of its editions were very large impressions. Its only serious rival arrived in 1763 as *The Complete Guide to all Persons who have any Trade or Concern with the City of London and Parts Adjacent*, a work reprinted six or seven times before 1780. As a true street guide, the first successful alphabetical listing was John Bew's *Ambulator* of 1767, an instant best-seller that was republished and imitated many times by the end of the century.[42] If the advertisements are to be believed, however, it was not until 1789 that with Samuel Fores's *New Guide* came 'the only pocket map ever published with the names of the streets'.[43] Some booksellers became specialists in these works. Henry Kent held shares in the *Foreigner's Guide*

---

41   Research in the publication history of this work, as of many others considered in this study, was led by ESTC online searches.

42   Anon., *Universal Directory consisting of Alphabetical Lists of Merchants, Banks, Notaries, Shopkeepers, Doctors with distinct List of Booksellers* (London, 1763), is of interest for its connection with the book trades, but does not appear to have gone through any subsequent editions.

43   Cited by Harris, 'London Guidebooks', p. 51.

and nearly a dozen other directories, while William Lowndes produced the *London Directory*, the *Travellers Companion*, a *Guide to Stage Coaches* and numerous street and town directories in the 1780s.[44]

The general commercial guides (in successive editions) of Thomas Mortimer, Henry Kent, Thomas Lowndes, William Bailey and William Holden, among others, offered listings of the major firms in all London trades. The directories were, however, problematic publications to consult, not least in their ordering, even if, when examining them today, the organizing principle of the directories reveals much about the originators' perceptions of place and trades. Many trade directories were useless in certain circumstances. A comparison might be with modern-day French telephone directories where you must know the exact village (which are arranged alphabetically) before you can find your person. In some eighteenth-century directories, like Holden's, alphabetical ordering assumed that the individual's name was all that you needed to know for the directory to be of use, whereas those like Mortimer's, arranged by trade, assumed that (as with the contemporary British *Yellow Pages*) profession or service was your only useful starting point (and about whose exact trade description you had to take an educated guess). You would, for example, in searching for a paper merchant and stationery business like that of John Bloss & Co., or of the even larger firm of Mount & Page or of the later Goadby & Berry, have to guess whether it would be under 'S' for 'stationer', as it was in some directories, or 'W' for 'wholesale stationer', as it was (if at all) in others.

Directories to towns other than London and trade directories proper largely date from the second half of the century. The earliest examples of individual handbooks are probably Thomas Gent's guides to York and Hull in the 1730s. About twenty years later, pocket guides were printed and sold by Collins, Binns, Lockett and many other regional booksellers. From Dorchester, Lockett issued various guides to Weymouth and other neighbouring towns. In the final third of the century many regional town and county trade directories became virtually annual productions. Liverpool boasted a directory in 1766, Birmingham in 1767, and Manchester and Salford in 1772. The first Edinburgh directory was issued by Peter Williamson in 1773. Sheffield was provided with a directory in 1774, Bristol

44 The London directories, many updated at intervals, are listed and surveyed in Charles William Frederick Goss, *The London Directories, 1677–1855* (London: Denis Archer, 1932), and P. J. Atkins, *The Directories of London, 1677–1977* (London: Mansell, 1990).

in 1775, Newcastle upon Tyne in 1778, Dundee in 1782, Glasgow in 1784 and Cardiff in 1796. Of the spa resorts, Margate issued a guidebook in 1770, Southampton in 1775, Brighton in 1778 and Tunbridge Wells in 1780. Three years later, William Bailey's *Northern Directory* attempted the widest alphabetical commercial listings yet seen and included in its coverage London and all principal English towns north of the Trent. Thereafter came an avalanche of town directories together with the first comprehensive county and regional commercial guides. Ten different Birmingham directories were published before 1800 and seven for Liverpool, all of which went through various new editions and reprintings. In the south, John Sadler printed the first Hampshire guide at Winchester in 1784.[45]

Many, such as William Chase's *Norwich Directory: Or, Gentlemen and Tradesmen's Assistant*, included tables and charts for calculations and making notes. Bailey followed his *Northern Directory* with a *Western and Midland Directory* in 1783 and, the year after that, the *British Directory*, the first attempt at a national trades register. After an apparently unsuccessful attempt to launch a further part-by-part national guide in 1787, a rival partnership of Peter Barfoot and the Winchester printer, John Wilkes, published their *Universal British Directory* between 1790 and 1798. The project was undertaken on a grand scale: agents were appointed in the major towns to collect information and take subscriptions, and each of the completed sections included both descriptive accounts and alphabetical lists of tradesmen and businesses.

What is plain is the marriage of interests between local trading concerns and the publisher of the directory. Many of the compilers of directories were printers who also practised as local auctioneers or general storekeepers. One of the earliest county guides, *The Merchant's Miscellany and Traveller's Complete Compendium ... of the County of Bedford for 1785* was compiled and printed by John Henington, who was also the town's leading auctioneer. The Brosters, printers of Chester, edited the 1781 *Chester Guide ...* [and] *Directory of City and Market Towns in the County*. The composer and publisher of the earliest *Birmingham Directory* (1767), James Sketchley, had moved to the town in 1759 to commence work as a printer, bookseller, estate agent, lottery-ticket seller and auctioneer. In 1774 he also issued *Sketchley's Sheffield Directory* and in 1775, setting

---

45   The major works are checklisted in Jane E. Norton (comp.), *Guide to the National and Provincial Directories of England and Wales* (London: Royal Historical Society, 1950), and Kazuhiko Kondo, 'Town and County Directories in England and Wales 1677–1822', *Kenkyu Roshu*, 31:92 (Spring 1985), 47–55.

up as auctioneer in Bristol, a further guide to his new town. In addition to advertising their publishing and general commercial services, other writers of directories boasted of the quality of their printing. McSwinney, the type founder, issued his *New Birmingham Directory* in 1773, proudly announcing his use of up-to-the-minute, locally produced Baskerville type.

By the final third of the century, production of most of these types of directory was immensely competitive. Some of the most hotly disputed struggles over copyright in the century concerned guidebooks. Many were optimistically emblazoned with a royal licence and a notice that the work had been entered at Stationers' Hall. Various struggles between rival guides intensified as the potential for profits became clear. In the 1750s, hostilities broke out between a number of leading firms over the publication and supply of the *Court and City Register*. In the 1790s, rights to Bew's *Ambulator* were settled in a bitter and prolonged dispute. In the same decade George Kearsley pleaded with the public not to buy pirated copies of his *Tax Tables*. By the end of the century, heavy investment was also made in guides to the spas and seaside resorts. Obviously the guides to the great tourist 'lions' of the capital, including the pleasure gardens and the promenades, also assisted the general trade of these districts. Local traders advertised in the directories and many also sold them, acting as booksellers' agents. Other more general guides incorporated discreet advertising by including particular shops in tours of towns. Nor should 'trade' directories be too narrowly defined. Some gentlemen readers of newspapers and guidebooks were in search of more than tea and porcelain. One of the best selling of all guidebooks was *Harris's List of Covent Garden Ladies*, and although some descriptions appear too imaginative, they were certainly sold as genuine.[46] If they did fail in accuracy they would not be the only trade guides of the period to do so.

Almanacs and pocketbooks

During the eighteenth century, more copies of almanacs were sold than all other types of publication put together. As a ready calendar and diary, the almanac was often expanded to include a variety of miscellaneous

---

46 The guides have been credited with a certain veracity and usefulness in Hallie Rubenhold, *Harris's List of Covent-Garden Ladies; Sex in the City in Georgian Britain* (Stroud: Tempus, 2005).

material. It was also the last of the chapbooks to be bought by readers right across the social scale. A small book or single sheet with a calendar of astronomical and terrestrial events, expected weather, health signs and other predictions, the almanac also charted moveable feasts and quarters of the year, provided blank space for recording and planning engagements, and (according to the specific type of work) listed times of fairs, distances between towns, coach times, embarkation points, and weights, measures and other calculating tables. Traditionally structured to serve an agricultural community, particular attention was given to the phases of the moon and to notes on times of sowing and harvesting.

The huge demand for these books or sheets, selling from between a penny and eightpence each, made them extremely valuable publishing property. Produced under an exclusive patent granted in 1603, almanacs were for two centuries the tightly controlled mainstay of the 'English Stock' of the Stationers' Company. At its height, this monopoly brought in a gross profit of about £2,000 per year, involved an estimated turnover of some £10,000 and included thirty-five different works from the single-sheet broadside to the 24-page pocketbook.[47]

During the eighteenth century, nearly half a million almanacs were sold in the final two months of each year, almost half of which were single-sheet publications.[48] Contributory booksellers included Baldwin, Bladon, Longman and most of the leading operators of the century.[49] During at least the first third of the century, most of their almanacs were distributed by chapmen from stocks ordered by regional booksellers. Divided into

47   At mid-century, the hawking of unstamped almanacs was punishable by three months in gaol and rewards of twenty shillings were offered for the apprehension of offenders: 16 Geo. II, c. 26, fol. 546. The patent is considered in Cyprian Blagden, 'Thomas Carnan and the Almanack Monopoly', *Studies in Bibliography*, 14 (1961), 23–40. Local guilds of stationers were also keen to protect the monopoly. Of many regional examples, William Knight, chapman, had his goods seized and was fined five shillings by the Hereford magistrates for infringement of the Company's 'Compacion': HCL, Minute Books of the Guild of Haberdashers, Barbers, etc., 3 Nov. 1662.

48   SH, Misc. Box C.3, 'Almanacks'; records of printing ordered to replenish stock after the Great Fire reveal twenty almanac titles, totalling 318,850 copies; SH, Warehouseman's Records, 1667. The total printing costs were £2,887 15s 8d; in 1779, when 130,000 copies alone were printed of Francis Moore's almanac, *Vox stellarum*, better know as *Old Moore's Almanack* and first printed in 1700. At the same date of 1779, prior to distribution, the Stationers' Hall warehouses stored 20,000 copies of the *Ladies Diary* and 24,000 copies of *Rider's Almanack*.

49   SH, Misc. Box C.4, 'Almanack accounts'.

'blanks' and 'sorts', the almanacs were sold at wholesale trade prices to the country suppliers. The Stationers' Company advertised heavily in both London and provincial newspapers, carefully recording the entries and paying particular attention to the marketing of works aimed – if only on the title page – at different readerships.[50] In Scotland, where the Company's patent did not apply, almanacs were printed in Edinburgh from the 1620s and also in Glasgow and Aberdeen shortly after mid-century.[51] Even in the 1680s, John Forbes of Aberdeen had an annual sale of over fifty thousand such works.[52]

Many of the reckoners and other guides, such as those containing book-keeping advice, were combined with diaries and blank pocketbooks. Compared to the almanac proper, demand for the separate diary was slow to develop. The interleaving of diaries with blank and ruled pages from the 1730s was the key to their popularity.[53] Robert Dodsley published his *New Memorandum Book* in 1748 and a year later, Richard Baldwin II launched a rival *Gentleman's and Tradesman's Daily Journal*. By the 1760s the diary was clearly undermining the Company's monopoly in the higher social market for almanacs. From the 1720s, in fact, various notices from the Company warned of this wider infringement of copy. It was established early on that interleaving and the insertion of miscellaneous, often very obscure, information could avoid the monopoly, and when in 1775 the Company's sole rights were successfully challenged by Thomas Carnan, the victor was in reality only one of many who had been pressing the Company after mid-century. Led by his *New London Almanack* and his one-sheet diary 'by Reuben Burrow', Carnan's victory was in the short term to profit London booksellers rather than provincial ones.[54] Among many rivals, Carnan made the most of his victory. At Christmas, 1780, he was advertising no less than thirty-eight differently named almanacs.[55]

50   SH, Misc. Box C.2, 'Bills and receipts for almanack advertisements in provincial newspapers'.
51   The earliest Scottish almanac seems to be Raban's, printed in 1623; details are given in William R. McDonald, 'Scottish Seventeenth-century Almanacs', *Bibliotheck*, 4:7/8 (1966), 257–322.
52   *Register of the Privy Council of Scotland*, 3rd ser., 8 and 28 Feb. 1684.
53   Michael Harris, 'Astrology, Almanacks and Booksellers', *Publishing History*, 8 (1980), 87–104, a review of Bernard Capp, *Astrology and the Popular Press. English Almanacs 1500–1800* (London: Faber and Faber, 1979).
54   SH, Misc. Box D, 'Carnan Dispute'.
55   *Public Advertiser*, 20 Nov. 1780.

The Revd Dr John Trusler, the eccentric and notoriously productive literary entrepreneur, responded with his eight-year, one-sheet almanac.

Although provincial publishers were keen to compete, it was not until the 1790s that locally produced almanacs sold more than a few thousand copies. Nevertheless, most of the major regional printer-stationers were issuing their own almanacs or diaries by the late 1770s. By then, for example, Simmons and Kirkby of Canterbury and Thomas Fisher of Rochester were producing an annual *Kentish Companion* as an account book 'for the pocket or desk'. Claiming to be the first such guide for the county, the title page makes special reference to its fifty-two double-ruled blank pages designed 'to keep an Account of Monies received and paid'. No fewer than twenty-six dealers are named in *Kentish Gazette* advertisements for the *Companion*.[56] In 1775, the partnership published its first annual *Kentish Almanack*, a single sheet which could be pinned up as it was or folded and bound. It was republished by the firm and its successors until the mid nineteenth century.

The increase in pocketbook publication is dramatic after 1730. At least four hundred different titles were published between then and the end of the century. Works were advertised as 'sized to be worn in the pocket', to be always handy to correct errors and check on pricing. The inclusion of discount tables became commonplace, while other pocketbooks provided blank sections for calculations and jottings. In advertisements for his *Daily Journal or the Complete Annual Account Book*, Baldwin announced that as 'many friends and purchasers of this usefull Book have expressed a wish for an Almanack to be annexed to it, the Publisher has now procured one of a Size adapted to the Book'.[57]

Only a fraction of the hundreds of such works advertised in the newspapers now survive. Among those lost are some of the most interesting, locally published works, aimed – if the adverts are to be believed – at what must have been a very specific and small market. Of more general appeal were the many reckoners and advisers designed for ladies, gentleman and estate owners who had to deal directly with local tradesmen. Here there is no clear division between many of the manuals designed for the owner of private property and those which might also be used to advantage by the small tradesman. *The Universal*

56   The work is surveyed in David Knott, 'Competition and Co-operation in the Kent Almanack Trade', *Factotum*, Occasional Paper 3 (1982), 14–20.
57   *Public Advertiser*, 7 and 14 Dec. 1780.

Pocket-Book printed by various London bookselling congers during its dozen or more editions from 1730 to 1760 was a particular success. At 2s 6d it was not cheap, but does seem to have been one of the best selling of all such general works, with its tables of useful information and its reckoners. Local equivalents were also extremely successful ventures. *The Liverpool Memorandum Book*, published annually at least from 1753, included fifty-two pages prepared for the entry of cash accounts. *The Newcastle Memorandum Book* reached its forty-third edition in 1797. In December 1775, a small village shopkeeper ordered three dozen *Kentish Almanacks*.[58] In 1795, Trusler boasted that his *Country Almanack* had increased its sales from three thousand copies in 1791 to twenty thousand in 1794. Blank ledgers and ruled diaries were hardly new to this period, but business needs had never been of this scale before.

---

58   Knott, 'Competition and Co-operation', p. 18.

10

Wider Discussion

Literary historians and sociologists have spoken of the social impact of print as a form of restructuring consciousness. Historical reconstructions of attitudinal change have been greatly assisted by broad questions about the penetration of literature in society through studies of production, retail, borrowing and circulation, about the use to which books were put, and about the objective of writers and the confidence placed in their message.[1] The broader question of 'printedness' raised issues, as also addressed by earlier chapters here, particularly in relation to jobbing printing and the production of small printed items. The history of publishing that informed and assisted business does benefit, however, from revisiting the more traditional focus of the 'book'. The widening of the type and volume of publication and the extension of distribution networks have already been seen in relation to the servicing of the business community. Print replicated and circulated business news, standardized teaching and supported proposition and protest. In the full community, one effect of literature was to establish tacit rules affecting the direction of subsequent writing. Contributors were urged to consider the improvement of society and search for both explanatory and predictive laws.

By the end of the century, more Britons than ever before had been able to read about the characteristics of commerce and industry. The expansion of both print and trade intensified debate over the origins and consequences of financial and commercial transactions. Professional

---

1   Notably (but very selectively): Leo Lowenthal, *Literature, Popular Culture and Society* (Englewood Cliffs, NJ: Prentice-Hall, 1961); Robert Darnton, *The Forbidden Best-Sellers of Pre-Revolutionary France* (New York: W. W. Norton, 1995); Elizabeth Eisenstein, *The Printing Revolution in Early Modern Europe*, rev. 2nd edn (Cambridge: Cambridge University Press, 2005); Asa Briggs and Peter Burke, *A Social History of the Media: from Gutenberg to the Internet*, 2nd edn (Cambridge: Polity, 2005); and see Sabrina Alcorn Baron, Eric N. Lindquist and Eleanor F. Shevlin (eds), *Agent of Change: Print Culture Studies after Elizabeth L. Eisenstein* (Amherst, MA: University of Massachusetts Press, 2007).

disputants, from Grub Street hacks to scholarly writers on ethics and political arithmetic, were occupied by questions concerning the intended or unintended consequences of what is now loosely called 'economics'. Country gentlemen, clerics and amateur followers of commerce took to publishing tracts about trade for themselves. Even the general use of language was transformed. Increasing familiarity with economic acts brought a semantic narrowing of such words as 'fortune', 'corruption' and 'interest'. The words 'tradesman' and 'manufacturer' assumed completely new interpretations.

The history of popular inquiry into such topics as trade, finance and population, and the actual dynamic of print in the transmission of economic theories and histories in the eighteenth century, still requires more research, despite the vast literature that engages with the intellectual origins of political economy and political arithmetic.[2] Among others, for example, Mary Poovey has investigated the intellectual pedigree of distinctions between moral philosophy, from which political economy is said to have derived, and an older 'science of government' as a forerunner to political arithmetic.[3] Yet, within the scope of the history of book trades, there is certainly a place for a reassessment of the contemporary interest in economic matters created by the opening up of markets, the new availability of texts and the changing relationships between authors, booksellers and readers. In this, the recovery of a greater breadth of eighteenth-century publications does not diminish the earlier importance of John Graunt and William Petty in the espousal of political arithmetic[4]

2   See (among many others) Phyllis Deane, *The State and the Economic System: An Introduction to the History of Political Economy* (Oxford: Oxford University Press, 1989); Lars Magnusson, *Mercantilism: The Shaping of an Economic Language* (Abingdon: Routledge, 1994); Andrea Finkelstein, *Harmony and the Balance: An Intellectual History of Seventeenth-Century English Economic Thought* (Ann Arbor: University of Michigan Press, 2000); John A. Taylor, *British Empiricism and Early Political Economy: Gregory King's 1696 Estimates of National Wealth and Population* (Westport, CT and London: Praeger, 2005); and Sophus Reinert, *Translating Empire: Emulation and the Origins of Political Economy* (Cambridge, MA: Harvard University Press, 2011).

3   Mary Poovey, 'Between Political Arithmetic and Political Economy', in *Regimes of Description: In the Archive of the Eighteenth Century*, ed. John Bender and Michael Marrinan (Stanford, CA: Stanford University Press, 2005), pp. 61–76.

4   See Julian Hoppit, 'Political Arithmetic in Eighteenth-Century England', *EcHR*, 49:3 (Aug. 1996), 516–40; Paul Slack, 'Government and Information in Seventeenth-Century England', *Past and Present*, 184 (Aug. 2004), 33–68; Paul Slack, 'Measuring the National Wealth in Seventeenth-Century England', *EcHR*, 57:4 (Nov. 2004), 607–35; and Michael Donnelly, 'From Political Arithmetic to Social Statistics: How Some Nineteenth-Century

or of Hume, Smith, Malthus and other contributors to the long-term development of a science of economics.[5] The origins of such disciplines, if such they may be called, and the influence of Scottish Enlightenment writers upon the direction of early economic thought, continues to be debated by a comprehensive literature.[6] What is apparent, however, is that the most popularly reprinted of the writings on trade theory do not square with the texts now regarded as the most influential in terms of the subsequent development of economic thought. Nor does either reading list accord precisely with various eighteenth-century impressions of the types of work to be consulted for specific information about English (or British) commerce.[7]

The larger question concerns not so much the intellectual history of economic reasoning as the development of a print-led system of public discourse about trade and economics. The moral parameters and evidential basis of much argument about the economy not only depended upon the perception and intention of the writer, but were also guided by the author's means of communicating his work to a known public. Early economic writing is, of course, often as much about political ideology or the justification of specific proposals as it is about attempts at scientific explanation. Whatever the motivation of the writer, however, the actual or perceived methods for getting work into print, and for replicating and circulating it, had an essential bearing upon the form in which the

Roots of the Social Sciences Were Implanted', in *The Rise of the Social Sciences and the Formation of Modernity: Conceptual Change in Context, 1750–1850*, ed. Johan Heilbron, Lars Magnusson and Björn Wittrock (Dordrecht and Boston, MA: Kluwer Academic Publishers, 1998), pp. 225–39.

5   See in particular Emma Rothschild, *Economic Sentiments: Adam Smith, Condorcet and the Enlightenment* (Cambridge, MA: Harvard University Press, 2001).

6   William Letwin, *The Origins of Scientific Economics. English Economic Thought 1660–1776* (London: Methuen, 1963); Jacob Oser, *The Evolution of Economic Thought* (New York: Harcourt Brace, Jovanovich, 1963); Joyce O. Appleby, *Economic Thought and Ideology in Seventeenth-century England* (Princeton, NJ: Princeton University Press, 1978); Istvan Hont and Michael Ignatieff (eds), *Wealth and Virtue. The Shaping of Political Economy in the Scottish Enlightenment* (Cambridge: Cambridge University Press, 1983); D. C. Coleman, *Revisions in Mercantilism* (London: Methuen, 1969); Albert O. Hirschman, *The Passions and the Interests. Political Arguments for Capitalism before its Triumph* (Princeton, NJ: Princeton University Press, 1977).

7   See in particular the outstanding study by Richard B. Sher, *The Enlightenment and the Book: Scottish Authors and Their Publishers in Eighteenth-Century Britain, Ireland, and America* (Chicago and London: University of Chicago Press, 2006; pbk, with new preface, 2010).

argument was presented. In many cases, it should be added, original intention did not always correspond to eventual result. Like that recurrent problem for so many of the early economists, of the wider social conse-quences of purely private action, the original self-interest of the propa-gandist or apologist became of public interest when the printing-press lifted tracts and their imitators or objectors into a general circulation.[8]

A point made earlier about the publishing origins of guides to the merchant and accountant should also be repeated in relation to general publication. Broader discussion of trade in early modern England included consultation of books in foreign languages printed abroad and imported or bought during foreign travels, but the eighteenth-century vernacular tide was a strong one. Translation was also made of certain popular foreign titles, and the commercial treatise in French or some other language (such as Savary's *Dictionnaire universel de commerce* in the original) was a rare read (although one whose reading and citation might be deployed with superior authority in other English publications). The further and critical issue for English readers of books about commerce and the economy is that home production was British as much as English, and that the books crossing the borders were those from Glasgow and Edinburgh (and to a lesser extent reprints from Dublin).

Interest in trade

Two general trends can be identified at the outset: the increasing interest in commerce shown by authors of almost all types of literature and the increasing specialization and diversity of printed material available to the public. It was from a very great variety of work that discussion of trade was advanced. Book production, sales and edition reprinting rates, booksellers' stocks and advertisements, and commercial and private library catalogues, all reveal an extraordinarily wide selection of works which informed readers about the workings and consequences of commerce.

The restructuring of the book trades and the changing commercial base of their operation affected the content of literature at all levels. Over

8 Conceptual analysis of transmission is surveyed by Denis McQuail, *Mass Communication Theory* (London: Sage Publications, 1983), but see also the pioneering Harold D. Lasswell, 'The structure and formation of communications in society', in *The Communication of Ideas*, ed. L. Bryson (New York: Institute for Religious and Social Studies, 1948), 37–51.

the century, greater per capita expenditure on books and the widening of readerships brought various responses, from a choice of daily newspapers to the advent of the encyclopaedia salesman. Regional press activity in particular promoted greater engagement with trading issues. The extension of middle-class education, local political activity and the means to circulate printed works, generated new approaches to instruction and the articulation of ideas.

On issues of commerce, greatest publicity and profit for the writer and the book trades still came from pamphlet warfare, not from reflective writing about economics. By the early eighteenth century, more conceptual discussion of what we now call 'economics' either derived from the objectifying quantification generally known as political arithmetic[9] or within moral and political philosophy, usually at a level of abstraction that required no practical evidence relating to commercial policy or the specific actions of investors or tradesmen. The career of Defoe is instructive. The pre-eminent journalist of his day, he was supported in turn by government and aristocratic political patronage, but finally, after the 1720s, by successful public subscription. Subscription proposals were still the most common form of testing a market and launching a new work, and this was certainly true of writings about trade. Prominent supporters of such ventures were still few, however. Before the 1740s, larger dedicated works on commercial questions were rarely contemplated and several prominent subscription schemes failed to attract the required number of takers. Various voices complained of a general lack of interest in understanding the workings of trade. If mid-century Scotland produced a clutch of well-connected peers, gentlemen and émigrés promoting discussion of trade, in England the eccentric 3rd Viscount Townshend was almost the sole aristocratic sponsor of interest in trade theory before the 1760s.[10]

Nevertheless, even by the 1740s, the modest annual publication of books and pamphlets specifically devoted to trade theory was increasing. General surveys of publishing in the eighteenth century suggest not only

9   See Peter Buck, 'Seventeenth-Century Political Arithmetic: Civil Strife and Vital Statistics', *Isis*, 68:1 (Mar. 1977), 67–84.

10   According to Josiah Tucker he was 'ye only Nobleman I can find who expresses any concern for the preservation of Trade': Tucker to Townshend, 13 July 1752, HMC, Townshend MSS, 379. Despite being the dedicatee of various works on trade in the 1740s and 1750s, Charles Manners, Duke of Rutland, seems to have had no personal interest in the subject at all: see James Raven, 'Viscount Townshend and the Cambridge Prize for Trade Theory 1754–1756', *Historical Journal*, 28:3 (Sept. 1985), 535–55.

a sharp upturn in publication totals after the 1760s, but also an increasing secularization of literary output over the full century. By one estimate, some 40% of the total of just over 200,000 titles published in Britain during the century was devoted to social sciences (including politics, history and geography).[11] The continuing *ESTC* now comprises about 335,000 records for the period 1701–1800, including all imprints and significant variants of books and pamphlets published in Great Britain, her colonies and North America, and those publications in English originating abroad. A further estimate, based on sampling of the *ESTC* for every year ending in a '3', suggests that titles categorized in that particular exercise as 'business and finance' comprised 9% (146 titles) of the total number of book titles published in 1703, 7% (169 titles) of the total in 1763 and 16% (821 titles) in 1793. A pronounced dip in 'business and finance' publications appears in 1723 (84 titles) and 1743 (80 titles), although as a proportion of total estimated publication by titles, 1723 'business and finance' titles are 19% of the total (more, proportionately, than in 1793).[12] The verdict is that such counting, with all the caveats about categorization of titles, inclusion within the database, sampling difficulties and non-survival rates, becomes little more than the most general of guides, of which the most and perhaps only secure conclusion is that overall publication rates and those of publications about trade and finance followed the very common eighteenth-century 'growth curve', with its sharp and escalating take-off in the final third of the century.

For a more enlightened assessment of the development of interest in publishing, acquiring and consulting books and pamphlets on trade, the historian needs to examine records of specific publication strategies, and the purchasing, collecting and borrowing habits of consumers. As a breakdown of the 1723 *ESTC* count reveals, both more titles and more editions of titles on commerce were issued. The success of particular titles is a marked feature of mid-century publishing on commercial and financial topics. Josiah Tucker's *Essay on Trade* of 1749, for example, went through four rapidly successive editions, a feat equalled by none of the late-seventeenth-century tracts on commerce. Above all, the corresponding

11   John Feather, 'British Publishing in the Eighteenth Century a Preliminary Subject Analysis', *The Library*, 6th ser., 8 (1986), 32–46.
12   Michael F. Suarez, 'Towards a Bibliometric Analysis of the Surviving Record, 1701–1800', in *The Cambridge History of the Book in Britain: Volume V*, ed. Michael F. Suarez and Michael L. Turner (Cambridge: Cambridge University Press, 2009), pp. 39–65 (p. 46, table 1.1, 'Genre of books published between 1703 and 1793').

marketing of publications was more narrowly directed, commencing with the most obvious quarry. From the end of the seventeenth century, parliamentarians were the targets for the majority of printed proposals and counter-proposals relating to commerce and manufacturing. An analysis of one early dispute over commercial policy has shown how the Anglo-French treaty of 1713 was played out amid a blaze of newsprint and pamphlet pushing. The *Mercator* was published thrice-weekly in 181 numbers throughout the episode, statistics were lobbed from one publication to the next and, it is argued, the Tories lost the issue primarily through the poor public presentation of their cause.[13] The Whig–Tory debates of the first two decades were directly linked to the tracts fuelling disputes between landed and commercial interests at mid-century and beyond. As has been detailed, the *Craftsman* campaigned eagerly for new audiences in its bid to win the propaganda battle in and outside Westminster.[14]

By mid-century, new reasons were also being proffered for publishing such writings. The increasing identification of trade with the national interest, and the consequential need to promote commerce and cleanse it of impurities, spawned a variety of printed material, with some writers praising British achievements, others attacking certain social groups for undermining commercial progress. The diversity of writing was again related to changing opportunities for transmitting ideas to particular audiences. Different and differently packaged types of works were issued for gentlemen, women, clerics, intellectuals, children and the barely literate. Some title pages listed in great detail the profession of their intended readers; others gave more elliptic designations. The days when the gentleman read the chapbook were now over (at least in public admission). Discussion was further stimulated by the increasingly quicker rate at which texts could be circulated and writers react. The advance of political lobbying through print was clearly related to the increasing effectiveness of the book in debate. In any debate, the rate at which copy can be produced and sent out or reprinted is vital. This changed noticeably after about 1730 with the popularity of reprinting in part-form and, from the late 1740s, of reproduction in periodical reviews

13   D. C. Coleman, 'Politics and Economics in the Age of Anne', in *Trade, Government and the Economy in Pre-Industrial England: Essays Presented to F. J. Fisher*, ed. D. C. Coleman and A. H. John (London: Weidenfeld and Nicolson, 1976), pp. 187–211.
14   Simon Robertson Varey, 'The Craftsman 1726–52: An Historical and Critical Account' (unpubl. Ph.D. dissertation, Cambridge University, 1977).

and journals. The message conveyed was usually one-directional but, after mid-century, magazines and journals introduced a limited feedback from readers. With more discrimination on the part of an expanding audience and greater gambles taken by publishers in launching works quickly and without prior subscription, it was also in booksellers' interests to investigate more closely market demands and promotional possibilities. The 'widening circle' of readers in the provinces brought further opportunities for promotion and writing, and as a result economic works aimed at new markets were compiled by what appears as an often eccentric assortment of individuals.

In the discussion of trade there were no proscriptive borders to the sort of set disciplines that modern writers have to cross to explore similar themes. Those calling for investigation into trade theory did not view their subject as divorced from moral, legal or religious considerations. Smith, Ferguson and other professed tutors published works to instruct in the civic morality that all gentlemen were expected to study as citizens or legislators of a commercial polity.[15] In the middle decades of the century, more specific and secular discussion of trade and industry was increasingly woven into publications offering particular religious or political perspectives in relation to society and the individual. Writers from Tucker to Smith, for example, extended their discussion of the economic agency in part as a consequence of their interest in the question of an adequate subsistence for the poor. As has been discussed in influential works on the intellectual constructs adopted by the leading economic writers of the early modern period,[16] within the modernist framework of an historical, causal and systematic analysis of the development of commercial society, both Hume and Smith were also informed by a jurisprudential approach very much removed from many of the civic humanist critiques of an earlier generation. In both approaches, however, ethics and economics were inextricably bound up in questions concerning the individual and

15 This is fully discussed in Nicholas Phillipson, 'Adam Smith as Civic Moralist', in Hont and Ignatieff (eds), *Wealth and Virtue*, pp. 179–202.

16 Notably, J. G. A. Pocock, *The Machiavellian Moment: Florentine Political Thought and the Atlantic Republican Tradition* (Princeton, NJ: Princeton University Press, 1975) and see also his *Virtue, Commerce and History* (Cambridge: Cambridge University Press, 1985); Hirschman, *Passions and the Interests*; Donald Winch, *Adam Smith's Politics: An Essay in Historiographic Revision* (New York and London: Cambridge University Press, 1978); Andrew Skinner, *A System of Social Science: Papers Relating to Adam Smith* (New York: Oxford University Press, 1979); and Istvan Hont and Michael Ignatieff, 'Needs and justice in the Wealth of Nations', in Hont and Ignatieff (eds), *Wealth and Virtue*, pp. 1–44.

his pursuit and use of wealth, the consequences of a growing population, and the tensions between private property and an equitable distribution of goods.[17]

Popular, best-selling literature reproduced both current and venerable verdicts about wealth creation and deployment. Commerce was included as an integral part of political argument, of historical writing and those discussions of law, ethics and belief that underpinned new literary analyses of society. In the early years of the eighteenth century, about a third of all titles published annually can be attributed to the general category 'religion, philosophy and ethics'.[18] The vast sermon literature increasingly addressed specific trading issues as questions affecting moral choice. Advice and opinion became more pragmatic and founded upon informed, often statistical accounts, rather than upon biblical or classical evidence. Statistics and calculations were commonly unreliable, but their inclusion was based on an expectation of such proof in argument. Most tracts were penned not only to explain and instruct, but also to predict.

The readership

Changes in the treatment of commerce were especially related to the scale and composition of the readership. A major difference between the economic debate of the mid seventeenth century and that of the mid eighteenth century was the size of the audience. Seventeenth-century readership of economic tracts was very limited. Fewer than two thousand copies of the *Discourses* claimed to be by Dudley North[19] were printed during the century. Davenant's work of the 1690s only reached a major audience when it was reprinted in part-issue nearly a hundred years later. These editions compare with a possible publication total of Hatton's *Comes commercii* manual of six thousand copies between 1699 and 1722.[20] Many tracts, handbills, broadsides and pamphlets relating to

17   For political aspects, see 'Managing the "Great Machine of Trade"', in Nancy F. Koehn, *The Power of Commerce: Economy and Governance in the First British Empire* (Ithaca and London: Cornell University Press, 1994), pp. 61–104.

18   Suarez, 'Towards a Bibliometric Analysis', p. 47, 34% in his *ESTC* 1703 sample.

19   See William Letwin, 'The Authorship of Sir Dudley North's Discourses on Trade', *Economica*, n.s., 18:69 (Feb. 1951), 35–56.

20   Natasha Glaisyer, *The Culture of Commerce in England, 1660–1720* (London: The Royal Historical Society and Boydell, 2006), p. 105.

economic matters printed between 1660 and 1700 were issued in editions
of under five hundred copies. Most of the economic writing of this period
that found greater readerships is found primarily as part of religious
or political addresses or within more general didactic literature. Broad
readership also supported the republication of books on husbandry and
the sort of variegated stock of guides found in the bookshop of George
Conyers of Little Britain. Conyers's post-mortem sales catalogue of
1740 (including dozens of titles printed in the late seventeenth century)
has become a much-visited resource for historians of popular print of
this period but, in fact, the edition size of many of his titles remained
relatively modest.[21] Publications which were concerned only with matters
of trade and industry comprised a very small proportion of total annual
publications. The audience for the works discussed by Joyce Appleby in
her seminal study of seventeenth-century economic thought was in effect
a small, highly educated elite, residing largely in London.

Before about 1740, therefore, the market for retailing books should not
be overstressed. The limitations here are important counterpoints to the
hugely expanding use of jobbing print, of the appearance of small printed
items in everyday and business use. From 1700 until about mid-century,
the audience for larger published texts increased only gradually, although
there were probably several dramatic but short-lived surges in purchases
from the bookshops during the 'pamphlet wars'. These broke out with
increasing ease in the first half of the century, especially in time of conflict
abroad, and many were concerned with trading issues. Pamphlets relating
to specific episodes, such as the lottery schemes of the 1690s and 1710s
or the South Sea Bubble of 1720, found a ready audience in coffee-houses
and private societies. The most popular of these were issued in editions of
a thousand copies at a time. A considerable circulation of the pamphlets
was also maintained among the disputants and those personally involved
in the events. In turn, print became much more clearly appreciated as an
agent in the spread of ideas and as a means for furthering debate.

Readership numbers are notoriously difficult to calculate, but after

---

21   See James Raven, *Bookscape: Geographies of Printing and Publishing in London
before 1800* (London: The British Library, 2014), pp. 81, 94, 163–4; and Michael Harris,
'The Pleasant Art of Money Catching: The Expansion of the Trade in Cheap Books around
1700', in *Craft and Capital in Book Trade History. Part I: A Skilled Workforce: Training
and Collaboration in the Book Trades. Part II: Balancing the Books: Financing the Book
Trade from the 16th Century*, ed. Robin Myers, Michael Harris and Giles Mandelbrote, 2
vols (forthcoming, 2015).

mid-century there was a steady increase both in the number of people per head of population buying books and in the average number of books bought by each purchaser. Edmund Burke's contemporary estimate of a reading public in the 1790s of some eighty thousand has been much cited, as has Paul Korshin's identification of a newspaper readership of ten thousand in 1776.[22] The percentage of families denoted as nobility, gentlemen and clergy and the higher echelons of those classified as farmers, all by Joseph Massie (d.1784) in one of his many pamphlets on economic affairs, can be correlated with modern estimates of the English and Welsh population figures for 1761 (6.2 million) and 1791 (7.7 million). Assuming a constant family size between social groups and a rough correction for (another artificially constant) age structure (a generous 30% deduction from the total to account for those below reading age), we might posit a rough and ready maximum of those of sufficient age and position to comprise an 'at risk' readership of 350,000 in 1760 and 440,000 in 1790.[23] In terms of purchasing power, D. E. C. Eversley suggests 150,000 households with an annual income of between £50 and £400 in 1780 (15% of all households in 1750; 25% by 1780), while Neil McKendrick suggests this is an underestimate.[24]

The even greater increase in the number borrowing books far eclipsed the rate of population growth. Many others gained access to print in ways other than by purchase or commercial borrowing. From the first decades of the century, the audience for print was enlarged by literary and scientific societies, coffee-houses and informal associations. London remained the

22   Paul J. Korshin, 'Introduction', in *The Widening Circle: Essays on the Circulation of Literature in Eighteenth-Century Europe*, ed. Paul J. Korshin (Philadelphia: University of Pennsylvania Press, 1976), pp. 3–10 (p. 7).

23   Social groups from Massie as classified by Peter Mathias in 'The Social Structure in the Eighteenth Century', in *The Transformation of England: Essays in the Economic and Social History of England in the Eighteenth Century* (London: Methuen, 1979), pp. 171–89 (esp. pp. 188–9); population estimates from E. A. Wrigley and R. S. Schofield, *The Population History of England, 1541–1871: A Reconstruction* (Cambridge, MA: Harvard University Press, 1981), pp. 576–80.

24   D. V. Glass and D. E. C. Eversley (eds), *Population in History: Essays in Historical Demography: General and Great Britain*, new edn (London: E. Arnold, 2008); Neil McKendrick, 'Home Demand and Economic Growth: A New View of the Role of Women and Children in the Industrial Revolution', in *Historical Perspectives: Studies in English Thought and Society in Honour of J. H. Plumb*, ed. Neil McKendrick (London: Europa Publications, 1974), pp. 152–210 (pp. 172–3); see also essays in Isabel Rivers (ed.), *Books and Their Readers in Eighteenth-Century England: Volume 2: New Essays* (London: Bloomsbury, 2003).

centre of publication (but with increased regional publishing activity, and most notably of newspapers, of course) but London booksellers were increasingly serving a widening readership, supported by an increasingly competent and complex distribution network. The provincial market certainly came to offer rich rewards, enhanced by the postal service and by the advertising and distributional assistance of country town and city booksellers. The business structure of the printing trades changed markedly from the 1740s, with fewer subscription proposals and more gambles taken on the commercial market. Some of the non-subscription works considering economic issues were intended for city merchants and financiers, but many others sought to interest groups not directly involved in trade and manufacturing. For the country customer requiring the latest books on commerce, the usual procedure was to order through the local bookseller. Such customers invariably acted on the bookseller's or the original publisher's advertisements in the local newspaper. Carriage was paid by the bookseller and the customer could also enjoy account or credit facilities. With so few booksellers' business records now surviving, it is very difficult to reconstruct the exact transactions, although some information about the receipt of commercial books and the profession of the customers is available through the memoirs of the purchasers or borrowers. From various autobiographies we can learn of remote West Country agents and tradesmen receiving manuals from the productive London bookshops of a Robert Dodsley or Thomas Longman, or of interested subscribers in Westmorland receiving works from Edinburgh and Glasgow.

The growth of gentlemen's clubs and discussion groups further supported a growing amateur interest in trade. A readership for tracts and small volumes of commercial essays was clearly identified in leading booksellers' advertisements by the end of the century. As gentlemen considered the education of their sons, they were also fed books on commercial training and explanations of trade written specifically for the young. The didactic essay tradition of Addison and Steele was directed towards informing laymen and novices of matters relating to the organization of modern society. Writing as a practical moralist to instruct not only his students but also men of middling rank about their commercial society, Adam Smith was keenly aware of the necessity to include graphic examples to illustrate his points. By the 1760s, the high prices offered to certain authors for economic works for the young and inexperienced is another indication of the new market potential of such books.

As a result of increased interest and greater means of purchasing volumes, private collections of books, quite aside from institutional and commercial libraries, also continued to grow in number, location and size.[25] The range of the holdings of the libraries, especially as attested by sales catalogues to private collections – a major feature of the trade and auction in books in the eighteenth century – fully supports the change noted by Perry Gauci and others that while in the 1680s numerous contemporary writers lamented how poorly commerce was served by the press and how relatively few guides were published in England, this opinion had fundamentally altered by the second half of the eighteenth century.[26]

The writers

A survey of best-selling economic writing in eighteenth-century England might commence with familiar names, but those appearing from the reprinted items in the *ESTC* and eighteenth-century catalogues and publishing records include many authors now consigned to the margins of specialist bibliography. The early editions of works greatly respected today were also often modestly sized, and bought and read by a very specific audience. The style and emphasis of publication was changed greatly during the century by significant changes to the ranks of those interested in economic issues.

The writers of treatises on commercial matters in the eighteenth century are distinguishable from their seventeenth-century predecessors in the first instance because of their more varied backgrounds and professions. Almost without exception, the major economic writers of the seventeenth century had been leading merchants or commercial dealers. Thomas Mun (d.1641) was an East India Company director. Edward Misselden (d.1654) was a merchant adventurer. Sir Dudley North (d.1691) and Sir Josiah Child (d.1699) were eminent and very wealthy city merchants (and Child was the son of a merchant). Nicholas Barbon (d.1698) was a notorious mortgage banker and insurance broker. Before entering government service, Sir William Petty (d.1687) succeeded to his father's

---

25   See Rebecca Bowd (ed.), special issue of *Library and Information History*, 29:3 (Aug. 2013).

26   Perry Gauci, *The Politics of Trade: The Overseas Merchant in State and Society, 1660–1720* (Oxford: Oxford University Press, 2001), p. 161.

cloth business.[27] However much the authors protested their impartiality, such mercantile backgrounds provoked accusations of special pleading. As a result, many of the tracts were published anonymously while the publication of others – notably the works of Child – were complicated by disputes over authorship and booksellers' claims about the ownership of copyrights.

By contrast, relatively few eighteenth-century economic writers were merchants. Malachy Postlethwayt (1707–67) had direct mercantile experience, although it gave him neither great riches nor civic office. His *Universal Dictionary of Trade* (1751–55) was the product of twenty years' labour but he also produced many other works on commerce. Sir Matthew Decker (1679–1749), author of influential tracts on import duties (1743) and on foreign trade (1744), was a Flemish merchant who arrived to live in London in 1702. Almost the only other eighteenth-century merchant to publish economic works other than instructional manuals, or short, highly specific propagandist tracts, was Joshua Gee, and of his life relatively little is known.[28] A few company clerks and government revenue and customs officials published works on the public revenues and other financial matters, but again most were responding to immediate issues. Of their number, Adam Anderson (1692–1765), a native of Aberdeen and a clerk of the South Sea House for at least forty years, did produce the two-volume *Historical and Chronological Deduction of the Origin of Commerce* in 1764.

As a group, however, writers on commerce were most notable for the diversity of their occupations. Authors included clergymen, school-teachers and administrators, some writing as moralists and improvers, others acting as lobbyists for national or local causes. Most contributors were independent gentlemen, often removed from the centres of

---

27 Erich Strauss, *Sir William Petty: Portrait of a Genius* (London: Bodley Head, 1954); E. Fitzmaurice, *The Life of Sir William Petty* (London: John Murray, 1985); and Tony Aspromourgos, 'New Light on the Economics of William Petty (1623–1687): Some Findings from Previously Undisclosed Manuscripts', *Contributions to Political Economy*, 19 (2000), 53–70.

28 His *Trade and Navy of Great-Britain Considered* was first published in 1729; in 1742 he wrote one of the earliest economic inquiries into woollen manufacture: see 'Joshua Gee' by Peter Groenewegen in *ODNB*. John Bennet, whose *National Merchant* was issued in 1736, had some mercantile experience: see David Fairer, 'Persistence, Adaptations and Transformations in Pastoral and Georgic Poetry', in *The Cambridge History of English Literature, 1660–1780*, ed. John Richetti (Cambridge: Cambridge University Press, 2005), pp. 259–86 (p. 280).

financial or even commercial activity. Some, like Joseph Massie, were prolific writers of tracts on economics, often syntheses of previous pamphlets.[29] Others, like the prolific Scots writer, Sir John Sinclair, were great landowners. A few, like Jonas Hanway (d.1786), the champion of many causes but also a contributor to various commercial issues, set themselves up as writers of means after varied working careers. Hanway had for several years been apprenticed to a merchant. The greatest of those eventually able to make a living from pamphleteering, both officially commissioned and independent, however, was Defoe. He was probably the most widely read of all the early contributors to economic debate in the new century. Extravagantly versatile and prolific, Defoe penned some four hundred pieces and over 250 separate works (allowing for continued and often intemperate debate about the authorship of many publications attributed to him).[30] His contribution to economic writing spanned the *Review* and the *Mercator*, political squibs, guidebooks for the common man, comprehensive treatises and the influential *Tour thro' the Whole Island of Great Britain*, with its descriptive accounts of commercial progress. Other gentlemen penned short pieces in response to specific events or in support of specific lobbies. Short tracts on finance, trading regulations and questions of credit, poverty and population had burgeoned in post-Restoration Britain, but the output of writers swelled even more from the middle decades of the new century. Some of their number were considered mad, several quite reasonably so. George Edwards (d.1823) wrote forty-two books between 1779 and 1819, most propounding fantastic schemes.[31] The prolific Irish pamphleteer and millenarian, Francis Dobbs (1750–1811), was finally locked up for his own safety.

In one key respect, however, it is misleading to stress the greater 'secularization' of economic literature during the century. Against the diversification of writers, few of whom were now practising traders, clerical commentaries on commercial matters were also more numerous than in previous centuries. This is partly because of the increasing

29 William Arthur Shaw (comp.), *A Bibliography of Joseph Massie* (London: G. Harding, 1937).

30 See P. N. Furbank and W. R. Owens, *A Critical Bibliography of Daniel Defoe* (London: Pickering and Chatto, 1998); and P. N. Furbank and W. R. Owens, *A Political Biography of Daniel Defoe* (London: Pickering and Chatto, 2006).

31 J. M. Scott, in the 1888 *DNB*, delicately remarked that 'it may be conjectured that his sanity was imperfect'. The new *ODNB* entry is more charitable.

relevance of commerce to state-of-the-nation addresses by leading clerics, but during the second half of the century there also seems to have been stronger personal interest in the nature of trade among divines, both Anglican and Nonconformist. A recent and fascinating addition to the literature on this subject has argued that late-seventeenth-century political arithmetic was 'sacred' in the sense that it was essentially apologetic, providentialist, antideist discourse, based on polemical foundations laid by latitudinarian foundations of the Restoration, and able to incorporate an increasing corpus of demographic observation and analysis.[32] Such objectives were soon regarded as peripheral to the mainstream of mid and later eighteenth-century secular political arithmetic, which was taken up with fiscal policy, public health and increasingly refined calculation of annuities. As Ted McCormick puts it, 'while the Anglican clergy was still well represented among commentators on population, moreover, rational Dissenters like Richard Price and deists like Benjamin Franklin were at the forefront of new developments. Quantitative discussions of population were more likely to fuel projects for hospitals or pension schemes than defences of Mosaic history.'[33] Nevertheless, while many clerics were allied to a particular political lobby and some increasingly taken up by specific economically productive or evaluative projects, clergymen were also increasingly drawn to discussions of trade as salient moral discourses.[34] As Norman Sykes confirmed, authorship of pamphlets defending government policy was the easiest avenue for clerical advancement.[35] Perhaps because of this, Nonconformist writing was commonly the most perceptive and unconstrained. Robert Wallace, Presbyterian minister and student of population, was a founder member of the Rankenian club in Edinburgh. Richard Price (1723–91), who made his mark with a much republished work on the national debt in 1771 and his *Essay on Population* in 1780, was also a Nonconformist minister and voluminous writer. Of the many clerics contributing to economic writing during the century, however, the best known was Josiah Tucker, Dean of Gloucester and the author of the

---

32 Ted McCormick, 'Political Arithmetic and Sacred History: Population Thought in the English Enlightenment, 1660–1750', *Journal of British Studies*, 52 (Oct. 2013), 829–57 (esp. p. 849).

33 McCormick, 'Political Arithmetic and Sacred History', p. 854.

34 One of the most sensational and certainly best selling of their number was John Brown, the increasingly unstable curate who committed suicide in 1763.

35 Norman Sykes, *From Sheldon to Secker. Aspects of English Church History 1660–1768* (Cambridge: Cambridge University Press, 1959).

1749 *Essay on Trade* and of multiple economic tracts thereafter. A staunch Hanoverian and critic of monopoly and high wages, Tucker held fast to the possibility of constructing a science of economics.[36] His later work also made great use of statistical material drawn from discussions with merchant parishioners and an extensive correspondence with like-minded students of trade.

Of the other professions, most attention, of course, has been centred upon the professorial writers from Hutcheson and Ferguson to Smith and Millar. Others of the Scottish Enlightenment, such as the Court of Session judge, Lord Kames, further swelled the ranks of a lay intelligentsia, actively engaged in academic dispute about the conception and direction of society. Historical writing, led by Bolingbroke, Strutt, Robertson and Gibbon, was similarly occupied, though most affected consideration of commerce more through contributions to the debate about the origins of imperial decline than through any direct observations. Of the historical writers who specifically considered modern trade, Thomas Mortimer (1730–1810) had perhaps the greatest influence. After being dismissed in 1768 from his office as vice-consul for the Austrian Netherlands, he published many works by subscription. Parliamentarians were also prominent. Westminster men like George Rose and Thomas Whately contributed several influential works on the practice of trade. William Guthrie (1708–70) was a reporter of parliamentary debates for the *Gentleman's Magazine* and engaged in almost continuous political writing before achieving recognition for his 1770 *Commercial Grammar*. Towards the end of the century, a new breed of hack writer, exemplified by publisher-author John Trusler, wrote solely for the market. A dozen or more writers courted what was now clear general public interest in commercial issues, ranging from personal finance to the national polity. Many of the titles produced were deliberately sensationalist, reaching a peak during the East India inquiries and trials from the late 1770s to the early 1790s. A surprisingly large number of these writers can be classified either as rogues or cranks, and a select group of them as both.

---

36   Robert L. Schuyler, *Josiah Tucker. A Selection from his Economic and Political Writings* (New York: Columbia University Press, 1931); Walter E. Clark, *Josiah Tucker, Economist: A Study in the History of Economics* (New York: Columbia University Press, 1903); George Shelton, *Dean Tucker and Eighteenth-century Economic and Political Thought* (London: Macmillan, 1981).

The press and education

By the time of the surge in pamphleteering in the 1750s, the structure of the book trades, and with it printed discourse about economics, had changed from that of even twenty years before. Public interest and the expansion of (in particular) the London publishing business enabled authors to consider contributions more substantial than the 36-page pamphlet. The further stimulus came with the foundation of the annual journals and reviewing periodicals, led by the *Gentleman's Magazine* in 1731, the *Monthly Review* in 1749 and the *Critical Review* in 1756.[37] For at least the first thirty years of their publication, these journals and many of their imitators attempted a comprehensive reviewing policy. The weightier journals also extracted works at great length. In addition, the *Annual Register; a review of public events at home and abroad* opened its account in 1758. The club or private subscriber taking the monthly periodicals was introduced to the latest economic literature without having to buy the actual books. The whole range in reviewed form was before him, with the name of the bookseller as well as its price if he decided to order the work. For the reader interested in particular branches of financial or commercial expertise, such reviewing invariably gave a clear idea of content, irrespective of title or the profession of the author.

As an increasing volume of lobbying material was released, proposals were circulated to use the press competitively to set standards of debate and advance economic learning. Malachy Postlethwayt's *Universal Dictionary* and *Merchant's Public Counting House* of 1750 and 1751 included a plan of practical education, a call to establish a national mercantile college and a design to launch an annual prize-essay competition on trade theory. Apart from a much later and equally ineffectual suggestion by Tucker, the only other such initiative in England was the short-lived Townshend institution in the University of Cambridge at mid-century.[38] However evident the desire to instruct in practical aspects of trade, with large numbers of manuals published and dozens of amateur writers submitting works for teaching purposes, until the first decades of the nineteenth century the English universities' conception of providing gentlemen with a liberal education did not embrace economic thought. The few works on trade

37 Later but extremely popular rivals included the *Town and Country*, established in 1768, and the *European*, commenced in 1782.
38 The episode is described in Raven, 'Viscount Townshend and the Cambridge Prize for Trade Theory'.

produced by Cambridge and Oxford scholars during the century were all published in London by subscription or by highly commercial booksellers, and not by the university presses. Support from high places was also hesitant. Tucker was commissioned to write an educational treatise on commerce for the Prince of Wales, but the enthusiasm of the Court was very temporary. With the exception of brief consideration of the *Economica* which led to some limited study of the economics of the family, systematic analyses of wealth, poverty and population were deemed outside the bounds of proper learning. In London and the English towns, commercial learning was primarily advanced by the private academies, where English replaced Latin as the natural language of instruction and where current debates were introduced to wider audiences.

For most of the century, Scotland offered more and became the most important 'importing' centre for publications on commercial and financial subjects for English readers. In contrast to Oxford and Cambridge, the Scottish university presses fostered intellectual discussion of what 'trade' meant. The Glasgow press of the Foulis brothers, established in the precincts of the College in 1741, reprinted an impressive collection of economic literature, including Mun, Law, Child and Gee, as well as sixpence part-issues of the Postlethwayt dictionary.[39] The availability of texts had an immediate effect upon the system of university teaching. The use of modern, set books for illustration and discussion was widely adopted in the Scottish universities, leading eventually to the first published lectures on commerce. Change was also marked outside formal education. A large number of gentlemen's clubs had been founded, including the Easy Club in 1712 and various societies for improvement in the 1720s and 1730s, culminating in the establishment of the Select Society in 1754. In Glasgow, the Political Economy Club was founded by Andrew Cochrane in 1743 and directly influenced the decision by the Foulis brothers to launch their series of reprints. In 1752, the Literary Society of Glasgow was established and, six years later, the Philosophical Society of Aberdeen.[40] Taverns and coffee-houses and other semi-formal institutions for the middling ranks flourished in the northern cities. Henry

---

39   See Stephen W. Brown and Warren McDougall (eds), *The Edinburgh History of the Book in Scotland Vol. 2 Enlightenment and Expansion, 1707–1800* (Edinburgh: Edinburgh University Press, 2012).

40   The history of the clubs is comprehensively charted in D. D. McElroy, 'Literary Clubs and Societies of Eighteenth-Century Scotland' (unpubl. Ph.D. dissertation, Edinburgh University, 1952).

Mackenzie's *Mirror* and *Lounger*, direct descendants of the *Spectator*, were penned by an Edinburgh man.

The expanding market for economic textbooks, however, encouraged new ventures not only in the two leading Scottish centres but also in mid-century London, where particular bookselling firms specialized in educational or children's works and moral primers. Longmans, Cadell and Rivingtons despatched dozens of large, dense advertisements familiarly known as 'clouds' to be inserted in the London and provincial newspapers, listing up to fifty different titles at a time. Edinburgh's close relationship with the book trades of Antwerp and other continental towns enabled the rapid import of the latest foreign works considering trade. The incentive for cheap book production, where Scotland had originally been outside the Stationers' Company monopoly, was also maintained. Thomas and Walter Ruddiman and Gavin Hamilton, printers and publishers in Edinburgh, reprinted many tracts relating to topical commercial questions but whose copy was strictly held elsewhere. By mid-century, Scottish booksellers were left free to reprint and distribute, within and outside Scotland, books in which copyright had expired or did not apply. English booksellers rarely took action, even through the English courts. The imports from Dublin, which allegedly so damaged London traders, even seem to have done some harm to the Scottish trade. It has also been suggested, however, that London booksellers could also have benefited from the publicity brought by Irish piracies, and certainly that readerships were increased by their circulation in Britain.[41] The extent of the reprinting of works on commercial and financial issues, and the extent of the import (and smuggling) trade into England, have still to be fully established, however.[42]

Individual printers also directly promoted interest in trading publications by their own personal enthusiasm for the subject and the contacts they made with both popular and academic authors. The pre-eminent example is William Strahan who maintained a long-standing correspondence with, among many others, Smith and Hume, and acted as go-between for various publications undertaken by Cadell and the London

41   Richard Cargill Cole, *Irish Booksellers and English Writers 1740–1800* (London: Mansell, 1986).
42   For piracies see Warren McDougall, 'Smugglers, Reprinters, and Hot Pursuers: The Irish-Scottish Book Trade, and Copyright Prosecutions in the Late Eighteenth Century', in *The Stationers' Company and the Book Trade, 1550–1990*, ed. Robin Myers and Michael Harris (New Castle, DE: Oak Knoll, 1997), pp. 151–83.

booksellers.[43] Balfour of Edinburgh did regular business with Charles-Joseph Panckoucke, bookseller of Paris (d.1798). In another dimension of the book trades, London translators and compilers ensured that foreign authors including Cantillon and Turgot were swiftly available in English. Within five years of the publication of Montesquieu's *l'Esprit des Lois* in Paris in 1748, Tucker and Townshend were assuming common familiarity with his concepts. The first subject of Townshend's prize institution supposed full knowledge of Montesquieu's recent tenets. In Edinburgh, Hamilton and Balfour had published *l'Esprit des Lois* in 1749 – a venture which so impressed Hume that he asked them to undertake the revised edition of his *Essays*.

All this further enhanced the reputation of known centres for the study of commerce and served to attract like-minded men. In London and the provincial cities, private clubs and libraries were established as centres for debate and enlightenment. The London Library Society, founded in 1785 and organized by a distinguished Nonconformist committee and membership, stocked most of the leading commercial works.[44] Subscription libraries opened at Liverpool in 1758, Manchester in 1765, Leeds in 1768, Sheffield in 1771, Bristol in 1774, Hull in 1775, Birmingham in 1779 and at Newcastle in 1787. By 1800, Bristol boasted two hundred members, Leeds had four hundred and Birmingham, five hundred. By the same date, all the libraries held at least five thousand volumes. At Liverpool, the 1760 *Catalogue* listed the huge majority of members as merchants, and most of the remainder as brokers, attorneys and general traders. Among the merchant clientele of Bristol, where borrowing records uniquely survive for such a library, economic works, ranging from Tucker's tracts to the weighty compilations of Guthrie, Mortimer and Lewis, were extremely popular, being almost continuously on loan and even in need of replacement.[45] By 1800, over a hundred subscription libraries were in operation in the provinces.[46] In Wales, up to a dozen subscription libraries followed the foundation of earlier institutions by the Society for Promoting Christian Knowledge.[47]

---

43   Strahan's interests are described in J. A. Cochrane, *Dr Johnson's Printer: The Life of William Strahan* (London: Routledge and Kegan Paul, 1964), esp. ch. 10.

44   Anon., *Catalogue of the Books of the London Library Society* (London, 1786).

45   Bristol Library Society Borrowing Records, 1774–1800, Bristol Public Library.

46   Details are given in Paul Kaufman, 'The Community Library', *Transactions of the American Philosophical Society*, n.s., 57:7 (1967), 3–67.

47   The history of some of these is considered in Paul Kaufman, 'Community Lending Libraries in Ireland and Wales', *The Library*, 5th ser., 33 (1963), 299–312.

In addition, commercial libraries and local book clubs opened in their hundreds during the final third of the century.[48] Three hundred and eighty commercial lending libraries and book clubs have been identified in eighteenth-century England and Wales, twenty-one in Ireland and twenty-five (probably the greatest underestimate of the actual total) in Scotland.[49] The most commercial library initiatives were led by the Noble brothers of London from the late 1740s, with Hookham, Vernor and Bell joining them in the next twenty years. In the 1770s, Lane and then Cooke extended such enterprise by offering to supply fully stocked libraries to any part of the country. In Dublin, the Hoey family sponsored commercial circulating libraries from 1737, with similar establishments founded by Watts in 1754, Armitage in 1762 and Williams in 1765. In the provinces, bookshops, such as those of Binns of Leeds and Halifax, long served as surrogates for local lending libraries. Full catalogues do not always survive, but those remaining, such as that of Hookham, show that many works on commerce and industry were stocked even by commercial libraries primarily lending fiction and plays.[50] One of the few personal reading lists to have been made at the time, that of a student in a remote part of Wales, indicates that by the 1760s, and even in regions far from the metropolis, works on commerce from Salmon, Guthrie and Ward's instructional works to Defoe's *English Tradesman* were available, borrowed and reborrowed.[51]

From about mid-century, several scientific, literary and radical philosophical societies promoted investigations into economic issues. Of the many dissenting academies, the most famed were those founded by Joseph Priestley. Their activities were recorded in separate publications as well as in journal reviews and appreciations. The *Memoirs of the Literary and Philosophical Society of Manchester* was published in 1785 and, like many similar accounts, appeared in extracted form in national periodicals.

48 Many are considered in Hilda M. Hamlyn, 'Eighteenth-century Circulating Libraries in England', *The Library*, 5th ser., 1 (1947), 197–218.

49 James Raven, 'Libraries for sociability: the advance of the subscription library, c.1700–1850', in *The History of Libraries in Britain and Ireland: Volume II 1640–1850*, ed. Giles Mandelbrote and Keith Manley (Cambridge: Cambridge University Press, 2006), pp. 241–63.

50 Hookham catalogues, 1791 & 1794, Bodleian Library, Don.e.206 and 207.

51 Cardiff Public Library, MS 1.169, reading list of Thomas Benyon of Llansadwrn; the MS is considered in R. George Thomas, 'The Complete Reading List of a Carmarthenshire Student 1763–7', *Journal of the National Library of Wales*, 9 (1955–56), 356–64.

Edinburgh's Select Society was also closely linked to the book trade.[52] Lunatick Clubs (so named after their time of meeting at the full moon) were founded in many towns including Dolgelly and Bala in Wales and also in Coventry and Colchester, although by far the most famous of the small private groups was the fourteen-member Lunar Society of Birmingham.[53] In such ways the opportunity to debate trading issues in company with other educated men was increased, supported consistently by print. Even in small rural towns, debating or philosophical societies were founded. Gentlemen members were usually drawn from the town's professions and neighbouring gentry. Such groups supported their own libraries and many had certain of their papers printed and circulated by the local bookseller. Many of the invited speakers were made known to members through print. At Bungay in Suffolk, for example, a book society was established in 1770, maintained a regular meeting and was closely connected to the small but distinguished book trade and local writing fraternity, as well as to the town's leading businessmen and neighbouring gentry.[54] Wrexham's coffee-house, operating by 1675, was holding regular book auctions by the 1740s, as were the coffee-houses at the Exchange in Chester and the George in Liverpool. At Shrewsbury, the coffee-house was on Pride Hill where Wood had his printing office – a connection repeated in several county towns and new urban centres.[55] Certain large private libraries of economic literature were also established and gained a particular reputation among those interested in the subject. Joseph Massie petitioned the City of London in 1754 for a public library to house his collection of 'old, scarce, curious and valuable tracts and treatises on the history of commerce'. Massie's 2,500 tracts and manuscripts were more numerous even than those in the impressive library amassed by Defoe.[56] Records survive relating to at least two hundred separate major, catalogued private libraries in Ireland before 1800. Four belonged to merchants and contained an average of 1,500 volumes each.[57]

---

52 Peter Jones, 'The Scottish Professoriate and the Polite Academy 1720–1746', in Hont and Ignatieff (eds), *Wealth and Virtue*, pp. 89–117.
53 Studied by Robert E. Schofield, *The Lunar Society of Birmingham* (Oxford: Clarendon Press, 1963).
54 ESRO, HD476/1–5, Ethel Mann Papers, vols 1–3.
55 Development in Wales is sketched by Cecil J. L. Price, 'Polite Life in Eighteenth-Century Wales', *Yr Einon*, 5 (1953), 89–98.
56 Anon., *Librorum ex Bibliotensis Philip Farewell et Daniel Defoe* (London, 1731).
57 Richard Cargill Cole, 'Private Libraries in Eighteenth-Century Ireland', *Library Quarterly*, 44:3 (July 1974), 231–47.

Greater discussion of trade was generated by all the changes described: the encouragement of new readerships and specialist interests; new recruitment to the ranks of economic writers; the increasing preoccupation of all authors with economic issues; and the shifting structure of the book trades. Published investigations were increasingly detailed and probing, and the book-by-book construction of a literature of economics produced vast numbers of derivative works attempting synthesis, voicing disagreement and offering new explanations of causality or prediction. Economic literature was promoted not only to advance a science, but also to further British prosperity by informing and advising. This is most clearly seen by examining literary output from the perspective of the object of most of the booksellers' promotional efforts of the century – the gentleman reader.

II

Business, Publishing and the Gentleman Reader

Through the mediation of print, propertied gentlemen and gentlewomen, principal customers of the booksellers, viewed economic progress in their world and the moral implications of new wealth and new methods of business. With eighteenth-century presses providing more people with more information upon economic matters than ever before, a broad range of readers were offered unprecedented advice on how to conduct their financial affairs and how to understand the nature of commerce. Newspapers, pamphlets, manuals and magazines popularized current intellectual debate, often absurdly simplifying intricate propositions but also widening their audience and inviting public response. Booksellers and compilers made handsome profits from handbooks on trade and financial management. Such commercial venturing was not without its effect on the manner in which arguments were presented and counsel tendered.

The 'gentleman reader' was also a consciously constructed ideal. Many of those reading the commentaries on the economy were women and many of the propertied added to or resisted the ascription of gentlemen: clerics, scholars, merchants, lawyers, other professionals. Many owners of land and capital did not conform to the 'gentlemanliness' increasingly characterized in literature and drama. The literary fashioning of social stereotypes during the eighteenth century focused particularly on the negative, in which the avaricious tradesman, or the man or woman of all too rapid or squandered wealth, became the butt of jokes and a caricature of rapacity and idiocy. Yet the goal of many of those penning these stereotypes was to defend moderate wealth creation and point to ideal values by demonstrating the limits of proper behaviour. Those limits were described, often in outrageously negative lampoons, to defend capitalist values. In other words, the early-eighteenth-century revulsion for the financial market, and the distrust of credit so evident in literary commentaries and on the stage, was replaced by the end of the century by an acceptance in a wide range of writing of the merits of the wealth creation by merchants and of the good of trade, so long as it followed civilized parameters.[1]

The final question pursued by this book is how the broader representation of trade, finance and industry related to the expanding commercial and financial press and jobbing printing that have been the central concern of earlier chapters, but which have so often been neglected. For both writers and readers, questions relating to business in society were reformulated according to changes in personal holdings of wealth and patterns of expenditure. As A. W. Coats has written, 'historians of literature seem much more aware of the significance of this point than historians of economics'.[2] Changing perspectives affected not only works specifically addressing economic theory, but also the increasing amount of popular journalism, biography, imaginative literature and miscellanies touching on commercial issues. For the eighteenth-century bookseller, one of the safest and most rapidly expanding sections of this market was the production of works to help men (and some women) of means plan their financial affairs. Such books ranged from the diaries and almanacs already discussed to full do-it-yourself guides to estate and business management. Many were combined with descriptions of the operation and consequences of trade.

Guides to good management

Publications advising thrift and prudent management had a pedigree stretching back to the sixteenth century. Two of the most popular seventeenth-century works included the 1642 *Art of Living in London* and the 1647 *Worth of a Penny; or, a Caution to Keep Money* both by 'H. P.', or Henry Peacham junior (1578–c.1644). Between 1700 and 1750 over a hundred similar new titles were added to the lists. Old favourites like *The Pleasant Art of Money Catching* (apparently first published by John Dunton in 1684 and comprising extracts from Peacham's *Compleat Tradesman, or, the Exact Dealers Daily Companion*) were updated and printed in regional editions, many outside England. One so-named '5th'

1 This is the central argument of James Raven, *Judging New Wealth: Popular Publishing and Responses to Commerce in England, 1750–1800* (Oxford: Oxford University Press, 1992).
2 A. W. Coats, 'The Relief of Poverty. Attitudes to Labour and Economic Change in England 1660–1782', *International Review of Social History*, 21 (1976), 98–115 (p. 103).

edition of *The Pleasant Art* was published at Glasgow in 1740. Various London editions were issued throughout the century. The last eighteenth-century editions seem to have been printed in Dublin in 1793 and in Falkirk in 1799. The most noticeable change introduced into the later editions was in the particularity of the subjects and financial calculations. John Sowter's *The Way to be Wise and Wealthy*, apparently first printed in Exeter in 1716 and then much reprinted in London down to at least 1760, included a long and detailed section on the trader. *The Bachelor's Monitor, being a modest estimate of the expences attending the married life*[3] was among various manuals, of lesser or greater seriousness, printed by John Osborne in Paternoster Row in the 1730s and 1740s.[4] Gentlemen's guides to investments and shares proved another popular line from at least the time of Thomas Lydal's *New Interest Pocket Book*. Lydal's 144-page book, with its tables of simple and compound interest, was designed to provide advice and calculating tables for a range of investors. It was printed by Andrew Bell, printer and bookseller (and druggist) at the Cross-Keys and Bible in Cornhill, and co-published by Gosling the banker in 1710.

Fifty years later, Thomas Mortimer's *Every Man his Own Broker: or, A Guide to Exchange-Alley, in which the Nature of the several Funds, Vulgarly called the Stocks, is clearly explained* attained enormous popularity, achieving at least a dozen London editions between 1761 and 1798. It was published at first by Samuel Hooper, print, map and music-seller of the Strand and then Ludgate Hill, and then by the prolific Robinsons in the Row and in the Royal Exchange.[5] As the 1782 new preface to the ninth edition explained, *Every Man his Own Broker* was intended as a warning against 'the knavish tricks carried on in the stock-jobbing transactions of the [Exchange] Alley' and designed to suppress and circumvent brokers, teaching every man indeed to be his own broker. The new preface recounted the early newspaper puffs for the book and the engagement of many correspondents whose letters and advice Mortimer claimed to have incorporated in subsequent editions.[6] In 1775, John

---

3 Also published as *The Batchelor's Monitor: With healthy and pleasant advice for married men in the governing a wife. To which is added, an essay against unequal marriages* (possibly by Edward Ward).

4 *Gentleman's Magazine*, Feb. 1741, Register of Books.

5 Thomas Mortimer, *Every Man his Own Broker: or, A Guide to Exchange-Alley*, 1st edn (London, 1761).

6 Mortimer, *Every Man his Own Broker*, 9th edn (1782), pp. iv, vi.

Trusler, with a similar eye to the market, produced his much-reprinted *The Way to be Rich and Respectable, Addressed to Men of Small Fortune.* As the title explained, 'in this Pamphlet is given an Estimate, shewing that a Gentleman, with Economy, residing in the Country, may, with a few Acres of Land, live as well for 500£ a Year, and make an Appearance in Life equal to those who spend double that sum without these Advantages'. Thereafter, works became even more sophisticated. Trusler's *London Adviser and Guide* provided unprecedented detail. Under the heading 'Houses', for example, Trusler explained in twenty-six pages how to rent or buy accommodation, which auctioneers to approach, the comparative merits of fire insurances, the levels of house tax, and the means to secure water supplies. In addition to the usual guide material, he offered a series of 'marketing tables' by which the gentleman could estimate the cost of provisions, leading to 'estimates of housekeeping' that calculated the weekly budgets of families of differing incomes.[7]

Across this diverse collection of economic advisers there were subtle changes of emphasis over the century, as the provincial book market deepened and as writers saw new prospects for work. Companion manuals on how to prevent personal and business financial loss were produced in large numbers and the dangers of personal ruination repeated in countless printed works. Such counsel went hand in hand with fears of the consequences of living beyond one's means. Overexpenditure in desperate attempts to maintain or extend appearances was said to devastate families and threaten the prosperity of the nation. It was argued that financial crises affecting the whole community could originate from action by an individual, and that there was a determinable relationship between a right to a fortune and its usage. To some extent, familiarity with the national debt and share investment had eased anxieties by the end of the century, but concern was also focused more on the use, or rather misuse, of wealth than on the manner of its accumulation. For many writers and their readers, the dangers were clearly related to concern over the temptations of London life. Reissued, usually pocket-sized protests from Charles Davenant (d.1714) to Mortimer (d.1810) regarded non-residence in the country as a threat to personal solvency and to the balance of local society. Handbooks warned of the economic ruin facing those who were

7 Anon., *The London Adviser and Guide; Containing Every Instruction and Information Useful and Necessary to Persons Living in London and Coming to Reside There* (London, 1786).

beguiled by the fashionable life of the city. Mortimer was one of several who claimed that communities would collapse if landowners were continually absent from their seats.[8]

Reasons for such pessimism are not hard to seek. As John Brewer writes, economic crises 'seemed just as arbitrary and cruel as a death, flood or plague'.[9] Certainly, the gathering speed of domestic demand and of industrial output did not preclude short-term or individual failure. Competitive enterprise was often forced to carry larger overheads and credit burdens, and bankruptcy proceedings increased dramatically in the very midst of rampant demand.[10] Given the recurrence of local and national liquidity crises, the increasing facility with which credit could be obtained served to swell the number of defaulters, with perceptions of risk varying according to local conditions and the nature of personal credit arrangements.

Word of mouth spread news and rumours of failure. Confidence and the assessment and avoidance of risk remained informed by personal (and sometimes public, communal) exchange that, before the telephone or other long-distance means of immediate communication between people, depended essentially on the place and site of exchange. Emphasis on certain streets such as Exchange (or 'Change) Alley and on coffeehouses, taverns and the Royal Exchange itself is explained by their role in inaugurating gossip or offering face-to-face confirmation. The parish as an active communal sphere within the city of London also embraced many specific sites of exchange from vestries (the meeting places of office holders) to the churches themselves – sites, as Perry Gauci acknowledges, of multiple marble monuments and mercantile self-regard but worthy of continuing research as spaces of information exchange.[11] It was the word

---

8   Thomas Mortimer, *The Elements of Commerce, Politics and Finances* (London, 1772; new edn, 1780), p. 44.

9   John Brewer, 'Commercialization and Politics', in *The Birth of a Consumer Society: The Commercialization of Eighteenth-Century England*, ed. Neil McKendrick, John Brewer and J. H. Plumb (London: Europa, 1982), pp. 197–264 (p. 212).

10   L. S. Pressnell, *Country Banking in the Industrial Revolution* (New York: Oxford University Press, 1956), pp. 291, 330–1; T. S. Ashton, *Economic Fluctuations in England 1770–1800* (Oxford: Oxford University Press, 1959), esp. pp. 125–30. Bankruptcies peaked in 1772–73, 1778 and 1788. Ashton calculated that of the bankruptcies between 1731 and 1800, 40% fell in the years after 1782, a level noted as the mark of an expanding economy: *An Economic History of England: The Eighteenth Century* (London: Oxford University Press, 1955), p. 125.

11   Perry Gauci, *The Politics of Trade: The Overseas Merchant in State and Society,*

in print, however, which not only reinforced awareness of the failures but increasingly provided first news of changes in fortune, especially as information networks spread miles beyond the sites of personal communication. The replication of printed information in further printed works enlarged such publication still further. Many provincial newspapers carried extracts from the columns of the *Gazette*, and the leading magazines contained listings or summary articles of the most recent bankrupts alongside births, marriages, deaths and promotions. Monthly returns were given in the *Gentleman's Magazine* from its foundation in 1732. Some sixty years later, William Bailey, of *Northern Directory* fame and himself a bankrupt in 1787, even published a *List of Bankrupts, Dividends and Certificates from the year 1772 to 1793* as a comprehensive guide to defaulters. Although not so publicized as the official bankrupts, many other victims of financial failure were also featured in local commentaries by the end of the century.[12] Many best-selling works considered the collapse of great men or famous attempts to mend fortunes, whether by fair means or foul. However conveyed, default was not anonymous. Print published specific details to a wide community. The increasingly sophisticated borrowing on bond and mortgage was based far more upon localized, face-to-face undertakings than upon central or institutionalized development.[13] This placed a premium on trust and heightened anxieties over any tremor in economic fortunes. As the pamphlets stressed, honesty was the mainspring of a system seen to rely on individual goodwill.

The advice books urged their reader to live within real cash limits, and debated what was and was not a legitimate risk in business and estate management. The search for reasons for failures, publicized by newspapers and cheap tracts, nevertheless faced a mechanism largely mysterious beyond personal transactions. In the early decades of the

1660–1720 (Oxford: Oxford University Press, 2001), pp. 76–81, 88–94; continuing study includes Roze Hentschell, 'The Cultural Geography of St Paul's Cathedral Precinct', in *The Age of Shakespeare*, ed. R. Malcolm Smuts (Oxford: Oxford University Press, 2014), forthcoming.

12 Julian Hoppit, *Risk and Failure in English Industry, 1700–1800* (Cambridge: Cambridge University Press, 1987), p. 89.

13 Peter Mathias, 'Capital, Credit and Enterprise in the Industrial Revolution', in *The Transformation of England: Essays in the Economic and Social History of England in the Eighteenth Century* (London: Methuen, 1979), pp. 88–115; B. A. Holderness, 'Credit in a Rural Economy 1660–1800', *Midland History*, 3:2 (1975), 94–115; B. L. Anderson, 'Provincial Aspects of the Financial Revolution of the Eighteenth Century', *Business History*, 11:2 (1969), 11–20.

century, the greatest concern was over notes of credit which, as discussed in chapter 5, were now circulating in unprecedented quantity. As Defoe brooded,

> Yet tho' our Foreign Trade is lost,
> Of mighty Wealth we vapour,
> When all the Riches that we boast,
> Consists in Scraps of Paper.[14]

Later, more works focused upon personal expenditure and conspicuous consumption as most likely to bring down the whole edifice of credit and confidence. If the precise timing of changes in consumption patterns remains difficult to determine,[15] the modest work on eighteenth-century domestic inventories suggests increasing expenditure on consumer goods throughout the period.[16] Such research supports contemporary impressions of an increase in material possessions at almost all levels of society. The key variable to the support of fashion industries, however, was not so much change in average consumption levels as change in the distribution of income and the stimulation of demand among the middle orders.[17] Whatever the precise cause of the consumer boom, tracts such as the *Pleasant Art of Money Catching* continued to provide the inveterate

---

14   *Mercurius Politicus*, Sept. 1720, p. 37.
15   Such patterns are, of course, subject to regional variation and to differential rates of growth between commodity types. P. Deane and W. A. Cole, *British Economic Growth 1688–1959* (Cambridge: Cambridge University Press, 1962), ch. 2, discusses difficulties in calculating the volume of imports retained for consumption. See also the pioneering work on the expansion of consumer-goods industries in Walther G. Hoffmann, *British Industry 1700–1950*, trans. W. O. Henderson and W. H. Chaloner (Oxford: Blackwell, 1955), esp. Part B.iii and table.
16   John S. Moore (ed.), *The Goods and Chattels of our Forefathers: Frampton Cotterell and District Probate Inventories, 1539–1804* (London and Chichester: Phillimore & Co. Ltd, 1976).
17   W. A. Cole, 'Factors in Demand, 1700–80', in *The Economic History of Britain since 1700*, ed. Roderick Floud and Donald McCloskey, 2 vols (Cambridge: Cambridge University Press, 1981), vol. 1, pp. 36–65; D. E. C. Eversley, 'The Home Market and Economic Growth in England, 1750–1780', in *Land, Labour and Population in the Industrial Revolution*, ed. E. L. Jones and G. E. Mingay (London: Edward Arnold, 1967), pp. 206–59; and Neil McKendrick, 'Home Demand and Economic Growth: A New View of the Role of Women and Children in the Industrial Revolution', in *Historical Perspectives: Studies in English Thought and Society in Honour of J. H. Plumb*, ed. Neil McKendrick (London: Europa Publications, 1974), pp. 152–210.

comparison between bygone days and the immoral abundance of the present. Moral virtues of integrity, honesty, economy, even charity, were emphasized as essential for stability.

The future of the nation

Two broad themes came to dominate printed discussions of trade and industry intended for the general reader: the idea of progress or development, and a fear of economic retardation and the relinquishing of present prosperity. The first involved a reconsideration of the history of society; the second drove a succession of essayists and antiquarians to search for potential national weaknesses and continued to kindle the debate over luxury. By mid-century, these dual perspectives were not only pervasive but might be considered in terms of what Michael Polanyi expounded as the 'tacit dimension', properties and opinions so obviously shared by a group that they were never systematically articulated.[18] Whether the verdict was optimistic or otherwise, ideas of development, decline and luxury were adopted unhesitatingly by a very wide range of publications, all regarded by contemporaries as practical and reasoned contributions.[19]

From the beginning of the century, commerce was popularly perceived as the fundamental conveyor of national greatness. However strident the specific objections of the later decades of the century, this basic trust in the underlying virtue of trade was never diminished. In presenting their particular arguments, writers of histories and social essays, as well as pamphleteers, sermon writers and political lobbyists, shared broadly agreed ideals for the preservation of liberty, security and national prosperity. Commerce fathered honesty, regularity, integrity and sobriety, taught economy and toleration, and ensured the equitable distribution of wealth. Commerce induced industry and acted as the buttress for civilization and liberty. The civilization given by commerce – the 'douceur' stressed by Montesquieu – was the starting point for countless English tracts from the mid-1750s. Liberty, with Whig connotations of security for contract and property rights, was also always worthy of restatement: civil liberty and traffic were fundamentally inextricable, it was claimed. Developing

18 Michael Polanyi, *The Tacit Dimension* (London: Routledge, 1966).
19 For a comparative perspective see Jean-Claude Perrot, *Une histoire intellectuelle de l'économie politique, XVIIe-XVIIIe siècle* (Paris: Editions de l'Ecole des hautes études en sciences sociales, 1992).

commerce was a safeguard against despotism, with the separation of powers or interests that it promoted working to a common good.

By about 1760, the key assumption which had been adopted by most writers on the economy was the idea of developmental historical processes.[20] In stage-orientated explanatory theories, belief in an advanced state of society was consequent upon the progressive 'improvement' of civilization derived from particular modes of subsistence. Notions of successive ages of hunting, pasturage, agriculture and commerce reinforced the belief that it was necessary to examine the historical mechanism of a society in order to understand its present structure. The stage-led paradigm created a sense of inevitability about charted progress to the 'last stage of Improvement', that of Commerce, now upholding the nation. By the same argument, a commerce which was failing the nation could be considered as having advanced unhindered by moral checks, or as having been restrained or undermined by harmful forces. It was a debate encouraged by a wide variety of popular publications, and one led in the first instance by historians and economic writers.[21]

The question of the adverse effects of trade, increasingly debated during the century, focused on the dangers from luxury. An increasingly portmanteau term, 'luxury' was capable of application to a broad range of social, political and economic matters.[22] As the *Monthly* remarked as late as 1773, 'there is scarce any subject that has been more frequently

20   Ronald L. Meek, *Social Science and the Ignoble Savage* (Cambridge: Cambridge University Press, 1976), but also Malcolm Jack, review of Meek, *Journal of the Philosophy of History*, 16:1 (Jan. 1978), 110–12.

21   The intellectual basis of these constructs may be traced in writings on the origin of property (for example, from the emphasis of Locke's 1690 *Two Treatises of Government* on the state of nature and the original community of goods), from the so-called 'providential' theory of history and from the outcome of the 'battle of the ancients and moderns', which challenged the idea of degeneration and supported concepts of progress. The subject is surveyed in J. B. Bury, *The Idea of Progress: An Inquiry into its Origin and Growth* (London: Macmillan & Co., 1920), and Lois Whitney, *Primitivism and the Idea of Progress* (Baltimore: Johns Hopkins Press, 1934).

22   'Luxury is a word of the most vague and indeterminate signification; and admits of almost infinite degrees', complained Nathaniel Forster in *An Enquiry into the Causes of the Present High Price of Provisions* (London, 1767), p. 36. A great many writers agreed. 'Luxury is a word of very uncertain signification', wrote Hume, 'and may be taken in a good as well as a bad sense': *Political Discourses* (Edinburgh, 1752), discourse II, 'Of Luxury', p. 23. Luxury is considered by John Sekora, *Luxury. The Concept in Western Thought, from Eden to Smollett* (Baltimore: Johns Hopkins University Press, 1977), and S. M. Wade, 'The Idea of Luxury in Eighteenth-century England' (unpubl. Ph.D. dissertation, Harvard

treated by political writers than that of luxury, yet few have been treated in a more vague and superficial manner'.[23] Mandeville's heretical claim that private vice was public virtue, and hence that conspicuous consumption might be a social good, nourished writers and publishers for more than half a century. In fact, Davenant had accepted luxury as a 'necessary evil' and Barbon had stressed in 1690 that prodigality, however it might run against morality, might also be commercially beneficial.[24] In the fallout from The Fable of the Bees, however, disgusted scholars, moralists and hacks raced to condemn what was regarded as a reversal of truths, that frugality or 'necessity' was an abomination, that luxury was a prerequisite for national greatness and prosperity, and that self-interest might become a public benefit.[25] The South Sea Bubble crisis further fuelled the attack on Mandeville's uncompromising thrust against the self-deception involved in the luxury debate.[26]

University, 1969). My Judging New Wealth and other studies dissent from Wade's conclusion that the doctrine of beneficial luxury enjoyed but a brief victory at mid-century.

23 Monthly Review, 47 (July 1772), 508.

24 Anon. [Nicholas Barbon], A Discourse of Trade (London, 1690). This is discussed in William Letwin, The Origins of Scientific Economics. English Economic Thought 1660–1776 (London: Methuen, 1963), ch. 2; Neil McKendrick, 'The Consumer Revolution of Eighteenth-Century England', in McKendrick, Brewer and Plumb (eds), Birth of a Consumer Society, pp. 9–33; and Joyce O. Appleby, Economic Thought and Ideology in Seventeenth-century England (Princeton, NJ: Princeton University Press, 1978), esp. pp. 25–6, 83–7.

25 Bernard Mandeville (?1670–1733), The Fable of the Bees, or Private Vices, Public Benefits (London, 1714), an enlargement of his The Grumbling Hive: or Knaves Turn'd Honest (London, 1705; 6th edn, 1729; 9th edn, 1755). Mandeville was attacked by Richard Fiddes, General Treatise of Morality (London, 1724; 3rd edn, 1762); William Law, Remarks upon ... the Fable of the Bees (London, 1724); John Dennis, Vice and Luxury (London, 1724); Thomas Bluett, An Enquiry whether ... Virtue Tends to the Wealth ... or Disadvantage of a People (London, 1725), and his True Meaning of the Fable of the Bees (London, 1726); [James Arbuckle], Hibernicus's Letters: Or A Philosophical Miscellany (London, 1729); Sir John Thorold, A Short Examination of ... The Fable of the Bees (London, 1726); and Archibald Campbell, Aretē-logia, or An Inquiry into the Original of Moral Virtue (Edinburgh, 1728). The response is assessed in Bernard Mandeville, The Fable of the Bees, ed. F. B. Kaye, 2 vols (Oxford: Oxford University Press, 1924), vol. 1, pp. xciv–xcviii, cxxxvi–cxxxix; Andre Morize, L'Apologie du Luxe au XVIIIe siècle et 'Le Mondain' de Voltaire (Paris: H. Didier, 1909; repr. Geneva: Slatkine, 1970), pp. 73–8; and Gordon Vichert, 'The Theory of Conspicuous Consumption in the Eighteenth Century', in The Varied Pattern: Studies in the Eighteenth Century, ed. Peter Hughes and David Williams (Toronto: A. M. Hakkert, 1971), pp. 253–67.

26 Hector Monro, The Ambivalence of Bernard Mandeville (Oxford: Oxford University Press, 1975).

For half a century after Mandeville, the idea of luxury was further refashioned to present an even greater contrast both to new intellectual appreciation of the benefits of progressive levels of spending, and also to the public's own increasing conspicuous consumption. As a defence against the charge of luxurious living, ladies and gentlemen supporting the consumer boom were assured that certain luxury was not only acceptable but required, and that a very particular luxury was responsible for the outcries within contemporary literature. A beneficial luxury, originally and dramatically popularized by Mandeville, gained qualified support from writers as eminent as Hume and as commercially successful as Trusler.[27]

For both writers and booksellers, great potential was provided by the topicality of the enquiry and also by the imprecision of the argument. After mid-century, the most powerful of the London booksellers, including Hookham, Longman, Rivington and the Dillys, gave particular prominence to their works on morality and society. The real coup for the publishing community, however, was the attraction of new middle-class readers. The attack on the rich and indolent was sharpened and, by the 1760s, the social relocation of the luxury charges was clear. A conception of luxury that identified the wasteful rich as the enemies of society was even purposefully derived from a growing sympathy for the poor. Essayists, historians and economists, from Davenant to Bolingbroke, had focused on the lower orders when envisaging luxury as the harbinger of indolence, effeminacy, insubordination and social and political debility.[28] From Mun to Henry Fielding, pamphleteers stressed luxury as undermining the labour necessary for the support both of the poor and of the existing structure of society.[29] By mid-century, however, greater humanitarian consideration of the poor was also apparent. Barrow, Tillotson and Hutcheson (reworking Shaftesbury) made significant contributions to the development of the idea of 'benevolence' as applied to the indigent. Belief in the efficacy of a more positive work stimulus gradually displaced necessarian doctrines of the social utility of poverty. By at least 1770, a chorus

---

27 In essays in *Political Discourses*, Hume attempted to refute many long-standing objections to luxury, although not without heavy qualification.
28 James William Johnson, *The Formation of English Neo-Classical Thought* (Princeton, NJ: Princeton University Press, 1967), pp. 49–50, 59–68.
29 Fielding blamed 'a vast torrent of luxury' for the unrest of the poor in his *Enquiry into the Cause, of the late Increase of Robbers* (London, 1751). In his early writings, Josiah Tucker argued in favour of maintaining low wages for the poor. Defoe and Mandeville gave emphatic warnings against giving alms to beggars.

of economic writers held that the raising of living standards of even the poorest members of society worked to improve the prosperity of all.[30]

In the second half of the century, a popular succession of tracts aimed at the gentleman reader continued to isolate the intemperate luxury of individuals in order to explain the apparent contradiction between unprecedentedly large fortunes accrued from trade, manufacturing and service under the East India Company, and the ever-predicted fall in the rate of British economic expansion. This was sustained by a continuing but extremely anxious pride in the mercantile and constitutional achievements of the previous hundred years. Current 'luxury' was testified by extravagance, speculation, gambling and a lust for money. Personal dishonesty was paralleled by financial irresponsibility and the corrupting influence of new money. Redundant wealth and its promotion of worthless and rapidly changing fashion was associated unquestioningly with excessive luxury. Essayists reformulated the familiar bogey of an individual intriguing against state and community in terms of a growing disparity between rich and poor.[31]

Histories

One of the most successful new markets for the London and Edinburgh booksellers came from the publication of histories. Works ranged from the massive tome to the short popular work surveying world history in thirty-six pages. Much historical writing, both academic and popular, was designed to instruct and warn. Chesterfield urged his son to understand the past in order to understand the present, and Thomas Blackwell and Edmund Burke considered that great lessons were to be learnt from reading history.[32] Common to most works was an interest in prediction and an increasing concern to include commerce in the narrative. Some histories were indeed written specifically for the appreciation of trade. Self-congratulation upon the volume of Traffick, which had been a staple of prefaces to commercial manuals since

---

30   Including Mortimer, *Elements* (1780 edn); Francis Moore, *Considerations on the Exorbitant Price of Provisions* (London, 1773); and Smith's proposition that no society could prosper and be happy if a majority of its members were impoverished: *An Inquiry into the Nature and Causes of the Wealth of Nations* (London: 1776), vol. 1, p. 70.

31   Such arguments were first popularized in the form of attacks on the nouveaux riches in Samuel Fawconer's *Essay on Modern Luxury* (London, 1765).

32   Johnson, *English Neo-Classical Thought*, pp. 33–45; and George H. Nadel, 'Philosophy of History before Historicism', *History and Theory*, 3:3 (1964), 291–315.

the early years of the century, was carried into accounts of the past. English history was indisputably the history of freedom, and writers repeated at length the cardinal relationship between Commerce and Liberty. Both Mortimer's and Joseph Hudson's popular histories assumed throughout a connection between trade and the maintenance of public liberty and civic rights.[33] Anderson confirmed commerce as the principal means of conveying all benefits to mankind.[34] Most historical writers were convinced of the indispensability of commerce to British prosperity, arguing with varying shrillness that the alleged harmful effects of trade were only the result of recent sidetracking from the true course of economic progress. Much discussion centred therefore upon the extent to which commerce and industry might progress before early and agreed benefits developed socially damaging effects. Many inquirers did not project beyond the ambiguous 'last' stage of civilization, and concluded that society had peaked at a present stage of 'maturity'. Borrowing ancient analogies with the human body, more pessimistic writers conceived of an approaching decline into old age.[35]

For many, the conclusions served only to reinforce a classical theory of the decline of empires as the history of luxury following trade.[36] In considering the unwholesome effects of trade, the new histories advanced theories of luxury from severely limited sources. Few writers either possessed or deemed necessary a working knowledge of commercial or manufacturing concerns to substantiate their arguments. Neoclassical parables of decline after mid-century were dependent upon two well-rehearsed beliefs: that the vice of luxury and extravagance threatened the fabric of society, and that the decline of empires was essentially one of self-destruction. Published translations of the ancients proved the point with new directness, especially when such translations were directed at gentlemen anxious to display their classical learning without having had to tackle the original.[37] Historians of Rome and ancient Greece provided

33   Thomas Mortimer, *A New History of England*, 3 vols (London, 1764); Joseph Hudson, *Remarks upon the History of the Landed and Commercial Policy of England*, 2 vols (London, 1785).
34   Adam Anderson, *An Historical and Chronological Deduction of the Origin of Commerce*, 2 vols (London, 1764).
35   As for example in James Dunbar (d.1798), *Essays on the History of Mankind in Rude and Uncultivated Ages* (London, 1780).
36   For a wide-ranging exploration of this, see Peter Burke, 'Tradition and Experience: The Idea of Decline from Bruni to Gibbon', *Daedalus*, 105:3 (Summer 1976), 137–52.
37   Direct examples could be culled from a mass of passages in Tacitus and Polybius. Notable among the popular English translations was John Rowe's *Caius Crispus Sallustius*,

a surfeit of evidence. Montagu explained in detail the advance of luxury, the corruption of manners and the withering of martial powers.[38] Thomas Leland catalogued the sordid gratifications, such as money-lust, gaming and lavish sauces, which constituted the 'total corruption and depravity' of Athens on the eve of its downfall.[39]

Confidence in Roman and Hellenic parallels was founded, in many instances, upon a belief that the learning of the ancients provided an applicable world to the present. This resort to classical learning and history is marked at times of national crisis, notably in the aftermath of the South Sea Bubble and during the initial tense period of the Seven Years War.[40] Knowledge of the classics was an expected attribute of the gentleman and the informed reader.[41] If the presumed erudition of the readership was a myth, it was not one to be readily avowed. Pamphlets and treatises designed to prove specific political or economic arguments constantly relied upon analogies between classical commercial or libertarian empires and modern-day European tyrannies.[42] Given the stated similarities between the origins and animus of the ancient and British republics, it was deemed almost a certainty that, in the absence of reform, Britain would share the fate of the unfortunate Romans. This was certainly stressed in the collected, brief, histories aimed at a mass market and issued

the Historian made English (London, 1709), on the decline of Rome (reprinted in 1715, 1726, 1727 and 1739, and much quoted in the magazines).

38 Edward Wortley Montagu, Reflections on the Rise and Fall of Antient Republicks, 2nd edn (London, 1760).

39 Thomas Leland, History of the Life and Reign of Philip King of Macedon, 2nd edn (London, 1761), p. 86.

40 Dennis's Vice and Luxury, noting vicious parallels between ancient Sparta, Rome and Britain, was published immediately after the Bubble, while Thomas Blackwell and John Mills, Memoirs of the Court of Augustus (Edinburgh and London, 1753–63), and M. P. Macquer, A Chronological Abridgment of the Roman History, From the Foundation of the City to the Extinction of the Republic, trans. Thomas Nugent (London, 1760), as well as Leland and Montagu, were all published or reprinted during the Seven Years War.

41 The classical influence in education is discussed in Sheldon Rothblatt, Tradition and Change in English Liberal Education (London: Faber and Faber, 1966).

42 Of many examples, Thomas Cole, Discourses on Luxury (London, 1761), pp. 54–5; [Francis Forster], Thoughts on the Times, But Chiefly on the Profligacy of our Women, and It's Causes (London, 1779), p. 12; John Naismith, Thoughts on Various Objects of Industry (Edinburgh, 1790), pp. 32–3; Revd John M'Farlan, Tracts on Subjects of National Importance (London and Edinburgh, 1786), p. 4; and the concluding proof of William Hazeland, A View of the Manner in which Trade and Civil Liberty support each other (London, 1756).

in great numbers from the 1770s.[43] Cadell's *An Historical Miscellany*, first issued in 1771, carried a great range of short extracts. Its successor, *The Historical Pocket Library*, was matched, volume for volume, by *Riley's Historical Pocket Library*, one of at least three pocket historical miscellanies issued in the same year by the Riley–Hazard partnership at Bath and London.[44] In 1780, Cooke published Charles Egerton's *The History of England in Verse* amid a blaze of publicity. Many of these pamphlet books and short essays crudely represented neoclassical theories of the imminent self-destruction of Britain. A typical magazine contribution of this period employed the Roman parable as clinching proof that luxury, if initially beneficial, must now be curbed.[45] The Row bookseller, John Bew, issued his *Historical Mirror* in 1775 'for the instruction and entertainment of youth'. It relied upon classical quotation and excerpts from modern historians of the classical period. The parallels with the decline of Greece and Rome reached even the chapbooks: 'What but the introduction of luxury, the inseparable concealment of riches, by the great Cyrus himself rendered his hardy followers effeminate, and in the sequel proved the subversion of his extensive empire?'[46] At the end of the 1780s, letters to respectable magazines still bemoaned the neglect of classical learning by the young.[47]

Sermons

During the century, sermon literature continued to be an industrious and profitable sector of the publishing trade. Collections of sermons appeared on the shelves of many gentlemen's libraries and compilers broadcast to a much wider audience than just those listening to the printed addresses reproduced on a Sunday morning. Aside from continuous clerical demand,

43 Of the larger popular histories, the best selling were almost certainly Smollett's *The Complete History of England* (London, 1757–58), *The Continuation of the Complete History* (London, 1760–65) and the *Modern Part of the Universal History* (London, 1759–65).

44 Anon., *Riley's Historical Pocket Library*, 6 vols (London and Bath, 1790); Anon., *A Biographical History of the Roman Empire* (London and Bath, 1790); Anon., *A New Biographical and Chronological History of England* (London and Bath, 1790).

45 *T&C*, xix (Sept. 1787), 394–6, 'On the Bad Consequences of National Avarice'.

46 Anon., *Affecting History of the Innkeeper of Normandy* (London, 1780), p. 14.

47 For example, letter to the editor, signed 'Senex', *Biographical and Imperial*, 1 (June 1789), 372–3.

prefaces and the waves of advertisements in the press suggest strong interest from middle-class readers, especially in the provinces.[48] Equally, the published sermon commonly considered wider subjects than did most of those delivered from the pulpit, and the audience was often intended to be national. This was particularly so from the 1730s with the increased popularity of part-issue publications and the improvement in transport facilities from London. The Rivingtons of St Paul's Churchyard, known for high Anglican piety, built up their very prosperous firm from a range of serious literature in which sermons and works of divinity were to the fore. Trusler boosted his career by printing single-sheet sermons in 'copperplate' type avowedly designed to imitate clerical handwriting and fool inquisitive parishioners. By the 1770s, collections of sermons were streaming from the London presses at a rate of twenty or more per year.[49] Also by this decade, however, the number of individual titles locally and often privately published far exceeded those from the capital. The main publishing ventures of very many regional printer-stationers were local addresses about special events or the reprinting of a national sermon in response to some natural or martial disaster.

The future state of society was clearly always a concern of published sermons, but many writers were also quick to incorporate recent, if basic, concepts of historical causality, and relate their homilies to current commercial change. By the 1730s, many clerics incorporated specific examples drawn from the Tory critiques of the City and financier. Tucker and Berkeley continued to support the idea of a beneficial luxury, but many more seized upon the arguments propounded by Mandeville's opponents or took to reading and then denouncing *The Fable of the Bees* for themselves. The 'fast sermons' of Ashton, Bayley, Doddridge, Hall and Stebbing, which so influenced the ideas of the populist, John Brown, may have been rhetorical set pieces, but during the 1750s many of them itemized specific points raised about corn bounties, the state of the poor and the distribution of wealth.[50] In this respect, these very practically oriented sermons might support Ted McCormick's suggestion that the mid

---

48 Johnson was one of several who commented on their popularity: G. B. Hill (ed.) and L. F. Powell (rev.), *Boswell's Life of Johnson*, 6 vols (London: Oxford University Press, 1934–50), vol. 4, p. 105.

49 Six leading contributors are considered in James Downey, *The Eighteenth-Century Pulpit: A Study of the Sermons of Butler, Berkeley, Secker, Sterne, Whitefield and Wesley* (Oxford: Clarendon Press, 1969).

50 For bibliographical assistance I am indebted to Anne Barbeary who most generously

eighteenth century was 'the moment that demographic quantification was definitively secularized, its sacred historical applications retreating under fire from Voltaire and Hume even as its scientific pretensions were super-annuated by French and Scottish political economy'. As he adds, however, the distance between sacred and secular political arithmetic looks larger in retrospect.[51] Dean Tucker incorporated much recent economic thinking into his *Seventeen Sermons* published at Gloucester in 1776. In 1782, John Wesley published his pungent 'On the Use of Money' in the *Estimate of the Manners of the Present Time*. Others, such as the Revd John M'Farlan, wrote a series of papers which were, in his words, 'an attempt to shew that manufactures, commerce and great towns produced by them are not so hurtful as some have supposed to the welfare of a nation'.[52] Argument was often well informed and the incorporation of questions of trade theory far from incidental to the wider moral issues.

However optimistic the writings of a Tucker or M'Farlan, most religious writers of the second half of the century highlighted moral dangers arising from increased prosperity. Both Anglican clerics and dissenting ministers were in the vanguard of those fearful of the changes wrought by new manufacturing and greater domestic spending on consumer goods. In 1785, for example, the Revd Fawel condemned the views contained in Trusler's pamphlet, advocating luxury as a stimulus to the economy, as an unnecessary evil 'in an Age, when both Art and Nature seem almost exhausted by the varied, ingenious Invention of new Luxuries; and are tortured, ransacked, and plundered on every side, in order to create new Appetites and Desires'.[53] Jeremiads against materi-alism were nothing new of course, but more people than ever before were buying them, whether or not as a salve to heightened anxiety. As John Brown wrote, in one of his more lucid passages, an underlying fear of the Country lobby was that commercial progress was reaching its self-inflicted nemesis:

allowed me to consult her 'To Make the Best of Both Worlds? Religion and Luxury in the Sermon Literature c.1740–1789' (unpubl. B.A. dissertation, Cambridge University, 1985).

51   Ted McCormick, 'Political Arithmetic and Sacred History: Population Thought in the English Enlightenment, 1660–1750', *Journal of British Studies*, 52 (Oct. 2013), 829–57 (p. 854).

52   M'Farlan, *Tracts*, pp. 1–2.

53   Revd J. Fawel, *Observations on a Pamphlet entituled 'Luxury No Political Evil'* (Wigan, 1785), p. 40.

There never was an Age or Nation that had not Virtues and Vices peculiar to itself: And in some Respects, perhaps, there is no time nor Country delivered down to us in Story, in which a wise Man would so much wish to have lived, as in our own. Notwithstanding this, our Situation seems most dangerous: We are rolling to the Brink of a Precipice that must destroy us ... we shall probably find, that in its first and middle stages [Commerce] is beneficent; in its-last, dangerous and fatal.[54]

Brown concluded that 'There seems no other Expedient than this, that Commerce and Wealth be not discouraged in their Growth; but checked in their Effects.'[55]

Also in line with other writings of the period, however, sermon writers emphasized the importance of thrift and the productive use of savings, and offered specific advice on domestic economy and the most socially profitable use of a gentleman's resources. Similarly, many clerics revised familiar charges against the 'luxuriousness of the poor' to attack the manners and conspicuous consumption of the rich and newly wealthy.[56] Tucker, known in his early ministry for his concern over the failings of the indigent, concentrated in his later sermons upon the luxury of great men.[57] Sermons on the behaviour of the propertied classes became a staple of the evangelical revival, of Wesleyan Methodism and many late-century Quaker addresses. For all Wesley's admiration of businessmen, he adopted a very traditionalist perspective upon the concept of luxury, preaching upon personal austerity and simplicity. He too, however, came to concentrate on the dangers of great riches by the end of his life.[58]

54   John Brown, *An Estimate of the Manners and Principles of the Times. By the Author of Characteristics, etc.* (London, 1757), pp. 13, 59–60; Brown's *Estimate* achieved at least a further dozen editions in 1757 and 1758.

55   Brown, *Estimate*, p. 152.

56   Of many examples, the Revd Walter Harper, *The State of the Nation with Respect to Religion and Manners. A Sermon Preached at Uxbridge Chapel, Middlesex on Sunday, 25th October 1789* (London, Cambridge, Oxford, Uxbridge and Hereford, 1789).

57   Josiah Tucker, *Six Sermons on Important Subjects* (Bristol, 1772); Josiah Tucker, *Sermons on Political and Commercial Subjects* (Gloucester, 1776).

58   Notably sermons 87, 108 and 126, from *The Works of John Wesley*, 14 vols (London: John Mason, 1872); the controversy over Wesley's economic thinking is given in Bernard Semmel, *The Methodist Revolution* (London: Basic Books, 1974). Wesleyan attitudes to luxury are neatly summarized in Barbeary, 'Best of Both Worlds?', ch. 5; during his lifetime, 133 of Wesley's sermons were published.

Tracts and magazines

As has been observed by Perry Gauci, 'the key to the advancement of the mercantile press was diversification in the format of commercial debate, and the most important sign of growing interest in trade was the appearance of several periodicals dedicated to commerce'.[59] John Houghton's *A Collection of Letters for the Improvement of Husbandry and Trade* offered an innovative and influential model for the future. His *Collection* was published in twenty-one issues in the 1680s and then ran weekly (with a lightly modified title) in a second and more significant series of 583 issues in nineteen volumes between 1692 and 1703. Houghton's aim was that 'trade may be better understood, and the whole kingdom made as one trading city'.[60] The environment in which Houghton's publications circulated, however, was in certain quarters becoming more hostile to trade as well as more familiar with it. Following the lively debates over financing standing armies and war policies under first William and Mary and then Anne, fierce attacks upon projectors and the dealings of the City continued well into the next two reigns. Familiarity could bring contempt. Davenant's scathing *Picture of a Modern Whig* was published in 1702 and Defoe's *Review*, founded in 1704, ran until 1713. The *Spectator* sustained lively debate between 1711 and 1714[61] and the *Craftsman*, with its remorseless sniping at both City and Walpolean corruption, was published continuously from 1726 to 1742. Substantial government subsidy of publications such as Defoe's *Mercator* (technically given sole access to official statistics) and heavy-handed attempts at control and suppression, reflected high-level concern over the effects of the new literature.[62]

The projector, financier and stock-jobber – 'that ravenous Worm in

---

59   Gauci, *Politics of Trade*, p. 164.

60   See Natasha Glaisyer, 'Readers, Correspondents, and Communities: John Houghton's *A Collection of Letters for the Improvement of Husbandry and Trade* (1692–1703)', in *Communities in Early Modern England: Networks, Place, Rhetoric*, ed. Alexandra Shepard and Phil Withington (Manchester: Manchester University Press, 2000), pp. 235–51.

61   One of the earliest periodical assertions of the classical decline theory as applicable to Britain, was Addison's quotation of Perseus and Sallust from Dryden in no. 55 of the *Spectator* (3 May 1711), and including the lines, 'A Tradesman thou! and hope to go to Heav'n'.

62   Three papers were printed to oppose the *Craftsman*, its circulation by the Post Office blocked, and manuscript materials seized: Simon Varey, *Lord Bolingbroke. Contributions to the Craftsman* (Oxford: Clarendon Press, 1982).

the Entrails of the State'[63] – had been under almost constant attack since the end of the seventeenth century, with publications such as Ned Ward's *London Spy* colourfully depicting fraud at the Exchange and coffee-houses. The onslaught continued after Davenant's influential portrait of Tom Double, shoeless before 1688 but worth £50,000 after twenty-four years as a stock-jobber.[64] Speculation in stocks was credited with the deaths of good men impetuously trying to revive their fortunes. Hundreds of prints released after the South Sea Bubble fiasco illustrated the ruin of the City, the corruption of the times and the malignity of money. One subscript ran, 'Trade is a dying woman, Honesty is being broken on the wheel, and Honour is being scourged by Villainy'.[65] In 1764, William Mildmay still condemned stock-jobbing as dependent upon deceit, and Mortimer's *History* referred to the 'avarice and oppression' of contractors and jobbers.[66]

Other attacks against financial corruption were linked to the abstract enemy, luxury. John and Francis Noble, the notorious and aggressively commercial booksellers of mid-century, launched their 1s 6d *Tryal of Lady Allurea Luxury* in 1757. After long courtroom speeches, the prisoner is found guilty of conspiring to destroy the morals of the people. At the same time, while the cheap pamphlet or journal essay remained the most likely medium for charges against particular trading activities or government policy, popular magazines also echoed enthusiasm for the progress of commerce. Tracts and ephemeral publications borrowed from the major writers, urging that the advantages gained from overseas trade should not be lost. Magazines and periodicals dating from the second half of the century reprinted essays on trade, as well as publishing new contributions. Neglect of trade was a national sin, however disturbing the side effects of commerce might be.[67]

---

63 Richard Steele, *The Englishman*, no. 4, 13 Oct. 1713.
64 Charles Davenant, *The Picture of a Modern Whig* (London, 1701).
65 *An Emblematic Print on the South Sea Bubble*, reproduced in Dorothy M. George, *English Political Caricature to 1792. A Study of Opinion and Propaganda* (Oxford: Clarendon Press, 1959), p. 73.
66 William Mildmay, *The Laws and Policy of England* (London, 1764), pp. 122–3; Mortimer, *History of England*, vol. 3, p. 793.
67 A typical pamphlet reaffirmed the orthodoxy of 'Commerce the fair sister of liberty and common friend of mankind', and that 'an extensive trade and flourishing manufacturies, tend to soften the manners of men, to render them capable of social impressions, to extend their views over the habitable globe and to eradicate narrow prejudices': Anon., *Thoughts on Commerce and Liberty* (London, 1786), pp. 1–3, 14.

From the 1750s to the 1790s, all the leading journals and magazines considered the luxury question. Essays and letters in the *Town and Country*, the *Lady's* and the *New Lady's* accepted as axiomatic the appropriateness of the luxury debate. As consumer industries disgorged a torrent of new wares, the consensus of magazine discussions was an acceptance of the necessity of luxury, while demanding a variety of measures to prevent its excess. It was not only the advice books which warned of the dangers of imprudence. Magazine essays boasted much practical advice. Mrs Grey's 'Matron', the long-running column in the *Lady's*, advised husbands upon restraining wives' expenses. In the 1770s, the balance was clearly against luxury,[68] but later decades brought more complex arguments. In the *Town and Country*, 'An Admirer of Ease and Conscience' of October 1781 debated the advantages of luxury, settling for a balanced compromise only after tortuous argument. Luxury was said to promote industry and support labour, but also to encourage wantonness, subvert manners and undermine the state.[69] A piece on 'National Luxury' of the same year decided that luxury did produce vice, and vice, misery, but that luxury remained a fundamental stimulus to national greatness.[70] A letter 'On Luxury' of January 1782, signed 'Voltaire', wholly championed luxury, claiming that it clothed the poor.[71] Many writers and booksellers clearly stimulated the debate for commercial reasons, with Trusler arguing both for and against luxury in consecutive publications.[72] When Trusler's defence of luxury was savagely condemned in a pamphlet put out by another publishing cleric, it was only to Trusler's commercial advantage.[73]

Mid-century journals such as the *London Magazine* concentrated upon the dangers of the vice to the lower orders, but increasingly the perspective shifted to worries over the habits of gentlemen and the example they were setting to their inferiors.[74] On the way back from her trial, the condemned

68 Articles by 'Poplicola' ('Friend of the People') clearly identified the most flourishing branches of trade as the most significant carriers of luxury, *T&C*, x (Jan. 1778), 24–6, 'Essay on the State of the Nation'. The author added, 'blind is the man who maintains that private vices are public benefits'.
69 *T&C*, xiii (Oct. 1781), 577, to the editor 'On Luxury'.
70 *T&C*, xiii (June 1781), 318, no. iv of 'The Literary Budget, containing Select Pieces adapted to the Times'.
71 *T&C*, xiv (Jan. 1782), 31.
72 John Trusler, *The Way to be Rich and Respectable* (London, ?1776); and John Trusler, *Luxury No Political Evil* (London, ?1779).
73 Fawel, *Observations on ... Luxury No Political Evil*.
74 Numerous letters including, *London Magazine*, xxv (1750), 15–16, 439–40; esp.

Lady Allurea Luxury is rescued 'by a mob of Nobility and Gentry'.[75] Mortimer believed that the cause of the complaint, which 'resounds from all parts', that Old English hospitality had been banished, was the stock-jobber and other 'useless slaves of luxury, many of them foreigners'.[76] Trusler also stressed the necessity for economy and country virtues, especially in *The Way to be Rich and Respectable*. Such pieces stressed the social as much as the economic threat of luxury, and, in illustration, accused parvenu families of self-indulgent and antisocial behaviour. The 1782 edition of the greatly reprinted *Pleasant Art of Money Catching* warned the propertied classes that, for the genuinely needy, 'Charity (in this last and iron age of the world) is grown as cold, that there is scarce anything to be got upon that account'.[77] In imaginative literature and in the contributions to the magazines, asperity escalated as frivolous spending became associated with social and even political pretension.[78] In the final three decades of the century, scholars and publicists inveighed against the abandonment of traditional codes of conduct and implored the 'rising generation' to look to their standards of behaviour.[79] The *Biographical and Imperial Magazine*, first published in 1789, was one of several popular monthlies to include advice on manners and economic obligations.

Almost without exception, writers depicted London as the crucible of fashion and the source of all vice.[80] John Trusler's *London Adviser* warned that the metropolis provided both the social example and the financial enticements which led to economic ruin. The capital was credited with a destructive magnetism which attracted the young and ambitious away from an honest home to new and terrible temptation. Alarmed essays and serial stories in the new magazines reported that London diseases were spreading to the provinces.[81] While many sober essays related luxury to the material progress of society, at less refined levels of thought such associations

'Civis', xxiii (1754), 409–10; 'Britannicus', xxvii (1758), 223–4; and xxxiii (1764), 28–31, 653–5.

75 Anon., *The Tryal of the Lady Allurea Luxury, before the Lord Chief-Justice Upright, on an Information for a Conspiracy* (London, 1757), p. 91.

76 Mortimer, *Elements* (1780 edn), p. 44.

77 Anon., *The Pleasant Art of Money Catching* (1705; London, 1782), p. 10.

78 Detailed in Raven, *Judging New Wealth*.

79 Anon., *Thoughts on the Times*; and Hannah More, *Thoughts on the Importance of Manners of the Great to General Society* (London, 1788), pp. 58–9.

80 Of many magazine examples, *T&C*, ix (July 1777), 378–9, 'on London being over-built'.

81 *Lady's*, xi (Apr. 1780), 171.

became all-out attacks upon newfangled and manufactured extravagancies and fashions. The very success of emulative spending[82] and the outpouring of home-produced commodities from the 1780s were major stimuli to the literary fulminations against extravagance. New luxuries were charged with both following and directing weathercock fashions.

Pamphlet and magazine literature clearly personalized the debate much more than most scholarly works. Simplification often meant characterization. Financiers were the victims of the early Tory propagandists, as the new industrialists were of late-century invective. By the end of the century it was the consensus of popular moralists that the extravagance of unthinking individuals could bring about not only their own ruin but that of the whole nation. The starting point for an explanation of national crisis was a consideration of the state not of the national debt, as had been common in early century moralities, but of the health of private – and identifiable – finances. It was another proof offered against extravagance, and one which may have contributed to the blurring of the distinctions between public and private credit. In attacking conspicuous wastage and warning of economic ruin, popular writers isolated culprits who were said to have no right to their fortunes.

Above all, pamphlets and tracts were concerned with identifying luxury or extravagance as it most affected their readers, not only in terms of spending on consumer goods but also of the misuse of resources through gambling and speculation. Steele popularized the type for the dissolute gamester early in the century.[83] The *Pleasant Art of Money Catching* extensively surveyed the 'quicksands' of extravagance and gambling,[84] and the moralizing Erasmus Jones presented gaming as derived from covetousness and cheating.[85] In the two decades after 1775, print focused public attention on a succession of extraordinary disputes and sensational suicides brought about by gambling debts.[86] Novels and moral

82   The distinguishing feature of a 'leisure class', according to Thorstein Veblen, *The Theory of the Leisure Class*, ed. J. K. Galbraith (Boston: Houghton Mifflin, 1973).

83   *The Guardian*, 1st collected edn, 2 vols (London, 1714), vol. 2, pp. 189–94, no. 120 (29 July 1713); the satirical stereotype for the gambler had been established in 1705 by Mrs Centlivre (Susanna Carroll) in *The Gamester: a Comedy* [from *Le Jouer* of J. F. Regnard] (London, 1705).

84   *Pleasant Art of Money Catching* (1782 edn), p. 28.

85   [Erasmus Jones], *Luxury, Pride and Vanity*, 3rd edn (London, ?1737), p. 24.

86   The private career of Fox was a centrepiece of town gossip, and Damer's suicide in 1776 was discussed avidly in newspapers and magazines throughout the nation: Lewis Melville [pseud.] (ed.), *The Berry Papers. Being the correspondence hitherto unpublished*

tracts envisaged a contagion of ruin, resulting from the indebtedness and time-wasting of an army of gamblers. The state lottery, supported by so many men of property, was a favourite target. In the 1770s, magazine essays on 'The Mischief of Lotteries' vied with letters describing symptoms and prognoses of the current 'Lottery Influenza'.[87] The 1780s produced still more vivid accounts.[88]

Such commentary maintained strong links with the popular guides to economic management. The stewardship of riches was re-emphasized, often in biblical terms. As an ideal of the gentleman, it was carefully moulded and perpetuated by both imaginative and serious literature. As the contribution entitled 'The Abuse of Riches' explained in a 1775 *Town and Country*:

> The man who squanders his money with a wanton profusion, and the man who hoards it with a sordid parsimony, are equally strangers to the true use of riches ... Avarice and extravagance are undoubtedly the two rocks which men of fortune should, with the greatest caution avoid; but it is a very nice point to draw the line of moderation between them.[89]

The dangers of luxury were illustrated in great detail and effectiveness by a flood of colourful and didactic works, magazine contributions, potted biographies, trial stories, and educative tracts for children and the poor. The anxieties of a John Brown were those of many hack journalists. Serialized or one-part magazine stories in particular, offered short, pungent moral parables against profligacy, hoarding and unacceptable social behaviour. By the time of the impeachment trial of Sir Thomas Rumbold and also that of Warren Hastings, the tone was strident, if not hysterical. As early as 1776 the *Town and Country* had carried a letter confident that 'luxury and dissipation were never at so high a pitch'.[90] The *General Magazine*, in the introduction to its first number, proudly justified its publication as 'to turn the tide of public partiality against every species

of *Mary and Agnes Berry 1763–1852* (London: John Lane, 1914), p. 20; and M. D. Archenholz, *A Picture of England* (Dublin, 1790), p. 112.
87   Contributions included *T&C*, vii (Nov. 1775), 571; xi (Dec. 1779), 619–21.
88   Notably, *T&C*, xix (Jan. 1787), 30–2.
89   *T&C*, vii (July 1775), 361–3.
90   *T&C*, viii (July 1776), 377.

of luxury'.[91] Similarly, the *Town and Country* – subtitled the *Universal Repository of Knowledge, Instruction, and Entertainment* – was as obsessed by social taste, manners and popular lore as it was dependent upon them for its sales, circulation, and readers' contributions.

By the end of a century which boasted an eventual intellectual appreciation of the benefits of increased consumer spending and an equation of the notion of private credit with the public good, the shelves of many private gentlemen were stocked with works which stridently attacked any such accommodation. However great the concern about the continuing success of British overseas trade, demand for detailed investigations into trade theory remained slight. Most property-owners were interested in technical argument about the economy only in so far as it affected their own financial circumstances. Amid confusion and recrimination over the origins and effects of commercial change and instability, an insistent economic puritanism was popularized exactly because it was never widely followed. Tracts and pamphlets reinforced notions of the importance of active circulating and redeployable wealth, and attempted a layman's analysis of unacceptable commercial behaviour and its consequences. As the range of consumer products widened, dozens of writers from very different political and religious backgrounds insisted that excessive expenditure could be even more dangerous than selfish accumulation. The charity of the gentleman would prevent non-use of riches, his economy and natural good sense, its misuse. Counsel against living beyond one's means supported an increasing obsession with taste, propriety and social mobility. The literary warnings about personal extravagance also left their mark on the history of the period. Contemporary best-sellers provided the basis for the persistent legends of conspicuous consumption and familial decline in a socially fluid, money-into-land England. Such themes were introduced for very particular reasons, but the images presented have not been easily removed.

The greatest difference between printing for the commercial world and printing about the commercial world was that, in servicing the economy, print was almost wholly positive in its effect. The response of printers and booksellers to the needs of a commercial society was various: the enabling of greater efficiency and reliability; the standardizing of techniques; the reduction of time in teaching; the provision of ready-made distributional networks for goods; the promotion of particular markets; the assistance to

91   *General Magazine*, I (1788), 5–7.

manufacturers and importers in forging direct links with consumers; and the furtherance of lobbying. In explaining economic change to inexpert readers, however, the effect of print could be more inhibiting. Printed discussion proved wide-ranging and able to reach greater readerships than ever before, but the cultivation of new audiences also extended the life of the luxury debate and rekindled mistrust of commercial dealings and men of business, as writers (and readers) sought new legitimation for new forms of wealth-holding and new explanations for economic crises.

Conclusion

This study identifies consequential connections between diverse types of late seventeenth- and eighteenth-century printed and semi-printed materials, and productive relationships between small items such as jobbing forms and documents, and larger publications including newspapers, pamphlets and books that communicated commercial and financial information, guidance and opinion. Also at issue is the connection between the matter carried by print and how print conveyed it, the most important products of that connection being knowledge, accuracy, efficiency, security, authority and the creation of trust. In the 120 years between 1680 and 1800, stationers, printers, engravers and booksellers contributed to a multiplication of material publications that enhanced economic confidence and engineered beneficial (as well as some disadvantageous) conformities of practice and principle.

In 1726, the French visitor de Saussure observed that 'you often see an Englishman taking a treaty of peace more to heart than he does his own affairs'.[1] Sixty years later, a greatly matured and more sophisticated press presented various reports in anticipation of the Versailles Treaty of 21 November 1787. At the beginning of that month, the *World and Fashionable Advertiser* recounted that 'a prodigious number of new faces, male and female, were seen at the Bank yesterday, investing their property, in consequence of the Peace appearance; and the Three per Cent, Consols, felt the influence of returning Confidence'. This followed, said the article, misreporting and a volatility in trading and fortune. Now, 'it is expected that *to-morrow and Tuesday* next will witness the greatest rise when the *Stocks* will increase before Christmas, and most probably will ascertain the *standard price* of the Funds; so that those who are fortunate enough to get in *this day*, will receive the best interest for their money'.[2] This report

---

1 César de Saussure, *A Foreign View of England in the Reigns of George I and II*, trans. Madame van Muyden (London: John Murray, 1902), p. 162.
2 *World and Fashionable Advertiser*, 250, Thurs. 1 Nov. 1787.

from the *World and Fashionable Advertiser* then listed 'the reasons which lead us to this opinion' (and the editorial ploy of the 'us' was significant). Five explanations were advanced in some detail, namely that there was no doubt about the permanency of peace, that a vast sum which had been transferred away from the market would now return upon peace, that the country gentlemen were receiving news of all of this in their mails and would send in to invest, that 'previous to the publication of the gazette' several bankers and merchants warned their country correspondents by post of a failure in negotiations but that would now be 'obviated by last night's post', and finally, that Great Britain would henceforth be regarded by other powers 'with confidence and respect'. Such printed reports offered news and guidance favourable to investment and trade but they were also self-referential (in some cases, self-absorbed) and often, as in this example, circulated an opinion that discussed the agency of the press in economic performance.

'Print culture' has become a familiar expression in the writing of early modern European history. Yet it is an elusive concept, whose general application has not always been helpful in advancing our understanding of the dynamics of the relationship between medium, message and outcome. The charting of the evolution of printing has its challenges, but more problematic is the evaluation of its impact. Modernity, it is often asserted, arrived with gunpowder, the compass and the printing press. The introduction of printing by moveable type followed from the recovery of population after the Black Death, the greater movement of peoples, and a modest increase in discretionary and disposable income that broadened demand for consumables. Early modern print undoubtedly contributed to the transformation of politics, religion, commerce, and intellectual and cultural life, but when is it possible to speak of a 'print culture' given that so much continued to depend on oral communication? A popular perspective in the history of printing concerns the identification of pervasive change to individual mental worlds as much as to collective politics, commerce or devotion. Nevertheless, changes to the practice of communications are subtler than often appear. An emphasis on new technologies can disguise a broader historical context in which material objects (namely books changing from script to print) continued to be socially highly specific. The number of people in England in the seventeenth century who engaged directly or extensively with written words and numbers must not be overstated. If needed at all, basic literacy and numeracy enabled labourers to mark down numbers of livestock or products, or create simple calendars. Many tradesmen and craftsmen required more advanced literacy or numeracy but their proficiency remained well below that of clerks and clerics, whose activities depended more perceptibly on counting, reading and writing. Given that knowledge of Latin was often demanded, 'literacies' might be a better skill description than 'literacy'. Even so, much was memorized and the oral continued to dominate the written. A limited elite enjoyed or endured reading manuscripts, some on parchment, some on paper. Roughly the same elite exchanged some degree of correspondence, both public and private. A great many people remained largely unaffected by the production of books. For most men and women, however, knowledge related to the natural world, to practical skills and handed-down lore, and depended more on observation, listening and memory than on material texts. The reading of print reached the ears of the illiterate, but only occasionally.

A rather different perspective in understanding the history of the social penetration of print is given by attention to the full range of printed and part-printed items that were produced by printers and in printing houses than by the more restricted consideration of books or even of books and newspapers. In the late seventeenth century, more people, in more ways, engaged with printing by moveable type and the refinement of engraving for illustration and display. Gradually, but increasingly, the means of doing business, of domestic trading and overseas commerce was assisted and influenced by the printed text. Print, however, must not be confused with, or at least restricted to, books and what we usually think of as 'publications'. By the mid eighteenth century, only a minority of Europe's population confidently read pamphlets, newspapers and books, even including bibles, prayer-books and hymn books. In England, literacy levels and the supply and cost of cheap literature probably ensured that more people read simple books than did not. An especially refined minority engaged with works of great learning, fastidious devotion or sophisticated entertainment. Yet in these same years, almost no life was untouched by print. By 1800, almost all men and women directly or indirectly encountered the multiple products of the printing house. As much as books, it was the diverse jobbing work of the printers that recast the production, material form and reception of everyday knowledge. Small pieces of printed paper (and sometimes other material) reshaped intimate, private worlds and human relationships. Individuals and groups were bound, freed and defined by printed and filled-in forms of understanding and obligation. People were baptized, married and buried by forms and documents, and the eighteenth-century business world – finance, commerce and industry – proceeded on a raft of printed and blank chits, certificates and authorizations.

This book has attempted to demonstrate some of the specific, practical ways in which letterpress printing and engraving supplied the means to reshape social and cultural practices and the direction of the economy in eighteenth-century England. In an economy which outdistanced all its rivals by 1800, the intervention of print ensured the transformation of the conveyance of information and knowledge, and of the methods of recording, filing and writing things down on prepared and standardized forms. The overarching result was that print and its publication ensured greater confidence in modes of transaction, communication and exchange, and did so through a number of critical characteristics: reliability, reputation, regularity, authority and familiarity. These features were supported by practical aspects of printing, engraving and publication techniques, by readability and conveyance, and also by design and aesthetics.

This is not to say that print was uncontentious or immutable – far from it – and the charges made against print as the bearer and instigator of the fraudulent, corrupt and seditious were shrill and continuous throughout the century. Ultimately, the interpretation of printed words and images rested with the recipient, whether as an individual or as part of a group. However, even in the 1790s when the reaction against print was strident and widespread, opponents of tracts and newspapers exactly demonstrated their fear of its authority and power. The press and print, after several centuries of development, had seemingly come of age in a century of self-congratulatory financial and commercial progress. The role of print was accepted and valued within social and economic affairs, but it was also subject to greater discrimination. In other words, while trust in print and trust by print was shared across a very great variety of printed publications, numerous exclusions were also identified. Fraud and misinformation, for example, remained features of printing and publication that by their isolation from generally accepted good practice helped define the normative. A normative media world therefore paralleled the broader literary depiction of financial and commercial virtue by the vilification of the abnormal (often through crude and negative stereotypes of corrupt and overreaching traders).[3] Fraudulent tickets and tricksters contrasted with secure banknotes, helpful advertisements and upstanding merchants.

---

3   Continuing the argument of James Raven, *Judging New Wealth: Popular Publishing and Responses to Commerce in England, 1750–1800* (Oxford: Oxford University Press, 1992).

The account given here has been one of incremental development, of an increasing volume and diversity of printed matter and of types of publication, of an increasing number of printers and publishers, of a spreading network of distribution and information. Most of these outputs and employment patterns conform to the common profile of development in the 1690s and to the eighteenth-century growth curve that shows a strong upward inclination in the 1740s, continues to rise and then markedly accelerates in the last two decades of the century. Such a curve is very general, however, rather like the running average constructed from the title counting of printed items in the *ESTC*. In fact, *ESTC* annual title counts (rather than ones averaged over several years) actually produce a graph of successive and highly volatile peaks and troughs, and a graph that disguises significant variations in the volume of print that made up the individual titles of publications.[4] Similarly, the course of printing and publication in this period did not run smoothly. This book has been at pains to indicate the setbacks, the contradictions and the pauses in productive output: the unpredictable consequences of early experiments in financial journalism; the stop–start publication of so many early currents and financial guides; the natural hesitancy of printers in the 1710s, fearful of a reimposition of licensing laws; the surge in business publication in the 1720s in *relative* terms, while overall publication totals fell back; the glut of provincial newspaper production in the 1740s that caused problems for the pioneers; and many more instances besides. The inadequacy of information and services, the failures of printed forms to fulfil their intention (and, therefore, having to be amended), the discarding of the ephemeral because of its limited application rather than overuse, the incitement to fraud and malpractice by poor security printing, all these factors need to be kept in mind as we read in this book (among others) of the successes, and of the overall critical, beneficial contribution that printing and publishing made to business.

That conclusion, of advancing confidence and maturity, is inescapable. The study builds on research such as that of Anne Murphy who points to an inherently flawed investment market in England in the late seventeenth century and cautions against assuming too great a proficiency in the gathering of financial information in the early eighteenth century. Although the evidence is problematic, and tensions and weaknesses are

---

4   The peaks and troughs also include distortions caused by the attribution of undated materials to end-of-decade or mid-decade dates: 1700, 1705, 1710, etc.

indeed apparent in the early part of the period considered here, by the mid eighteenth century the collection and dissemination of information became much more reliable, regular and authoritative, and the types of printed materials that offered guidance were much more integrated into literary and business infrastructures. Reliability, regularity and authoritativeness are similar and connected characteristics but each also stands alone. A regular newspaper notice of official exchange rates or shipping news, for example, might be reliable because of a sound, established history of regularity of appearance and of the proven trustworthiness of its data, but its authority might also be a wider consideration, judged in relation to the standards of other newspapers and publications, and by the shared and broadcast testimony of other recipients, users and beneficiaries of the information conveyed by the notices in the past.

The definition of publishing most useful to these considerations is the making public of every type of print and material that involved printing and engraving. The attempt to understand the agency of that publication in economic change in eighteenth-century England is best served by discussing print in broad material forms and certainly in relation to the scribal and the part-printed. The evidence is at once overwhelming in its range and prone to partiality and incompleteness. Intuitively, it is obvious that expansion in print and the expansion in finance and commerce in general are interconnected, but the evidence for exactly how is elusive. The discernable changes to commerce and finance and the massively increasing volume and diversity of print during the eighteenth century are, in different ways, challenges to historical reconstruction.

In pursuit of business publishing, this book has explored the production and circulation of many different types of manuals, guides and small books but it has also investigated two neglected and importantly related histories: that of jobbing printing in the printing house, and that of jobbing printing in the economic revolution of the eighteenth century. Neither history can be divorced from broader deliberations about publication, and each reaches importantly beyond the metropolis. Neither history has been given the attention it deserves. Most studies of the development of printing with moveable type since the mid fifteenth century elucidate, in one way or another, the production of books, periodicals and newspapers. This is especially so in the Enlightenment, in the age of *illuminés* and *philosophes*. The history of Enlightenment is the history of the book, of print bound in leather volumes, of print issued in separate collectable parts, of print combining text and illustration in new ways, of print offering instruction and entertainment, of print as 'book'. What is almost entirely ignored is the printer's output of jobbing work: the myriad of quick, unromantic, practical productions that grounded the printer's trade. Without his or her production of jobbing work the vast majority of printers would have failed. Almost every printer from the fifteenth century to modern times has depended on the regular income afforded by jobbing work. It has been a hidden history. It is also a history of the social construction of knowledge.

The neglect of the second hidden history of printing is just as significant We have hundreds of accounts of the commercial and industrial revolution of Europe from Carlo Cipolla onwards (and indeed before Cipolla), but nowhere in this is the printer given due significance for lowering transaction costs by the provision of jobbing and small-item printing that extended from advertisements to receipts and a myriad of blank forms, legal and commercial. The economic transformation to which the printers' products and services contributed was one of astonishing range and complexity. Printers and stationers promoted and serviced unprecedented commercial, financial and industrial expansion. From the late seventeenth century in particular, the volume, quality and location of jobbing printing was transformed, despite a virtual technological standstill in the design of the common printing press.

As assessed by the preceding chapters, the commercial-assistance activity of the printer divides loosely into three general types. First, there are general treatments of the economy from extended philosophies and essays in political arithmetic in the seventeenth century, to small essays in moral (and what became known as political) economy, advancing in the 1730s and then greatly boosted by the support of periodicals and critical reviewing from after mid-century. Supply from abroad was supplemented, if not supplanted, by the strength of Scottish contributions in the second half of the century (although many were first published in London), and the profile of popular reading comprises many long-forgotten names and titles, often deviating from texts later studied as landmark publications in intellectual history. Second, there is practical guidance, including, for example, currents, advertisements and newspapers but also printed books and pamphlets that advanced new techniques in accounting and business management. Many such titles, first published in the 1680s and 1690s and often based on earlier exemplars, gained steadily in numbers, reputation and rivalry through the eighteenth century. Guides for specialist trades, professions and investments proliferated, as did general all-encompassing guides for gentlemen and general readers. Much other printing assisted in selling wares and advertising services. In businesses both small and large, efficiency and accuracy was aided and gauged by ready reckoners, trade calculating tables, timetables and charts for travel by road and water. The third category of print and publication for business is jobbing printing proper and allied stationery sales, a constant of the printing office, but subject to hugely increased demand especially after the foundation of so many new newspapers in the 1740s, and again with a second wave of newspaper activity in the 1780s. Booksellers and stationers supplied an unparalleled volume of ledgers and account books. Printers undertook a new and vast range of business jobbing, including printed bills, tickets, receipt forms, commercial and financial blanks, secure promissory notes, warrants, indentures and authorizations.

There was inevitable overlap between these categories, especially where jobbing printing merged work into something wider. Thus, for example, print raised subscriptions to public works and helped organize commercial institutions. It promoted new transport, marketing and rating schemes and it enabled protest against them. Many printers' and booksellers' premises became an integral part of local business development, offering a diverse range of services including carriage, warehousing, public notification and even banking. Turnpike and canal developments in the second half of the eighteenth century were promoted by print (and printed subscription schemes) and, once built, were served and policed by printed tickets, and themselves enabled the speedier, more reliable and extensive distribution of advertising newspapers and other printed products. The interconnection and self-involvement of printed contributions to English navigations and road building typified the deepening, reciprocal engagement of printing, publishing and business ventures by the end of the eighteenth century. It was a markedly more complex and productive relationship at that time than anywhere else in the world. Print, as the surviving inventories and business ledgers of the printer-stationers show, offered a critical contribution to the development of financial and commercial, and ultimately industrial, organization.

In consideration of the printed and the published, the application of bibliographical techniques and perspectives, and much lateral thinking in the archives, can recover evidence of small printed items, just as patience in the library and the more recent searching techniques of digital archives can recover long-ignored but once popular publications. Both assist in the understanding of a subject long neglected or, if treated at all, resident in antiquarian listings that have been unrelated to larger historical analysis.

What is also at issue, and has been much debated, is the identification of normative attitudes and behaviour. How did people perceive the local economy and act upon that perception? Ideas about finance and commerce are testing examples of the historical search for an understanding of what 'knowledge' was and how that knowledge related to practice. It is so broad and complex a search that it seems not to matter whether we call this cultural or social or political, but examination of the production and use of jobbing print as well as more obvious forms of publication, in all their accelerating profusion, allows an identification of specific features of the construction of new social knowledge. The profusion might be immeasurable and survival rates erratic, as this study reiterates, but individual exemplars offer real insight into a changing society and changing societal awareness.

What was normative is not always what was most striking. In the same way that anti-business, usually personalized, literary stereotypes have been repeated over and over again, and taken as evidence of pervasive hostility to business (when the norm was a subtly and more supportive understanding of commercial and financial expansion), so the identification of what was taken for granted as the normal means and material forms of doing business is the more elusive. This is particularly the case when the evidence is ephemeral, discarded, hidden in archives and, in some ways most significantly, offered little commentary in its own time. Many writers in the late eighteenth century did, in popular tracts and guides, allude to the processes of recording economic affairs, and, moreover, to literary and press involvement in supporting industry and commerce. Many newspaper reports were especially self-referential. The *World and Fashionable Advertiser* notice cited above typifies late-eighteenth-century pride in the communication by the press of news favourable to investment and trade. Such newspapers were usually silent when outcomes were unfavourable.

Besides commentary on specific projects and investment risks, however, the day-to-day use of print in easing and enabling transactions is largely unmentioned. The normative makes for invisibility. Evidence of the physical use of reckoners and scribbled marginalia can be found (all too rarely perhaps) in books and manuals, but contemporary comments on usage are elusive. We do not make remarks on what is familiar or obvious. Before at least the digital revolution and the relentless commentaries of social media (few of which perhaps will be saved for posterity) we have rarely recorded our reactions when washing dishes or having a bath. More pertinently, even in the Internet age, we rarely record our reactions to using 'plastic' for purchases and in credit transactions. Most people are uninterested in recording what they think of the role of modern media in promoting and enabling economic change, or if they do, their contribution is likely to be made at a broad, conceptual level. In the absence of many eighteenth-century comments on business publishing, we have a vast material range of archival survivals, including long-neglected examples of jobbing print (often catalogued as 'ephemera' and often dismissed by historians), ledgers recording orders for print, and a formidable range of books and pamphlets representing broader social thought and an indirect appreciation of economic change. Newspapers and their advertisements survive in hundreds of copies, and certain letters of merchants and brokers give occasional glimpses of the usage of adverts, small printed items and guides. The rare business archives of printers assist in the reconstruction of printing-house practice although day-to-day activity in the shops of stationers and country booksellers is often obscure. The different types of evidence have been presented together here, side by side, in order to suggest connections and the agency of the press. It is the best we can do in the absence of an eighteenth-century reviewer of the business contribution of the press – of a Gilbert White[5] of Exchange Alley or of the port of Bristol (either of which might have been subject to a highly parochial focus).

The trust required for an economy to flourish is far reaching and dependent on the maturity of social and political relationships. Even competitors must be trusted to adhere to shared and agreed rules. Just as Adam Smith placed great importance upon trust as the means to build viable societies, so trust was the key variable in the description of normative social behaviour in the hundreds of tracts published in increasing numbers in the second half of the eighteenth century, describing commercial society and the activities of merchants and brokers. Trust and confidence were sponsored by the medium of print and by processes of publication at many different levels: in textual commentaries but also by the assurance of standardized and widely accepted documents and security printing. Standardized information allowed the calibration and confirmation of data received from a range of different origins.

5   Gilbert White, *A Naturalist's Calendar, with observations in various branches of natural history, extracted from the papers of the late Rev. Gilbert White of Selborne, Hampshire, Senior Fellow of Oriel College, Oxford: Never before published*, ed. John Aikin (London: Printed for B. and J. White, Horace's Head, Fleet Street, 1795).

Print formalized relationships and allowed the creation, conveyance and reception of knowledge. As Diego Gambetta has argued, an extensive range of activities has served to 'circumscribe the extent to which we need to trust agents or cope with them in case of distrust'. This safety net, as he adumbrates it, includes coercion, commitment, contracts and promises, all made 'with varying degrees of subtlety, mutuality, legitimation, and success'.[6] Although Gambetta does not explore this, for the historian of eighteenth-century England it is print and printed communication and the processes of communication that create and deliver the practical modes by which the knowledge is created, circulated, further modified, challenged and relied upon in what continued to be, in large measure, a face-to-face society. Trust continued to be based on personal communication, but was a verbal and visual intercourse that more and more required written and especially printed support – and, over distance, substitution.

The range of printed products, some given the authority of penned signatures or with filled-in blank sections to supply or authenticate critical parts of information, offered the means to reduce distrust. To borrow Gambetta's theoretical formulation, 'men and women have tried to overcome the problem of trust by modifying the feasible set of alternatives open not only to others but also to themselves'.[7] The authoritative price and exchange rate currents, the forms to be filled in, the publication in newspapers of sailings and market prices, the guides to merchants, the security printing of banknotes, the manuals on accounting practices, and the ready reckoners that enabled or confirmed calculations (even if, like other printed items, they were occasionally corrected by users), all offered the framework to develop and uphold a trust that eliminated the risk of misinformation and fraud. Ultimately, of course, what someone does with information that they read might not follow a rational or expected course. Emotion can override the logic of the printed news and printed argument. What we might assume from surviving textual evidence to have been a wilful rejection of printed advice might also have been a simple misreading. Print, in the end, cannot account for all: nonetheless, printing for business, in all the diverse ways described, accelerated over the course of the eighteenth century, and commercial and financial information gathering hugely improved.

6   Diego Gambetta, 'Can we Trust Trust?', in *Trust: Making and Breaking Co-operative Relations*, ed. Diego Gambetta (Oxford: Basil Blackwell, 1988), pp. 213–37 (p. 220).
7   Gambetta, 'Can we Trust Trust?', p. 220.

Reputation offered a means of avoiding deception and poor quality advice. It was built up by reliability founded on widely accepted credibility or also on the assured regularity and efficiency of a production, and often on all of these things. The excellence of typographical design or fine engraving contributed to the authority and hence reputation of a production. Reputation was further enhanced by the rectitude of publishing agents. In other words, print enabled trust and repute among persons and agencies by the quality of its transmission as well as by the perceived quality of the object transmitted. This was further and perhaps most obviously exemplified by the various bills of exchange and banknotes, with their successive modifications and increased volume and circulation during the century. For a range of manuals and guides, the name of the publisher and the historical profile of the author ensured repute. For many titles first published without attribution, market success ensured the addition of 'by the author of' tags in subsequent writing issued by the bookseller-publishers (and by many authors who had a share in or financed publication themselves).

Authorship and anonymity were also equivocal. Some declared authorships alerted readers to the qualities anticipated, but also, in the case of many established forms of print, anonymity offered an impersonality that lent itself to objectivity, impartiality and repute. The absence of an 'author' was, indeed, one mark of jobbing print and the identification of even a printer something to be discouraged by many clients such as local corporations, committees or magistrates ordering jobbing print. Printing anonymity was also the case for most of the great multitude of general vouchers, tickets and blanks. Typographical assuredness, the familiarity of a selected type and design, including the continuation of a newspaper and price or exchange current masthead, and many other devices, all acted to reassure. Such typographic reassurance might also be contrasted to scribal equivalents. This is not quite the same as the 'fixity' of print, an argument which runs foul of the reading history of the object, of the inherent instability of the text as consumed.[8] Texts were read by different readers with different abilities and motives at different times and in different places. Rather, the

8   For debate of these issues, see Elizabeth L. Eisenstein, Anthony Grafton and Adrian Johns, 'AHR Forum: How Revolutionary Was the Print Revolution?', *American Historical Review*, 107:1 (2002), 84–128; Sabrina Alcorn Baron, Eric N. Lindquist and Eleanor F. Shevlin (eds), *Agent of Change: Print Culture Studies after Elizabeth L. Eisenstein* (Amherst, MA: University of Massachusetts Press, 2007); and Paul N. Edwards, Lisa Gitelman, Gabrielle Hecht, Adrian Johns, Brian Larkin and Neil Safier, 'AHR

reassurance of print in a particular formation is that it lent familiarity by its unchanged nature. As established English newspaper information columns and hundreds of different types of official document did by the final quarter of the eighteenth century, print reassured and invited automatic verification of the reports and information it offered by the standardized, familiar vessel in which it was contained. Such considerations also force more attention to 'the scribal': to the difference between scripted documents which were replaced by apparently more reliable printed versions, and the script which by signature or filled-in information actually authorized or certified the printed form (and notably the ticket, voucher or passport).

The repeatability of printed forms and the regularity of their appearance added to reputation and authority. In this respect, study of the role of printers, engravers and stationers certainly supports Anne Murphy's insistence that English endeavours in developing financial systems deserve much more credit than is offered by accounts that give special emphasis to Dutch prototypes and energies.[9] Publication by postal services, and by established financing booksellers able to adhere to a set timetable for publication, enabled merchants and brokers (and indeed general investors and purchasers) to receive information and guidance at set, anticipated times without fearing disruption or uncertainty. Just as in the Internet age, where we have seen a series of experiments in the means to acquire and receive purchased goods online, both form and conveyance were crucial. During the eighteenth century, both form and conveyance, the staples of publication, offered increasingly greater certitude, respectability, assurance and authority. In turn, improved expectations enhanced trust. As Partha Dasgupta writes, 'even though there are no obvious units in which trust can be measured, this does not matter, because in any given context you can measure its value, its worthwhileness. In this respect, trust is not dissimilar to commodities such as knowledge or information.'[10] As he also concludes, such trust is based on reputation and that 'reputation has to be acquired in well-understood circumstances'.[11]

Conversation: Historical Perspectives on the Circulation of Information', *American Historical Review*, 116:5 (2011), 1392–435.

9   Anne L. Murphy, *The Origins of English Financial Markets: Investment and Speculation before the South Sea Bubble* (Cambridge: Cambridge University Press, 2009), p. 4.

10   Partha Dasgupta, 'Trust as a Commodity', in Gambetta (ed.), *Trust: Making and Breaking Co-operative Relations*, pp. 49–72 (p. 51).

11   Dasgupta, 'Trust as a Commodity', p. 53.

What Dasgupta's insight left unanswered was the character of 'well-understood circumstances'. That question, for a specific place and time, has been given particular attention by this book, which has suggested, in a series of examples, that the volume and quality of production became central to those 'well-understood circumstances'. Popularity of objects and transactions contributed to the sense of reliability. Within particular networks, as Larry Neal has argued, the usefulness of 'knowledge products' depends on how many consumers continue to use them. Most consumers restrict themselves to concentrating on a single, popularly recommended source. The shared focus further increases the chances of discussing performances with other knowledge consumers, a discussion valued for refining and perfecting one's own ability to appreciate products and their information.[12] The addictive quality of public price and exchange currents, for example, resulted in an increased marginal utility with an increase in use. How and why such items became addictive, however, requires a consideration of form and regularity of appearance, and above all, of reliability and confidence as much as the concentration upon a single source. It was, for example, the combination of all these characteristics that apparently guaranteed *de facto* monopoly publishing to the *Course of the Exchange* by the late eighteenth century.

Preceding chapters have also much expanded on what Neal seeks to understand: 'what profit opportunities were available in providing printed and public, as opposed to hand-written and confidential information on financial markets'.[13] That proposed opposition between the scripted and the printed is not absolute. The difference between the privately circulated list and the public document is often cited, but there is an important overlap between the two. The combination, indeed, of the written and the print strengthened during the eighteenth century and especially with the multiplication of bureaucratic forms in the closing decades of the century; certification and authority was often given by taking a pen to a printed form. This was not only the extension of information but also the provision of confidence. In practical terms, elaborate and delicate security printing ensured a greater prevention of fraud and counterfeit, but new trust was also founded on the public acceptance of the standardized form and the commonplace item. The commonplace gave a security whose

12 Larry Neal, 'The Rise of a Financial Press: London and Amsterdam, 1681–1810', *Business History*, 30:2 (April 1988), 163–78 (pp. 164, 176), drawing on Paul David's research on selection and monopoly of theatre performance.
13 Neal, 'The Rise of a Financial Press', p. 165.

recognition was indeed too commonplace to leave convenient historical comment. Historical imagination must deepen where evidence thins.

Reliability, trust and confidence was achieved not only by an increased volume of print but also by its valorization in a developing literary infrastructure of new publishing modes, more intricate distribution networks, and greater public feedback and exchange with readers and users. Trust within the book trades was variable. Many booksellers and printers were quick to identify miscreant or recalcitrant practices. Membership of the Stationers' Company ensured reputation and an authority over printing by entry to apprenticeships and the official freedom to trade. Not all London and local publishers and not all printers in the provinces were members of the Company, however, and the *de facto* control by a monopolizing and effectively price-fixing cartel of leading bookseller-publishers raised tension in the trade that erupted finally in the dispute over copyright in the 1760s and 1770s. That tension, even though it divided the trade and created new publishing opportunities as well as disputes,[14] little affected the appraisal of the day-to-day business of the printers and stationers discussed here. Of much greater importance to local valuation and reputation was a consistent record of publication, the quality of printing and delivery, opening hours and services, and the general proficiency and expansiveness of business.

Since the elaboration by Neil McKendrick, John Brewer and J. H. Plumb of the 'birth of a consumer society', a spirited literature has engaged with the history of ways in which consumers shaped and were themselves shaped by different tastes and practices. More recently, interest in material culture and the history of particular objects has revived and redirected attention to the nature of a consumer culture in which emulative buying, new advertising techniques and the stimulation of demand resulted in both the appreciation and disparagement of luxury goods. Key agents of change in consumption patterns were the mediation of print and the way in which printed communication enabled things to be created, sold and transferred. The market was a public venue made visible not only by face-to-face observation and debate, but also by the printed pages that circulated in increased profusion during the century. The printed and graphic response to this market was also one that promoted and developed new services that ranged from newspaper advertisements to

14   See James Raven, *The Business of Books: Booksellers and the English Book Trade 1450–1850* (London and New Haven, CT: Yale University Press, 2007), chs 8 and 10.

tickets and transaction vouchers. It was a process in which women were particularly evident in imprint and in participation. Many advertisements and services were specifically directed towards women, and several were directed by them. Not all of the printers in this study, and not all of the most prominent, were men. Several notable widows maintained and preserved important printing concerns, becoming established in their own right as respected and innovative contributors to local commerce. Many women operatives do fall beneath the record, however, an absence to be remembered when the execution of much jobbing work, the folding, cutting and presentation of orders, was often carried out by apprentices and by women members of the household. This is an invisible presence not only in the historical record but also in the accounting practice of the time which did not include the labour and time of female family members in the calculations of profit and loss within the printing house. By contrast, the encouragement to participate in markets and in social activities by advertisement and tickets is identifiable along gender lines. The promotion of female social involvement and the representation of particular female spheres (that can be all too misleading if taken at face value) were prominent features of both press advertising and the vouchers and ticketing commissions undertaken by local printers.

A still broader question concerns the political and legal context of changing economic performance in Britain, as much as England, in this period. This study has focused on England and Wales, although developments in Scotland and Ireland are inescapably bound to the trade by import of materials and the source of authorship (books, although less so jobbing printing, keep to few borders). Deepening political and legal frameworks but also social and cultural arrangements in which business might develop are self-evidently reported in, and also exemplified by, many of the objects and processes assessed in this book. By 1800 and the eve of the formal Union with Ireland, the state offered an overarching political construct and self-conception whereby finance, commerce and industry might be encouraged and protected, and notably in a British rather than English context.[15] Recent arguments about the empowering state have certain affinities (as well as disagreements) with older assertions that the birthing of a modern state by the Glorious Revolution enhanced

15 As Julian Hoppit concludes, 'not least of the achievements of the British state was to provide various ways in which political and legal power might be used to pursue economic opportunities': 'The Nation, the State, and the First Industrial Revolution', *Journal of British Studies*, 50:2 (April 2011), 307–31 (p. 331).

confidence by convincing people that it was now safe to invest in instruments of long-term debt. Ending this book, as it began, with a Nobel Prize-winning commentator, economic transformation has further been attributed by Douglass C. North to the singular establishment of a framework of governance and law that assisted and expedited economic transactions.[16] Julian Hoppit has noted that 72% of the more than 14,200 Acts passed at Westminster in the eighteenth century applied to specific rather than general concerns. Notable among them were private Acts relating to the turnpikes, navigation schemes and other transport projects appearing in this study, but the broader point is one of a legislatively and judicially enshrined language and behaviour that accommodated business and financial initiatives as well as protecting and promoting the exchange of information. The mundane, workaday consolidation of information promoters, and the expanding contribution of publishing and printing to commercial enterprise are easily overshadowed in accounts that focus on a post-1688 or post-1695 relationship between the press, liberty and political maturation.

There are also further political ramifications which, in terms of the history of the press, suggest certain cautions against accepting the developing commercial benevolence of political and legal structures. Consideration of the larger framework highlights points at which the state intervened to control the press. Several incidents are described in the preceding chapters, but the history of printing as it relates to business activity is often less detained by trials, civil action, and judicial and political intervention than is the broader history of the book trade in the eighteenth century. The 1799 Act to police the press was telling. Just as the Reformation state and Church introduced controls over printing presses from the mid sixteenth century, so at the turbulent end of the eighteenth century did the foremost economic power in Europe engage with new determination and fastidiousness in the activities of its printers. Usually, this turn of events is considered simply in terms of political repression and the examination of published 'sedition' in the courts. Unlike in France and several other countries, censorship in England since the late seventeenth century had been a post-publication affair. The commercial world of printing and publishing, however, was increasingly turbulent in the sense

---

16   Douglass C. North, 'The Paradox of the West', in *The Origins of Modern Freedom in the West*, ed. R. W. Davis (Stanford, CA: Stanford University Press, 1995), pp. 1–34 (esp. pp. 8, 19).

that new centres of production and escalating output, certainly including vast outputs of jobbing printing, were increasingly beyond the command of London and of the Stationers' Company. The 1799 Act demanding returns printed by printers, and recording the number of presses in each printing house, locations and certain actions, is a marvellous instance of commercial activity undertaken to monitor and even restrict itself. Even in jobbing and the intervention of government at the end of the eighteenth century, we are not far from engagement with Foucault's idea of surveillance as an element of the bourgeois liberal state, and a surveillance that turns into punishment.

As stated at the outset of this history, the dissemination of practical knowledge has much in common with the consciously undertaken but also state-surveyed and state-policed social activities outlined by E. P. Thompson and Antonio Gramsci: the quotidian world of the England of 1800, in which men and women (and witnesses) signed their troth on printed forms, taking a pen to gridded blanks, just as recruits and apprentices marked or signed paper processed by stationers and printers. Suspects and criminals were arraigned and sentences passed on forms; geographical mobility and the life of labour were determined, and vagrants and travellers were moved on or allowed to rest, by print-ordered settlement papers and passes; merchants and richer tourists used passports; mariners and sea-captains and their clients depended on bills of lading, schedules and preprinted marine wills; the propertied were taxed by paper forms and protected themselves by printed contracts, inheritance documents and insurance forms; rich and poor prayed on special occasions by reading from or listening to printed prayer sheets; and further examples abound.

A more organized world was not necessarily, of course, a more liberated one. Indeed, the collection of information, from civic and fiscal enumeration to the civil registration of familial (or what demographers call 'vital') events, represented a new ordering, social arrangement and 'control' that linked intolerance with modernity, regimentation with progress. For historians like Thompson, this was the replacement of customary social bonds by a new, inherently more ruthless political economy of discipline, wage structures and greatly more organized and centralized employment.[17] The legitimating defence of traditional rights and customs was, according to Thompson, shared across a wide community consensus and at least

---

17   E. P. Thompson. 'The Moral Economy of the English Crowd in the Eighteenth Century', *Past and Present*, 50:1 (1971), 76–136.

partly sanctioned by local and even national political and religious authorities. Yet conformity is not the same as control. Conformity reassures and
can be in response to the need for the regularity and familiarity which
assures reliability, confidence and trust. Standardization, if broadly rather
than thoroughly applied, allows for local differences. Printed outcomes
also reflect technologies and human competences, and the copying of
exemplars was often imperfect and botched. Much turned on what 'publication' meant.

The pioneering insight of Peter Mathias into the nature of credit
relations and the trust ensured by an essentially 'face-to-face' society in
mid-eighteenth-century England[18] has now to be placed within our much
expanded understanding of culture and society of the time. The evidence
brought together in this book attests to a deepening trade structure of
printing and publishing in which forms of communication were increasingly multidirectional. No longer were newspapers and commercial correspondence simply supplying information from London to the provinces,
but information (such as prices of market goods) was exchanged
between provincial towns and London, and between regional towns,
each of which also developed extensive radiating networks of exchange.
Like the standardized forms used to record events and activities, the
newspapers that underpinned these information networks were mutable
but also conformist. Thus an advertisement in a newspaper printed and
published in Exeter looked much the same as one in a newspaper printed
and published in York or Liverpool. The wording differed, the services
or objects on offer differed, the typography differed, but the overall
presentation was similar. Parameters were set by experience and general
imitation; styles were transferable; typologies were recognizable across
the country. This was a unifying conformity that allowed for difference:
a controlling form of print that also allowed for certain resistance and
adaptability. In 1680, variation between many types of publication and
between individual exemplars of items like currents and official recording
forms subverted any sense of uniformity and undermined assertions of
value and reliability; in 1800, variation was subject to broad conformities
that established trust and confidence. It was a reassurance that included

---

18   His inspirational chapter 5 on this subject in Peter Mathias, *The Transformation of
England: Essays in the Economic and Social History of England in the Eighteenth Century*
(London: Methuen, 1979) is augmented by his 'Risk, Credit and Kinship in Early Modern
Enterprise', in *The Early Modern Atlantic Economy*, ed. John J. McCusker and Kenneth
Morgan (Cambridge: Cambridge University Press, 2000), pp. 15–35.

regularity of appearance and uniformity of material forms – of corn returns, of circulating banknotes, of exchangeable vouchers that might be tendered remotely and at a great distance. The anonymity introduced by new modes of publication began to replace the face-to-face society with something that was institutionalized, widespread, objectified, culturally acceptable and engineered by the medium of print and paper, engraving and ink.

Bibliography of Printed Sources

Anon., *An Account of Public Charities in England and Wales* (London, 1828).

——, *Affecting History of the Innkeeper of Normandy* (London, 1780).

——, *A Biographical History of the Roman Empire* (London and Bath, 1790).

——, *The Case Between the Proprietors of News-Papers, and the Coffee-Men of London Fairly Stated* (London, 1729).

——, *The Case of the Coffee-Men of London and Westminster. Or, An Account of the Impositions and Abuses, put upon Them and the Whole Town by the Present Set of News-Writers* (London, 1728).

——, *Catalogue of the Books of the London Library Society* (London, 1786).

——, *The Coal Dealer's Assistant. Being Tables Calculated for the ready and easy finding out the true value of any number of chalderns from 1 to 200, at any of the usual prices* (Newcastle upon Tyne, 1759).

——, *A Compleat Guide to All Persons Who Have Any Trade or Concern with the City of London and Parts Adjacent*, 4th edn (London, 1749).

——, *The Compleat Tradesman* (London, 1790).

——, *The Death and Burial of Mistress Money: with her Will she made at her departure and what happened afterwards to the Usurer that buried Her* (London, 1678).

——, *A General Description of all Trades* (London, 1747).

——, *A Letter to the Chairman of the Committee by a Merchant, Reasons Humbly Offered Against the Societies of Mines Royal* ([London, 1720]).

——, *Librorum ex Bibliotensis Philip Farewell et Daniel Defoe* (London, 1731).

——, *The London Adviser and Guide; Containing Every Instruction and Information Useful and Necessary to Persons Living in London and Coming to Reside There* (London, 1786).

——, *A New Biographical and Chronological History of England* (London and Bath, 1790).

——, *The Pleasant Art of Money Catching* (1705; London, 1782).

——, *Proposals modestly offered for the full peopling and inhabiting the City of London, and to restore the same to her ancient flourishing trade, which will suite her splendid structure* (London, 1672).

——, *Riley's Historical Pocket Library*, 6 vols (London and Bath, 1790) [printed by and sometimes attributed to George Riley].

——, *Thoughts on Commerce and Liberty* (London, 1786).

——, *The Tryal of the Lady Allurea Luxury, before the Lord Chief-Justice Upright, on an Information for a Conspiracy* (London, 1757).

——, *Universal Directory consisting of Alphabetical Lists of Merchants, Banks, Notaries, Shopkeepers, Doctors with distinct List of Booksellers* (London, 1763).

Acres, William Marston, *The Bank of England from Within, 1694–1900*, 2 vols (London: Oxford University Press, 1931).

Albert, William, *The Turnpike Road System in England, 1663–1840* (Cambridge: Cambridge University Press, 1972; new edn, 2007).

Alexander, David, '"Alone Worth Treble the Price": Illustrations in 18th-Century English Magazines', in *A Millennium of the Book: Production, Design and Illustration in Manuscript & Print 900–1900*, ed. Robin Myers and Michael Harris (Winchester and New Castle, DE: Oak Knoll, 1994), pp. 107–33.

Allan, D. G. C., *William Shipley: Founder of the Royal Society of Arts*, new edn (London: Scolar Press, 1979).

Amory, Hugh and David Hall (eds), *A History of the Book in America: Volume 1: The Colonial Book in the Atlantic World* (Cambridge: Cambridge University Press, 2000).

Anderson, Adam, *An Historical and Chronological Deduction of the Origin of Commerce*, 2 vols (London, 1764).

Anderson, B. L., 'Provincial Aspects of the Financial Revolution of the Eighteenth Century', *Business History*, 11:2 (1969), 11–20.

Appadurai, Arjun (ed.), *The Social Life of Things: Commodities in Cultural Perspective* (Cambridge: Cambridge University Press, 1986).

Appleby, Joyce O., *Economic Thought and Ideology in Seventeenth-century England* (Princeton, NJ: Princeton University Press, 1978).

[Arbuckle, James], *Hibernicus's Letters: Or A Philosophical Miscellany* (London, 1729).

Archenholz, M. D., *A Picture of England* (Dublin, 1790).

Arkle, A. H., 'Early Liverpool Printers', *Transactions of the Historic Society of Lancashire and Cheshire*, n.s., 32 (1917), 73–84.

Ashton, John, *Social Life in the Reign of Queen Anne: Taken from Original Sources*, 2 vols (London: Chatto and Windus, 1882).

Ashton, T. S., *Economic Fluctuations in England 1770–1800* (Oxford: Oxford University Press, 1959).

——, *An Economic History of England: The Eighteenth Century* (London: Oxford University Press, 1955).

Aspinall, A., 'Statistical Accounts of the London Newspapers in the Eighteenth Century', *EHR*, 63 (1948), 201–32.

Aspromourgos, Tony, 'New Light on the Economics of William Petty (1623–1687): Some Findings from Previously Undisclosed Manuscripts', *Contributions to Political Economy*, 19 (2000), 53–70.

Atkins, P. J., *The Directories of London, 1677–1977* (London: Mansell, 1990).

Bain, Ian, 'Thomas Bewick and his Contemporaries', in *Maps and Prints*, ed. Robin Myers and Michael Harris (Oxford: Oxford Polytechnic Press, 1984), pp. 67–80.

Baker, J. H., 'English Law Books and Legal Publishing', in *The Cambridge History of the Book in Britain: Volume IV 1557–1695*, ed. John Barnard and D. F. McKenzie (Cambridge: Cambridge University Press, 2002), pp. 474–503.

Ball, Johnson, *William Caslon, 1693–1766: The Ancestry, Life and Connections of England's Foremost Letter-Engraver and Type-Founder* (Kineton: Roundwood Press, 1973).

Barbeary, Anne, 'To Make the Best of Both Worlds? Religion and Luxury in the Sermon Literature c.1740–1789' (unpubl. B.A. dissertation, University of Cambridge, 1985).

[Barbon, Nicholas], *A Discourse of Trade* (London, 1690).

Barker, Hannah, 'Medical Advertising and Trust in Late Georgian England', *Urban History*, 36:3 (2009), 379–98.

——, *Newspapers, Politics and English Society, 1695–1855* (London: Longman, 2000).

——, *Newspapers, Politics and Public Opinion in Late Eighteenth-Century England* (Oxford: Oxford University Press, 1998).

——, *The Business of Women: Female Enterprise and Urban Development in Northern England, 1760–1830* (Oxford: Oxford University Press, 2006).

Barker, Hannah and Elaine Chalus (eds), *Gender in Eighteenth-Century*

England: Roles, Representations and Responsibilities (London: Longman, 1997).

——, *Women's History: Britain, 1700–1850* (London: Routledge, 2005).

Barker, Hannah and Jane Hamlett, 'Living above the shop: home, business, and family in the English "Industrial Revolution"', *Journal of Family History*, 35:4 (2010), 311–28.

Baron, Sabrina Alcorn, Eric N. Lindquist and Eleanor F. Shevlin (eds), *Agent of Change: Print Culture Studies after Elizabeth L. Eisenstein* (Amherst, MA: University of Massachusetts Press, 2007).

Barry, Jonathan, 'Publicity and the Public Good: Presenting Medicine in Eighteenth-Century Bristol', in *Medical Fringe and Medical Orthodoxy, 1750–1850*, ed. William Bynum and Roy Porter (London: Croom Helm, 1987), pp. 29–39.

Barry, Jonathan and Kenneth Morgan (eds), *Reformation and Renewal in Eighteenth-Century Bristol* (Bristol: Bristol Record Society, 1994).

Baudino, Isabelle, Jacques Carré and Cécile Révauger (eds), *The Invisible Woman: Aspects of Women's Work in Eighteenth-Century Britain* (Aldershot: Ashgate, 2005).

Beawes, Wyndham, *Lex Mercatoria Rediviva: or the Merchant's Directory* (London, 1751).

Beer, E. S. de, 'The English Newspapers from 1695 to 1702', in *William III and Louis XIV*, ed. R. Hatton and J. S. Bromley (Liverpool: Liverpool University Press, 1968), pp. 117–29.

Berg, Maxine and Helen Clifford, 'Selling Consumption in the Eighteenth Century: Advertising and the Trade Card in Britain and France', *Cultural and Social History*, 4:2 (2007), 145–70.

Bidwell, John, 'Printers' Supplies and Capitalization', in *A History of the Book in America: Volume 1: The Colonial Book in the Atlantic World*, ed. Hugh Amory and David Hall (Cambridge, MA: Cambridge University Press, 2000), pp. 163–82.

Bisschop, W. R., *The Rise of the London Money Market, 1640–1826* (London: Cass, 1968).

Black, Jeremy, *The English Press in the Eighteenth Century* (London: Croom Helm, 1987).

Blackwell, Thomas and John Mills, *Memoirs of the Court of Augustus* (Edinburgh and London, 1753–63).

Blagden, Cyprian, 'A Bookseller's Memorandum Book, 1695–1720', in *Studies in the History of Accounting*, ed. A. C. Littleton and

B. S. Yamey (Homewood, IL: Richard D. Irwin, and London: Sweet and Maxwell, 1956), pp. 255–65.

——, 'Thomas Carnan and the Almanack Monopoly', *Studies in Bibliography*, 14 (1961), 23–40.

Blair, Ann M., *Too Much to Know: Managing Scholarly Information before the Modern Age* (London and New Haven, CT: Yale University Press, 2010).

Bluett, Thomas, *An Enquiry whether …Virtue Tends to the Wealth … or Disadvantage of a People* (London, 1725).

——, *True Meaning of the Fable of the Bees* (London, 1726).

Botein, Stephen, 'Meer Mechanics and an Open Press: The Business and Political Strategies of Colonial American Printers', *Perspectives in American History*, 9 (1975), 127–225.

Bowd, Rebecca (ed.), special issue of *Library and Information History*, 29:3 (Aug. 2013).

Braudel, Fernand, *Capitalism and Material Life, 1400–1800* (New York and London: Harper Collins, 1973).

Brenni, Vito J., *Book Illustration and Decoration: A Guide to Research* (Westport, CT: Greenwood Press, 1980).

Brewer, John, 'Commercialization and Politics', in *The Birth of a Consumer Society: The Commercialization of Eighteenth-Century England*, ed. Neil McKendrick, John Brewer and J. H. Plumb (London: Europa, 1982), pp. 197–264.

Brewer, John and Roy Porter (eds), *Consumption and the World of Goods* (London: Routledge, 1993).

Briggs, Asa and Peter Burke, *A Social History of the Media: from Gutenberg to the Internet*, 2nd edn (Cambridge: Polity, 2005).

Bristol Presentments, 1770–1917, ed. Walter E. Minchinton (Wakefield: Microform Academic Publishers, 1986).

Brown, Stephen W. and Warren McDougall (eds), *The Edinburgh History of the Book in Scotland Vol. 2 Enlightenment and Expansion, 1707–1800* (Edinburgh: Edinburgh University Press, 2012).

Brown, John, *An Estimate of the Manners and Principles of the Times. By the Author of Characteristics, etc.* (London, 1757).

Brown, P. S., 'Medicines Advertised in Eighteenth-Century Bath Newspapers', *Medical History*, 20:2 (Apr. 1976), 152–68.

——, 'The Venders of Medicines Advertised in Eighteenth-Century Bath Newspapers', *Medical History*, 19:4 (Oct. 1975), 352–69.

Bruttini, Adriano, 'Advertising and the Industrial Revolution', *Economic Notes*, 4:2–3 (May–Dec. 1973), 90–[116].

Bryden, D. J., 'A Short Catalogue of the Types used by John Reid, Printer in Edinburgh, 1761–74', *Bibliotheck*, 6:1 (1971), 17–21.

Buchanan, B. J. 'The Evolution of the English Turnpike Trusts: Lessons from a Case Study', *EcHR*, n.s., 39:2 (May 1986), 223–43.

Buck, Peter, 'Seventeenth-Century Political Arithmetic: Civil Strife and Vital Statistics', *Isis*, 68:1 (Mar. 1977), 67–84.

Burke, Peter, 'Tradition and Experience: The Idea of Decline from Bruni to Gibbon', *Daedalus*, 105:3 (Summer 1976), 137–52.

Bury, J. B., *The Idea of Progress: An Inquiry into its Origin and Growth* (London: Macmillan & Co., 1920).

Bywater, M. F. and B. S. Yamey (eds), *Historic Accounting Literature: A Companion Guide* (London: Scolar Press, and Tokyo, Yushodo Press, 1982).

Cameron, A. and R. Farndon (eds), *Scenes from Sea and City. Lloyds List 1734–1984* (Colchester: Printed for Lloyds, 1984).

Campbell, Archibald, *Aretē-logia, or An Inquiry into the Original of Moral Virtue* (Edinburgh, 1728).

Campbell, R., *The London Tradesman* (London, 1747).

Capp, Bernard, *Astrology and the Popular Press. English Almanacks 1500–1800* (London, 1977).

Carlson, David R., *English Humanist Books: Writers and Patrons, Manuscript and Print, 1475–1525* (Toronto, Buffalo and London: University of Toronto Press, 1993), pp. 131–41.

——, 'A Theory of the Early English Printing Firm', in *Caxton's Trace: Studies in the History of English Printing*, ed. William Kuskin (Notre Dame: University of Notre Dame Press, 2006), pp. 35–68.

Centlivre, Mrs [Susanna Carroll], *The Gamester: a Comedy* (London, 1705).

Cheney, C. R., *John Cheney and his Descendants: Printers in Banbury since 1767* (Banbury: Cheney and Sons, 1936).

Christianson, C. Paul, 'Evidence for the Study of London's Late Medieval Manuscript-Book Trade', in *Book Production and Publishing in Britain, 1375–1475*, ed. J. Griffiths and D. Pearsall (Cambridge: Cambridge University Press, 1989), pp. 87–108.

——, 'The Rise of London's Book-Trade', in *The Cambridge History of the Book in Britain: Volume III 1400–1557*, ed. Lotte Hellinga and

Joseph B. Trapp (Cambridge: Cambridge University Press, 1999), pp. 128–47.

Clapham, Sir John, *The Bank of England: A History 1694–1914*, 2 vols (Cambridge: Cambridge University Press, 1944).

Clark, Geoffrey Wilson, *Betting on Lives: The Culture of Life Insurance in England, 1695–1775* (Manchester: Manchester University Press, 1999).

Clark, Walter E., *Josiah Tucker, Economist: A Study in the History of Economics* (New York: Columbia University Press, 1903).

Coats, A. W., 'The Relief of Poverty. Attitudes to Labour and Economic Change in England 1660–1782', *International Review of Social History*, 21 (1976), 98–115.

Cochrane, J. A., *Dr Johnson's Printer: The Life of William Strahan* (London: Routledge and Kegan Paul, 1964).

Coke, David E. and Alan Borg, *Vauxhall Gardens: A History* (New Haven, CT: Yale University Press, 2011).

Cole, Richard Cargill, *Irish Booksellers and English Writers 1740–1800* (London: Mansell, 1986).

——, 'Private Libraries in Eighteenth-Century Ireland', *Library Quarterly*, 44:3 (July 1974), 231–47.

Cole, Thomas, *Discourses on Luxury* (London, 1761).

Cole, W. A., 'Factors in Demand, 1700–80', in *The Economic History of Britain since 1700*, ed. Roderick Floud and Donald McCloskey, 2 vols (Cambridge: Cambridge University Press, 1981), vol. 1, pp. 36–65.

Coleman, D. C., *The Paper Industry, 1495–1860: A Study in Industrial Growth* (Oxford: Clarendon Press, 1958).

——, 'Politics and Economics in the Age of Anne', in *Trade, Government and the Economy in Pre-Industrial England: Essays Presented to F. J. Fisher*, ed. D. C. Coleman and A. H. John (London: Weidenfeld and Nicolson, 1976), pp. 187–211.

——, *Revisions in Mercantilism* (London: Methuen, 1969).

——, *The Economy of England, 1450–1750* (Oxford: Oxford University Press, 1977).

Coleman, D. C. and A. H. John (eds), *Trade, Government and the Economy in Pre-Industrial England: Essays Presented to F. J. Fisher* (London: Weidenfeld and Nicolson, 1976).

[Collinges, John], *The Weaver's Pocket-Book; Or, Weaving Spiritualiz'd* (Glasgow, 1766).

Corbett, Margery and Ronald Lightbown, *The Comely Frontispiece: The*

Emblematic Title-Page in England 1550–1660 (London: Routledge and Kegan Paul, 1979).

Corfield, P. J., *The Impact of English Towns 1700–1800* (Oxford: Oxford University Press, 1982).

Crafts, N. F. R., *British Economic Growth during the Industrial Revolution* (Oxford: Oxford University Press, 1985).

Craig, Mary Elizabeth, *The Scottish Periodical Press, 1750–1789* (Edinburgh: Oliver and Boyd, 1931).

Cranfield, G. A., *The Development of the Provincial Newspaper, 1700–1760* (Oxford: Oxford University Press, 1962).

Crawford, W. H. and B. Trainor (eds), *Irish Social History: Aspects of Irish Social History 1750–1800: Documents* (Belfast: HMSO, 1969).

Crouzet, François, 'Toward an Export Economy: British Exports during the Industrial Revolution', *Explorations in Economic History*, 17 (1980), 48–93.

Cullen, K. J., *Famine in Scotland: The 'Ill Years' of the 1690s* (Edinburgh: Edinburgh University Press, 2010).

Cullen, L. M. and T. C. Smout, 'Economic Growth in Scotland and Ireland', in *Comparative Aspects of Scottish and Irish Economic and Social History, 1600–1900*, ed L. M. Cullen and T. C. Smout (Edinburgh: John Donald, 1977), pp. 3–18.

Dale, Richard, *The First Crash: Lessons from the South Sea Bubble* (Princeton, NJ: Princeton University Press, 2004).

Darnton, Robert, *The Forbidden Best-Sellers of Pre-Revolutionary France* (New York: W. W. Norton, 1995).

Dasgupta, Partha, 'Trust as a Commodity', in *Trust: Making and Breaking Co-operative Relations*, ed. Diego Gambetta (Oxford: Basil Blackwell, 1988), pp. 49–72.

Daunton, Martin, *Progress and Poverty: An Economic and Social History of Britain, 1700–1850* (Oxford: Oxford University Press, 1995).

Davenant, Charles, *The True Picture of a Modern Whig* (London, 1701).

Davis, Ralph, *A Commercial Revolutions: English Overseas Trade in the Seventeenth and Eighteenth Century* (London: Historical Association, 1967).

——, *The Industrial Revolution and British Overseas Trade* (Leicester: Leicester University Press, 1979).

Deane, Phyllis, *The State and the Economic System: An Introduction to the History of Political Economy* (Oxford: Oxford University Press, 1989).

Deane, P. and W. A. Cole, *British Economic Growth 1688–1959* (Cambridge: Cambridge University Press, 1962).

Defoe, Daniel, *The Complete English Tradesman, in Familiar Letters; Directing him in all the several Parts and Progressions of Trade*, 2 vols (London, 1726–27).

Dennis, John, *Vice and Luxury* (London, 1724).

Devine, T. M., C. H. Lee and G. C. Peden (eds), *The Transformation of Scotland: The Economy Since 1700* (Edinburgh: Edinburgh University Press, 2005).

Dickson, P. G. M., *The Financial Revolution in England: A Study in the Development of Public Credit, 1688–1756* (London: Macmillan, 1967).

——, *The Sun Insurance Office, 1710–1960: The History of Two and a Half Centuries of British Insurance* (London: Oxford University Press, 1960).

Doherty, Francis, *A Study in Eighteenth-Century Advertising Methods: The Anodyne Necklace* (Lewiston, NY: Edwin Mellen Press, 1992).

Dolphin, Laurie (ed.), *Evidence: The Art of Candy Jernigan* (San Francisco: Chronicle Books, 1999).

Donnelly, Michael, 'From Political Arithmetic to Social Statistics: How Some Nineteenth-Century Roots of the Social Sciences Were Implanted', in *The Rise of the Social Sciences and the Formation of Modernity: Conceptual Change in Context, 1750–1850*, ed. Johan Heilbron, Lars Magnusson and Björn Wittrock (Dordrecht and Boston, MA: Kluwer Academic Publishers, 1998), pp. 225–39.

Dowell, Stephen, *A History of Taxation and Taxes in England*, 3 vols, 3rd edn (London: Longmans, 1965).

Downie, Alan, 'The Growth of Government Tolerance of the Press to 1790', in *The Development of the English Book Trade, 1700–1899*, ed. Robin Myers and Michael Harris (Oxford: Oxford Polytechnic Press, 1981), pp. 36–65.

Downey, James, *The Eighteenth-Century Pulpit: A Study of the Sermons of Butler, Berkeley, Secker, Sterne, Whitefield and Wesley* (Oxford: Clarendon Press, 1969).

Dunbar, James, *Essays on the History of Mankind in Rude and Uncultivated Ages* (London, 1780).

Edwards, A. S. G. and Carol M. Meale, 'The Marketing of Printed Books in Late Medieval England', *The Library*, 6th ser., 15 (1993), 95–124.

Edwards, Paul N., Lisa Gitelman, Gabrielle Hecht, Adrian Johns, Brian Larkin and Neil Safier, 'AHR Conversation: Historical Perspectives on the Circulation of Information', *American Historical Review*, 116:5 (2011), 1392–435.

Eisenstein, Elizabeth L., Anthony Grafton and Adrian Johns, 'AHR Forum: How Revolutionary Was the Print Revolution?', *American Historical Review*, 107:1 (2002), 84–128.

Eisenstein, Elizabeth, *The Printing Revolution in Early Modern Europe*, rev. 2nd edn (Cambridge: Cambridge University Press, 2005).

Eisermann, Falk, 'Mixing Pop and Politics: Origins, Transmission, and Readers of Illustrated Broadsides in Fifteenth-Century Germany', in *Incunabula and their Readers: Printing, Selling and Using Books in the Fifteenth Century*, ed. Kristian Jensen (London: British Library, 2003), pp. 159–77.

Elliott, Blanche B., *A History of English Advertising* (London: B. T. Batsford, 1962).

Elton, G. R., 'The Sessional Printing of Statutes, 1484–1547' in *Wealth and Power in Tudor England: Essays Presented to S.T. Bindoff*, ed. E. W. Ives *et al.* (London: Athlone Press, 1978), pp. 68–86.

Eversley, D. E. C., 'The Home Market and Economic Growth in England, 1750–1780', in *Land, Labour and Population in the Industrial Revolution*, ed. E. L. Jones and G. E. Mingay (London: Edward Arnold, 1967), pp. 206–59.

Fairer, David, 'Persistence, Adaptations and Transformations in Pastoral and Georgic Poetry', in *The Cambridge History of English Literature, 1660–1780*, ed. John Richetti (Cambridge: Cambridge University Press, 2005), pp. 259–86.

Fawconer, Samuel, *Essay on Modern Luxury* (London, 1765).

Fawel, Revd J., *Observations on a Pamphlet entituled 'Luxury No Political Evil'* (Wigan, 1785).

Feather, John, 'British Publishing in the Eighteenth Century a Preliminary Subject Analysis', *The Library*, 6th ser., 8 (1986), 32–46.

——, 'John Clay of Daventry: The Business of an Eighteenth-Century Stationer', *Studies in Bibliography*, 37 (1984), 198–209.

——, *The Provincial Book Trade in Eighteenth-Century England* (Cambridge: Cambridge University Press, 1981).

Ferdinand, C. Y., *Benjamin Collins and the Provincial Newspaper Trade in the Eighteenth Century* (Oxford: Clarendon Press, 1997).

——, 'Benjamin Collins: Salisbury Printer', in *Searching the Eighteenth Century*, ed. M. Crump and M. Harris (London: British Library, 1983), pp. 74–92.

Fergus, Jan and Ruth Portner, 'Provincial Bookselling in Eighteenth-century England: The Case of John Clay Reconsidered', *Studies in Bibliography*, 40 (1987), 147–63.

Fiddes, Richard, *General Treatise of Morality* (London, 1724; 3rd edn, 1762).

Fielding, Henry, *Enquiry into the Cause, of the late Increase of Robbers* (London, 1751).

Finkelstein, Andrea, *Harmony and the Balance: An Intellectual History of Seventeenth-Century English Economic Thought* (Ann Arbor: University of Michigan Press, 2000).

Finn, Margot C., *The Character of Credit: Personal Debt in English Culture, 1740–1914* (Cambridge: Cambridge University Press, 2004).

Fitzmaurice, E., *The Life of Sir William Petty* (London: John Murray, 1985).

Floud, R. and D. N. McCloskey (eds), *The Economic History of Britain since 1700*, 2 vols (Cambridge: Cambridge University Press, 1981).

Floud, Roderick and Paul Johnson (eds), *The Cambridge Economic History of Modern Britain*, 3 vols (Cambridge: Cambridge University Press, 2004).

[Forster, Francis], *Thoughts on the Times, But Chiefly on the Profligacy of our Women, and It's Causes* (London, 1779).

Forster, Nathaniel, *An Enquiry into the Causes of the Present High Price of Provisions* (London, 1767).

Fox, Adam, *Oral and Literate Culture in England 1500–1700* (Oxford: Oxford University Press, 2000).

Frank, Joseph, *The Beginnings of the English Newspaper, 1620–1660* (Cambridge, MA: Harvard University Press, 1961).

[Fry, Joseph], *Specimen of Metal Cast Ornaments, Curiously Adjusted to Paper, By Edmund Fry and Isaac Steele* (London, 1794).

——, *A Specimen of Printing Types made by Joseph Fry and Sons, Letter-Founders, Worship-Street, Moorfields* (London, 1785).

Furbank, P. N. and W. R. Owens, *A Critical Bibliography of Daniel Defoe* (London: Pickering and Chatto, 1998).

——, *A Political Biography of Daniel Defoe* (London: Pickering and Chatto, 2006).

Gambetta, Diego, 'Can we Trust Trust?', in *Trust: Making and Breaking Co-operative Relations*, ed. Diego Gambetta (Oxford: Basil Blackwell, 1988), pp. 213–37.

—— (ed.), *Trust: Making and Breaking Co-operative Relations* (Oxford: Basil Blackwell, 1988).

Gaskell, Philip, *A New Introduction to Bibliography* (Oxford: Clarendon Press, 1972).

Gauci, Perry, *The Politics of Trade: The Overseas Merchant in State and Society, 1660–1720* (Oxford: Oxford University Press, 2001).

George, Dorothy M., *English Political Caricature to 1792. A Study of Opinion and Propaganda* (Oxford: Clarendon Press, 1959).

Gibb, D. E. W., *Lloyd's of London: A Study in Individualism* (London: Macmillan and Co., 1957).

Gillespie, Alexandra, 'Balliol MS 354: Histories of the Book at the End of the Middle Ages', *Poetica*, 60 (2003), 47–63.

——, 'Caxton and After', in *A Companion to Middle English Prose*, ed. A. S. G. Edwards (Cambridge: D. S. Brewer, 2004), 307–25.

——, *Print Culture and the Medieval Author: Chaucer, Lydgate, and their Books, 1473–1557* (Oxford: Oxford University Press, 2006).

Gillespie, Vincent, 'Vernacular Books of Religion', in *Book Production and Publishing in Britain, 1375–1475*, ed. J. Griffiths and D. Pearsall (Cambridge: Cambridge University Press, 1989), pp. 317–41.

Glaisyer, Natasha, 'Readers, Correspondents, and Communities: John Houghton's *A Collection of Letters for the Improvement of Husbandry and Trade* (1692–1703)', in *Communities in Early Modern England: Networks, Place, Rhetoric*, ed. Alexandra Shepard and Phil Withington (Manchester: Manchester University Press, 2000), pp. 235–51.

——, *The Culture of Commerce in England, 1660–1720* (London: The Royal Historical Society and Boydell, 2006).

Glaisyer, Natasha and Sara Pennell (eds), *Didactic Literature in England, 1500–1800: Expertise Constructed* (Aldershot: Ashgate, 2003).

Glass, D. V. and D. E. C. Eversley (eds), *Population in History: Essays in Historical Demography: General and Great Britain*, new edn (London: E. Arnold, 2008).

Goldgar, Anne, *Impolite Learning: Conduct and Community in the Republic of Letters 1680–1750* (London and New Haven, CT: Yale University Press, 1995).

Goodfellow, James, *The Ready Calculator ... exhibiting at one view, the solid contents of all kinds of packages* (London, 1794).

Goodman, Stanley, 'A Collection of Lewes Handbills, 1768–1777', *Sussex Archaeological Collections*, 97 (1959), 58–68.

Gordan, John D., III, 'John Nutt: Trade Publisher and Printer "In the Savoy"', *The Library*, 7th ser., 15 (2014), 243–60.

Goss, Charles William Frederick, *The London Directories, 1677–1855* (London: Denis Archer, 1932).

Graham, William, *The One Pound Note in the History of Banking in Great Britain*, 2nd edn (Edinburgh: J. Thin, 1911).

Grassby, R., 'The Rate of Profit in Seventeenth-Century England', *EHR* 84 (1969), 721–51.

Green, James N., 'English Books and Printing in the Age of Franklin', in *A History of the Book in America: Volume 1: The Colonial Book in the Atlantic World*, ed. Hugh Amory and David Hall (Cambridge, MA: Cambridge University Press, 2000), pp. 248–97.

Greenfeld, Liah, *The Spirit of Capitalism: Nationalism and Economic Growth* (Cambridge, MA: Harvard University Press, 2001).

Greg, W. W., *A Companion to Arber* (Oxford: Clarendon Press, 1967).

Griffiths, Antony, *Prints and Printmaking: An Introduction to the History and Techniques*, 2nd edn (London: British Museum, 1996).

Griffiths, J. and D. Pearsall (eds), *Book Production and Publishing in Britain, 1375–1475* (Cambridge: Cambridge University Press, 1989).

Groebner, Valentin, *Who are You? Identification, Deception, and Surveillance in Early Modern Europe* (New York: Zone Books, 2007).

The Guardian, 1st collected edn, 2 vols (London, 1714).

Haig, Robert Louis, *The Gazetteer, 1735–1797: A Study in the Eighteenth-Century English Newspaper* (Carbondale, IL: Southern Illinois University Press, 1960).

Hainsworth, D. R. (ed.), *The Correspondence of Sir John Lowther of Whitehaven, 1693–1698, a Provincial Community in Wartime* (New York: Oxford University Press for the British Academy, 1983).

Hamilton, Henry, *An Economic History of Scotland in the Eighteenth Century* (Oxford: Oxford University Press, 1963).

Hamlyn, Hilda M., 'Eighteenth-century Circulating Libraries in England', *The Library*, 5th ser., 1 (1947), 197–218.

Hammelmann, Hanns and T. S. R. Boase, *Book Illustrators in Eighteenth-Century England* (New Haven, CT: Yale University Press, 1975).

Handover, P. M., *Printing in London from 1476 to Modern Times* (London: George Allen & Unwin Ltd, 1960).

Hans, Nicholas, *New Trends in Education in the Eighteenth Century* (London: Routledge & Kegan Paul, 1951).

Harper, Revd Walter, *The State of the Nation with Respect to Religion and Manners. A Sermon Preached at Uxbridge Chapel, Middlesex on Sunday, 25th October 1789* (London, Cambridge, Oxford, Uxbridge and Hereford, 1789).

Harris, Michael, 'Astrology, Almanacks and Booksellers', *Publishing History*, 8 (1980), 87–104.

——, 'London Guidebooks before 1800', in *Maps and Prints. Aspects of the English Booktrade*, ed. Robin Myers and Michael Harris (Oxford: Oxford Polytechnic Press, 1984), pp. 31–66.

——, *London Newspapers in the Age of Walpole: A Study of the Origins of the Modern English Press* (London: Associated University Presses, 1987).

——, 'The Pleasant Art of Money Catching: The Expansion of the Trade in Cheap Books around 1700', in *Craft and Capital in Book Trade History. Part I: A Skilled Workforce: Training and Collaboration in the Book Trades. Part II: Balancing the Books: Financing the Book Trade from the 16th Century*, ed. Robin Myers, Michael Harris and Giles Mandelbrote, 2 vols (forthcoming, 2015).

——, 'The Structure, Ownership and Control of the Press, 1620–1780', in *Newspaper History from the Seventeenth Century to the Present Day*, ed. George Boyce, James Curran and Pauline Wingate (London: Constable, 1978), pp. 82–97.

Hatton, Edward, *Arithmetick Made Easy* (London, 1726).

——, *Comes Commercii: Or, The Trader's Companion* (London, 1699).

——, 'A Dictionary, or Alphabetical Explanation of the most difficult Terms commonly used in Merchandise and Trade', *Merchant's Magazine* (1699), 223–39.

Hazeland, William, *A View of the Manner in which Trade and Civil Liberty support each other* (London, 1756).

Heal, Ambrose, *London Tradesmen's Cards of the XVIII Century* (London: Batsford Ltd, 1925).

——, 'The Trade-Cards of Engravers', *Print Collector's Quarterly*, 14:3 (July 1927), 219–50.

Heal, Ambrose and Stanley Morison, *The English Writing-Masters and their Copy Books* (Cambridge: Cambridge University Press, 1931).

Hellinga, Lotte, 'Importation of Books Printed on the Continent into England and Scotland before c.1520', in *Printing the Written Word: The Social History of Books circa 1450–1520*, ed. Sandra Hindman (Ithaca and London: Cornell University Press, 1991), pp. 205–24.

Hellinga, Lotte and Joseph B. Trapp (eds), *The Cambridge History of the Book in Britain: Volume III 1400–1557* (Cambridge: Cambridge University Press, 1999).

Hentschell, Roze, 'The Cultural Geography of St Paul's Cathedral Precinct', in *The Age of Shakespeare*, ed. R. Malcolm Smuts (Oxford: Oxford University Press, 2014), forthcoming.

Hernlund, Patricia, 'William Strahan, Printer' (unpubl. Ph.D. dissertation, University of Chicago, 1965).

——, 'William Strahan's Ledgers', *Studies in Bibliography*, 20 (1967), 89–111 and 22 (1969), 179–95.

Higgs, Edward, *Identifying the English: A History of Personal Identification from 1500 to the Present* (London and New York: Continuum, 2011).

——, *The Information State in England: The Central Collection of Information on Citizens, 1500–2000* (London: Palgrave Macmillan, 2004).

Higgs, H. (ed. and trans.), *Essai sur la Nature du Commerce en géeacuteral by Richard Cantillon* (London: Frank Cass and Co., 1931).

Hill, G. B. (ed.) and L. F. Powell (rev.), *Boswell's Life of Johnson*, 6 vols (London: Oxford University Press, 1934–50).

Hill, Joseph, *The Book Makers of Old Birmingham* (Birmingham: Shakespeare Press for Cornish Bros Ltd, 1907).

Hindle, Steve, 'Dependency, Shame and Belonging: Badging the Deserving Poor, c.1550–1750', *Cultural and Social History*, 1 (2004), 6–35.

——, *On the Parish? The Micro-Politics of Poor Relief in Rural England, c.1550–1750* (Oxford: Clarendon Press, 2004).

Hirschman, Albert O., *The Passions and the Interests. Political Arguments for Capitalism before its Triumph* (Princeton, NJ: Princeton University Press, 1977).

Hitchcock, Tim, *Down and Out in Eighteenth-Century London*, 2nd edn (London: Hambledon and London, 2004).

Hitchcock, Tim and Robert B. Shoemaker, *London Lives, 1690–1800: Crime, Poverty and Social Policy in the Metropolis* (ongoing searchable database, www.londonlives.org, accessed 11 June 2014).

Hodnett, Edward, *Francis Barlow, First Master of English Book Illustration* (London: Scolar Press, 1978).

Hoffman, Walther G., *British Industry 1700–1950*, trans. W. O. Henderson and W. H. Chaloner (Oxford: Blackwell, 1955).

Holderness, B. A., 'Credit in a Rural Economy 1660–1800', *Midland History*, 3:2 (1975), 94–115.

Hont, Istvan and Michael Ignatieff, 'Needs and justice in the Wealth of Nations', in *Wealth and Virtue. The Shaping of Political Economy in the Scottish Enlightenment*, ed. Istvan Hont and Michael Ignatieff (Cambridge: Cambridge University Press, 1983), pp. 1–44.

—— (eds), *Wealth and Virtue. The Shaping of Political Economy in the Scottish Enlightenment* (Cambridge: Cambridge University Press, 1983).

Hoon, Elizabeth, *The Organization of the English Customs System, 1696–1786* (London: Greenwood Publishing Group, 1968).

Hopkins, A. E. (ed.), *Ralph Allen's Own Narrative, 1720–1761* (London: Postal History Society, 1960).

Hoppit, Julian, 'Political Arithmetic in Eighteenth-Century England', *EcHR*, 49:3 (Aug. 1996), 516–40.

——, 'The Nation, the State, and the First Industrial Revolution', *Journal of British Studies*, 50:2 (April 2011), 307–31.

——, *A Land of Liberty? England 1689–1727* (Oxford: Clarendon Press, 2000).

——, *Risk and Failure in English Industry, 1700–1800* (Cambridge: Cambridge University Press, 1987).

Hudson, Joseph, *Remarks upon the History of the Landed and Commercial Policy of England*, 2 vols (London, 1785).

Hughes, Edward, *Studies in Administration and Finance, 1558–1825* (Manchester: Manchester University Press, 1934).

Hume, David, *Political Discourses* (Edinburgh, 1752).

Hunt, Margaret R., *The Middling Sort: Commerce, Gender, and the Family in England 1680–1780* (Berkeley: University of California Press, 1996).

——, 'Women and the Fiscal-Imperial State in the late 17th and early 18th Centuries', in *A New Imperial History: Culture, Identity and Modernity in Britain and the Empire, 1660–1840*, ed. Kathleen Wilson (Cambridge: Cambridge University Press, 2004), pp. 29–47.

Hunter, Michael and Annabel Gregory, *An Astrological Diary of Samuel Jeake of Rye, 1652–1699* (Oxford: Oxford University Press, 1988).

Hunter, P. W., 'Containing the Marvellous: Instructions to Buyers and Sellers' in *Didactic Literature in England, 1500–1800: Expertise Constructed*, ed. Natasha Glaisyer and Sara Pennell (Aldershot: Ashgate, 2003), pp. 169–85.

Hutt, Allen, *Fournier: The Compleat Typographer* (London: Frederick Muller, 1972).

Isaac, Peter C. G., *William Davison of Alnwick: Pharmacist and Printer, 1781–1858* (Oxford: Clarendon Press, 1968).

Jack, Malcolm, review of Meek, *Journal of the Philosophy of History*, 16:1 (Jan. 1978), 110–12.

Jackson, Ian, 'Print in Provincial England: Reading and Northampton, 1720–1800' (unpubl. D.Phil. dissertation, University of Oxford, 2003).

Janin-Thivos, Michèle, 'Pratiques commerciales, pratiques linguistiques. Les langues du commerce entre gênes et lisbonne (fin XVIIe–début XVIIIe siècle)', *La Revue Historique*, 7 (2010), 59–75.

Jenkins, David, 'Newspapers for the Historian', *Journal of the Welsh Bibliographical Society*, 11:1 (1973–74), 68–84.

Jenner, Mark, 'London', in *The Oxford History of Popular Print Culture Volume One: Cheap Print in Britain and Ireland to 1660*, ed. Joad Raymond (Oxford: Oxford University Press, 2011), pp. 294–307.

Jewitt, Llewellyn (ed.), *The Life of William Hutton* (London: Frederick Warne, 1872).

John, A. H., 'Aspects of English Economic Growth in the First Half of the Eighteenth Century', *Economica*, n.s., 28:110 (May 1961), 176–90.

——, 'The London Assurance Company and the Marine Insurance Market of the Eighteenth Century', *Economica*, n.s., 25:98 (May 1958), 126–41.

Johnson, A. F., 'Type-Designs and Type-Founding in Scotland', *Edinburgh Bibliographical Society Transactions*, 2 (1938–45), 255–61.

Johnson, James William, *The Formation of English Neo-Classical Thought* (Princeton, NJ: Princeton University Press, 1967).

Johnson, John, 'The Development of Printing, other than Book-Printing', *The Library*, 4th ser., 17 (1937), 22–35.

Johnson, Samuel, *The Idler*, 2 vols (London, 1761).

Jones, Erasmus, *Luxury, Pride and Vanity*, 3rd edn (London, ?1737).

Jones, Eric L., 'Fashion Manipulators: Consumer Tastes and British Industries, 1660–1800', in *Business Enterprise and Economic Change*, ed. L. P. Cain and P. J. Uselding (Kent State, OH: Kent State University Press, 1973).

Jones, Peter, 'The Scottish Professoriate and the Polite Academy 1720–1746', in *Wealth and Virtue. The Shaping of Political Economy in the Scottish Enlightenment*, ed. Istvan Hont and Michael Ignatieff (Cambridge: Cambridge University Press, 1983), pp. 89–117.

Kaufman, Paul, 'Community Lending Libraries in Ireland and Wales', *The Library*, 5th ser., 33 (1963), 299–312.

——, 'The Community Library', *Transactions of the American Philosophical Society*, n.s., 57:7 (1967), 3–67.

Klein, Lawrence E., 'Politeness for Plebes: Consumption and Social Identity in Early Eighteenth-Century England', in *The Consumption of Culture, 1600–1800: Image, Object, Text*, ed. Ann Bermingham and John Brewer (London: Routledge, 1995), pp. 362–82.

Knott, David, 'Aspects of Research into English Provincial Printing', *Journal of the Printing Historical Society*, 9 (1973–74), 6–21.

——, 'Competition and Co-operation in the Kent Almanack Trade', *Factotum*, Occasional Paper 3 (1982), 14–20.

Koehn, Nancy F., *The Power of Commerce: Economy and Governance in the First British Empire* (Ithaca and London: Cornell University Press, 1994).

Kondo, Kazuhiko, 'Town and County Directories in England and Wales 1677–1822', *Kenkyu Roshu*, 31:92 (Spring 1985), 47–55.

Korshin, Paul J. (ed.), *The Widening Circle: Essays on the Circulation of Literature in Eighteenth-Century Europe* (Philadelphia: University of Pennsylvania Press, 1976).

Korshin, Paul J., 'Introduction', in *The Widening Circle: Essays on the Circulation of Literature in Eighteenth-Century Europe*, ed. Paul J. Korshin (Philadelphia: University of Pennsylvania Press, 1976), pp. 3–10.

Kruse, Jürgen Elert, *Allgemeiner und besonders Hamburgischer Contorist*, 3rd edn, 3 vols (Erfurt, 1772).

Langley, Batty, *The Builder's Jewel* (London, 1741).

——, *London Prices of Bricklayers Materials and Works* (London, 1750).

Lasswell, Harold D., 'The structure and formation of communications in society' in *The Communication of Ideas*, ed. L. Bryson (New York: Institute for Religious and Social Studies, 1948), 37–51.

Law, William, *Remarks upon … the Fable of the Bees* (London, 1724).

Leland, Thomas, *History of the Life and Reign of Philip King of Macedon*, 2nd edn (London, 1761).

Lenman, Bruce, *An Economic and Social History of Modern Scotland, 1660–1976* (London: Harper Collins, 1977).

Letwin, William, *The Origins of Scientific Economics. English Economic Thought 1660–1776* (London: Methuen, 1963).

——, 'The Authorship of Sir Dudley North's Discourses on Trade', *Economica*, n.s., 18:69 (Feb. 1951), 35–56.

Lewis, John, *Printed Ephemera: The Changing Uses of Type and*

Letterforms in English and American Printing (Ipswich: W. S. Cowell, 1962).

Leybourn, William, *Panarithmologia: Or, The Trader's Sure Guide* (London, 1693).

Lippincott, Louise, *Selling Art in Georgian London: The Rise of Arthur Pond* (New Haven, CT: Yale University Press, 1983).

Littleton, A. C. and B. S. Yamey (eds), *Studies in the History of Accounting* (Homewood, IL: Richard D. Irwin, and London: Sweet and Maxwell, 1956).

Lloyd, Sarah, 'Ticketing the British Eighteenth Century: "A thing ... never heard of before"', *Journal of Social History*, 46:4 (2013), 843–71.

Lowenthal, Leo, *Literature, Popular Culture and Society* (Englewood Cliffs, NJ: Prentice-Hall, 1961).

McCormick, Ted, 'Political Arithmetic and Sacred History: Population Thought in the English Enlightenment, 1660–1750', *Journal of British Studies*, 52 (Oct. 2013), 829–57.

McCusker, John J., 'European Bills of Entry and Marine Lists: Early Commercial Publications and the Origins of the Business Press', *Harvard Library Bulletin*, 31:3 (1984), 209–55 and 31:4 (1984), 316–39.

——, 'British Commercial and Financial Journalism before 1800', in *The Cambridge History of the Book in Britain: Volume V*, ed. Michael F. Suarez and Michael L. Turner (Cambridge: Cambridge University Press, 2009), pp. 448–65.

——, 'The Business Press in England before 1775', *The Library*, 6th ser., 8 (1986), 205–31.

McCusker, John J. and Cora Gravesteijn, *The Beginnings of Commercial and Financial Journalism: The Commodity Price Currents, Exchange Rate Currents, and Money Currents of Early Modern Europe* (Amsterdam: NEHA, 1991).

McDonald, William R., 'Scottish Seventeenth-century Almanacs', *Bibliotheck*, 4:7/8 (1966), 257–322.

McDougall, Warren, 'Smugglers, Reprinters, and Hot Pursuers: The Irish-Scottish Book Trade, and Copyright Prosecutions in the Late Eighteenth Century', in *The Stationers' Company and the Book Trade, 1550–1990*, ed. Robin Myers and Michael Harris (New Castle, DE: Oak Knoll, 1997), pp. 151–83.

McDowell, Paula, *The Women of Grub Street: Press, Politics and Gender in the London Literary Marketplace, 1678–1730* (Oxford: Clarendon Press, 1998).

McElroy, D. D., 'Literary Clubs and Societies of Eighteenth-Century Scotland' (unpubl. Ph.D. dissertation, Edinburgh University, 1952).

MacGhie, Alexander, *The Principles of Book-keeping Explain'd* (Edinburgh, 1718).

McKendrick, Neil, 'The Commercialization of Fashion', in *The Birth of a Consumer Society: The Commercialization of Eighteenth-Century England*, ed. Neil McKendrick, John Brewer and J. H. Plumb (London: Europa, 1982), pp. 34–99.

——, 'The Consumer Revolution of Eighteenth-Century England', in *The Birth of a Consumer Society: The Commercialization of Eighteenth-Century England*, ed. Neil McKendrick, John Brewer and J. H. Plumb (London: Europa, 1982), pp. 9–33.

——, 'Home Demand and Economic Growth: A New View of the Role of Women and Children in the Industrial Revolution', in *Historical Perspectives: Studies in English Thought and Society in Honour of J. H. Plumb*, ed. Neil McKendrick (London: Europa Publications, 1974), pp. 152–210.

——, 'Josiah Wedgwood and the Commercialization of the Potteries', in *The Birth of a Consumer Society: The Commercialization of Eighteenth-Century England*, ed. Neil McKendrick, John Brewer and J. H. Plumb (London: Europa, 1982), pp. 100–45.

McKendrick, Neil, John Brewer and J. H. Plumb, *The Birth of a Consumer Society: The Commercialization of Eighteenth-Century England* (London: Europa, 1982).

Mackenzie, A. D., *The Bank of England Note: A History of its Printing* (Cambridge: Cambridge University Press, 1953).

McKenzie, D. F., *The Cambridge University Press, 1696–1712: A Bibliographical Study*, 2 vols (Cambridge: Cambridge University Press, 1966).

——, 'The London Book Trade in the Later Seventeenth Century' (unpubl. typescript of the Sandars Lectures, Cambridge, 1975–76).

McKenzie, D. F. and J. C. Ross (eds), *A Ledger of Charles Ackers: Printer of The London Magazine* (Oxford, Oxford Bibliographical Society, 1968).

McKitterick, David, 'Histories of the Book', *The Book Collector* (Spring 2000), 9–26.

——, *Print, Manuscripts and the Search for Order, 1450–1830* (Cambridge: Cambridge University Press, 2003).

Maclean, Ian, 'The Market for Scholarly Books and Conceptions of Genre in Northern Europe, 1570–1630', in *Die Renaissance im Blick der Nationen Europas*, ed. Georg Kauffmann (Wiesbaden: Harrassowitz, 1991), pp. 17–31.

Macquer, M. P., *A Chronological Abridgment of the Roman History, From the Foundation of the City to the Extinction of the Republic*, trans. Thomas Nugent (London, 1760).

McQuail, Denis, *Mass Communication Theory* (London: Sage Publications, 1983).

Magens, Nicolas, *An Essay on Insurances*, 2 vols (London, 1755).

Magnusson, Lars, *Mercantilism: The Shaping of an Economic Language* (Abingdon: Routledge, 1994).

Mandeville, Bernard, *The Fable of the Bees, or Private Vices, Public Benefits* (London, 1714).

——, *The Fable of the Bees*, ed. F. B. Kaye, 2 vols (Oxford: Oxford University Press, 1924).

——, *The Grumbling Hive: or Knaves Turn'd Honest* (London, 1705; 6th edn, 1729; 9th edn, 1755).

Martin, Frederick, *The History of Lloyd's and of Marine Insurance in Great Britain: With an appendix containing statistics relating to marine insurance* (London: Macmillan, 1876).

Martin, Henri-Jean, *Print, Power, and People in Seventeenth-Century France*, trans. David Gerard (Metuchen, NJ: Scarecrow Press, 1993).

Maslen, Keith, *An Early London Printing House at Work: Studies in the Bowyer Ledgers* (New York: Bibliographical Society of America, 1993).

Maslen, Keith and John Lancaster (eds), *The Bowyer Ledgers* (London: The Bibliographical Society, 1991).

Masters, B. R. (ed.), *Chamber Accounts of the Seventeenth Century* (London: London Record Society, 1984).

Mathias, Peter, *The First Industrial Nation: An Economic History of Britain, 1700–1914* (London: Methuen & Co. Ltd, 1969).

——, 'Risk, Credit and Kinship in Early Modern Enterprise', in *The Early Modern Atlantic Economy*, ed. John J. McCusker and Kenneth Morgan (Cambridge: Cambridge University Press, 2000), pp. 15–35.

——, *The Transformation of England: Essays in the Economic and Social History of England in the Eighteenth Century* (London: Methuen, 1979).

Maxted, Ian, 'Four Rotten Corn Bags and Some Old Books: The Impact of the Printed Work in Devon', in *The Sale and Distribution of Books from 1700*, ed. Robin Myers and Michael Harris (Oxford: Oxford Polytechnic Press, 1982), pp. 37–76.

——, *The London Book Trades, 1775–1800* (London: Dawson, 1977).

——, 'Single Sheets from a County Town: The Example of Exeter', in *Spreading the Word: The Distribution Networks of Print, 1550–1850*, ed. Robin Myers and Michael Harris (Winchester: St Paul's Bibliographies, 1990), pp. 109–29.

Meek, Ronald L., *Social Science and the Ignoble Savage* (Cambridge: Cambridge University Press, 1976).

Melton, Frank, 'Robert and Sir Francis Gosling: Eighteenth-Century Bankers and Stationers', in *Economics of the Book Trade 1605–1939*, ed. R. Myers and M. Harris (Cambridge: Chadwyck-Healey, 1985), pp. 60–77.

Melville, Lewis [pseud.] (ed.), *The Berry Papers. Being the correspondence hitherto unpublished of Mary and Agnes Berry 1763–1852* (London: John Lane, 1914).

M'Farlan, Revd John, *Tracts on Subjects of National Importance* (London and Edinburgh, 1786).

Middleton, Bernard C., *A History of English Craft Bookbinding Technique*, 4th edn (London: Oak Knoll Press, 1996 [1st edn, 1963]).

Mildmay, William, *The Laws and Policy of England* (London, 1764).

Mitchell, B. R., *British Historical Statistics* (Cambridge: Cambridge University Press, 1988).

Mitchell, C. J., 'Provincial Printing in Eighteenth-Century Britain', *Publishing History*, 21 (1987), 5–24.

Mizuta, Hiroshi, *Adam Smith's Library. A Supplement to Bonar's Catalogue with a Checklist of the Whole Library* (Cambridge: Cambridge University Press, 1967).

Mokyr, J., 'Demand vs. Supply in the Industrial Revolution', *Journal of Economic History*, 37 (1977), 981–1008.

Money, John, *Experience and Identity: Birmingham and the West Midlands, 1760–1800* (Manchester: Manchester University Press, 1977).

Monro, Hector, *The Ambivalence of Bernard Mandeville* (Oxford: Oxford University Press, 1975).

Montagu, Edward Wortley, *Reflections on the Rise and Fall of Antient Republicks*, 2nd edn (London, 1760).

Mooney, Linne R., 'Scribes and Booklets of Trinity College, Cambridge, MSS R.3.19 and R.3.21', in *Middle English Poetry: Texts and*

Traditions: Essays in Honour of Derek Pearsall, ed. Alastair Minnis (Woodbridge: Boydell and Brewer, 2001), pp. 241–66.

Moore, Francis, *Considerations on the Exorbitant Price of Provisions* (London, 1773).

Moore, John S. (ed.), *The Goods and Chattels of our Forefathers: Frampton Cotterell and District Probate Inventories, 1539–1804* (London and Chichester: Phillimore & Co. Ltd, 1976).

More, Hannah, *Thoughts on the Importance of Manners of the Great to General Society* (London, 1788).

Morgan, F. C., 'A Hereford Bookseller's Catalogue', *Transactions of the Woolhope Naturalists' Field Club*, 1942–44, pt 1, 22–36.

Morgan, Marjorie, *Manners, Morals and Class in England, 1774–1858* (London: Macmillan, 1994).

Morgan, Paul, *Warwickshire Printers' Notices, 1799–1866* (Oxford: Dugdale Society, 1970).

Morison, Stanley, *The English Newspaper, 1622–1932* (Cambridge: Cambridge University Press, 1932).

Morize, Andre, *L'Apologie du Luxe au XVIIIe siècle et 'Le Mondain' de Voltaire* (Paris: H. Didier, 1909; repr. Geneva: Slatkine, 1970).

Mortimer, Thomas, *The Elements of Commerce, Politics and Finances* (London, 1772; new edn, 1780).

——, *Every Man his Own Broker: or, A Guide to Exchange-Alley* (1st edn, London, 1761; 9th edn, 1782).

——, *A New History of England*, 3 vols (London, 1764).

Muldrew, Craig, *The Economy of Obligation: The Culture of Credit and Social Relations in Early Modern England* (New York: St Martin's Press, 1998).

Munter, Robert, *The History of the Irish Newspaper, 1685–1760* (Cambridge: Cambridge University Press, 1967).

Murphy, Anne L., 'Lotteries in the 1690s: Investment or Gamble?', *Financial History Review*, 12:2 (2005), 227–46.

——, *The Origins of English Financial Markets: Investment and Speculation before the South Sea Bubble* (Cambridge: Cambridge University Press, 2009).

Myers, Robin, 'Sale by Auction: the Rise of Auctioneering Exemplified', in *Sale and Distribution of Books from 1700*, ed. Robin Myers and Michael Harris (Oxford: Oxford Polytechnic Press, 1982), pp. 126–63.

Myers, Robin and Michael Harris (eds), *Maps and Prints. Aspects of the English Booktrade* (Oxford: Oxford Polytechnic Press, 1984).

——, *A Millennium of the Book: Production, Design and Illustration in Manuscript & Print 900–1900* (Winchester and New Castle, DE: Oak Knoll, 1994).

——, *Sale and Distribution of Books from 1700* (Oxford: Oxford Polytechnic Press, 1982).

Myers, Robin, Michael Harris and Giles Mandelbrote (eds), *Craft and Capital in Book Trade History. Part I: A Skilled Workforce: Training and Collaboration in the Book Trades. Part II: Balancing the Books: Financing the Book Trade from the 16th Century*, 2 vols (forthcoming, 2015).

Nadel, George H., 'Philosophy of History before Historicism', *History and Theory*, 3:3 (1964), 291–315.

Naismith, John, *Thoughts on Various Objects of Industry* (Edinburgh, 1790).

Neal, Larry, 'The Rise of a Financial Press: London and Amsterdam, 1681–1810', *Business History*, 30:2 (April 1988), 163–78.

——, *The Rise of Financial Capitalism* (Cambridge: Cambridge University Press, 1990).

Neal, Larry and Stephen Quinn, 'Networks of Information, Markets, and Institutions in the Rise of London as a Financial Centre, 1660–1720', *Financial History Review*, 8:1 (April 2001), 7–26.

Nichols, John, *Literary Anecdotes of the Eighteenth Century*, 9 vols, 2nd rev. edn (London, 1812–20).

Norris, J. M., 'Samuel Garbett and the Early Development of Industrial Lobbying in Great Britain', *EcHR*, 2nd ser., 10:3 (April 1958), 450–60.

North, Douglass C., 'The Paradox of the West', in *The Origins of Modern Freedom in the West*, ed. R. W. Davis (Stanford, CA: Stanford University Press, 1995), pp. 1–34

Norton, Jane E. (comp.), *Guide to the National and Provincial Directories of England and Wales* (London: Royal Historical Society, 1950).

Ogborn, Miles, *Spaces of Modernity: London's Geographies, 1680–1780* (London: Guilford Press, 1998).

Oldham, J. B., 'An Ipswich Master-Stationer's Tiff with his Journeyman', *TCBS*, 2 (1958), 381–4.

Oser, Jacob, *The Evolution of Economic Thought* (New York: Harcourt Brace, Jovanovich, 1963).

Overton, Mark, *Agricultural Revolution in England: The Transformation of the Agrarian Economy, 1500–1850* (Cambridge: Cambridge University Press, 1996).

Pardoe, F. E., *John Baskerville of Birmingham: Letter-Founder and Printer* (London: Frederick Muller, 1975).

Parsons, Brian, 'The Behaviour of Prices on the London Stock Market in the Early Eighteenth Century' (unpubl. Ph.D. dissertation, University of Chicago, 1974).

Paulson, Ronald, *Hogarth: His Life, Art and Times*, 2 vols (London and New Haven, CT: Yale University Press, 1971).

Pendred, J[ohn], *The London and Country Printers, Booksellers and Stationers Vade Mecum* (London, 1785).

Perrot, Jean-Claude, 'Les dictionnaires de commerce au XVIIIe siècle', *Revue d'histoire moderne et contemporaine*, 28 (1981): 36–67.

——, *Une histoire intellectuelle de l'économie politique, XVIIe-XVIIIe siècle* (Paris: Editions de l'Ecole des hautes études en sciences sociales, 1992).

Pettegree, Andrew, *The Book in the Renaissance* (London and New Haven, CT: Yale University Press, 2010).

Philip, I. G., *William Blackstone and the Reform of the Oxford University Press in the Eighteenth Century* (Oxford: Oxford Bibliographical Society, 1955 [1957]).

Phillipson, Nicholas, 'Adam Smith as Civic Moralist', in *Wealth and Virtue. The Shaping of Political Economy in the Scottish Enlightenment*, ed. Istvan Hont and Michael Ignatieff (Cambridge: Cambridge University Press, 1983), pp. 179–202.

Pickford, Christopher, 'Bedford Stationers and Booksellers', *Factotum*, 15 (Oct. 1982), 21–7.

Playford, John, *Vade Mecum; Or, The Necessary Companion* (London, edns since at least 1679).

Plomer, H. R., 'The Booksellers of London Bridge', *The Library*, 4 (1903), 28–46.

——, *A Dictionary of the Booksellers and Printers Who Were at Work in England, Scotland and Ireland from 1668 to 1725* (London: Bibliographical Society, 1922).

——, *A Short History of English Printing* (London: Kegan Paul, Trench, Trubner & Co. Ltd, 1915).

Plumb, J. H., 'The Commercialization of Leisure in Eighteenth-Century England', in *The Birth of a Consumer Society: The Commercialization of Eighteenth-Century England*, ed. Neil McKendrick, John Brewer and J. H. Plumb (London: Europa, 1982), pp. 265–85.

Pocock, J. G. A., *The Machiavellian Moment: Florentine Political Thought and the Atlantic Republican Tradition* (Princeton, NJ: Princeton University Press, 1975).

——, *Virtue, Commerce and History* (Cambridge: Cambridge University Press, 1985).

Polanyi, Michael, *The Tacit Dimension* (London: Routledge, 1966).

Poovey, Mary, 'Between Political Arithmetic and Political Economy', in *Regimes of Description: In the Archive of the Eighteenth Century*, ed. John Bender and Michael Marrinan (Stanford, CA: Stanford University Press, 2005), pp. 61–76.

Presbrey, Frank, *The History and Development of Advertising* (New York: Doubleday, Doran & Co., 1929).

Pressnell, L. S., *Country Banking in the Industrial Revolution* (New York: Oxford University Press, 1956).

Price, Cecil J. L., 'Polite Life in Eighteenth-Century Wales', *Yr Einon*, 5 (1953), 89–98.

Price, J. M., 'Notes on some London Price Currents, 1667–1715', *EcHR*, 2nd ser., 7:2 (1954), 240–50.

Pryor, Alan, *Beer, Brewhouses and Businessmen: The Transformation of the London Brewing Trade 1700–1850* (Manchester: Manchester University Press, 2014).

P.T.P., 'Pope and Woodfall' and 'Woodfall's ledger, 1734–1747', *Notes & Queries*, 11 (1855), 377–8, 418–20.

Quid, Oliver [pseud.], *A Letter of Advice Addressed to All Merchants, Manufacturers and Traders, of Every Denomination in Great Britain* (London, 1783).

——, *A Second Letter of Advice Addressed to All Merchants, Manufacturers and Traders, of Every Denomination in Great Britain* (London, 1783).

Rabuzzi, D. A., 'Eighteenth-Century Commercial Mentalities as Reflected and Protected in Business Handbooks', *Eighteenth-Century Studies*, 29 (1995–96), 169–89.

Raimbach, M. T. S. (ed.), *Memoirs and Recollections of the late Abraham Raimbach, Esq., Engraver* (London: Frederick Shoberl, Junior, 1843).

Raistrick, Arthur, *Quakers in Science and Industry*, 2nd edn (Newton Abbot: David & Charles, 1968).

Ramsey, Peter, 'Some Tudor Merchant Accounts', in *Studies in the History of Accounting*, ed. A. C. Littleton and B. S. Yamey (Homewood, IL: Richard D. Irwin, and London: Sweet and Maxwell, 1956), pp. 185–201.

Raven, James, 'The Abolition of the English State Lotteries', *Historical Journal*, 34 (1991), 371–89.

——, *Bookscape: Geographies of Printing and Publishing in London before 1800* (London: The British Library, 2014).

——, *The Business of Books: Booksellers and the English Book Trade 1450–1850* (London and New Haven, CT: Yale University Press, 2007).

——, 'Choses banales, imprimés ordinaires, "travaux de ville": l'économie et le monde de l'imprimerie que nous avons perdus', *Histoire et civilisation du livre: Revue international*, 9 (2013 [2014]), 243–58.

——, 'Imprimé et transactions économiques: représentation et interaction en angleterre aux XVIIe et XVIIIe siècles', *Revue d'histoire moderne et contemporaine*, 43:2 (1996), 234–65.

——, 'Jobbing: Was it the financial mainstay of the printing house?', in *Craft and Capital in Book Trade History. Part I: A Skilled Workforce: Training and Collaboration in the Book Trades. Part II: Balancing the Books: Financing the Book Trade from the 16th Century*, ed. Robin Myers, Michael Harris and Giles Mandelbrote, 2 vols (forthcoming, 2015).

——, *Judging New Wealth: Popular Publishing and Responses to Commerce in England, 1750–1800* (Oxford: Oxford University Press, 1992).

——, 'Letters, correspondents and correspondence', *Electronic Enlightenment On-line* (Oxford: Voltaire Foundation, 2010), www.e-enlightenment.com/letterbook/colloq2010/raven,james.html, accessed 28 June 2014.

——, 'Libraries for sociability: the advance of the subscription library, c.1700–1850', in *The History of Libraries in Britain and Ireland: Volume II 1640–1850*, ed. Giles Mandelbrote and Keith Manley (Cambridge: Cambridge University Press, 2006), pp. 241–63.

——, 'The Novel Comes of Age', in *The English Novel 1770–1829*, ed. Peter Garside, James Raven and Rainer Schöwerling, 2 vols (Oxford: Oxford University Press, 2000), vol. 1, pp. 15–121.

——, 'Print and Trade in Eighteenth-Century Britain' (unpubl. prize dissertation, Thirlwall Prize and Seeley Medal, University of Cambridge, 1986, Cambridge University Library).

——, 'Viscount Townshend and the Cambridge Prize for Trade Theory 1754–1756', *Historical Journal*, 28:3 (Sept. 1985), 535–55.

Raynes, Harold E., *A History of British Insurance* (London: Pitman, 1950).

Reed, Talbot Baines, *A History of the Development of Old English Letter Foundries*, ed. and rev. A. F. Johnson (London: Faber and Faber, 1952).

Reinert, Sophus, *Translating Empire: Emulation and the Origins of Political Economy* (Cambridge, MA: Harvard University Press, 2011).

Relton, Boyer, *An Account of the Fire Insurance Companies, Associations, Institutions, Projects and Schemes Established and Projected in Great Britain and Ireland during the Seventeenth and Eighteenth Centuries* (London: Swan Sonnenschein & Co., 1893).

Rickards, Maurice, *The Encyclopaedia of Ephemera: A Guide to the Fragmentary Documents of Everyday Life for the Collector, Curator and Historian*, ed. Michael Twyman, Sarah du Boscq de Beaumont and Amoret Tanner (London: British Library, 2000).

——, *The Public Notice: An Illustrated History* (Newton Abbot: David & Charles, 1973).

The Rise of Note-Taking in Early Modern Europe, intr. Richard Yeo, special issue of *Intellectual History Review*, 20:3 (Aug. 2010).

Rivers, Isabel (ed.), *Books and Their Readers in Eighteenth-Century England: Volume 2: New Essays* (London: Bloomsbury, 2003).

Robertson, J. C., 'Reckoning with London: Interpreting the *Bills of Mortality* before John Graunt', *Urban History*, 23:3 (Dec. 1996), 325–50.

Robinson's Merchants Weekly Remembrancer of the Present-Money-Prices, etc. 1708–?1714.

Roche, Daniel, *Histoire des choses banales: Naissance de la consommation des les sociétés traditionnelles (XVIIe–XIXe siècles)* (Paris: Fayard, 1997).

Roget, John Lewis, *A History of the Old Water-Colour Society*, 2 vols (London and New York: Longmans, Green and Co., 1891).

Rostow, W. W., 'The Take-Off into Self-Sustained Growth', *Economic Journal*, 66:261 (Mar. 1956), 25–48.

Rothblatt, Sheldon, *Tradition and Change in English Liberal Education* (London: Faber and Faber, 1966).

Rothschild, Emma, *Economic Sentiments: Adam Smith, Condorcet and the Enlightenment* (Cambridge, MA: Harvard University Press, 2001).

Rouse, Richard R. and Mary A. Rouse, *Manuscripts and their Makers: Commercial Book Production in Medieval Paris 1200–1500* (Turnhout: Harvey Miller Publishers, 2000).

Rowe, John, *Caius Crispus Sallustius, the Historian made English* (London, 1709).

Rubenhold, Hallie, *Harris's List of Covent-Garden Ladies; Sex in the City in Georgian Britain* (Stroud: Tempus, 2005).

Russell, Gillian, *Women, Sociability and Theatre in Georgian London* (Cambridge: Cambridge University Press, 2007).

Sale, William M., Jr, *Samuel Richardson: Master Printer* (Ithaca, NY: Cornell University Press, 1950).

Sampson, H., *A History of Advertising from the Earliest Times* (London: Chatto and Windus, 1874).

Saussure, César de, *A Foreign View of England in the Reigns of George I and II*, trans. Madame van Muyden (London: John Murray, 1902).

Savage, N. L., 'On the Make-up of Certain Eighteenth-century Architectural Books', *Factotum*, 20 (May 1985), 20–7.

Savage, William, *A Dictionary of the Art of Printing* (London: Longman, Brown, Green and Longmans, 1841).

Schofield, Robert E., *The Lunar Society of Birmingham* (Oxford: Clarendon Press, 1963).

Schürer, Norbert (with Chris Mounsey and Debbie Welham), *Jane Austen's Bookshop: An Exhibition* (Alton, Hampshire: Chawton House Library, 2012).

Schuyler, Robert L., *Josiah Tucker. A Selection from his Economic and Political Writings* (New York: Columbia University Press, 1931).

Sekora, John, *Luxury. The Concept in Western Thought, from Eden to Smollett* (Baltimore: Johns Hopkins University Press, 1977).

Semmel, Bernard, *The Methodist Revolution* (London: Basic Books, 1974).

Sharpe, Pamela, *Adapting to Capitalism: Working Women in the English Economy, 1700–1850* (New York: St Martin's Press, 1996).

Shaw, William Arthur (comp.), *A Bibliography of Joseph Massie* (London: G. Harding, 1937).

Shelton, George, *Dean Tucker and Eighteenth-century Economic and Political Thought* (London: Macmillan, 1981).

Sher, Richard B., *The Enlightenment and the Book: Scottish Authors and Their Publishers in Eighteenth-Century Britain, Ireland, and America* (Chicago and London: University of Chicago Press, 2006; pbk, with new preface, 2010).

Shiller, Robert J., *Irrational Exuberance* (Princeton, NJ and Oxford: Princeton University Press, 2000).

Shoemaker, Robert B., *Prosecution and Punishment: Petty Crime and the Law in London and Rural Middlesex, ca. 1660–1725* (Cambridge: Cambridge University Press, 1991).

——, *Gender in English Society, 1650–1850: The Emergence of Separate Spheres?* (London and New York: Longman, 1998).

Shorter, Alfred H., *Water Paper Mills in England* (London: Society for the Protection of Ancient Buildings, 1966).

Skinner, Andrew, *A System of Social Science: Papers Relating to Adam Smith* (New York: Oxford University Press, 1979).

Slack, Paul, 'Measuring the National Wealth in Seventeenth-Century England', *EcHR*, 57:4 (Nov. 2004), 607–35.

——, 'Government and Information in Seventeenth-Century England', *Past and Present*, 184 (Aug. 2004), 33–68.

Slater, Donald, 'Advertising as a Commercial Practice: Business Strategy and Social Theory' (unpubl. Ph.D. dissertation, Cambridge University, 1986).

Smith, Adam, *An Inquiry into the Nature and Causes of the Wealth of Nations* (London, 1776).

Smollett, Tobias, *The Complete History of England* (London, 1757–58).

——, *The Continuation of the Complete History* (London, 1760–65).

——, *Modern Part of the Universal History* (London, 1759–65).

Snyder, Henry L., 'The Circulation of Newspapers in the Reign of Queen Anne', *The Library*, 5th ser., 23 (1968), 206–35.

——, 'A Further Note', *The Library*, 5th ser., 31 (1976), 387–9.

Soll, Jacob, 'From Note-Taking to Data Banks: Personal and Institutional Information Management in Early Modern Europe', in *The Rise of Note-Taking in Early Modern Europe*, intr. Richard Yeo, special issue of *Intellectual History Review*, 20:3 (Aug. 2010), 355–75.

Spufford, Margaret, *Small Books and Pleasant Histories: Popular Fiction and its Readership in Seventeenth-Century England* (Cambridge: Cambridge University Press, 1981).

——, *The Great Reclothing of Rural England: Petty Chapmen and their Wares in the Seventeenth Century* (London: Continuum, 1984).

Stallybrass, Peter, '"Little Jobs": Broadsides and the Printing Revolution', in *Agent of Change: Print Culture Studies after Elizabeth L. Eisenstein*, ed. Sabrina Alcorn Baron, Eric N. Lindquist and Eleanor F. Shevlin (Amherst, MA: University of Massachusetts Press, 2007), pp. 315–41.

Steele, Richard, *The Englishman*, no. 4, 13 Oct. 1713.

Stobart, Jon, *Sugar and Spice. Grocers and Groceries in Provincial England, c.1650–1830* (Oxford: Oxford University Press, 2013).

Stoker, David, 'Another Look at the Dicey-Marshall Publications: 1736–1806', *The Library*, 7th ser., 15 (2014), 111–57.

——, 'The establishment of printing in Norwich', *TCBS*, 7:1 (1977), 94–111.

Stower, Caleb, *The Compositor's and Pressman's Guide to the Art of Printing* (London, 1808).

——, *The Printer's Grammar* (London, 1808).

Strauss, Erich, *Sir William Petty: Portrait of a Genius* (London: Bodley Head, 1954).

Suarez, Michael F., 'Towards a Bibliometric Analysis of the Surviving Record, 1701–1800', in *The Cambridge History of the Book in Britain: Volume V*, ed. Michael F. Suarez and Michael L. Turner (Cambridge: Cambridge University Press, 2009), pp. 39–65.

Suarez, Michael F. and Michael L. Turner (eds), *The Cambridge History of the Book in Britain: Volume V* (Cambridge: Cambridge University Press, 2009).

Supple, Barry, *The Royal Exchange Assurance: A History of British Insurance 1720–1970* (Cambridge: Cambridge University Press, 1970).

Sutherland, James R., 'The Circulation of Newspapers and Literary Periodicals, 1700–30', *The Library*, 4th ser., 15 (1934), 110–24.

——, *The Restoration Newspaper and its Development* (Cambridge: Cambridge University Press, 1986).

Sutherland, Lucy Stuart, *A London Merchant, 1695–1774* (London: Oxford University Press and Humphrey Milford, 1933).

Swanson, R. N., 'Printing for Purgatory: Indulgences and Related Documents in England, 1476 to 1536', *Journal of the Early Book Society*, 14 (2011), 115–44.

Sweet, Rosemary, 'Corrupt and corporate bodies: attitudes to corruption in eighteenth-century and early nineteenth-century towns', in *Corruption in Urban Politics and Society, Britain 1780–1950*, ed. James R. Moore and John Smith (Aldershot: Ashgate, 2007), pp. 41–56.

Sweet, Rosemary and Penelope Lane (eds), *Women and Urban Life in Eighteenth-Century England* (Aldershot: Ashgate, 2003).

Sykes, Norman, *From Sheldon to Secker. Aspects of English Church History 1660–1768* (Cambridge: Cambridge University Press, 1959).

Tattersfield, Nigel, *Thomas Bewick, The Complete Illustrative Work*, 3 vols (London and New Castle, DE: British Library, Bibliographical Society and Oak Knoll, 2011).

Taylor, John A., *British Empiricism and Early Political Economy: Gregory*

King's 1696 Estimates of National Wealth and Population (Westport, CT and London: Praeger, 2005).

Thomas, R. George, 'The Complete Reading List of a Carmarthenshire Student 1763–7', *Journal of the National Library of Wales*, 9 (1955–56), 356–64.

Thompson, E. P., 'The Moral Economy of the English Crowd in the Eighteenth Century', *Past and Present*, 50:1 (1971), 76–136.

Thomson, Alistair G., *The Paper Industry in Scotland, 1590–1861* (Edinburgh: Scottish Academic Press, 1974).

Thorold, Sir John, *A Short Examination of The Fable of the Bees* (London, 1726).

Timelli, Maria Colombo, 'Dictionnaires pour voyageurs, dictionnaires pour marchands, ou la polyglossie au quotidien au XVIe et XVIIe siècle', *Linguisticae Investigationes*, 16:2 (1992), 395–420.

Treadwell, Michael, 'A New List of English Master Printers, c.1686', *The Library*, 6th ser., 4 (1982), 57–61.

——, 'London Printers and Printing Houses in 1705', *Publishing History*, 7 (1980), 5–44.

Trebilcock, Clive, *Phoenix Assurance and the Development of British Insurance*, 2 vols (Cambridge: Cambridge University Press, 1985–99).

Troyer, Howard William, *Ned Ward of Grubstreet: A Study of Sub-Literary London in the Eighteenth Century* (Cambridge, MA: Harvard University Press, 1946).

Trusler, John, *The London Adviser and Guide; Containing Every Instruction and Information Useful and Necessary to Persons Living in London and Coming to Reside There* (London, 1786).

——, *Luxury No Political Evil* (London, ?1779).

——, *The Way to be Rich and Respectable* (London, ?1776).

Tucker, Josiah, *Sermons on Political and Commercial Subjects* (Gloucester, 1776).

——, *Six Sermons on Important Subjects* (Bristol, 1772).

Turner, M. L. (comp.), *The John Johnson Collection: Catalogue of an Exhibition* (Oxford: Bodleian Library, 1971).

Twyman, Michael, *Printing, 1770–1970: An Illustrated History of its Development and Uses in England* (London: Eyre and Spottiswoode, 1970).

Twyman, Michael and William Rollinson, *John Soulby, Printer, Ulverston: A Study of the Work Printed by John Soulby, father and son, between*

1796 and 1827 with an account of Ulverston at the time (Reading: Museum of English Rural Life, 1966).

Tyacke, Sarah, *London Map-Sellers 1660–1720* (Tring: Herts Map Collector Publications, 1978).

Unwin, George, *Samuel Oldknow and the Arkwrights: the Industrial Revolution at Stockport and Marple* (Manchester: The University Press, and London and New York: Longmans, Green & Co., 1924).

Updike, Daniel Berkeley, *Printing Types: Their History, Forms and Use: A Study in Survivals*, 2 vols (Cambridge, MA: Harvard University Press, 1962).

Valenze, Deborah, *The Social Life of Money in the English Past* (Cambridge: Cambridge University Press, 2006).

Varey, Simon Robertson, 'The Craftsman 1726–52: An Historical and Critical Account' (unpubl. Ph.D. dissertation, Cambridge University, 1977).

——, *Lord Bolingbroke. Contributions to the Craftsman* (Oxford: Clarendon Press, 1982).

Veblen, Thorstein, *The Theory of the Leisure Class*, ed. J. K. Galbraith (Boston: Houghton Mifflin, 1973).

Vichert, Gordon, 'The Theory of Conspicuous Consumption in the Eighteenth Century', in *The Varied Pattern: Studies in the Eighteenth Century*, ed. Peter Hughes and David Williams (Toronto: A. M. Hakkert, 1971), pp. 253–67.

Wade, S. M., 'The Idea of Luxury in Eighteenth-century England' (unpubl. Ph.D. dissertation, Harvard University, 1969).

Walford, Cornelius, *The Insurance Cyclopaedia*, 5 vols & 1 part [unfinished] (London: Charles and Edwin Layton, 1871–80).

Walker, R. B., 'Advertising in London Newspapers, 1650–1750', *Business History*, 15:2 (July 1973), 112–30.

——, 'The Newspaper Press in the Reign of William III', *Historical Journal*, 17:4 (Dec. 1974), 691–709.

[?Ward, Edward], *The Batchelor's Monitor: With healthy and pleasant advice for married men in the governing a wife. To which is added, an essay against unequal marriages* (London, 1743 edn).

Ward, Edward, *The Wealthy Shopkeeper: or, The Charitable Citizen: A Poem* (London, 1700).

Ward, J. R., *The Finance of Canal Building in Eighteenth-Century England* (Oxford: Oxford University Press, 1974).

Weskett, John, *A Complete Digest of the Theory, Laws, and Practice of Insurance* (London, 1781).

Wesley, John, *The Works of John Wesley*, 14 vols (London John Mason, 1872).

[Whiston, James], *The Merchants Remembrancer* (London, 1680–86).

Whiston's Merchants Weekly Remembrancer of the Present-Money-Prices of their Goods Ashoar in London, ?1689–1707.

White, Gilbert, *A Naturalist's Calendar, with observations in various branches of natural history, extracted from the papers of the late Rev. Gilbert White of Selborne, Hampshire, Senior Fellow of Oriel College, Oxford: Never before published*, ed. John Aikin (London: Printed for B. and J. White, Horace's Head, Fleet Street, 1795).

Whitney, Lois, *Primitivism and the Idea of Progress* (Baltimore: Johns Hopkins Press, 1934).

Whyman, Susan, *The Pen and the People: English Letter Writers* (Oxford: Oxford University Press, 2009).

Wiles, R. M., *Freshest Advices: Early Provincial Newspapers in England* (Columbus, OH: Ohio State University Press, 1965).

Willan, T. S., *The Early History of the Don Navigation* (Manchester: Manchester University Press, 1965).

——, *An Eighteenth-Century Shopkeeper: Abraham Dent of Kirkby Stephen* (Manchester: Manchester University Press, 1970).

——, *Navigation of the River Weaver in the Eighteenth Century* (Manchester: Chetham Society Publications, 1951).

Winans, R. B., *A Descriptive Checklist of Book Catalogues Separately Printed in America 1693–1800* (Worcester, MA: American Antiquarian Society, 1981).

Winch, Donald, *Adam Smith's Politics: An Essay in Historiographic Revision* (New York and London: Cambridge University Press, 1978).

Wright, Charles and C. Ernest Fayle, *A History of Lloyd's from the Founding of Lloyd's Coffee House to the Present Day* (London: Blades, East & Blades, 1928).

Wright, William, *The Complete Tradesman: or, A Guide in the Several Parts and Progressions of Trade* (London, 1789).

Wrigley, E. A., 'British population during the "long" eighteenth century, 1680–1840', in *The Cambridge Economic History of Modern Britain*, ed. Roderick Floud and Paul Johnson, 3 vols (Cambridge: Cambridge University Press, 2004), vol. 1, *Industrialisation, 1700–1860*, pp. 57–95.

——, 'The Growth of Population in Eighteenth-Century England: A Conundrum Resolved', *Past & Present*, 98 (Feb. 1983), 121–50.

——, *People, Cities and Wealth: the Transformation of Traditional Society* (Oxford: Oxford University Press, 1987).

Wrigley, E. A. and R. S. Schofield, *The Population History of England, 1541–1871: A Reconstruction* (Cambridge, MA: Harvard University Press, 1981).

Wroth, Warwick, 'Tickets of Vauxhall Gardens', *Numismatic Chronicle*, 3rd ser., 18 (1898), 73–92.

Yamey, B. S., *Essays on the History of Accounting* (New York: Arno Press, 1978).

——, 'Scientific Bookkeeping and the Rise of Capitalism', *EcHR*, 2nd ser., 1:2/3 (1949), 99–113.

Yamey, B. S., H. C. Edey and Hugh W. Thomson (eds), *Accounting in England and Scotland: 1543–1800* (London: Sweet & Maxwell, 1963).

Yanaihara, Tadao, *A Full and Detailed Catalogue of Books which Belonged to Adam Smith* (Tokyo: Iwanami Shoten, 1951).

Young, Timothy G., 'Evidence: Toward a Library Definition of Ephemera', *RBM: A Journal of Rare Books, Manuscripts, and Cultural Heritage*, 4 (2003), 11–26.

Zucker, Lynne G., 'Production of Trust: Institutional Sources of Economic Structure, 1840–1920', in *Research in Organizational Behavior 8*, ed. B. M. Staw and L. L. Cummings (Greenwich, CT: JAI Press, 1986), pp. 55–111.

Index

Printed and bound by CPI Group (UK) Ltd, Croydon, CR0 4YY

13/04/2025